LOCATING BRICS IN THE GLOBAL ORDER

BRICS is conceivably the most formidable organisation to have emerged in the post–Cold War period in the non-Western world. This book highlights the significance of BRICS in a wider global context and foregrounds the long-pending demand for the reform of global governance institutions.

The volume:

- Traces how the organisation came into being and looks at the distinct norms and principles espoused by it
- Discusses the glaring limitations of the existing institutions of global governance
- Explores the economic growth and the rising political influence of BRICS states
- Analyses the internal threats to the survival of the organisation and assesses its prospects in the foreseeable future.

A significant intervention in situating BRICS as one of the major players in global governance, the book will be of great interest to students and scholars of international political economy, international business and finance, international relations, politics, and Global South studies.

Rajan Kumar, Associate Professor, Jawaharlal Nehru University, New Delhi, India.

Meeta Keswani Mehra, Professor, Jawaharlal Nehru University, New Delhi, India.

G. Venkat Raman, Professor, Indian Institute of Management, Indore, India.

Meenakshi Sundriyal, Assistant Professor, Jawaharlal Nehru University, New Delhi, India.

LOCATING BRICS IN THE GLOBAL ORDER

Perspectives from the Global South

Edited by Rajan Kumar, Meeta Keswani Mehra, G. Venkat Raman, and Meenakshi Sundriyal

Routledge
Taylor & Francis Group
LONDON AND NEW YORK

Cover image: @gettyimages

First published 2023
by Routledge
4 Park Square, Milton Park, Abingdon, Oxon OX14 4RN

and by Routledge
605 Third Avenue, New York, NY 10158

Routledge is an imprint of the Taylor & Francis Group, an informa business

British Library Cataloguing-in-Publication Data
A catalogue record for this book is available from the British Library

Library of Congress Cataloging-in-Publication Data
Names: Kumar, Rajan, editor. | Mehra, Meeta Keswani, editor. | Venkat Raman, G., Dr., editor. | Sundriyal, Meenakshi, editor.
Title: Locating BRICS in the global order : perspectives from the Global South / edited by Rajan Kumar, Meeta Keswani Mehra, G. Venkat Raman and Meenakshi Sundriyal.
Description: London ; New York, NY : Routledge, Taylor & Francis Group, 2023. | Includes bibliographical references and index. | Summary: Provided by publisher.
Identifiers: LCCN 2022019528 (print) | LCCN 2022019529 (ebook) | ISBN 9780367643089 (hardback) | ISBN 9780367708085 (paperback) | ISBN 9781003148074 (ebook)
Subjects: LCSH: International organization. | International cooperation. | BRIC countries—Foreign relations. | BRIC countries—Politics and government
Classification: LCC D887 .L63 2023 (print) | LCC D887 (ebook) | DDC 341.2—dc23/eng/20220811
LC record available at https://lccn.loc.gov/2022019528
LC ebook record available at https://lccn.loc.gov/2022019529

ISBN: 978-0-367-64308-9 (hbk)
ISBN: 978-0-367-70808-5 (pbk)
ISBN: 978-1-003-14807-4 (ebk)

DOI: 10.4324/9781003148074

Typeset in Bembo
by Apex CoVantage, LLC

To Late Professor Tulsi Ram under whose stewardship we started a project on BRICS which finally culminated in this book. His legacy continues to inspire us.

CONTENTS

FIGURES

TABLES

NOTES ON CONTRIBUTORS

Sk. Md. Azharuddin, Doctoral Candidate in Economics, School of International Studies Jawaharlal Nehru University, Delhi, India.

Júlio Vicente Cateia, Postdoctoral Researcher in Economics at the University of Laval, Canada.

Surbhi Choudhary, Research Scholar, School of International Studies, Jawaharlal Nehru University, India.

Bruno De Conti, Associate Professor, University of Campinas, Brazil.

Oxana Kharitonova, Associate Professor, MGIMO, Moscow, Russia.

Rajan Kumar, Associate Professor, School of International Studies, Jawaharlal Nehru University, New Delhi, India

Khush-Hal S. Lagdhyan, Associate Professor, Jaipuria Institue of Management, Jaipur, India.

Subodh N. Malakar, Professor, Jawaharlal Nehru University, Delhi, India.

Meeta Keswani Mehra, Professor, School of International Studies, Jawaharlal Nehru University, Delhi, India.

Himanshu Shekhar Mishra, Senior Political Correspondent, NDTV, Delhi, India.

Bappaditya Mukherjee, Former faculty, State University of New York, Genesco, USA.

Édivo de Almeida Oliveira, Research Fellow, University of Campinas, Brazil.

Aparaajita Pandey, Assistant Professor at the Institute of Public Policy, Amity University, Noida, India.

Ajay K. Patnaik, Professor, School of International Studies, Jawaharlal Nehru University, Delhi, India.

Rohan, Assistant Professor, Delhi University, India.

Ashok Sharma, Visiting Fellow at the Strategic and Defence Studies Centre, Coral Bell School of Asia-Pacific Affairs, The Australian National University.

Shradha, Professor, School of Humanities & Social Sciences, Sharda University, India.

Huma Siddiqui, Senior Editor, The Financial Express, India.

Meenakshi Sundriyal, Assistant Professor, Jawaharlal Nehru University, Delhi, India.

G. Venkat Raman, Professor, Indian Institute of Management, Indore, India.

Liu Zongyi, Secretary-General & Senior Fellow, South Asia and China Center (SACC) of Shanghai Institutes for International Studies, China.

PREFACE

This edited volume on BRICS comes when the world is facing unprecedented challenges in the domain of geopolitics, global governance, and economic cooperation. The Covid pandemic, growing rivalry between the United States and China, growing protectionism, and the rise of popular authoritarianism threaten to disrupt the liberal international order. The institutions of liberal international order are under severe strain because of the decline in the influence of the United States and the growing economic and political clout of China. The world is clearly multipolar in which regional powers are exerting far more influence than what they did during the Cold War or during the next two decades. Russia, India, Brazil, and South Africa have become influential regional players. The United States' capacity to protect the rules-based liberal international order is under doubt. The Biden administration is trying to revive the liberal order by rejecting the 'America First' approach and forging alliances and partnerships with the EU, Japan, the UK, Australia, and India, but it no longer carries the conviction and commitment of the Cold War period. Therefore, states have begun to reorient their policies with an underlying presumption that while America will remain a leading player in the foreseeable future, China will rival the United States in the field of economy, military, and science and technology.

The rise in the economic clout of regional players such as China, Russia, India, Brazil, and South Africa has made them question the hierarchy that exists in the institutions of the liberal international order. A general perception among the leading states of the Global South is that the existing institutions such as the International Monetary Fund, the World Bank, the World Trade Organization, and the United Nations must undergo urgent reforms to remain relevant in the fast-changing world order. BRICS provided a platform for these states to socialise, share information, and voice their dissatisfaction over the unrepresentative nature of many of the institutions.

BRICS does not represent the whole of the Global South, but it certainly is the most powerful institution of the Global South in the post–Cold War period. It functions like a club privileging members over others. Further, it has Russia as a member which is divided between the North and South. Nonetheless, every continent of the Global South, that is Asia, Africa, and Latin America, has at least one representation in this organisation. All the countries of BRICS, barring Russia, share a colonial past and are critical of the Western dominance in global governance. They are also the most powerful states in their respective regions, and therefore, their influences travel far beyond their borders.

The rise of BRICS is an interesting development in the domain of international politics. Most of the states do not share geography, have diverse political systems ranging from established democracies to outright authoritarianism, and are culturally poles apart. Yet these states came together to create an institution of global significance. BRICS is a unique institution with an ability to implement policies and influence global governance. Member states have ensured that internal contradictions do not disrupt the functioning of BRICS. BRICS has begun to discuss a wide range of issues, from climate change, terrorism, disaster management, public health to reforms in multilateral institutions. The complexities of these domains have motivated states to come together and address their concerns.

Western scholarship has largely been dismissive of BRICS' relevance for the following reasons: first, taking BRICS just as an economic cohort of 'emerging markets'; second, overstressing the intra-BRICS heterogeneity; third, the power asymmetry among its members; and finally, the dissipating growth stories of several of its members. Defying all these criticisms, BRICS has managed to acquire the status of a formal institution with solid financial and political backing from its members.

BRICS is a work in progress, and much will depend on the way the world order unfolds in the coming years. We hypothesise that a bipolar world will make BRICS lose its current sheen, while a multipolar world will enhance its significance in the coming years. Since the bipolar world has not yet evolved, BRICS will continue to play a bridging role in the coming years. It is also possible that it might open up its membership and include new states.

This edited volume is an endeavour to present the idea of BRICS from member states' perspective. To do justice and give legitimacy to this modest ambition, we have included chapters by scholars from each of the BRICS countries. We intend to bring forward non-Western perspectives on BRICS to the readers.

ACKNOWLEDGEMENTS

We want to acknowledge the generous assistance and support of a host of institutions to bring out this edited volume. The idea of such a volume was conceived when the editorial team of this book along with two other scholars were awarded an Indian Council of Social Science Research (ICSSR) grant to undertake a project on BRICS. The group visited various Brazilian, South African, and Russian institutes in completing the project. Some notable mentions are the Institute of Economics, University of Campinas, the University of São Paulo in Brazil, the University of Pretoria, the Centre for China Studies, Stellenbosch University, South Africa, National Institute of Humanities and Social Sciences, affiliated to the Department of Higher Education of the South African government, Moscow State University, and the MGIMO, Moscow, Russia. The colleagues in these institutes were very gracious in sharing information and ideas with us. This helped us develop a more informed understanding of BRICS from member states' perspective. We fondly remember the help of Bruno De Conti in the University of Campinas. We thank the Jawaharlal Nehru University, New Delhi, for granting the editorial team study leave and facilitating the field visits. We would also like to thank the Indian Institute of Management, Indore, for extending all possible support and generously granting study leave to one of the editorial team members. We express our sincere thanks to Tara Nair, who edited the volume with utmost rigour. Her exhaustive and meticulous editing and relentless persuasion have been a learning experience for all of us.

We also place on record our indebtedness to Late Professor Tulsi Ram, who was instrumental in conceiving the BRICS project. We are grateful to Ajay K. Patnaik for steering and leading the project. We would also like to thank our colleagues Anuradha Chenoy, Kamal Mitra Chenoy, Pushpesh Pant, R.K. Kale, Manoj Pant, Sanjay Pandey, Alka Acharya, Archana Upadhyay, Priti Das, Amitabh Singh, Phool Badan, Khush-Hal S. Lagdhyan, Sk. Md. Azharuddin, Sandesha Rayappa, Shandar

Ahmad, Nagesh Ojha, Dhrub Tara, and many more for their constant encouragement and support. We have always learnt from discussions with our students in the classroom.

We would like to thank our family members for bearing with us in difficult times. Rajasree, Reyansh, Rama, Nachiketa, Anvita, Atul, Aashna, Saumyaa, Samar, and Shakuntala deserve special thanks for being magnanimous in allowing us to take two long trips to Brazil and South Africa as part of our project.

We are delighted to have finished the book at last, but our journey has not been a smooth one. We lost a colleague, Sanjay Rajhans, who was supposed to write a chapter for this book. He succumbed to complications related to Covid. Three editors of the book were infected with the Delta variant of Covid. One of them had a hard time in the hospital. Nonetheless, the book project kept us moving when times were difficult for us. We are grateful to the contributors for responding to our requests to write chapters during the peak of Covid.

We also express our gratitude to anonymous reviewers of this book. Aakash Chakrabarty at Routledge has always been very kind and supportive.

Finally, the editors are responsible for omissions and errors.

1

INTRODUCTION

G. Venkat Raman and Rajan Kumar

BRICS, a grouping of Brazil, Russia, India, China, and South Africa, is conceivably the most formidable organisation to have emerged in the post–Cold War period in the Global South. What makes it worthy of attention is that, in a short period, it has demonstrated a capacity to institutionalise, learned to make consensual decisions, successfully executed policies, and endured border conflicts between two of its prime members. It has defied the doomsday arguments of experts who dismissed it as too incoherent to be consequential. Arguably, it has demonstrated a purpose and evolved mechanisms to address issues of common concern.

BRICS began as a discussion forum, focusing primarily on grievances regarding global financial governance. Over time, it became more ambitious and included political, social, and security concerns in its purview. It attracted widespread attention for two specific reasons: its projected growth potential and its vocal disapproval of Western financial dominance. The BRICS economies began to outperform the traditional economies of the West in aggregate terms. Economic growth spurred the aspiration of these states, and they began to question the financial dominance of the West.

The main grudge of the member states is that international institutions are not in tune with the emerging economic and political reality. An epochal change is underway, and the fulcrum of economic activity has shifted from the North Atlantic to the Asia-Pacific (Mohan and Kapur, IMF Working Paper 2015). This shift is the broader geopolitical context in which the idea of BRICS was mooted. Leading states of the Global South felt a need to create alternate institutions to voice their concerns and tackle issues of collective interest. BRICS was conceptualised to carry forward this sentiment. It did not intend to subvert existing institutions; rather, it was meant to complement them. The declaration of the first BRICS Summit explicitly recognised the centrality of the G20 in reviving the global economy and the role of the UN in maintaining peace (BRICS Summit, Yekaterinburg 2009).

DOI: 10.4324/9781003148074-1

BRICS emerged at a time when Western economies were facing an unprecedented financial crisis. It became apparent that without the active co-operation of the BRICS states, the concerns of global governance could not be addressed. However, the resounding optimism of the initial years gave way to serious apprehensions about its role and effectiveness in future. A growing body of literature began to question the growth potential and viability of BRICS. The Western literature remains largely dismissive of the relevance of this organisation. The slow down of the BRICS economies has lent further credence to such arguments. China's economic growth has decelerated, Brazil is yet to recover from the economic downturn that started in 2015–2016, India's economy is stumbling, Russia is under sanctions, and South Africa faces political and economic instability. BRICS is under pressure to retain its legitimacy amidst the pandemic, low growth rate, and strife among the member states.

This book attempts to explore the raison d'etre of BRICS as an organisation, describe its role in governance, and assess its prospects in the foreseeable future. It analyses the relevance of this organisation from the perspective of the member states. All the contributors have paid special attention to domestic contexts and narratives, which determine their state's orientation towards this organisation. They have addressed the following questions in the book: How did BRICS come into being? What are the economic and political justifications for the existence of this institution? What are the major financial and developmental initiatives taken by the organisation? Are there distinct norms and principles espoused by BRICS? What are the geopolitical and commercial interests of member states? How do they converge or diverge on governance issues? And finally, what are the internal threats to the survival of this organisation?

Origin of BRICS: Tracing the Ancestry

While the term 'BRICS' owes its origin to Jim O'Neill, the impulse for collective action by the leading states of the Global South dates to the late 1990s. The acronym 'BRIC' was coined by Jim O'Neill, an economist at Goldman Sachs (G.S.), a US multinational company. The acronym BRICs was used in his publication 'Building Better Global Economic BRIC' in 2001. He expected the fast-growing economies of China, India, Brazil, and Russia to surge ahead of the economies of the West in the foreseeable future.

The urge for collective action among the southern states was sui generis in its origin. Initiatives like the Russia, India, and China (RIC) trilateral; India, Brazil, and South Africa (IBSA); and the G7 'Outreach Five' (O-5) started taking shape to vent their collective aspirations in influencing global governance. The idea of a 'strategic triangle' in the form of RIC, comprising Russia, India, and China, conceived by Russian Prime Minister Yevgeny Primakov during his visit to India in 1998, took the shape of a triangular association (Mohan 2002). The foreign affairs ministers of Russia, China, and India – Igor Ivanov, Tang Jiaxuan, and Yashwant Sinha – met in New York on the sidelines of the United Nations General Assembly meeting in 2001. Our attempts to re-trace the history of collective action are not motivated by concerns related to chronology but to contend that the political foundation of BRICS was laid before the much-celebrated Goldman Sachs report. Politics preceded the economic rationale of the association.

Many of the collective forums mentioned earlier emerged in the 1990s when these states were viewed as unstable economies. India and Brazil had initiated liberal reforms but were vulnerable to economic and financial vicissitudes. Except for China, with a high growth rate of about 9 per cent, the other states had a modest growth rate. India grew at an average of about 5 per cent, Brazil 3 per cent, and the Russian economy was in deep turmoil. It may sound counterintuitive, but it was amidst this turmoil that collective forums like IBSA and RIC were conceived. Therefore, it can be safely argued that what brought them together was a certain kind of politics. The inclusion of South Africa added moral weight to the BRICS cause due to its long anti-apartheid struggle. South Africa was preferred over other African states because it had worked in earlier associations such as the BASIC, O-5 of the G8, and climate change negotiations.

This unique nature of BRICS got a shot in the arm with gradual recognition from some influential voices in the West. For instance, the former French President Jacques Chirac admitted in 2003 that the G8 was no longer inclusive and invited leaders from India and Brazil to attend the Evian Summit (Cooper 2016, p. 25). Thabo Mbeki, the President of South Africa, proposed a subgroup at the Evian Summit of G7 in 2003. With its first meeting in Brasilia, IBSA created the IBSA Business Council and several other civil society forums. The G8 institutionalised a mechanism through which five states of the Global South – Brazil, India, China, Mexico, and South Africa – known as 'Outreach Five' (O-5) were invited for dialogues at the G7 Summit meetings. The ministers of these O-5 countries started meeting on the sidelines of the G8 summits. These semi-formal and informal rendezvous of O-5 leaders perhaps contributed inadvertently to the origin of BRICS. The leaders of the BRIC countries met at the Tokyo Summit in Japan in 2008. This rendezvous is often taken as a precursor to the formal meeting of BRIC in Yekaterinburg in 2009 (Cooper 2016). The financial crisis of 2008 proved to be a turning point for BRICS. Unlike the non-Western origins of earlier crises, it had its epicentre in the United States and Europe. The financial crisis of 2008 infused new impetus into an organisation like BRICS.

BRICS is a unique organisation in terms of its composition, character, and regional representation. Juxtaposing it to the Organisation of Petroleum Exporting Countries (OPEC), the G7 and the Non-Aligned Movement (NAM) carries limited analytical value. Unlike the OPEC, it is not an organisation dedicated to a particular issue, nor can it be compared to the G7, a grouping of powerful economies. To project it as a successor of the NAM is equally misleading. Further, it is not a regional organisation such as the European Union, the African Union, or the Association of South-East Asian Nations. Simply put, BRICS is an organisation of emerging global leaders. It has restricted membership and privileges some states over others. It does not represent the whole of the Global South, but it is arguably the most significant organisation in the Global South.

Members of BRICS have divergent orientations, but they work on the principle of a common denominator. For China and Russia, this organisation is an instrument to offset the prominence of the West, particularly the United States. Cornered by the North Atlantic Treaty Organization (NATO) in its neighbourhood, Russia has temporarily pivoted eastward. China faces identical threats from the West. The trade and technology wars with the United States, the unilateral thrust of the Belt and Road Initiative, military modernisation, and its disputed claims over Taiwan and the South China Sea have created numerous friction points between the West and China. Their conflicting interests have led to increasing suspicion, hostility, and containment. Under these circumstances, China views BRICS as a platform to socialise with other regional powers of the Global South and cut down the influence of the West with incremental steps. However, India, South Africa, and Brazil do not share the revisionist dreams of Russia and China in containing the West. They are reasonably satisfied with their elevated status where they are viewed as vital poles in emerging multipolarity. Their motives are limited to reforming multilateral institutions, enhancing South–South co-operation, and taking up the common causes of terrorism, climate change, energy co-operation, and the pandemic. India's main grudge is its exclusion from the Security Council of the United Nations, and it believes that support from BRICS would be necessary for any such reform. India is always comfortable in an organisation where Russia is a leading player. India's comfort with the Russia factor explains its involvement in BRICS and the Shanghai Cooperation Organization (SCO), but not the Belt and Road Initiative. BRICS is often seen as a balancing strategy in a transitional and highly uncertain world. 'Status seeking' and 'hedging' are two core motives of India and China at BRICS. As China hedges against the United States, India employs the same strategy against China (Cooper 2016, p. 73). For New Delhi, BRICS is a useful forum and an exclusive club to protect and push forward its cross-regional interests (Kumar 2017).

BRICS states are conscious of their historical subjugation to Western imperialism in varying degrees. This common historical experience proved to be a formidable glue in voicing their dissatisfaction over existing global governance mechanisms. We do not contend that their histories determined current policies, but we believe that their past subconsciously oriented their worldview. They have customised their developmental paths following their unique historical and political experience.

Economic Growth of BRICS States

Some scholars have argued that BRICS' goal to craft grandiose global governance plans is ill-conceived. We contend that BRICS' credibility lies in the aggregate size of its economy, prospects of its growth in the next two decades, shared historical grief, a discrete sense of non-West, and its incredible regional outreach and influence. Having stagnated for centuries, countries like China and India began to grow rapidly towards the end of the twentieth century. In AD 1000, China and India contributed nearly 50 per cent of global output (Maddison 2001). China in the sixteenth century accounted for almost 25 per cent of world production. When the British came in 1600, India contributed around 17–20 per cent of global output, and, when they left India in 1947, it was down to only 2 per cent (Malone 2011). The colonial exploitation of Africa was marked by slavery, racism, and segregation. Brazil was under Portuguese rule, and the form of colonialism was equally exploitative. Russia and China have their grudge against Western imperialism.

However, towards the end of the twentieth century, states in the Global South began to grow at a remarkable pace. The trajectory of growth in each of the BRICS countries is different. As part of the Soviet Union, Russia went through a high phase of industrialisation since the 1930s. The Soviet Union became the second-most powerful economy after the United States. But after the disintegration of the Soviet Union, Russia underwent a long period of economic recession. It started growing after 1999, owing mainly to the depreciation of the rouble and high oil prices. It experienced high growth from 1999 to 2008. China has had double-digit growth since the 1980s. India opened its economy in 1991 following a balance of payment crisis. The reform was gradual, and the state remained heavily invested in several sectors of the economy. Its insulated character ensured that it was largely unaffected by the financial crises in 1998 (South-East Asian Financial crisis) and 2008 (US sub-prime crisis).

Two developments took place in the 1990s: the foreign investment boom and the rise of China (Kiely 2015). In the 1990s, developing countries constituted roughly 18 per cent of global output, which increased to 26 per cent in 2007; exports increased from 19 to 30 per cent (Dicken 2011). BRICS contributed roughly 30 per cent of global output in 2014. BRICS represents nearly 42 per cent of the worldwide population, 23 per cent of global GDP, 30 per cent of the territory, and 18 per cent of international trade. In the period between 2008 and 2017, the global growth rate was about 1 per cent, while BRICS grew at a pace of about 8 per cent. The key states that accounted for 52 per cent of world GDP growth in 2000–2020 were China, India, Russia, and Brazil (Kondratov 2021). In 2000–2020, China grew by 8.6 per cent, and India by 5.9 per cent; the growth rate was between 1.8 to 2.7 per cent in Russia, Brazil, and South Africa. China's share of global exports in 1990 was 1.9 per cent; this increased to 10.6 per cent in 2010. The United States had 11.6 per cent, which came down to 8.6 per cent (Farooki and Kaplinsky 2012). In the 1980s and 1990s, developed countries accounted for 75 per cent of global growth; this dropped to 50 per cent between 2000 and 2006 and further plummeted to only 26 per cent between 2006 and 2012 (UNCTAD 2012). The development of China is a fantastic story. In 2001, China accounted for 50 per cent of the BRICS GDP, but its contribution increased to two-thirds of the BRICS GDP in two decades (The Economist 2017). The GDP of China is more significant than the GDP of all other countries of BRICS put together. In terms of nominal GDP (2020), China has a US$14.34 trillion economy, India US$2.87 trillion, Brazil US$1.84 trillion, Russia US$1.70 trillion, and South Africa US$301 billion (Top 20 Economies of the World, Investopedia 2020). The economy of China is nearly 50 times bigger than that of South Africa and roughly five times bigger than that of India. With the current average growth rate, the GDP of BRICS countries by 2050 will be 2.4 times higher (46.2 per cent of the world GDP) than that of the G7 (Kondratov 2021).

In the last two decades, the nature of globalisation has created complex value chains tying countries between the Global North and the Global South and forming new value chains between South–South countries. BRICS countries in general and China in particular have developed close economic and commercial ties owing to their critical roles in global value chains. The growing economies of India and China and the resurgence of Russia as a vital player in the energy sector have added a new dimension to BRICS. Their high-tech information technologies, infrastructure construction, service industries, and sophisticated manufacturing have eroded the monopoly of the Western countries in several sectors.

From the investment perspective, BRICS emerged as attractive destinations for incoming foreign direct investment (FDI) and as a source of outward investments. The BRICS countries invested only US$7 billion in 2000, which went up to US$126 billion in 2012. They received only 6 per cent of the global FDI in 2000, which went up to 20 per cent, amounting to US$263 billion in 2012 (UNCTAD 2013). The significant outward FDIs in China, Russia, Brazil, and India amplify their growing relevance. Among the top FDI hosting countries in the world, four are from BRICS: China (3rd rank in 2016 and 2nd rank in 2017), Brazil (7th rank in 2016 and 6th rank in 2017), India (9th rank in 2016 and 10th rank in 2017) and the Russian Federation (10th rank in 2016 and 14th rank in 2017). These states have a clear advantage over other states. There was a sharp decline in FDI in Russia and Brazil in 2020 following the Covid crisis.

There was a marginal increase in FDI inflows to China of 4 per cent. FDI inflows into BRICS grew from about 6 per cent in 2000 to 20 per cent in 2018 (Hiratuka 2019). In the same period, FDI outflows from BRICS increased from less than 1 per cent to more than 16 per cent of global investment. A large amount of BRICS' overseas investment is in developed countries. However, BRICS countries have become one of the most prominent investors in Africa. Their share reached 25 per cent of total FDIs in Africa in 2010 (UNCTAD 2013). South Africa has emerged as one of the biggest investors in Africa. The BRICS countries are also investing a significant amount in neighbouring countries that are not BRICS members. Both China and Brazil have invested heavily in their adjacent regions. China is the biggest investor in BRICS states. Its worldwide investment is $425 billion, but only 2.2 per cent of this figure goes to BRICS countries. These trends indicate that BRICS is keen to expand trade and commercial ties with the Global South.

Africa is the biggest beneficiary of investment from BRICS. One-fourth of the assets in the region originate from BRICS (UNCTAD 2013), mainly in the manufacturing and service sectors. Indian investments are also in the same sectors. India has invested in Africa through the Mauritius route. Bharti Airtel acquired the Zain mobile networks for US$10.7 billion. India was the seventh-largest investor in 2011, with about $14 billion (UNCTAD 2013).

Distinct Multilateralism of BRICS

In international relations (IR) literature, multilateralism is widely viewed as a form of inter-state relations conducted among three or more states in a framework of a defined set of rules or principles (Ikenberry, 2003, pp. 533–550). Robert Keohane's 'co-ordination among three or more states' and John Ruggie's 'co-ordination based on rules and principles' are often combined to extract a standard definition of multilateralism. For Ruggie (1993), more than mere co-ordination among three or more states, the 'principles of ordering relations among those states' distinguish multilateralism from other forms of inter-state relations (Ruggie, 1993, p. 567). Given the scholarly interpretations of multilateralism, it is pertinent to examine whether BRICS qualifies as a multilateral institution, and if so, what its distinctive features are. The relevant question in this regard pertains to the generalised principles of conduct, indivisibility, and diffused reciprocity espoused by the BRICS.

As a caveat, we acknowledge that applying the concept of multilateralism in the non-Western context becomes a challenge given the absence of cross-cultural theorisation. The concept of multilateralism has primarily been hostage to a specific version of the liberal international order and its 'ideal types', drawn invariably from the West. One rarely comes across multilateralism studied in the context of the NAM, the G77, or even BRICS. The literature is still far from a cross-cultural understanding of multilateralism claiming universality (Bouchard and Peterson 2010, p. 21). Having said this, we argue that Morse and Keohane's concept of 'contested multilateralism' is an appropriate concept to explain the origin of BRICS.

Morse and Keohane argue that countries dissatisfied with existing institutions resort to threat, exit, or even creating alternative institutions (Morse and Keohane 2014, p. 385). Unable to alter the status quo, dissatisfied states engage in a multilateral contest in two principal forms: 'regime shifting' and 'regime creation'. Regime shifting refers to a situation when unhappy states either take recourse to 'parallel-institutionalisation' (Kumar 2022) or create a new one. BRICS and its affiliated institutions – namely, the New Development Bank (NDB) and the Contingency Reserve Fund (CRF) – are examples of the new form of multilateralism. In short, BRICS members engaged in 'regime shifting' or 'regime creation'.

In distinguishing BRICS' multilateralism, it must be borne in mind that it does not aspire to sabotage the rule-based international economic order. In all its Summit Declarations, BRICS has stressed the centrality of global institutions such as the United Nations, the World Trade Organization, and the G20. Member states recognise the benefits of an order based on the rule of law. Time and again, BRICS has reiterated the centrality of the UN in international governance. Despite internal differences between the elite membership of Russia and China in the P5 and the aspirations of remaining member states to expand the UN Security Council's permanent membership, its position on the UN has mainly been non-confrontational. Even China and Russia, which are critical of political liberalism, acknowledge the value of free trade and economic liberalisation. In the New Delhi Summit Declaration (2021), BRICS was critical of Western protectionism. Therefore, one can safely infer that BRICS is not an institution opposed to all the norms and institutions of liberal internationalism.

BRICS differs from the liberal order on issues of sovereignty, multipolarity, non-interference, and non-intervention. Sovereignty is prized, as the member states are highly suspicious of Western interventions in their territory or their neighbourhoods on the pretext of humanitarian intervention. For instance, Russia and China have vehemently contested Western invocation of democracy and human rights as a ruse for regime change. Russia turned hostile to the West following attempts of 'regime change' in Georgia and Ukraine. China is equally sensitive to any interference in its domestic affairs. It backed Russia in opposing the Western meddling in Iraq, Syria, Libya, Ukraine, and Afghanistan. On sovereignty and non-interference, India's official position is closer to Russia and China than to the West. It does not endorse Western intrusions on the pretext of promoting democracy and regime change. On several occasions, it has criticised these policies as hypocritical and destabilising. India abstained from voting against Sri Lanka in the United Nations Human Rights Council in March 2021 and against Myanmar at the United Nations General Assembly Resolutions in June 2021 (*The Print* 2021). Interestingly, China and Russia also abstained from voting against the military junta of Myanmar (Raj 2021). These resolutions were backed by the United States, the United Kingdom, France, and Germany. Brazil and South Africa are also cautious of Western interference in the name of responsibility to protect.

At a larger geopolitical level, BRICS is also seen as an ideological challenge to the logic of the Washington Consensus. In the case of China, Russia, and some other states, what we witness is a model where the state remains a dominant actor in the economic domain. The Beijing consensus conforming to state-led growth and characterised as 'state-capitalism' emerged as a viable competitor to the Washington Consensus (Kiely 2015). On the issues of fiscal discipline, the autonomy of central banks, and the stability of prices, BRICS states have shown the astuteness to abide by the virtues of the Washington Consensus. But a simultaneous message from BRICS to the rest of the world is that the state's role is crucial in economic transition. Without just and fair conditions, crony capitalism is likely to prosper in emerging countries. Russia of the 1990s is the best example of this development. Local capital cannot compete against multinational companies. India needs a 'developmental state for its market economy to improve the standards of living conditions of her people' (Nayyar 2017). The state and market complement each other, and they can work as checks and balances to regulate the economy as it grows. The model that has been championed by China and followed by Russia is to retain strategic sectors with the state and liberalise the remaining sectors. The declaration of the Summit Meeting at Durban (2013) categorically says, 'We acknowledge the important role that State-Owned Companies (SOCs) play in the economy and encourage our SOCs to explore ways of co-operation, exchange of information and best practices' (BRICS Summit Declaration, Durban 2013). This strategy seems to have worked quite well in the case of the two countries. But such a policy is antithetical and a threat to the neoliberal policies of the West.

BRICS: Criticism and Appraisal

Current scholarship is divided on the effectiveness of BRICS in making a significant impact on the 'structural transformation' of global governance. Will the rise of BRICS lead to a more effective, legitimate, and genuinely representative institutional mechanism for global governance? Optimists have described BRICS as a body with global political influence, having a 'unified political will' and 'institutional balance' (Cooper and Farooq 2013). India's Prime Minister Narendra Modi has described BRICS as a body that has been very adept at evolving mechanisms to develop its institutional skills. In the same vein, Stuenkel (2012) and Luckhurst (2013) have characterised BRICS as a 'successful co-operator'. Club dynamics has helped them overcome internal conflicts and recognise mutual interests (Cooper and Farooq 2013). It has created an informal institutional mechanism to iron out competitive intra-BRICS interests. Miller (2021) argues that many of the analysts in the West dismiss the relevance of BRICS due to a fundamental misunderstanding of non-familiar institutions like BRICS. She underlines three reasons why members participate in such institutions: these forums become channels of information-sharing; they represent their interests; and finally, they enhance the reputations of members and help them build consensus on shared norms and ideas.

BRICS has succeeded in creating valuable institutions such as the NDB and the Contingency Currency Reserve Arrangement (CRA). Some of the reforms in the International Monetary Fund (IMF) are often attributed to pressure from BRICS countries. The IMF increased the quota of the BRICS countries in 2016. India's voting rights increased from 2.3 to 2.6 per cent, and China's from 3.8 to 6 per cent. The share of quotas also changed: India's from 2.44 to 2.7 per cent, China's from 4 to 6.39 per cent, and Russia's from 2.5 to 2.71. Nearly 6 per cent of the allocation will shift from the developed countries to emerging states (George 2016). The executive director will also be elected rather than appointed. Such piecemeal reforms, however, have failed to satisfy the emerging economies. The former finance minister of India Arun Jaitley called for immediate reforms in the IMF and the World Bank (*The Economic Times*, April 23, 2017). He suggested that the World Bank needs to resolve the issue of selective capital increase to reflect the increasing weight of emerging economies and general capital increase to expand its annual lending (Ibid.). The New Delhi Declaration of the BRICS Summit 2021 expressed grave concern at the failure of the IMF to initiate quota reforms under the 15th General Review of Quotas (GRQ). It called for the successful completion of the 16th GRQ by December 15, 2023, to cut down the reliance of the IMF on temporary resources and address the issue of BRICS' under-representation. Yet another example is the proposal to set up the BRICS energy association. The proposal aligns closely with Putin's call for an anti-dollar alliance.

At the other end of the spectrum, sceptics question the credentials of BRICS in heralding a significant change in global governance. Jim O' Neill argued that BRICS is of 'little relevance' (O'Neill 2012). Scholars like Niu Haibin, Keukeleire, and Hooijmaijers characterise BRICS as a 'boom to bust decline' (Niu 2015).

Similarly, some experts argue that BRICS wears a 'facade of unity' at a cursory glance but has cracks beneath its surface. There are too many disputes and contradictions within BRICS. Although BRICS has emerged as an influential actor, it is 'far from a unified alliance or a geopolitical bloc' (Kulik 2014). The sceptics doubt the long-term relevance of BRICS given its heterogeneity, divergence of interests, differences in political systems, and rivalry between India and China. The book discusses these convergences and divergences of interests in detail. It has specific chapters devoted to each member country's interests authored by native citizens or recognised experts in that field.

Rivalry Within BRICS

While BRICS states have repeatedly urged for changes in the international order, these states confront a vast array of challenges. Arguments to this end usually centre on diversity and conflict of interests among the members. Their economic asymmetry and political competition stall any meaningful co-operation. The paradox of BRICS is that it challenges the same system that it wants to retain (Ladwig 2012). This dilemma leads BRICS to meander between the 'voice' (work within the current system) and the 'exit' options (work outside the current regime). Patrick Bond has characterised it as 'co-dependent BRICS from above, co-opted BRICS from the middle, and confrontational from below' (Bond 2015). Achin Vanaik, an Indian scholar, noted that a fundamental political-economic incompatibility rather than organisational handicaps limit the BRICS' capacity to function as a novel force in global politics.

A predominant concern is that China is likely to flex its muscles, dominate BRICS, and threaten its egalitarian spirit. Russia is under the influence of China; South Africa is too small; and Brazil is facing economic recession. Beijing has the financial leverage to influence the policies of other countries. India remains the sole member to resist Chinese pressure in BRICS. India objected to China's proposal of including other countries in the 'BRICS Plus'. It also objected to the Chinese design to integrate BRICS with its flagship project, the 'Belt and Road Initiative'.

The biggest threat to the viability of BRICS, nonetheless, is the potential escalation of border clashes between China and India. In recent years, such events occurred at Doklam (2017) and at the Ladakh border (2020). According to M.K. Narayanan, the former National Security Advisor of India, 'While professing friendship, both sides nurse a mutual suspicion of each other – at times prompting several degrees of alienation. Both countries remain wary of each other's intentions and actions' (Narayanan 2017). Their stances have become rigid, and the border tension between the two prime members can derail the progress of BRICS.

Future of the BRICS

BRICS countries have already started to become more assertive and stress the need for a path of global governance that is multipolar in character. A critical view of global governance holds that the prevailing international system favours big corporate through neoliberal policies and contingent norms. Concerns that the existing system has failed to ensure people's well-being are widespread. Such developments have cast doubt on policies promulgated by financial institutions.

A new set of political forces manifesting themselves in resurgent nationalism and authoritarianism is espousing values antithetical to traditional liberal ideas. Cornier and others have argued that there is pragmatic progress and accommodation despite the frequent criticisms of their natural diversity. At a time of massive geopolitical shifts, BRICS is looking to play an influential role. Hence, 'values and reputation are critical to the credibility of the BRICS' (Cornier 2012). It is not global governance per se but its skewed features in favour of the West that are contested by BRICS. With the rise of China, one witnesses a contest between state capitalism and liberal capitalism. BRICS seeks to work within the existing liberal international order and its affiliated institutions such as the G20.

The future of BRICS is contingent upon a number of developments in the coming years: first, the way the rivalry between the United States and China unfolds in the coming years. If there is polarisation and Russia throws its weight behind China, and India behind the United States, the institution of BRICS will crumble. In other words, a bipolar world will take away the sheen of BRICS. Second, if the uncertainty regarding the evolving world order prevails and polarisation does not hasten up, BRICS will remain relevant. The member states find BRICS extremely useful in navigating an uncertain world order. It is an institutional parachute for safe landing in a turbulent atmosphere. Third, BRICS is still considered a new institution and, therefore, is not judged as harshly as the older institutions. The role of the NDB and the CRA will face harsh scrutiny in the years to come. If the NDB and the CRA succeed in funding and financing developmental projects in developing countries, they will retain their legitimacy and provide an economic rationale for BRICS, which is often viewed with suspicion due to the political diversity and cultural heterogeneity. Finally, the border conflicts between India and China should never escalate to an extent that it begins to affect the functioning of BRICS. Member states must evolve a mechanism to discuss and share information on such thorny issues without interfering with the sovereignty of any state. To sum up, BRICS is a work in progress. It is likely to remain a flexible economic and political forum in the foreseeable future. It is certainly not disappearing from the scene of global governance.

References

'Top 20 Economies of the World', *Investopedia*. www.investopedia.com/insights/worlds-top-economies/ (accessed on 9 July 2021).

Bond, P. 2015. 'Co-dependent BRICS from Above, Co-opted BRICS from the Middle, and Confrontational BRICS from Below', in *BRICS: An Anti-Capitalist Critique*. Auckland Park: Jacana Media.

Bouchard, C. and J. Peterson. 2010. 'Multilateralism: Dead or Alive?', *Mercury E-paper*, 1(1), 1–31. https://dokumen.tips/documents/multilateralism-dead-or-alive-university-of-dead-or-alive-1-ugly-duckling.html?page=5 (accessed on 12 July 2021).

BRICS Summit Declaration, Durban. 2013. www.brics.utoronto.ca/docs/ (accessed on 12 February 2021).

BRICS Summit, Yekaterinburg. 2009. http://brics2019.itamaraty.gov.br/en/about-brics/previous-summits (accessed on 12 February 2021).

Cooper, A. F. 2016. *The BRICS: A Very Short Introduction*. Oxford: Oxford University Press.

Cooper, A. F. and A. B. Farooq. 2013. 'BRICS and the Privileging of Informality in Global Governance', *Global Policy*, 4(4), 428–433.

Cornier, T. 2012. 'The Urban Sustainable Development in European Union through Ranking: A Tool for Governance or a Report of Territorial Disparities?' *International Journal of Environment and Sustainable Development*, 11(1), 64–86.

Dicken, P. 2011. *Global Shift: Mapping the Changing Contours of the World Economy*. London: Sage. pp. 109–168.

The Economist. 2017. 'Four BRICs Don't Quite Make a Wall', June 10. www.economist.com/finance-and-economics/2017/06/08/four-brics-dont-quite-make-a-wall (accessed 10 July 2020).

The Economic Times. 2017. 'Arun Jaitley Calls for Urgent World Bank, IMF Quota Reforms', April 23. http://economictimes.indiatimes.com/news/economy/policy/arun-jaitley-calls-for-urgent-world-bank-imf-quota-reforms/articleshow/58328367.cms (accessed on 3 April 2021).

Farooki, M. and R. Kaplinsky. 2012. *The Impact of China on Global Commodity Prices: The Global Reshaping of the Resource Sector*. London: Routledge Studies in Global Competition. Taylor & Francis.

George, Varghese K. 2016. 'India Gets More Voting Rights in IMF Reforms', *The Hindu*, January 29. www.thehindu.com/business/India-gets-more-voting-rights-in-IMF-reforms/article14024758.ece, (accessed on 16 January 2021).

Hiratuka, C. 2019. 'Trade and Investment within BRICS', in *BRICS Winter School 2019*. UNICAMP. https://we.hse.ru/mirror/pubs/share/332816276 (accessed on 15 July 2021).

Ikenberry, G. J. 2003. 'Is American Multilateralism in Decline?' *Perspectives on Politics*, 1(3), 533–550.

Kiely, R. 2015. *The BRICs, US 'Decline' and Global Transformations*. Singapore: Springer.

Kondratov, D. I. 2021. 'Internationalization of the Currencies of BRICS Countries', *Herald of the Russian Academy of Sciences*, 91(1), 37–50. https://doi.org/10.1134/S1019331621010044 (accessed on 15 July 2021).

Kulik, J. 2014. 'A BRICS Alliance within the G20? Assessing the Performance of BRICS Members', *Os papel dos BRICS nas Relacoes Internacionais Contemporaneas" at the 2nd Seminario Internacional Sobre Potencias Intermediarias*, Belo Horizonte, Brazil, 12.

Kumar, R. 2017. 'India and the BRICS: A Cautious and Limited Engagement', *International Studies*, 54(1–4), 162–179.

Kumar, R. 2022. 'India's Multilateral Foreign Policy Strategy: Phases of its Evolution', *The Round Table* (*Special Issue*) 111(3), 426–439. https://doi.org/10.1080/00358533.2022.2082769

Ladwig, W. 2012. 'An Artificial Bloc Built on a Catchphrase', *The New York Times*, March 26. www.nytimes.com/2012/03/27/opinion/an-artificial-bloc-built-on-a-catchphrase.html (accessed on 20 October 2021).

Luckhurst, Jonathan. 2013. 'Building Cooperation between the BRICS and Leading Industrialized States', *Latin American Policy*, 4(2), 251–268.

Maddison, A. 2001. *The World Economy: A Millennial Perspective*. Paris: Development Centre Studies, OECD.

Malone, D. 2011. *Does the Elephant Dance? Contemporary Indian Foreign Policy*. London: Oxford University Press.
Miller, Manjari. 2021. 'Why BRICS Still Matters', *Foreign Policy*, September 27. https://foreignpolicy.com/2021/09/27/brics-members-summit-brazil-russia-india-china-south-africa/ (accessed on 14 December, 2021).
Mohan, R. 2002. 'Strategic Triangle in Focus During Putin's Visit', *The Hindu*, December 3.
Mohan, R. and M. Kapur 2015. 'Emerging Powers and Global Governance: Whither the IMF?' *IMF Working Paper*. www.imf.org/external/pubs/ft/wp/2015/wp15219.pdf (accessed on 20 October 2021).
Morse, J. C. and R. O. Keohane. 2014. 'Contested Multilateralism', *The Review of International Organizations*, 9(4), 385–412. https://doi.org/10.1007/s11558-014-9188-2 (accessed on 18 July 2021).
Narayanan, M. K. 2017. 'Understanding the Chinese Mind', *The Hindu*, September 1.
Nayyar, D. 2017. 'Economic Liberalisation in India', *Economic & Political Weekly*, 52(2), 41.
Niu, H. 2015. 'A Chinese Perspective on the BRICS in 2015', *Council of Councils*, February 6. www.cfr.org/councilofcouncils/global-memos/chinese-perspective-brics-2015 (accessed on 20 October 2021).
The Print. 2021. 'India Abstains from Voting on Sri Lanka Resolution at UNHRC', March 23. https://theprint.in/diplomacy/india-abstains-from-voting-on-sri-lanka-resolution-at-unhrc/627137/ (accessed on 15 July 2021).
Raj, Y. 2021. 'India Abstains from Voting on UNGA's Myanmar Resolution', *Hindustan Times*, June 20. www.hindustantimes.com/india-news/india-abstains-from-vote-on-unga-s-myanmar-resolution-101624129552897.html (accessed on 11 July 2021).
Ruggie, J. G. 1993. *Multilateralism Matters: The Theory and Praxis of an Institutional Form*. New York: Columbia University Press.
Stuenkel, O. 2012. *Can the BRICS Co-operate in the G-20? A View from Brazil*. South Africa: South African Institute of International Affairs.
UNCTAD. 2012. *Trade and Development Report, 1981–2011 (Three Decades of Development Thinking)*. New York and Geneva: United Nations.
UNCTAD. 2013. 'The Rise of BRICS FDI and Africa', *Global Investment Trends Monitor*, 12.

PART I

Locating BRICS in the Global Order

2

LIBERAL INTERNATIONAL ORDER AND THE EVOLUTION OF BRICS

Bappaditya Mukherjee

Introduction to the Chapter

In the past two decades, a group of leading non-Western powers have come together under a platform known by the acronym BRICS. This platform has emerged within an international system dominated by the ideational, material, and institutional architecture of the US-led liberal international order (LIO). Over the past few years, BRICS members have tried to grow their influence within the LIO. Although it remains a largely informal association with limited institutional features, BRICS nations have also laid the foundations of new structures of global governance favorable to their interests. As the LIO and its foundational idea, liberal internationalism, come under increasing duress, the alternative modes of global governance set by the BRICS group are likely to gain prominence. Even so, the BRICS group is operating in a world in which the ideas of liberal internationalism have taken hold. Liberal internationalism idealizes an interconnected and interdependent world of sovereign states based on mutually beneficial rules, norms, and multilateral institutions (Deudney & Ikenberry 2018). This chapter tries to understand the role of BRICS by situating it within some elements of the LIO. First, we discuss the LIO and the role of the United States in forging it; next, we examine the formation and subsequent functioning of the BRICS; and finally, we explore the interaction of the LIO with BRICS nations.

Liberal Internationalism and the BRICS

Liberal internationalism played an important role in shaping global politics since the end of World War II. It is the underlying philosophy of the LIO. For the LIO to function effectively, the compliance of states with the rules and norms of liberal global governance has to coexist with their sovereignty (i.e., their exclusive

DOI: 10.4324/9781003148074-3

jurisdiction over their respective territorial boundaries). In practice, however, this balance can be rather difficult to achieve. As Ikenberry has pointed out, the United States, its allies, and some of its client states formed the "core" of the LIO. These included the Western European liberal democracies, Canada, Australia, US allies in Europe, as well as Japan, in Southeast Asia and Latin America (Ikenberry 2018a: 16). Following the "unipolar moment" of the disintegration of the Soviet Union in 1991, an era of unparalleled US dominance over the international system followed. The core of the LIO expanded to include some of the newly independent nations that broke away from the former Soviet Union, the post-communist states of Eastern Europe, and China (Ikenberry 2018a: 16). The United States actively pushed these states to shift to market economy, join the US-dominated Bretton Woods international institutions – the International Monetary Fund (IMF), the World Bank (WB), and the World Trade Organization (WTO) – and adopt competitive electoral politics. LIO emerged as a dominant paradigm of global governance in the early 1990s after the end of the Cold War. From the account of the LIO given thus far, we can infer that the actions and capabilities of the United States shape its functioning to an overwhelming extent.

The BRICS is a relatively novel, informal multilateral forum with a low degree of institutionalization. Therefore, the bilateral ties of the United States with individual BRICS members are consequential for the functioning of this group vis-à-vis the LIO. US relations with Russia and China have nosedived in recent years. US-India relations appear to be on the upswing, particularly in the area of defense cooperation. The contradictory nature of these bilateral ties can create cross-pressures, thereby impacting the vision of the group vis-à-vis the LIO. The platform's effectiveness will also be impacted by the current and future course of the bilateral ties of the BRICS members with each other. For example, the latest episode in the India–China rivalry – the border skirmishes that began in May 2020 – presented a serious challenge to the functioning of BRICS.

The strategic impulse of the United States during the Cold War was to contain and isolate the Soviet Union, the precursor to the current Russian Federation. This orientation persisted after the Soviet Union disintegrated into Russia and the independent Central Asian Republics after the end of the Cold War. During this transitionary phase, the relations of the United States with the Soviet Union under the regime of Gorbachev and with the Russian Federation under Yeltsin remained stable. The stability seems to have rested on the asymmetrical power dynamic that favored the United States during this transitional phase. During 1992–1998 the Russian Federation suffered an average annual decline in the GDP of 6.8 percent, while in the subsequent decade it grew at an average of 6.9 percent. Since the economic upswing of Russia was largely a product of oil and gas exports, Russia's weak financial sector and the overall economy were hit particularly hard by the global financial crisis (GFC) of 2008 (Welt 2017). President Yeltsin was succeeded by Vladimir Putin in 1999, who has continuously held one of the two top-most positions in the executive branch – prime minister and president. The ten years of economic stability from 1998 to 2008 coincided with Putin's first tenure as president.

The competitiveness of Russian exports was boosted by a 75 percent devaluation in the ruble. The world's oil prices that stood at $12 in 1997 rose to $148 in 2008 (Rutland 2013: 351). These years of prosperity cum steadiness of the economy not only helped Putin consolidate his power at home but also emboldened him to undertake forceful actions abroad to counter US hegemony. Not surprisingly, this coincided with a deterioration in US-Russia relations.

The post–Cold War policy of the United States toward China was primarily guided by the ideology of commercial liberalism[1] (Doyle 1986). In the early 1990s, elite consensus in the United States was that the growing economic integration of autocratic countries like China could lead to its domestic political liberalization and a "managed" accommodation with the rest of the international community. Economic liberalization would create an indigenous Chinese middle class. This middle class would be dependent on economic openness for their material welfare, thereby acting as a lobby to make political liberalization self-reinforcing. They expected the Chinese middle class to act as a vanguard for political liberalization and representative democracy in China, as during the Industrial Revolution in some parts of Europe.

These expectations were dashed. The Chinese Communist Party (CCP) leadership used economic growth to invest in military modernization and consolidate autocratic power at home. China vigorously followed the goal of global economic integration and zealously guarded its political structure from external interventions. US policy makers and a large section of the Western academic community had encouraged this integration partly for the ideological reasons outlined earlier. In the policy debate that ensued, the integrationists in the United States had touted the principles of comparative advantage. Therefore, market access to Chinese goods would deliver cheaper goods for US consumers. Moreover, opening up the China market would increase foreign direct investment opportunities for Western firms. Western firms saw a golden opportunity to expand their bottom line by entering into another untapped market with a relatively lower cost of production. By the early 2000s, China emerged as a serious competitor to the United States in trade, high-tech, and communication sectors. Chinese indigenous technological productivity made it a serious competitor to the US-led advanced industrial states. The roots of the current problems in US-China relations date back to the Obama administration, which expressed concern over China's cyber-espionage practices and alleged military encroachment in the South China Sea. Populist hostility in the United States toward China came to the fore during the US presidential campaign of 2016. Candidate Trump's anti-China electoral rhetoric was translated into a trade war after he assumed office in January 2017. The Covid crisis has reinforced the mutual hardening of US-China relations. The United States has clearly decided to reorient its trade and security policies to counter China in the Asia-Pacific region.

The Covid crisis is likely to accelerate the structural shift from unipolarity to multipolarity that began during the first decade of this century. In a multipolar system, offensive realists expect great power rivalries to spin out of control. Therefore, compliance with international liberal rules and norms is less likely in a multipolar system in which a powerful authoritarian country like China constitutes one of the "poles" (Popescu 2020). The response of major powers to the Covid threat seems to align with the expectations of offensive realists. For example, Mearsheimer has argued that the behavior of great powers will ultimately be driven by strategic competition with each other (Mearsheimer 2001). Nonetheless, a unipolar system formed under US hegemony has witnessed recurring, hypocritical contraventions of the rules and norms of liberal internationalism. During the Cold War, these violations went largely unchallenged as states viewed everything through the prism of bipolar superpower competition between the United States and the Soviet Union. This is no longer the case as US hegemony is on the wane. The end of the Cold War reinforced the normative and material influence of the neoliberal philosophy of economic governance. Several of the new entrants in the LIO were compelled by the US-led Western powers to adopt some of the policies of the "Washington Consensus" to integrate them into the global market (Babb 2013). The transnational financial crisis of 1997–1998 in East Asia and the 2008 global contagion illustrated the problems of the economic elements of the LIO. In recent decades, countries that were at the "core" of the LIO have experienced cyclical economic recessions, rising inequality, unstable employment, and stagnant wages. The low-skilled workers were particularly hard hit due to the shift of manufacturing bases to low-wage markets in the developing world and rapid advances in automation and information technology.

Liberal Internationalism and Its Discontents

The organizing principles of liberal internationalism include free markets, trade, financial, and commercial relations among nations, international regulations, rules-based interaction among states in multilateral institutions, security cooperation, proselytization of representative democracy, and a faith in reform and progress (Deudney & Ikenberry 2018; Doyle 1986). The ideology of liberal internationalism helped solidify the US alliances of liberal democracies that successfully competed against the Soviet Union and its satellite states during the Cold War. Under US leadership, the Western European democracies formed a security alliance called the North Atlantic Treaty Organization (NATO) and an economic union now known as the European Union (EU). These were the two central pillars of liberal internationalism in practice. This was in contrast to the proletarian or socialist internationalism of the Soviet Union. The Soviet-led model privileged exclusive state ownership of property, preferential trade among ideologically aligned states, state-directed economic planning, and prioritized capital investment in heavy industries. Following World War II, the decolonization of Asia and Africa expanded the Westphalian global order of sovereign legally co-equal states. Along with the former Spanish colonies of Latin America that had gained independence a century earlier, these regions would come to be known as the developing or the Third World. During the Cold War, the United States and Soviet alliance systems fiercely competed to implement their respective visions of a global order by bringing these developing states into their orbit of influence.

At the same time, the objective of the global propagation and support of liberal democratic norms and practices were repeatedly sacrificed by the US-led alliance at the altar of Cold War realpolitik. The expansion of the anti-communist alliance led by the United States could not expand outside Europe without turning a blind eye to egregious violations of human rights by their partner regimes in the developing world. The strategic interventions in the domestic politics of states in the Middle East, Africa, and Latin America by the US-led Western alliance generally weakened the propagation of *political* liberal internationalism during the Cold War period. The professed fealty to democratic values of the Western alliance did not reflect the ground realities. In East Asia, under the hub-and-spokes system, the United States forged bilateral military alliances with Japan, South Korea, Taiwan, Vietnam, the Philippines, and Thailand with somewhat deleterious consequences. As Stubbs (1999, 2018) has illustrated, with the exception of Japan, the infusion of massive amounts of US military assistance contributed to the rise of authoritarianism and militarized disputes in the region. Economic liberal internationalism propagated the benefits of free trade, respect for private property, and minimal role of the state. Some of these East Asian nations resisted economic liberal internationalism with protectionist policies and adopted the import-substitution industrialization and infant industry model of development in which the state played a prominent role. A shift to export-oriented industrialization in the early 1980s accelerated the integration of the East Asian nations with the liberal economic order. It is plausible that US security guarantees in East Asia during the Cold War helped integrate these countries into certain aspects of the LIO (Beeson & Watson 2019; Deudney & Ikenberry 2018; Ikenberry 2018a, 2018b).

At the global level, liberal internationalism influenced the structure of the Bretton Woods institutions created to formalize mechanisms of interstate cooperation and coordination after World War II. These included the United Nations (UN), International Trade Organization, and, later, the General Agreement on Trade and Tariff (GATT) and the WTO, the IMF, and the WB. The IMF was tasked with managing currency exchange rates and assisting countries facing balance of payments difficulties. The WB was initially focused on managing the postwar reconstruction in Europe. A few years later, the WB's activities shifted to devising and funding development projects in middle- and low-income countries. The International Trade Organization, the precursor to the GATT and the WTO became the institutional vehicle for member states to negotiate rules for international commerce. The global trading regime sought to avoid a recurrence of the system-wide retaliatory protectionism by the major powers that accompanied the Great Depression of 1929. Incorporating the logic of Keynesianism, the Bretton Woods structure (BWS) lasted until the 1970s. Terms such as "embedded liberalism" (Ruggie 1982) or the "regulatory liberalism or federalism of free states" (Keohane 2002a) have been used to describe the BWS. This is because obligations of the member states under the global trade rules were sought to be reconciled with their autonomy as sovereign self-governing entities. The goal of the BWS was to counteract the negative effects of trade openness through countercyclical policies and a social safety net. This was different from the model of laissez-faire nineteenth-century classical liberalism, which envisioned a very limited role for the state in economic management.

The cornerstone of postwar international security governance was the UN Security Council (UNSC). It consisted of five veto-wielding permanent members in which the United States and two of its transatlantic allies – Great Britain and France – were in the majority. This system was based on the notion that the great power cooperation was essential to maintain international peace. In contrast, the balance of power system of shifting alliances in earlier eras was inherently unstable and conflict inducing (Ikenberry & Kupchan 1990: 299–307). However, over the past seven decades, the effectiveness of the UNSC to respond to breakdowns in international security has often been constrained due to disagreement among its permanent members.

The Cold War bipolarity of the international system ended with the collapse of the Soviet Union in 1989. This removed the fetters on US hegemony and the "core" of liberal internationalism (Ikenberry 2018a: 9), allowing the uninhibited propagation of the economic ideology of neoliberalism. The central tenet of neoliberalism is that higher growth rates for a country can be best ensured through an empowered private sector operating in a system of interstate economic interdependence and global capitalism. Since the election of conservative governments in the United States and the United Kingdom in the early 1980s, neoliberal economic policies became the default orientation of Western policy makers. Making a departure from the "embedded liberalism" of the post–World War II era (Ruggie 1982), the neoliberal revolution led to the implementation of the "Washington Consensus" policies of lowering trade barriers, capital account convertibility, privatization of state-owned enterprises, and deregulation of markets across the Western world as well as a large swathe of the non-Western world (Stephen 2014: 929). The major Western democracies and international financial institutions (IFIs) advocated these policies as the universal panacea for economic stagnation and distress across the developing world and the post-communist states that became independent after the break-up of the Soviet Union. The disbursement of financial assistance by the IFIs to countries undergoing economic crisis was made conditional on the adoption of neoliberal economic reforms (Babb 2013).

There has been evident dissatisfaction among the rising non-Western powers, including those that constitute the BRICS coalition in the previously described order. This arises from two sources: (1) their perceived unfairness of the rules that currently institutionalize liberal internationalism and (2) their limited representation in the influential nodes of the global governance architecture. At the same time, the complexity of the interaction of the BRICS with the LIO must be appreciated. In an interview to the *Financial Times* on the sidelines of the 2019 G20 summit in Osaka, Japan, the Russian President Vladimir Putin proclaimed that the "liberal idea" had "outlived its purpose". Putin's assessment rested on the challenges facing liberalism in the domestic politics of industrialized Western states that had brought to power reactionary leaders like President Donald Trump in the United States, Prime Minister Viktor Orban in Hungary, and Deputy Prime Minister Matteo Salvini in Italy (Barber *et al.* 2019). Putin's revelatory comments on the "liberal idea" notwithstanding, such rhetoric is not backed up by a concerted program by the BRICS platform to undermine rules-based global capitalism. In fact, there is a shared wariness among policy makers and opinion influencers among BRICS nations with the precipitous diminution of the "liberal idea" that undergirds an interconnected global economy. It is accepted as conventional wisdom within the policymaking and intellectual circles of the BRICS countries that some of the instrumentalist elements of the "liberal idea" (i.e., the various global governance mechanisms) have materially benefited them. The rules, treaties, and agreements formulated within the liberal order have accelerated cross-border capital flows, investments, and value-added production chains; created testing standards to ensure product quality; and boosted technological and research collaboration and trade in services.

At the same time, national policy discussions in most BRICS countries have accepted the current global economic system as given. Just like the majority of the Global South, there is little sign that the diplomatic energies of the BRICS group are being expended on dismantling or reversing global capitalism (van Apeldoorn *et al.* 2012). China predominates in setting the BRICS agenda vis-à-vis global economic integration. Although state capitalism remains the ideological and structural attribute of the domestic Chinese political economy, there has been no let-up in Chinese enthusiasm to participate in the global economy. In comparison, skepticism regarding economic openness is relatively more pronounced among the competing domestic political coalitions in Brazil and India (Stephen & Parizek 2018). However, this protectionist sentiment in Brazil and India is tempered by countervailing constituencies within the state structure and civil society that support greater integration with the global economy. Therefore, it is not implausible that global governance mechanisms spawned since World War II may survive as long as the overall level of economic interdependence remains high (Ikenberry 2018b). The decline in US preponderance and commitment to liberal internationalism and the unsettling effect of the Covid outbreak will not automatically trigger the complete collapse of the LIO.

The bigger source of uncertainty in the LIO arises from the problem of regulatory scale. Transnational issues requiring interstate policy coordination have become far too complex for a single multilateral institution to tackle. This is a plausible explanation for the increasing reliance on informal gatherings such as the G7 and G20 to negotiate important issues of mutual concern (Alcaro 2018: 4) rather than the "institutionalized" multilateral organizations. Writing in the context of the end of the Cold War three decades ago, David Lake had prophesized that in the long run, the costs of global public goods will exceed the willingness of the United States to pay. Consequently, only a working partnership between the United States and China – through informal gatherings like the G7 or G20, could stem the descent toward global instability (Lake 1993: 465). This thesis has proved overoptimistic. These groupings have largely failed to check the deterioration in US-China relations over the past decade.

However, informal gatherings at the G7 and G20 played an important role in creating the space for the BRICS platform to emerge. The roots of the current iteration of the BRICS coalition can be traced back to informal discussions among the senior cabinet officials of Russia, China, and India that had started in the late 1990s. During his visit to India in 1998, the Russian Prime Minister Yevgeny Primakov floated the idea of a triangular alliance between these three countries – the RIC (Cherian 1999; Raja Mohan 2002). The idea was advanced further during the deliberations among the RIC foreign ministers on the sidelines of the UN General Assembly meeting in 2001. India, Brazil, and South Africa then formed a coalition called IBSA on the basis of their shared identity as democratic nations from the Global South. These diplomatic initiatives in the early 2000s were accompanied by overtures from the G8, which is composed of the eight richest nations in the world. In 2003, French President Jacques Chirac took the initiative to invite India and Brazil to the G8 summit at Evian. The 'Outreach Five' (O – 5) created a structure when the five BRICS nations started getting invited to subsequent summits of the G8. Informal discussions among the representatives of the five nations at the G8 summits laid the groundwork for the eventual formation of a separate BRICS group. The precipitating event that hastened the diplomatic cohesiveness of the BRICS group was the global financial crisis of 2008. In retrospect, the G8 summit in Tokyo in the wake of the 2008 crash marked an inflection point after which significant diplomatic energies and material resources were devoted by the BRICS nations to fashion a cohesive response to serious global problems (Cooper 2016).

Sovereignty and Nonintervention

International threats to peace and security are an issue that often tests the cohesiveness of the BRICS coalition on the global stage. The BRICS coalition members are enthusiastic adherents to the organizing principles of the Westphalian state system – sovereignty, territorial integrity, and nonintervention norm. First, they tend to be unified in their opposition to the idea of political liberal internationalism that representative democracy is ideal and must be propagated and institutionalized. Second, all states must adhere to the basic standards of human rights. A variant of political liberal internationalism even provides legal and normative justifications for militarized humanitarian interventions. The hypocritical use of these principles to justify US-led foreign interventions engenders considerable disquiet among these powers. In general, BRICS members favor upholding the nonintervention norm in international law. This is in conflict with the broader LIO framework used to justify US diplomatic and material support for civil society and pro-democracy movements abroad. Suspicion abounds in the international community regarding US military interventions that adopt this rationale. US-led actions that are seemingly aligned with normatively appropriate causes such as democracy promotion and humanitarian aid also engender considerable controversy in international politics. These concerns have been validated as US military involvement in Iraq, Afghanistan, Libya, Syria, and others has generated chaotic and uncertain outcomes in recent years.

The BRICS nations take a dim view of doctrines like "Responsibility to Protect" (R2P) that run counter to the Westphalian norms of sovereignty, nonintervention, and territorial integrity. The R2P doctrine is of particular concern to the BRICS nations because it made sovereignty conditional (Colitt 2011). In other words, the rights of sovereign statehood would be qualified by the behavior of governments with their citizens. Governments that commit egregious violations of human integrity against their own citizens would forego the cloak of protection from external interference in their internal affairs that is granted by sovereign statehood. For example, BRICS nations were united in their criticism of the airstrikes by the US-led coalition to accelerate the fall from power of Libyan leader Muammar Gaddafi in 2011. Interestingly, South Africa initially voted in favor of the resolution establishing the "no-fly" zone over Libya in the UNSC but later joined fellow BRICS members in voicing deep disapproval of this escalation in the use of force (Colitt 2011). In the UNSC Open Debates on the Protection of Civilians during 2011–2012 following the fall of Gaddafi's regime, South Africa explicitly opposed the use of the R2P as grounds for regime change. Russia and China abstained on the resolution to the UNSC vote authorizing a no-fly zone in Libya. Putin (then Russia's prime minister) expressed disapproval of the proposed intervention as a violation of Libya's sovereignty. Since 2011, Russian diplomats have cited the NATO mission in Libya to support their claim that civilian protection provisions in UNSC resolutions can become the justification for Western powers to carry out regime change. The opposition of BRICS nations to US-led multilateral interventions like Libya has shorn the veneer of legitimacy from US-led military actions (Moore 2018: 858–859). Trump's transactional bilateralism is partly rooted in the waning of domestic support for humanitarian and democratization interventions in the United States. It remains to be seen whether the interventionist impulse within the US foreign policy establishment will return with the Biden administration.

Liberal internationalism of the Global North at the level of analysis of global society supersedes sovereign statehood. In contrast, the conception of internationalism favored by the Global South – the newly independent developing countries – places the sovereign state as the inviolable building block of the international system. This is the position that these developing states have consistently held since they emerged as legally co-equal autonomous actors in the current Westphalian international system. Unlike most other sub-groups of nations in the world today, the transnationalism of the BRICS nations is not rooted in their shared history, cultural ties, or geographical contiguity. The most obvious commonality that ties all these nations – except Russia – is their shared experience with some variant of colonialism/imperialism by some of the European powers and the United States in the past. As the successor of the Soviet Union, Russia has obvious reasons to retain a considerable residue of hostility against the US-led Western coalition that handed them a bitter defeat in the Cold War. Thus, a strain of suspicion of the Western powers permeates the foreign policy discourse in all the BRICS countries. However, the suggestions by some (e.g., Pant 2013) that opposition to the West is the overriding reason for the existence and sustenance of the BRICS group in the global order are far too facile.

As an informal anti-Western alliance of convenience, the ideological framework of BRICS can be located on the same continuum as the movement for transnational solidarity among formerly colonized nations against the former imperial powers of Europe and the two superpowers, the United States and the Soviet Union. There are certain overlapping rhetorical themes between the admittedly nebulous ideological perspective represented by BRICS and the broader multilateralism of the Global South represented by the Non-Aligned Movement (NAM). Historically, the Bandung Conference in 1955, the NAM in 1961, the formation of UNCTAD in 1964, and the New International Economic Order (NIEO) in 1974–1975 after the oil price rise of 1974 tried to create solidarity among the Southern states. The NAM declaration prioritized the inviolability of their sovereignty and noninterference in each other's internal affairs (Moore 2018). This made sense in the global order during the Cold War characterized by proxy superpower competition in the Third World. The frailty of their respective economic systems left them extremely vulnerable to exogenous shocks caused by the fluctuations in the global prices of essential commodities. Their foreign policy was subject to the strategic whims of the two competing alliances in the Cold War. When a number of these countries adopted neoliberal models – some voluntarily while others under Western pressure – in the early 1980s, it further eroded the ideological skepticism toward global capitalism in the developing world. The disintegration of the Soviet Union accelerated this process, and by the mid-1990s, the developing world politics of solidarity was largely trumped by the Atlantic project of neoliberalism (Prashad 2012).

Even if we were to exclude Russia, the shared experience of the other BRICS nations with European/US colonialism does not logically provide the cohesive ideological glue for the group. Among the BRICS members, India has a rather strong legacy of anti-colonial South–South diplomacy over the past few decades. Indian Cold War diplomacy was characterized by its leadership of the NAM that balanced its "soft" alignment with the Soviet Union in the Cold War with the United States. On the other hand, the constraints of Cold War dynamics weighed heavily on Brazilian orientation toward NAM. It could not even send an observer to the first NAM summit at Belgrade in 1961 because of US pressure (Hershberg 2007). Brazil has still not joined the organization as a full member. It currently maintains an observer status in the NAM. The same is true of China, which only began participating in the early 1990s (Raja Mohan 2006). South Africa's role in South–South diplomacy is of very recent vintage. During the apartheid rule, it played no role in the NAM. In fact, the NAM had led the global diplomatic charge to sustain sanctions against South Africa. However, since South Africa's readmission to the international community after the end of apartheid in 1994, it has played a very active role in the NAM to signal its disassociation from this policy (South Africa 2006).

Today, the rhetoric of the NAM meetings is reflected in the collective diplomatic voice of BRICS nations. The BRICS political agenda often advances the discourse of Global South solidarism, which privileges non-interference in the internal affairs of states over other norms of international law. The BRICS group on transnational concerns with human rights violations by governments against their own citizens captures the inherent contradictions in this internationalism of the Global South. Unfortunately, the multilateral engagement among the nations of the Global South through BRICS can sometimes turn into a conspiracy of silence on the rights of minorities in these nations. The waning of US support for global human rights standards imposed by major Western democracies under US President Trump serves the self-interest of political elites in the developing world. At the same time, there has been a rise in allegations of political intolerance and backsliding of liberal norms and practices in the three democratic BRICS nations – India, Brazil, and South Africa (IBSA) by transnational political actors. This has further eroded the commitment to appeal to universal standards and norms on human rights among these countries.

South Africa and Brazil's actions have provided brief, albeit noteworthy, exceptions to the overall dilution of human rights in the BRICS agenda set. The consensual opposition by BRICS nations to moral universalism on human rights was publicly resisted by Brazil and South Africa in 2011–2012. At the time, the UNSC had taken up the issue of the Libyan internal conflict that was causing considerable loss of civilian lives. Brazil espoused the doctrine of "non-indifference", and South Africa supported the UNSC resolution sanctioning the no-fly zone. Both these responses were characteristic of a liberal internationalist conception of universal human rights. Admittedly, neither country followed through the logic of liberal interventionism to justify the use of force by the international community and override the nonintervention norm to protect civilians (Moore 2018).

Overall the response of BRICS nations to human rights issues remains constrained. The democratic credentials of the IBSA are increasingly coming under international censure due to evidence of endemic corruption, restrictions on press freedoms, targeting of minorities, and uneven human development indices. Faced with this international pressure, the logic of the partnership of convenience of IBSA nations with China and Russia, which are more unabashedly vocal in opposing the humanitarian aspects of liberal internationalism, becomes clear. Hence, it is doubtful that the democratic credentials of IBSA nations will correlate with policy advocacy for liberal norms and practices in world politics (Öniş & Gençer 2018). Even if it so desired, the IBSA sub-group cannot challenge the agenda-setting power of China and Russia within a non-Western counter-hegemonic alignment such as BRICS to gain a greater foothold within the US-dominated multilateral system. A nebulous desire to act as a global upholder of democratic norms appears unlikely to be sufficient to bind the IBSA sub-group together vis-à-vis Russia and China.

In the next section, this chapter addresses the diffusion of the economic elements of the LIO under the rubric of the Washington Consensus and its impact on BRICS nations.

The Washington Consensus and the BRICS Nations

The elements of the Washington Consensus policy framework have impacted the political economy of each of the BRICS nations over the past three decades. Some BRICS nations adopted these policies due to exigent circumstances. For instance, Russia witnessed an uninhibited implementation of the IMF's "structural adjustment" programs during the 1990s. The so-called shock therapy proved harmful to the Russian economy, which was beset with crisis for several years. Following this period of volatility, Russia entered a phase of relative economic stability once the ruble was devalued in 1998. Since then, Russian economic performance has remained heavily reliant on exports of oil and gas, making it vulnerable to exogenous shocks from price changes in international commodity markets (Cooper 2016: 22). An important landmark in Russia's integration in the LIO was its accession to the WTO in 2012. Following its initial application in 1993, Russia's road to accession faced several obstacles despite reducing its import tariff barriers to the levels required by the WTO. Reservations of the United States regarding greater market access to Russia's financial sector and reforms in intellectual property protection held up accession for several years. The 2008 war in Georgia further delayed accession as it increased the tensions with the United States. The decision of the then prime minister, Vladimir Putin, to join the WTO was based on strategic self-interest rather than on pressure from Western advisers or IMF loan conditionality. Accession to the WTO served Putin's objective of signaling Russia's keenness to be accepted as a respected member of the international community (Rutland 2013: 354–355). Russia adopted currency convertibility and reduced tariffs under the rubric of policies dictated by the Washington Consensus. However, there was little to show for other consensus recommendations relating to privatization, rule of law, and property rights. Its privatization process was largely accessible only to insiders and its state-dominated oil and gas-dependent economy was nowhere near the competitive market that the Washington Consensus wished to create (Rutland 2013).

In India, ideational and policy orientation toward market reforms had begun taking root in the mid-1970s. However, they were stymied by a coalition of vested interests that included farmers, big industrialists, and the professional middle class. The balance of payments crisis of 1991 empowered pro-liberalization technocrats to take on the opposition and introduce the first generation of economic reforms that incorporated elements of the Washington Consensus (Mukherji 2013). The crisis was set in motion when in October 1990 Moody's recommended that commercial banks should stop lending to India considering its internal fiscal situation. When the exogenous shock of the Gulf War of 1991 occurred, it triggered severe foreign exchange shortages (Mukherji 2013: 364). This shortage compelled the anti-reform political and occupational constituencies to cave to the prescriptions of pro-liberalization technocrats. Ultimately, India also picked and chose which Washington Consensus recommendations to implement. Successive governments have largely ignored the Washington Consensus prescription of reducing deficits and social spending. They have also dissented from the Washington Consensus by largely preventing the complete capital account deregulation of the Indian rupee and confined it to the current account (Mukherji 2013: 379).

Under the influence of the Washington Consensus, Brazil moved toward economic openness since the early 1990s. Barriers to trade were reduced, and a host of bilateral and multilateral trade agreements were signed to promote economic interaction with the Americas and beyond. The banking sector was opened to foreign firms. At the same time, Brazil followed other BRICS nations in modifying these recommendations. For instance, Brazil instituted a ban on the privatization of state firms deemed as strategic (e.g., utilities and power companies). Its industrial policy continued to rely on subsidies. Capital controls were imposed during the economic downturn in 2009 (Ban 2013: 308–309). Highly demanding liquidity and solvency requirements were instituted. These measures helped prevent Brazil from experiencing the worst consequences of the global contagion of 2008 (Ban 2013: 313).

Like many other states in Africa, the South African ruling elite adopted the Washington Consensus policies of structural adjustment, privatization, and export orientation in the 1980s. This allowed South Africa to play the role of a junior partner in its alliance with the West and also bolstered its regional hegemony by accessing markets in other African nations. This trend continued after the emergence of the post-apartheid ANC government in the mid-1990s (Martin 2008; Williams & Taylor 2000). South Africa's dominant role in the continent has been undermined with the arrival of China as a major trading partner of the vast majority of African states (Martin 2008). At the same time, the dominance of exports of primary commodities (e.g. oil, mineral, cotton) from African nations is currently replicating rather than replacing the neoliberal policies that had created unequal terms of trade between them and the Western nations of the Global North (Martin 2008: 126).

Over the past three decades, China accepted two elements of the IMF/WB prescriptions – market liberalization and privatization – and resisted pressure to open up its capital account and make the yuan fully convertible (Liew 2005). When the East Asian crisis struck in 1998, the Chinese reticence to liberalize its financial sector helped it to escape relatively unscathed. Policy makers in several developing nations learned from the Chinese experience and followed suit (Rapley 2007). Such cautionary monetary policy gained further traction following the 2008 crisis that disproportionately impacted the Western advanced states. The differential impact of the 2008 crash on countries was in direct proportion to their relative exposure to the globalized capital markets.

Historically, China's market liberalization has taken care to protect its domestic firms – many of them state-owned – from foreign competition. Taking advantage of its large domestic market, its indigenous firms were able to realize economies of scale and lower production costs. In a world market marked by oligopolies, such intervention has proved to be beneficial (Liew 2005). This indigenous production and innovation capabilities have proved valuable for China to weather the twin storm of its trade war with the United States and the post-Covid hostility of major powers.

The Washington Consensus's global legitimacy came under serious threat following the 2008 financial crisis. Ironically, some of the loudest voices in opposition to the Washington Consensus have come from the advanced Western world rather than the BRICS nations. The LIO and the Washington Consensus were buffeted by a populist backlash in the advanced industrial nations in the past few years. This development fits with Robert Keohane's thesis on the adverse consequences of interdependence for workers in wealthier countries:

> Interdependence is characterized by continual discord within and between countries, since the interests of individuals, groups, and firms are often at odds with one another. . . . A stateless competitive world market economy, in which people as well as factors of production would move freely, would be extremely painful for many residents of rich countries: the quasi-rents they now receive as a result of their geographical location will disappear.
>
> *(Keohane 2002a: 73)*

Keohane's prognosis regarding the consequences of interdependence is currently being borne out by the crisis of unprecedented inequality, wage stagnation, and job market volatility within advanced Western states. These negative reactions to global capitalism in the Global North have triggered the following question: Is liberal internationalism "path dependent"? Will states voluntarily adhere to rules to ensure interstate cooperation through multilateral institutions in an open global economy? The path-dependent thesis holds that the longer international institutions survive, the more they become "inherited patterns of rules and relationships that can affect beliefs and expectations" of state and non-state actors (Keohane 2002b: 13; Mahoney 2009). One of the objectives of this study is to understand how and to what extent the individual and collective behavior of the BRICS coalition of nations is interacting with the elements of the post–World War II LIO. While some of the rules, beliefs, and expectations of the Washington Consensus are being reinforced by the BRICS nations, others are not. As Ban and Blyth have pointed out,

> although these countries went through their impressive growth spurts in an international context dominated by neoliberal economic ideas and narratives about the dos and don'ts of development, they nevertheless reclaimed the role of the state in development far beyond the limits of the Washington Consensus framework.
>
> *(Ban & Blyth 2013: 242)*

The diffusion of some of the Washington Consensus policies within the ideological construct of neoliberalism is likely to have contributed to the emergence of the BRICS as a significant player in the international system. It can be argued that the improvement in economic performance of BRICS nations like China and India is inextricably correlated with the acceleration in the globalized system of production and finance that this consensus engendered since the early 1990s. China is clearly the most potent member of this group with a clear vision of the role that BRICS can play in advancing its geostrategic goals. It has already committed significant resources to wield global diplomatic influence commensurate with the expanded scale of its economic might. These countries became key players in the formulation of a nebulous "post-Washington Consensus", particularly in the aftermath of the GFC of 2008 (Birdsall & Fukuyama 2011; Lutz 2015; Stiglitz 2005). Given the variance in their domestic administrative models and political systems, it is no surprise that BRICS nations pursued vastly different development strategies to interact with global capitalism. Higher growth rates transformed the domestic political economy in China and India. The dominant foreign policy orientation of the governing elite and opinion makers of the global South was also altered with the adoption of some of these recommendations. Yet skepticism about certain aspects of the Washington Consensus has remained. BRICS nations have wanted to maximize the benefits from global capitalism while minimizing their exposure to the associated risks. China's growth has been mainly driven by greater access to foreign market for its manufactured goods, while India's reforms have facilitated greater integration of its services sector with the global economy (Cooper 2016: 22).

Interestingly, members of the BRICS platform did not exploit the 2008 crash to push for an ideological alternative to global capitalism. While the overall structure of global capitalism survived the 2008 crash, the crisis strengthened the political resistance to specific Washington Consensus policies in many emerging markets. Prior to the 2008 crash, the dependence of developing nations with balance of payments difficulties on the IMF had been going down precipitously. Due to the East Asian currency crisis of 1998, policy makers in the non-Western world had become more sensitive to the dangers of unregulated integration of their domestic financial sector with foreign capital markets (Rapley 2007). In the decade following the 1998 contagion, many emerging markets shored up their reserves of foreign currency and resisted Western pressures to relax banking regulations. These measures provided an effective guardrail against the global negative externalities of the failures of multinational financial firms in the lead-up to the 2008 crash (Birdsall & Fukuyama 2011). The 2008 crash followed a boom in North–South foreign direct investment (FDI) that further propelled the rapid rise of China (Kiely 2015) and the overall share of developing countries in FDI, trade, and global output. Their portion in the global output increased from 18 percent in 1990 to 26 percent in 2007, while exports increased from 19 percent to 30 percent over the same time period (Dicken 2011).

While the general dissatisfaction with the US-led BWS exacerbated by the 2008 crash animated the consolidation of the BRICS coalition, the asymmetric performance and diversity of sectoral specialization within this group poses a challenge for intra-BRICS economic cooperation. While China, and to some extent India, has managed to sustain impressive rates of growth in recent years, the record of Russia,

South Africa, and Brazil has been relatively disappointing (Lele 2019). The growth of the BRICS countries, except that of China, was highly uneven in the 1990s. In the 1990s, India grew at an average of about 5 percent and Brazil at 3 percent, and Russia was facing an economic catastrophe. Only China was growing at a rate of about 9 percent. In the period since the 2008 crash, the variance in the economic performance of China vis-à-vis other BRICS nations has become even more glaring. China's share in the aggregate GDP of BRICS nations rose from 50 percent in 2001 to 68 percent in 2018 (Hooijmaaijers 2019; Lele 2019). In 2019, the US-headquartered ratings agency Standard and Poor withdrew its formerly bullish rating on the viability of BRICS as an economic bloc (Lele 2019). There is also very little prospect that a free trade agreement (FTA) among the BRICS nations can be negotiated in the near future, particularly as none of them have concluded even a bilateral agreement as yet (Patnaik 2019). At the same time, it would be erroneous to associate the relevance of BRICS merely with the combined economic power of these nations. Nations draw their power in world affairs from non-economic factors as well. For example, the interventionist zeal in recent Russian foreign policy makes it a significant global actor in its own right irrespective of the fluctuations in its economic growth. Similarly, the overwhelming regional influence of Brazil and South Africa is unlikely to be diminished even if they suffer from domestic economic mismanagement (Bershidsky 2019).

Conclusion

In summary, this chapter has posited that liberal internationalism and the LIO provide the background conditions within which the BRICS group emerged. The eventual goal of the BRICS is to fashion an alternative to the system of rules and institutions of the LIO. The United States is the central actor in the LIO, having coaxed and bullied other nations to adhere to its rules. Therefore, the bilateral relations of the United States with BRICS nations impact how they negotiate with one another in fashioning this alternative. Notwithstanding the challenges faced by the LIO in recent years, the policy prescriptions, institutional structures, and rules entailed by liberal internationalism are likely to shape the global order for the foreseeable future. Second, BRICS nations are united in their aversion to humanitarian intervention. As a policy prescription, humanitarian intervention is an offshoot of political liberal internationalism that emphasizes that states uphold a universal standard of human rights. BRICS nations share the belief that the United States and other Western powers couch their strategic objectives under the guise of civilian protection in conflict zones. This chapter has highlighted that the BRICS nations have shown considerable dexterity in picking and choosing elements of the liberal order that suited their circumstances. Despite the normative and material force of US hegemony backing these recommendations, BRICS nations showed considerable autonomy while adopting them. Finally, it is noteworthy that BRICS nations have never questioned the basic premises of global capitalism, just the rules and institutions governing them.

Note

1 Michael Doyle is one of the leading exponents of the tradition of liberalism in IR. Along with other contributors on the subject of interstate war, such as the authors of *Triangulating Peace*, Russett and Oneal, Doyle consolidated the influence of the research tradition of liberalism in Western academia and policy circles (Doyle 1986).

References

Alcaro, R. 2018. 'The Liberal Order and its Contestations. A Conceptual Framework', *The International Spectator, 53*(1): 1–10.

Babb, S. 2013. 'The Washington Consensus as Transnational Policy Paradigm: Its Origins, Trajectory and Likely Successor', *Review of International Political Economy, 20*(2): 268–297. https://doi.org/10.1080/09692290.2011.640435.

Ban, C. 2013. 'Brazil's Liberal Neo-Developmentalism: New Paradigm or Edited Orthodoxy?' *Review of International Political Economy, 20*(2): 298–331. https://doi.org/10.1080/09692290.2012.660183.

Ban, C., and Blyth, M. 2013. 'The BRICs and the Washington Consensus: An introduction', *Review of International Political Economy*, 20(2): 241–255. https://doi.org/10.1080/09692290.2013.779374.

Barber, L., Foy, H., and Barker, A. 2019. 'Vladimir Putin says Liberalism has Become Obsolete', *Financial Times*, June 28. www.ft.com/content/670039ec-98f3-11e9-9573-ee5cbb98ed36.

Beeson, M., and Watson, N. 2019. 'Is International Leadership Changing Hands or Disappearing? China and the USA in Comparative Perspective', *Asian Perspective, 43*(2): 387–415.

Bershidsky, L. 2019. 'BRICS is all about Geopolitics, not Economics', *The Print*, October 30.

Birdsall, N., and Fukuyama, F. 2011. 'The Post-Washington Consensus – Development after the Crisis', *Foreign Affairs, 45*(2): 45–53.

Cherian, J. 1999. 'The Primakov Visit', *Frontline, 16*(1) January 2–15.

Colitt, R. 2011. 'BRICS Powers Criticise Western Strikes in Libya – Source', *Reuters*, April 14. www.reuters.com/article/idINIndia-56321320110414.

Cooper, A. F. 2016. *The BRICS: A Very Short Introduction*. London: Oxford University Press.

Deudney, D., and Ikenberry, G. J. 2018. 'Liberal World: The Resilient Order', *Foreign Affairs, 97*(4): 16–24.

Dicken, P. 2011. *Global Shift: Mapping the Changing Contours of the World Economy*. London: Sage.

Doyle, M. W. 1986. 'Liberalism and World Politics', *American Political Science Review, 80*(4): 1151–1169. https://doi.org/10.1017/S0003055400185041.

Hershberg, J. G. 2007. 'High-Spirited Confusion: Brazil, the 1961 Belgrade Non-Aligned Conference, and the Limits of an 'Independent' Foreign Policy during the High Cold War', *Cold War History*, 7(3): 373–388. https://doi.org/10.1080/14682740701474840.

Hooijmaaijers, B. 2019. 'China, the BRICS, and the Limitations of Reshaping Global Economic Governance', *The Pacific Review, 34*(1): 1–27. https://doi.org/10.1080/09512748.2019.1649298.

Ikenberry, G. J. 2018a. 'The End of the Liberal Order?' *International Affairs, 94*(1): 7–23.

Ikenberry, G. J. 2018b. 'Why the Liberal World Order will Survive', *Ethics & International Affairs, 32*(1): 17–29.

Ikenberry, G. J., and Kupchan, C. A. 1990. 'Socialization and Hegemonic Power', *International Organization, 44*(3): 299–307.

Keohane, R. 2002a. 'International Liberalism Reconsidered', in R. Keohane (ed.), *Power and Governance in a Partially Globalized World*. New York: Routledge.

Keohane, R. 2002b. 'Introduction: From Interdependence and Institutions to Globalizations and Governance', in R. Keohane (ed.), *Power and Governance in a Partially Globalized World*. New York: Routledge.

Kiely, R. 2015. *The BRICs, US 'Decline'and Global Transformations*. London: Palgrave Macmillan.

Lake, D. A. 1993. 'Leadership, Hegemony, and the International Economy: Naked Emperor or Tattered Monarch with Potential?' *International Studies Quarterly*, *37*(4): 459–489. https://doi.org/10.2307/2600841.

Lele, A. 2019. 'BRICS Has Lost Relevance as Economic Grouping, Says Standard and Poor's', *Business Standard*, October 28. www.business-standard.com/article/economy-policy/brics-has-lost-relevance-as-economic-grouping-says-standard-poor-s-119102800903_1.html.

Liew, L. H. 2005. 'China's Engagement with Neoliberalism: Path Dependency, Geography and Party Self-Reinvention', *The Journal of Development Studies*, *41*(2): 331–352.

Lutz, S. 2015. 'From Washington Consensus to flexible Keynesianism? The International Monetary Fund after the Financial Crisis', *Journal of International Organizations Studies*, *6*(2): 85–110.

Mahoney, J. 2009. 'Path Dependence in Historical Sociology', *Theory and Society*, *29*(4): 507–548.

Martin, W. G. 2008. 'South Africa's Subimperial Futures: Washington Consensus, Bandung Consensus, or Peoples' Consensus?' *African Sociological Review/Revue Africaine de Sociologie*, *12*(1): 124–134.

Mearsheimer, J. J. 2001. *The Tragedy of Great Power Politics*. New York: W.W. Norton & Company.

Moore, C. 2018. 'Internationalism in the Global South: The Evolution of a Concept', *Journal of Asian and African Studies*, *53*(6): 852–865.

Mukherji, R. 2013. 'Ideas, Interests, and the Tipping Point: Economic Change in India', *Review of International Political Economy*, *20*(2): 363–389. https://doi.org/10.1080/09692290.2012.716371.

Öniş, Z., and Gençer, A. S. 2018. 'Democratic BRICS as Role Models in a Shifting Global Order: Inherent Dilemmas and the Challenges Ahead', *Third World Quarterly*, 1–21. https://doi.org/10.1080/01436597.2018.1438185.

Pant, H. V. 2013. 'The BRICS Fallacy', *The Washington Quarterly*, *36*(3): 91–105.

Patnaik, I. 2019. 'To Increase Cooperation, BRICS Countries Need a Bottom-up Approach, People to People Connect'. https://theprint.in/ilanomics/to-increase-cooperation-brics-countries-need-bottom-up-approach-people-to-people-connect/291062/.

Popescu, I. 2020. 'Its Time to get Real about Great Power Politics', *National Interest*, April 15.

Prashad, V. 2012. *The Poorer Nations: A Possible History of the Global South*. London: Verso.

Raja Mohan, C. 2002. 'Strategic Triangle in Focus during Putin's Visit', *The Hindu*, December 3. www.thehindu.com/2002/12/03/stories/2002120302761200.htm.

Raja Mohan, C. 2006. 'China and NAM', *Indian Express*. http://archive.indianexpress.com/news/china-and-nam/11629/.

Rapley, J. 2007. *Understanding Development: Theory and Practice in the Third World*. Boulder: Lynne Rienner.

Ruggie, J. G. 1982. 'International Regimes, Transactions, and Change: Embedded Liberalism in the Postwar Economic Order', *International Organization*, *36*(2): 379–415. https://doi.org/10.1017/S0020818300018993.

Rutland, P. 2013. 'Neoliberalism and the Russian Tradition', *Review of International Political Economy*, *20*(2): 332–362.

South Africa. 2006. 'Non-Aligned movement: History and Present Status'. www.dirco.gov.za/foreign/Multilateral/inter/nam.htm.

Stephen, M. D. 2014. 'Rising Powers, Global Capitalism and Liberal Global Governance: A Historical Materialist Account of the BRICS challenge', *European Journal of International Relations*, *20*(4): 912–938.

Stephen, M. D., and Parizek, M. 2018. 'New Powers and the Distribution of Preferences in Global Trade Governance: From Deadlock and Drift to Fragmentation', *New Political Economy*, *24*(6): 735–768.

Stiglitz, J. 2005. 'More Instruments and Broader Goals: Towards a Post-Washington Consensus', in UNUWIDE Research (ed.), *Wider Perspectives on Global Development*. London: Pelgrave Mcmillan.

Stubbs, R. 1999. 'War and Economic Development: Export-Oriented Industrialization in East and Southeast Asia', *Comparative Politics*, *31*(3): 337–355. https://doi.org/10.2307/422343.

Stubbs, R. 2018. 'Order and Contestation in the Asia-Pacific Region: Liberal vs Developmental/Non-interventionist Approaches', *The International Spectator*, *53*(1): 138–151.

van Apeldoorn, B., de Graaff, N., and Overbeek, H. 2012. 'The Reconfiguration of the Global State – Capital Nexus', *Globalizations*, *9*(4): 471–486. https://doi.org/10.1080/14747731.2012.699915.

Welt, C. 2017. *Russia: Background and U.S. Policy*. https://fas.org/sgp/crs/row/R44775.pdf.

Williams, P., and Taylor, I. 2000. 'Neoliberalism and the Political Economy of the "New" South Africa', *New Political Economy*, *5*(1): 21–40. https://doi.org/10.1080/13563460050001961.

3

EVOLUTION OF BRICS

History and Politics

Ajay K. Patnaik

Introduction

BRIC began as an informal grouping of four countries having the potential to exert a strong influence in global affairs due to the size of their population and economy. Subsequently, with the addition of South Africa, the organisation came to be known as BRICS, whose members account for as much as 42 per cent of the global population and 30 per cent of the land area of the world. They also accounted for 23 per cent of the world's GDP and 18 per cent of global trade in 2019 ('What is BRICS?' 2019).

With such a huge reach spanning over four continents and strong economic capabilities, a Research Paper of Goldman Sachs, whose Head of Economic Research Jim O' Neill coined the term 'BRIC' as an acronym for the original four founding countries in 2001, was not exaggerating when it made the projection that 'the rise of the BRICs and the emerging world has been one of the defining stories of the era' (Wilson et al. 2011, p. 3). With their economic weight and contribution to global growth rising rapidly, BRICS has the potential to redefine the rules of global governance and influence the way international institutions function.

Since the first summit meeting of BRICS in 2009 was held in the background of the global financial crisis, it has been argued by some scholars that economic imperatives lie at the heart of BRICS co-operation. For example, Oliver Stuenkel argues,

> an unprecedented combination in 2008 – a profound financial crisis among developed countries compared to the relative economic stability among emerging powers – caused a legitimacy crisis of the international financial order, which led to equally unprecedented cooperation between emerging powers in the context of the BRIC grouping.
>
> *(Stuenkel 2013, p. 611)*

DOI: 10.4324/9781003148074-4

Similarly, Luiza Peruffo (2020, p. 92–93) is of the view that the global financial crisis, which 'disrupted the dominant power structures' in the global financial and monetary architecture, provided the context that 'catalyzed this formal rapprochement' and induced the 'first joint actions' by BRICS members as a group.

However, BRICS was not just a response to the global financial crisis. It originated earlier than 2009, before the crisis happened. BRICS was formed when the foreign ministers of Brazil, Russia, India and China met in September 2006 on the sidelines of the UN General Assembly and decided to come together as a formal grouping. The issue around which the four countries came together was related to the prevailing international order that marginalised countries outside the Western bloc. The threat of unipolarity and unilateralism remains at the core of BRICS co-operation, especially concerns regarding certain powers dominating global institutions or bypassing international organisations in pursuit of their geopolitical interests.

There is no strict separation in reality, however, between the political and economic objectives of BRICS. The international order is both political and financial. The domination of the Western powers in the 1990s was based on their global political/geopolitical influence as well as control of international financial institutions. The weakening of one also weakens the other – weakening political influence results in weak financial control and vice versa. BRICS seeks to contest the Western-dominated international order in both these aspects so that not only the emerging powers but also the Global South in general can benefit.

Evolution of BRICS

Idea and Background

One can trace the origin of the idea of a multilateral organisation like BRICS to the vision of one of the most prominent statesmen of Russia – the late Yevgeny Primakov – who during his tenure as foreign minister floated the idea of a Russia–India–China 'strategic triangle' in 1996. The idea was again articulated during his visit to New Delhi in December 1998. Primakov's vision was to achieve a multipolar world order by building what he called a 'strategic triangle' between the aforementioned three powers (Cherian 1999; Simha 2015).

Coming as early as the mid-1990s, when Russia was pursuing a Euro-Atlantic partnership agenda, this was truly imaginative thinking. The idea also came at a time when India and China were building closer relations with the West. It was not until Putin's presidency that Russia seriously considered a multipolar world order as a strategic policy objective. Since Putin came to power in 2000, the United States and its allies began having a spree of regime changes, beginning with the invasion of Afghanistan in 2001, followed in 2003 by military actions and a change of regime in Iraq.

Primakov's vision was premised on constraints imposed by the prevailing international system on the rise and influence of Russia, India and China. It took a while for his ideas to shape policies since all three countries were reluctant in the mid-1990s to take any step that would negatively affect their growing ties with the United States and other European powers. The move to strengthen relations between the three countries advanced forward with the formation of the RIC (Russia, India and China) Grouping and IBSA (India, Brazil and South Africa) Dialogue forum (Das 2010).

In the background of some unilateral actions by the United States and its allies, the threat of a unipolar world order was becoming real. For example, the military actions against Yugoslavia and Iraq were taken outside the framework of the United Nations (UN). These developments brought the three RIC countries closer.

RIC and IBSA were two important mechanisms for the later evolution of BRICS, which came into existence in 2006 and held its first summit in 2009. In spite of the differences in terms of economic policies, political systems and foreign policy orientations, Russia, India and China were induced by international circumstances to come together when their foreign ministers met to form the RIC Dialogue Platform in 2002. Dongxiao and Shua (2016, p. 433) describe RIC co-ordination as a 'non-ideological pattern of major-power cooperation on regional security'. This co-operation, however, is based on a wide range of shared interests on global issues.

RIC members advocate the primacy of the UN in solving crises in various parts of the world, strict adherence to international law and non-interference in the internal affairs of sovereign states. Their foreign ministers have met annually and reiterated their opposition to externally managed regime changes and to the imposition of sanctions against any country without the authorisation of the UN. RIC foreign ministers have also stressed the need for more resources to be provided to countries in the Global South from international financial institutions. The three countries have emphasised the need for free and open markets, and opposed any steps to promote protectionism (Rajagopalan 2019).

The IBSA Dialogue Forum is another multilateral framework to promote South–South co-operation. Formed in 2003, IBSA held its first summit in the Brazilian city of São Paulo in 2006, the year when BRIC was launched in New York. Although trade and the Doha round of WTO negotiations remained the focus in the first two summits, from the 2008 New Delhi summit onwards, the global financial crisis, the Iranian issue, the West Asian conflict and the International Monetary Fund (IMF) reforms came to the agenda. On the issue of the UN Security Council (UNSC) reforms, there is complete consensus among IBSA members (Arruda and Slingsby 2014, p. 2).

Thus, RIC and IBSA did not just precede the formation of BRICS but prepared much of the ground for the future coming together of the five countries. Since then, these two forums have been very useful to pepper over differences before leaders meet at the BRICS Summits.

Post–Cold War International Order: Unipolarity and Unilateralism

The genesis of BRICS lies in the post–Cold War international order that emerged after the disintegration of the USSR. It was assumed that after the end of the Soviet

Union, the Cold War and its instrumentalities would become relics of the past. However, NATO not only remained intact but expanded eastward to the borders of Russia. The aggressiveness of this military alliance in different guises has been demonstrated in Europe (former Yugoslavia), West Asia (Iraq, Libya and Syria) and Asia (Afghanistan).

The growing trend of unilateral aggression and bypassing of the UN was worrying many countries outside the Western bloc, even if states around the world were seeking closer ties with the United States and its allies. Russia is a classic case whose leadership under President Yeltsin relentlessly pursued a policy of closer integration with Euro-Atlantic structures, but that did not stop NATO's eastward expansion. Russia, which has strong historical and ethno-cultural ties with Serbia, helplessly watched the NATO bombing of Belgrade.

In the 1990s, the world was reeling under the impact of an unfolding unipolar order, and the methods employed to achieve this were linking international aid and assistance to structural reforms, imposing economic sanctions and different forms of coercion, including invasion of sovereign states by the United States and its allies. Iraq was invaded and so was Libya; in both cases, regimes were changed by external military invasion. The same attempt was being made in Syria as well.

The global balance of forces was being changed in the West's favour through such unilateral actions. Russia and China as strong military powers have been at the receiving end, facing the threat of containment through alliance-building by the United States against them. India had always stood for an equitable international order that is against the hegemonic role of any power. Post–Cold War developments were obviously not in the long-term interests of India. With India's rise as an economic and nuclear power, Delhi aspired to have a bigger stake in the international system, both politically and economically.

Brazil, a leading power in South America, was changing its foreign policy orientation under Lula da Silva and his successor Dilma Roussef, both of whom put more emphasis on 'South–South co-operation'. Brazil became a leading voice from Latin America to oppose military intervention in sovereign states by Western powers. Some of the steps it took included abstention on the United Nations Security Council Resolution 1973 allowing for military intervention in Libya and favouring the recognition of Palestine as a non-member (UN) state in the face of US opposition. Brazil, like India, also favours reform of the UNSC, which they feel does not reflect contemporary realities. Both countries, along with Russia and China, support institutional reforms at the IMF and the World Bank (Jesus 2014; Marcondes and Mawdsley 2017).

South Africa's capability and its active role in the continent place Pretoria in a leading position in Africa. During its second term as an elected member of the Security Council from 2011 to 2012, South Africa prioritised African security issues. It has been working towards bringing peace and stability, especially in strife-torn countries such as Burundi, South Sudan and the Democratic Republic of the Congo.

According to some scholars like Maxi Schoeman et al. (2017), the location of South Africa marks it out as a 'gateway' into the continent, and, being on the southern tip of the continent, the country can also be considered as a 'bridge' between the North, the Global South and the African continent. Its membership in the G20 gives it additional importance as a global player from the continent.

In short, BRICS members are among the leading powers in their respective regions and have common interests in the search for a new world order where the voices and actions of countries outside the Western bloc would carry weight. BRICS is expected to provide the mechanism through which these countries can play effective roles in world affairs. Bilateral differences and different foreign policy orientations notwithstanding, there are some core issues on which the diverse group of countries forming BRICS has come together. These include strengthening a multipolar world order, reforming and expanding the role of the UN, supporting the Paris Agreement on climate change, reforming global financial institutions and supporting the countries of the Global South. There are of course differences in the nature of their relations with the West. India and Brazil today have excellent ties with the United States and its allies. On the other hand, Russia and China have faced sanctions from the Western powers. Yet the core issues highlighted here help the BRICS grouping to come together at the global level.

Multipolarity and the role of the UN have always been strategic goals of BRICS countries, which brought them together and have been reiterated since the first summit in the Russian city of Yekaterinburg in 2009. The joint statement after the first summit said:

> We underline our support for a more democratic and just multi-polar world order based on the rule of international law, equality, mutual respect, cooperation, coordinated action and collective decision-making of all states. We reiterate our support for political and diplomatic efforts to peacefully resolve disputes in international relations.

The leaders also called for comprehensive reform of the UN by recognising 'the status of India and Brazil in international affairs' and extending their support to the aspirations of these two countries 'to play a greater role in the United Nations' (Summit Declaration, Yekaterinburg 2009).

While these views have been expressed in subsequent summits, BRICS members have also strived to develop common alternative positions on various global challenges. At the time when the war in Libya was still going on and a multistate NATO-led coalition began a military intervention in Libya on the pretext of enforcing a UNSC resolution on ceasefire, the third BRICS Summit of 2011 was held in Sanya in China. The members were naturally worried about the actions being taken beyond the UN mandate and a regime change being enforced without respect for the sovereignty of a weaker state. BRICS members not only spoke on the Libya issue, but they also used the occasion to highlight the need for reform of the UNSC (Sanya Declaration 2011).

Illustrative of the alternative BRICS position to that of the West was its stand on the issue of Ukraine. The sixth BRICS Summit in Brazil took place when the

Ukraine crisis was deepening. As a demonstration of their global dominance, the West and its allies removed Russia from G8 after the Crimean referendum and the peninsula's integration with Russia in March 2014. Even the G8 meet, scheduled for June of that year at Sochi in Russia, was cancelled.

However, the BRICS grouping refused to be part of the efforts to isolate Russia. In fact, the Ukraine crisis also provided another opportunity to question the way Western powers dominate the narrative and actions in the international arena. In March 2014, the BRICS members abstained while voting at the UN General Assembly on a resolution condemning Russia over its actions in Crimea. Even India and China, which are normally very vocal on issues of territorial integrity and sovereignty, remained neutral on Crimea. India's then National Security Advisor Shivshankar Menon even stated:

> We would hope that whatever internal issues there are within Ukraine are settled peacefully and that the broader issues of reconciling the various interests involved, and there are after all legitimate Russian and other interests involved, are discussed, negotiated, and that there is a satisfactory resolution to them.
>
> *(Madan 2014, p. 1)*

Russia's partners in BRICS have avoided criticism of Putin's actions with respect to Ukraine in any way, and, subsequently, they helped Moscow with financial co-operation despite Western sanctions. A 30-year deal worth $400 billion, signed in May 2014 to bring gas from Siberian fields into China's northern industrial regions, is a strong example of BRICS countries co-operating to make sanctions irrelevant. Deals that could have taken much longer to materialise were completed faster due to Western actions against Russia. As a result, 300,000 barrels of gas a day from Sakhalin in Eastern Siberia began to be supplied to the industrial city of Daqing in China (Eckel 2014).

In 2016, Russia agreed to supply India with the latest weapons like the S-400 air defence systems (a deal worth US$5 billion) and construct frigates. Both sides also agreed to form a joint venture to manufacture Ka-226T helicopters in India. These deals were made despite the threat of US sanctions (Rajagopalan 2020).

Apart from the global geopolitical dynamics, the other development that brought the BRICS countries together was the global economic crisis of 2008–2009. The shock exposed the inadequacy of the global financial institutions to deal with the crisis and demonstrated the weakness of Western economies that were leading these institutions. The strength of the emerging economies was manifest during the crisis, and it was natural that they would demand their fair share in the decision-making structures of international financial institutions. The slow pace of reforms and reluctance to share power, especially in the IMF, pushed BRICS countries towards creating alternative institutions that could insulate them from future crises.

Global Financial Architecture: Search for Alternatives Institutions

BRICS countries came out of the economic crisis of 2008–2009 quickly without too much difficulty compared to developed economies. Following the crisis, the issue of global financial governance came to prominence in the BRICS agenda. The co-ordination of the finance ministers of the five countries had already resulted in some success at the London Summit of the G20 countries in 2009, where substantive recommendations of the finance ministers of four emerging economies – Brazil, Russia, India and China – made at their London meeting in April 2008 were endorsed, including the call for IMF quota reform (Stuenkel 2009, p. 611).

The first BRICS Summit of the grouping also took place in the background of the crisis and thus engaged the leaders who met in Yekaterinburg in 2009.

In fact, in the midst of the global economic crisis, BRICS leaders spoke of reforms in international financial institutions to minimise the impact of the crisis on poorer economies. The grouping since has become increasingly vocal about reforms, urging Western powers to undertake a comprehensive review of the quota formula and selecting the Heads of IMF and World Bank through a 'merit-based' transparent process (Fourth BRICS Summit – Delhi Declaration 2012).

Although the voting share change was finally agreed upon in 2010, it is still considered inadequate by BRICS members since it does not adequately reflect the economic weight of emerging markets. Today, the combined voting share of BRICS countries in the IMF is only 14.15 per cent, while the US vote share alone is 16.15 per cent, and it can block any proposal since at least 85 per cent is needed for approval (IMF 2020).

The reluctance of Western powers to move beyond symbolism and address the aspirations of BRICS countries made members of the group look for alternatives. The idea germinated first in the Delhi Summit of 2012, where the finance ministers agreed to study the feasibility and viability of setting up a new development bank. The process moved forward at the fifth summit next year in Durban, where the leaders signed an agreement to set up the New Development Bank (NDB). In 2014, two major BRICS institutions came into existence – the NDB and the Contingency Currency Reserve Arrangement (CRA). The BRICS NDB (with an initial capital of US$50 billion that rose over time to US$100 billion) and the CRA of US$100 billion have been functional since 2015. They would provide protection to member states against a liquidity crisis (Fourth BRICS Summit – Delhi Declaration 2012). By 2016, the NDB had approved projects worth US$1.5 billion in BRICS countries and had issued loans for 37 infrastructure projects by September 2019, with a total value of US$10.2 billion (Putin 2017, p. 20; CGTN 2019).

In short, BRICS countries have demonstrated their growing economic capacity by creating the NDB and CRA. However, the flaws in the global system were not merely economic or financial in nature. These are also related to the asymmetric power structure – the skewed representation in the UNSC being an example. Thus, the BRICS grouping prioritises its actions to address the discriminatory nature of an inequitable international order, at both the political and economic levels. However, other areas of global concern also needed BRICS' attention and action. As it evolved, the organisation included in its agenda issues related to development, human security, health, education and environment. Today, the BRICS countries are better poised to raise the level of welfare and development not only of their own population but also of those living in the Global South.

Africa became the focus of attention at the fifth summit on 27 March 2013, in Durban, South Africa, where the discussions under the theme 'BRICS and Africa: Partnership for Development, Integration and Industrialisation' resulted in the eThekwini Declaration. The members agreed to increase their engagement and co-operation with non-BRICS countries, in particular emerging market and developing countries. A meeting with leaders of other African countries under the theme 'Unlocking Africa's potential: BRICS and Africa Cooperation on Infrastructure' provided an opportunity for leaders from BRICS and African countries to discuss how to strengthen co-operation between the organisation and the continent.

A similar outreach to South American countries was tried in the next summit in 2014, where a joint session was held with the leaders of that region. The final Declaration recognised the importance of the Union of South American Nations (UNASUR) in promoting peace and democracy in the region and in achieving sustainable development and poverty eradication. It called for increasing dialogue of BRICS countries with South American countries (Sixth BRICS Summit – Fortaleza Declaration 2014).

Institutionalisation

BRICS took a formal shape in 2009, and, since then, the annual summit level meeting of top leaders of member countries with rotating presidency has been institutionalised. Similarly, following their first meeting in November 2008 in São Paulo to formulate a response to the global economic and financial crisis, BRICS finance ministers and governors of Central Banks have met on the sidelines of BRICS Summits and the UN General Assembly, as well as during G20, IMF and World Bank meetings. The foreign ministers of the group have been meeting during the UN General Assembly since 2006 to co-ordinate their response on matters of common concern. Ministers of trade traditionally meet on the eve of the BRICS Summits and at the margins of WTO ministerial meetings. There is a Contact Group for Economic and Trade Issues (CGETI), which proposes institutional frameworks and measures to expand co-operation on economic and trade issues among the BRICS (BRICS Meetings and Forums Website). The other formats of interaction among member states are the meetings of ministers of agriculture, communication, disaster management, education, energy, environment, finance, health, education, industry, labour and employment, migration, science, technology and innovation.

Institutionalising co-operation among members has been a work in progress. The most visible in this respect has been the establishment of the NDB and the

CRA. These institutional innovations, according to Abdenur and Folly, create new normative platforms similar to that of Western ones like the OECD, thus enhancing the role of BRICS countries as 'rule-makers in international development'. They further point out that in contrast to the 1990s, when strict conditionality like structural reforms and trade liberalisation were imposed for receiving northern aid either bilaterally or through the IMF, South–South co-operation that the BRICS promotes is based on 'horizontality, solidarity, non-conditionality and mutual benefits' (Abdenur and Folly 2015, p. 77). The NDB also can play an important role in addressing global environmental concerns.

BRICS co-operation is important to mitigate the effects of climate change. Since most of the BRICS member countries are large and fast-developing economies, they have greater responsibility to address the fallout of their growth on the environment. Brazil, Russia, India and China with a combined population of about three billion people and a GDP of nearly US$16 trillion have a major impact on global emissions (Wheeland Matthew 2015). Therefore, sustainable development in these countries is an imperative for improving the global environment.

At the first ever meeting of BRICS environment ministers held in Russia in April 2015, it was agreed to establish a working group on environment to 'identify priority areas of co-operation'. The working group also agreed to 'explore the potential of the BRICS New Development Bank (NDB) to fund environmental projects' and the possibility of 'establishing a collaborative platform of the BRICS countries to share best environmental practices and facilitate the exchange of environmentally sound technologies and know-how with participation of public and private stakeholders' (IISD News 2015).

The first BRICS project to be operational was a green energy project funded by the NDB, which involved a 17-year loan of US$76 million to Shanghai Lingang Distributed Solar Power Project sanctioned in December 2016 (The Indian Express 2017). According to K.V. Kamath, then the Bank's president, 80 per cent of its loans amounting to US$10.2 billion up to September 2019 went to transport, clean energy, water and sanitation sectors (CGTN 2019).

The 'Saint Petersburg initiative', as the meeting of environment ministers of 2015 came to be known, established a platform for sharing green technologies in certain areas in which some BRICS countries have made significant progress. There are areas where the BRICS members individually have become leaders in technologies such as solar – three of the top five solar photovoltaic firms are Chinese, while in the wind sector Indian and Chinese companies are among the leaders in this field (Maupin and Sidiropoulos 2015).

Non-transfer of technology and capital by the West pushed BRICS to focus on environmentally friendly projects. Individually, most of them are spending financial resources on renewable energy and enforcing strong domestic laws. But their role in international negotiations and multilateral co-operation has assumed critical importance following the United States' withdrawal from the Paris Accord. An important step in that direction was the 'BRICS Multilateral Co-operation and Co-financing Agreement for Sustainable Development', signed at the Durban Summit in 2013. The aim is to facilitate technological co-operation and co-financing that promote sustainable development and green economy (BRICS/Africa Partnership for Development 2014).

There are various other areas, apart from climate issues, where BRICS countries co-operate regularly. These include meetings of national security heads, meetings of heads of competition authorities and heads of revenue administration. Apart from these, summits of universities and youth summits are regularly held. These are important meetings that seek to co-ordinate policy-making in different areas as well as encourage non-state-level interactions. The BRICS Network University was established in 2016, and its annual meet includes participation from universities from emerging economies. BRICS has evolved a university ranking system based on its own parameters.

Another area of co-operation, Disaster Risk and Management, also figured conspicuously in the policies of BRICS in the last few years. At the ninth summit in Xiamen, China, on 4 September 2017, it was decided to endorse the Saint Petersburg and Udaipur Declarations of BRICS Ministers for Disaster Management and establish a BRICS Joint Taskforce on Disaster Risk Management. The purpose is to 'exchange of information on best practices concerning disaster risk management and co-operation in the field of forecasting and early warning for effective response to natural and human induced disasters' (9th BRICS Summit – BRICS Leaders Xiamen Declaration 2017).

As the world faced more and more health-related disasters, BRICS countries discussed ways and means to lessen these threats during summit meetings and through other mechanisms like minister-level meetings. Before the Covid-19 pandemic, the discussions were about saving lives from such prevailing diseases like tuberculosis and Ebola and even about milk shortages for the population. The BRICS TB Research Network was established in 2016 to promote 'new scientific, technological and innovative approaches to tackle the TB burden, by supporting scientific projects' on a wide range of issues related to the disease. In 2019, it was decided to establish the BRICS Human Milk Bank 'in order to expand sharing of knowledge and technologies focused on food and nutritional security in neonatal and nursing infant care, with the right to health as its central value' (10th BRICS Summit Johannesburg Declaration 2018).

The Covid-19 pandemic has tested the capability of not just individual members but also BRICS as an organisation at a time of grave crisis. The spread and extent of it is much larger than other viral epidemics in recent times. It also has challenged national and global responses to the virus. At a time when global co-operation is most needed and millions are affected with hundreds of thousands of deaths, the United States' decision to withdraw from the World Health Organization (WHO) dealt a serious blow to global efforts in fighting the pandemic. The role of BRICS under the circumstances becomes far more critical.

A co-ordinated response from BRICS came when the NDB announced a US$1 billion loan to China in the third week of March 2020, followed by a similar amount each being approved for India, South Africa and Brazil. This step, according Atul Aneja, could become 'a template to address natural disasters' in future as NDB also stated that it has the financial capacity to provide US$10 billion in 'crisis related assistance' to member countries (Aneja 2020).

Since the spread of the Covid-19 pandemic, BRICS countries have tried individually to help not just the member countries but also other nations, especially in the Global South. This was going on even before the formal video conference of the foreign ministers of BRICS on 28 April 2020. India has also been pushing for an inclusive BRICS-driven pharma alliance to actively explore the production of a vaccine.

Three countries – Russia, India and China – have the capacity to produce and deliver vaccines. For example, Sputnik V of Russia, Sinovac of China and Covaxin of India are strong candidates of a successful vaccine against the Covid virus. Given their capacity for medical research and production, there was a strong push by Russia to set up the BRICS Vaccine Research and Development Centre, which had been agreed upon in 2018 at the Johannesburg summit (BRICS Information Portal 2020).

Throughout the pandemic, the BRICS countries not only demonstrated their commitment to global institutions like the WHO but also came to the aid of poorer countries (Aneja 2020; Gupta 2020).[1] Following the United States' withdrawal, China extended another US$30 million donation to the WHO, and none of the BRICS members followed the US example of withdrawing from the organisation. India took over as the Chair of the WHO Executive Board on 22 May 2020. It is expected that this would rally BRICS' support for global health efforts under the auspices of the WHO.

Further Evolution: Challenges and Prospects

It could be argued that since BRICS members are from different continents, it would be difficult for them to find common ground on issues affecting various parts of the world. Krisztina Varro and Arnoud Lagendijk have discussed various strands of 'relational perspective' on regions in their article 'Conceptualising the Region – In What Sense Relational?' According to their opinion, the 'relational view', which has found wide acceptance among scholars of geography, goes beyond the notion of 'territorial contiguity' to conceptualise a region in an increasingly globalised and mobile world (Varro and Lagendijk 2013). From this perspective, as Meena argues:

> The underlying relational nature of the BRICS is that they are products of globalization and are regional powers in their respective regional locations. Such geopolitical imagination has resulted in strategic regionalization for the BRICS vis-à-vis the West because the defining relational element of the BRICS is that they have recently become capable of providing some semblance of global governance to the developing world.
>
> *(Meena 2015, p. 38)*

While BRICS might fit into the relational perspective framework, there are many bilateral problems between some BRICS countries that could hinder its progress as a cohesive organisation. Yet the relational elements, which brought them together in the first place, may help them transcend bilateral differences on issues of common interest. The organisation also could become a catalyst to smoothen relations by creating conditions like summit meetings and agreements on other areas of common concern even during periods of bilateral tensions.

Bilateral issues are relatively more complicated in India–China relations. Except for difficulties between these two, bilateral relations between and among others are not ridden with tension. India and China have excellent relations with the other three countries of the BRICS grouping. However, tensions between China and India in certain respects might create difficulties in the way of making BRICS a coherent and powerful organisation. The latest series of crises began with the standoff between the armies of the two countries in the Doklam Plateau at the tri-junction of Bhutan, India and China (The Hindu 2017). Next came the standoff in the Ladakh region, where the two armies have faced each other since May 2020.

The Sino-Indian tension also tests the resilience of BRICS as a multilateral organisation. In the background of the Doklam face off, the leaders of the two countries met along with other BRICS leaders on the sidelines of the G20 meeting in Hamburg on 7 July 2017, which sufficiently cooled temperatures for the subsequent meeting of India's National Security Advisor with his BRICS counterparts in China on 28 July 2017. The Doklam standoff ended just before the BRICS Summit in China (The Asian Age 2017).

A situation more serious than the Doklam crisis again emerged in the Ladakh region at various points of the Line of Actual Control (LAC), when soldiers of India and China were involved in skirmishes beginning on 5–6 May 2020. The face off resulted in tragic deaths for both sides on the night of 15–16 June 2020. The two countries have been amassing troops, ammunitions and fighter aircraft along the entire Indo-China border/LAC. The current standoff has taken military lives and threatens to spiral into more tensions between the two countries for a long time. The positive signal has been the talks at various military, diplomatic and political levels (India-China tensions 2020). In the meantime, India's actions against certain Chinese investments and companies have created a further gulf in the relationship, though negotiations for disengagement and de-escalation still go on.

India–China relations still suffer from unresolved border demarcation, apart from current geopolitical issues like differences on Chinese claims over the South China Sea and China's growing influence in India's neighbourhood. The evolving participation of India in a coalition of Pacific powers – the United States, Australia and Japan – is perceived by China as a threat to its position in the South China Sea. The co-operation of the four, now known as the Quadrilateral Security Dialogue or QUAD, began as an informal dialogue in 2007 and was revived in 2017. The members of the QUAD have been conducting joint large-scale naval exercises, known as Exercise Malabar.

However, the organisation has evolved over the years despite bilateral problems. For example, trade and economic ties between India and China have expanded from US$70 billion in 2014 to nearly US$85 billion in 2019 (Embassy of India in China 2019).

Apart from bilateral tensions between India and China, there are also apprehensions that some internal developments in the member countries could also slow down the progress of BRICS. Brazil, for example, has gone through some political turbulence and changes. The current leadership of the country has moved closer to the United States. Yet, given the global economic power of China, as well as Brazil's expanding trade ties with Russia, India and South Africa, it is not likely that Brasilia would weaken its ties with BRICS partners (*BrazilGovNews* 2017; Macauhub 2017).[2]

It is true that BRICS members are not the only important countries in their respective continents. There are other major economies and politically important states. That, however, does not take away the fact that each BRICS member is an important state in the region concerned. Some of them are even major global players. The multilateral agenda that brought the five countries together is yet to be substantially realised, and, despite bilateral problems between China and India, the objectives of BRICS remain a motivating factor for the participating states to remain together, which was demonstrated at the 12th virtual summit hosted by Russia under the theme 'Global Stability, Shared Security and Innovative Growth'. The summit was held in the background of the Covid-19 pandemic and the India–China standoff. Yet there were positive discussions on the reform of the multilateral system, measures to mitigate the impact of the ongoing Covid-19 pandemic and co-operation on counter-terrorism, among other issues.

Conclusion

Attempts to impose a post–Cold War hegemonic global order by the use of military force, regime change and sanctions without a UN mandate pushed the BRICS countries to come together to build a multipolar world order. BRICS members have been vocal about their growing frustration at the lack of reforms in the Bretton Wood institutions and the UNSC. It has developed alternative institutions like the NDB and CRA. These institutional innovations seek to create new normative platforms that are alternatives to Western ones like the OECD or G7, thus enhancing the role of BRICS countries as 'rule-makers' in the international system.

As the world becomes more multipolar and the threat of unilateral action by Western powers recedes, geopolitical elements might be less visible on the BRICS agenda, though Western sanctions and the Syria and Iran issues will still be on the radar. However, there are other issues of common challenges to humanity, like climate change and health epidemics, that guide the collective efforts of the BRICS countries. Bilateral issues and different political orientations of member states may come to the forefront from time to time as the spectre of a unipolar world order recedes. The greater challenge in future would be how to navigate between the trend in some states to pivot back to the United States and that in others to move farther away from the West. The divergent orientations amid bilateral tensions between China and India can affect the progress of BRICS. Further growth of BRICS thus depends on how they deal with their own differences by mutual accommodation and find some common orientation on global issues while continuing with their different political and economic paths. Clearly, none of the BRICS members would like to go back to a situation where a few powers in the West dominate the international order and impose their will on other states. This factor may remain a binding factor for BRICS countries in the future.

Notes

1 By the middle of April, China had sent medical aid to over 127 countries and four international organisations. Around the same time, New Delhi was providing pharma assistance to nearly 85 countries including many in Africa on a grant basis, apart from committing a grant of US$10 million (excluding transportation costs) to the South Asian Association for Regional Co-operation (SAARC). Atul Aneja, 'BRICS Foreign Ministers Expected to Brainstorm Joint Responses to Covid-19 Today', *The Hindu*, 28 April 2020; Shishir Gupta, 'Imran Khan Hits Mute on Saarc Covid-19 Pledge, India Sends $1.7 mn Relief', *The Hindustan Times*, 17 April 2020.

2 Brazil's annual trade with Russia reached US$4.6 billion in 2016, with agricultural segments being in the lead in terms of exports to Russia. 'Brazil-Russia Trade Reaches US$ 4.3 Billion a Year', *BrazilGovNews*, Presidency of the Republic of Brazil, 17 June 2017, www.brazilgovnews.gov.br/news/2017/06/brazil-russia-trade-reaches-us-4-3-billion-a-year (accessed on 10 December 2017); Brazil's trade with China amounted to over US$58.5 billion in 2016, with a trade surplus of more than US$11.7 billion in Brazil's favour. 'Brazil Posts Record Trade Surplus with China in 2016', *Macauhub*, 17 January 2017, https://macauhub.com.mo/2017/01/17/brazil-posts-record-trade-surplus-with-china-in-2016/ (accessed on 10 December 2017).

Bibliography

'9th BRICS Summit – BRICS Leaders Xiamen Declaration', Xiamen, China, September 4, 2017. Full text can be availed from Ministry of Foreign Affairs, Brazil, www.itamaraty.gov.br/en/press-releases/17427-9th-brics-summit-brics-leaders-xiamen-declaration-xiamen-china-september-4–2017 (accessed on 14 July 2017).

'10th BRICS Summit Johannesburg Declaration'. 2018. Full text is available Ministry of Foreign Affairs, Brazil, July 26. www.mea.gov.in/bilateral-documents.htm?dtl/30190/10th_BRICS_Summit_Johannesburg_Declaration (Accessed on 7 June 2020).

Aneja, Atul. 2020. 'India Sees RIC Meeting as Gateway to Eurasia', *The Hindu*, February 3.

Arruda, Pedro Lara de and Slingsby Ashleigh Kate. 2014. 'Digesting the Alphabet Soup: A Comparative Institutional History of IBSA and BRICS', *International Policy Research Brief*, Centre for Inclusive Growth, No. 43, June 2014, www.ipc-undp.org/pub/IPCPolicyResearchBrief43.pdf (accessed on 24 June 2020).

The Asian Age. 2017. 'India Wants to Solve Issues with China Based on Astana Consensus: MEA', July 27. www.asianage.com/india/all-india/270717/india-wants-to-solve-issues-with-china-based-on-astana-consensus-mea.html (accessed on 12 December 2017).

Atul, Aneja. 2020a. 'BRICS Foreign Ministers Expected to Brainstorm Joint Responses to Covid-19 Today', *The Hindu*, April 28.

Atul, Aneja. 2020b. 'BRICS against Covid-19', *The Hindu*, May 4.

BRICS Information Portal. 2020. 'Putin Advocates More BRICS Cooperation to Fight Pandemic', November 17. https://infobrics.org/post/32263 (accessed on 20 November 2020).

'BRICS Summit Brasilia Declaration, 15 November 2019'. Full text is available on www.xinhuanet.com/english/2019-11/15/c_138555948.htm (accessed on 7 June 2020).

CGTN (China Global Television Network). 2019. 'NDB Shows Further Commitment to Infrastructure Construction', November 10. https://news.cgtn.com/news/2019-11-10/NDB-shows-further-commitment-to-infrastructure-construction-LucqNerHK8/index.html (accessed on 28 November 2020).

Cherian, John. 1999. 'The Primakov Visit', *Frontline*, January 2. https://frontline.thehindu.com/world-affairs/article30256253.ece (Accessed on 15 November 2020).

CNBC TV 18. 2020. 'India-China Tensions: 'Casualties on Both Sides', Says Amended Army Statement', June 16. www.cnbctv18.com/politics/india-china-ladakh-stand-off-army-officer-2-soldiers-killed-in-violent-face-off-with-chinese-troops-in-galwan-valley-6145271.htm (accessed on 10 July 2021).

Das R. N. 2010. 'Russia-China-India Trilateral: Calibrating a Fine Balance', *IDSA Comment*, November 15, Manohar Parikar Institute for Defence Studies and Analyses (IDSA), New Delhi. https://idsa.in/idsacomments/RussiaChinaIndiaTrilateralCalibratingaFineBalance_rndas_151110 (accessed on 15 November 2020).

Declaration of the First BRICS Meeting on Human Milk Bank, Brasilia, Brazil, on August 30, 2019, *http://brics2019.itamaraty.gov.br/images/documentos/Declaration_of_thr_First_BRICS_Meeting_on_Human_Milk_Bank.pdf* (accessed on 19 November 2020).

Dongxiao, Chen and Shua Feng. 2016. 'The Russia-India-China Trio in the Changing International System', *China Quarterly of International Strategic Studies*, 2(4). www.worldscientific.com/doi/pdf/10.1142/S2377740016500275 (accessed on 15 November 2020).

Eckel, Mike. 2014. 'China May Be Biggest Winner From Ukraine Crisis', *Voice of America*, September 1. www.voanews.com/content/china-ukraine-russia-benefits/2432373.html (accessed on 14 July 2017).

Embassy of India. 2019. 'India-China Economic and Trade Relations', Embassy of India in China, Beijing. www.eoibeijing.gov.in/economic-and-trade-relation.php (accessed on 21 June 2019).

Erthal, Abdenur Adriana and Folly Maiara. 2015. 'The New Development Bank and the Institutionalisation of the BRICS', *Revolutions, Global Trends and Regional Issues*, 3(1).

'Fourth BRICS Summit – Delhi Declaration, March 29, 2012'. Ministry of External Affairs, Government of India. http://mea.gov.in/bilateral documents. htm?dtl/19158/Fourth+BRICS+Summit++Delhi+Declaration (accessed on 14 July 2017).

Gupta, Shishir. 2020. 'Imran Khan Hits Mute on Saarc Covid-19 Pledge, India sends $1.7 mn relief', *The Hindustan Times*, April 17.

The Hindu. 2017. 'All You Need to Know about Doklam and the India-China Border Standoff', July 25. www.thehindu.com/news/national/all-you-need-to-know-about-doklam-and-the-india-china-border-standoff/article19357499.ece (accessed on 12 December 2017).

IISD News. 2015. 'BRICS Environment Ministers Discuss Green Economy, Climate Change', International Institute for Sustainable Development, May 7. https://sdg.iisd.org/news/brics-environment-ministers-discuss-green-economy-climate-change/ (accessed on 21 November 2020).

IMF. 2020. 'IMF Members' Quotas and Voting Power, and IMF Board of Governors'. www.imf.org/external/np/sec/memdir/members.aspx (accessed on 24 November 2020).

The Indian Express. 2017. 'First Project of BRICS Bank Starts Operation', 4 September.

Jesus Diego Santos Vieira de. 2014. 'The Benign Multipolarity: Brazilian Foreign Policy under Dilma Rousseff', *Journal of International Relations and Foreign Policy*, 2(1), pp. 19–42. http://jirfp.com/journals/jirfp/Vol_2_No_1_March_2014/2.pdf (accessed on 15 November 2020).

Macauhub. 2017. 'Brazil Posts Record Trade Surplus with China in 2016', 17 January. https://macauhub.com.mo/2017/01/17/brazil-posts-record-trade-surplus-with-china-in-2016/ (accessed on 10 December 2017).

Madan, Tanvi. 2014. 'India's Reaction to the Situation in Ukraine: Looking Beyond a Phrase', *Brookings*, March 14. www.brookings.edu/blog/up-front/2014/03/14/indias-reaction-to-the-situation-in-ukraine-looking-beyond-a-phrase/ (accessed on 24 June 2020).

Marcondes, Danilo and Mawdsley Emma, 2017. 'South – South in Retreat? The Transitions from Lula to Rousseff to Temer and Brazilian development co-operation', *International Affairs*, 93(3). www.chathamhouse.org/sites/default/files/publications/ia/INTA93_3_10_MarcondesMawdsley.pdf (accessed on 15 November 2020).

Matthew, Wheeland. 2015. 'The BRIC Nations' Response to Climate Change is Critical to the Fate of the Planet', *The Guardian*, 4 May 2015 www.theguardian.com/sustainable-business/2015/may/04/brazil-china-russia-india-climate-change-labor-economy-sustainability (accessed on 24 June 2020).

Maupin, Agathe and Sidiropoulos Elizabeth. 2015. 'BRICS and Climate Change', South African Institute of International Affairs (SAIIA), July 6. www.saiia.org.za/opinion-analysis/brics-and-climate-change (accessed on 15 July 2016).

Meena, Krishnendra. 2015. 'Regions, Regionalisation and BRICS', *Revolutions, Global Trends and Regional Issues*, 3(1), p. 38, published by the Revolutions Research Centre, Adam Michiewicz University, Poznan, http://revjournal.org/wp-content/uploads/REV3/REVOLUTIONS_VOL.3.pdf (accessed on 14 July 2017).

Peruffo, Luiza, 2020. 'The BRICS Countries' Monetary and Financial Power: What has Changed Since the 2008 Global Financial Crisis and Why it Matters', *Conjuctura Austral, (Journal of Global South)*, 11(3), pp. 92–93. http://oaji.net/articles/2020/2137-1585666398.pdf (accessed on 14 November 2020).

Putin, Vladimir. 2017. 'BRICS: Towards New Horizons of Strategic Partnership', *The Times of India*, New Delhi, September 1.

Rajagopalan, Rajeswari Pillai. 2019. 'Russia-India-China Trilateral Grouping: More Than Hype?' *The Diplomat*, July 5. https://thediplomat.com/2019/07/russia-india-china-trilateral-grouping-more-than-hype/ (accessed on 24 June 2020).

Rajagopalan, Rajeswari Pillai. 2020. 'India-Russia Defense Ties Amid COVID-19', *The Diplomat*, May 1. https://thediplomat.com/2020/05/india-russia-defense-ties-amid-covid-19/ (accessed on 24 June 2020).

Report of the United Nations Economic Commission for Africa. 2014. 'BRICS/Africa Partnership for Development'. www.uneca.org/publications/bricsafrica-partnership-development (accessed on 15 July 2016).

'Sanya Declaration'. 2011. Ministry of External Affairs, Government of India, Ministry of External Affairs, Government of India, April 14. http://mea.gov.in/bilateral-documents.htm?dtl/4789/Sanya+Declaration (accessed on 14 July 2017).

Saran, Pankaj. 2017. 'Seventy Years of India-Russian Relations: A Historic Milestone', December, Embassy of India in the Russian Federation. https://indianembassy-moscow.gov.in/70-years-of-india-russia-relations-a-historic-milestone.php (accessed on 24 June 2020).

Schoeman, Maxi, Kefale Asnake and Alden Chris. 2017. 'It's time South Africa tuned into Africa's Views about Its Role on the Continent', *South African Institute of International Affairs (SAIIA)*, January 25. www.saiia.org.za/opinion-analysis/its-time-south-africa-tuned-into-africas-views-about-its-role-on-the-continent (accessed on 24 June 2020).

'Second BRICS Summit: Joint Statement'. 2010, Brasilia, April 16. http://brics6.itamaraty.gov.br/category-english/21-documents/66-second-summit (accessed on 20 June 2020).

Simha, Rakesh Krishnan. 2015. 'Primakov: The Man Who Created Multipolarity', *Russia Beyond*, June 27. www.rbth.com/blogs/2015/06/27/primakov_the_man_who_created_multipolarity_43919#:~:text=Yevgeni%20Primakov%20drafted%20the%20concept,counterbalance%20to%20the%20western%20alliance.&text=In%201996%2C%20as%20Foreign%20Minister,between%20Russia%2C%20India%20and%20China (accessed on 15 November 2020).

'Sixth BRICS Summit – Fortaleza Declaration'. 2014. Ministry of External Affairs, Government of India, July 15. www.mea.gov.in/bilateral-documents.htm?dtl/23635/Sixth+BRICS+Summit++Fortaleza+Declaration (accessed on 24 November 2020).

South African BRICS Think Tank (SABTT). 'BRICS Meetings and Forums', *South African BRICS Think Tank* (SABTT). http://sabtt.org.za/brics/brics-meetings-and-forums/ (accessed 19 November 2020).

Stuenkel, Oliver. 2013. 'The Financial Crisis, Contested Legitimacy, and the Genesis of Intra-BRICS Cooperation', *Global Governance*, 19(4).

Varro, Krisztina and Lagendijk Arnoud. 2013. 'Conceptualizing the Region – in What Sense Relational?' *Regional Studies*, 47(1). https://hal.archives-ouvertes.fr/hal-00790734/file/PEER_stage2_10.1080%252F00343404.2011.602334.pdf (accessed on 21 November 2020).

'What is BRICS?' 2019. *BRICS*, Brazil Government. http://brics2019.itamaraty.gov.br/en/about-brics/what-is-brics (accessed on 24 June 2020).

Wilson, Dominic, Trivedi Kamakshya, Carlson Stacy and Ursúa José. 2011. 'Global Economics Paper No: 208', December 7, p. 3, Goldman Sachs Global Economics, Commodities and Strategy Research. http://blogs.univ-poitiers.fr/o-bouba-olga/files/2012/11/Goldman-Sachs-Global-Economics-Paper-208.pdf (accessed on 24 June 2020).

'Yekaterinburg Summit Declaration'. 2009. Yekaterinburg, Russia, June 16. http://brics6.itamaraty.gov.br/category-english/21-documents/114-first-summit-2 (accessed on 24 June 2020).

4

BRICS IN BLUES

Potentialities of the Maritime World: Lessons from the History of Money, Metallism and Mercantilism

Rohan

Diplomacy among the nations is the politics of agreement while they disagree at best, deter at worse, while money, metal and merchandise all flow in between. One such conglomeration came into being not so long ago when a theoretical fascination of Goldman Sachs gave rise to a practical formulation called BRIC, and soon – S followed suit perfecting the monumentality of the twenty-first-century edifice. The economic endeavours of the global market were seen safe and prosperous in the able hands of the nations with fastest-growing GDPs across the globe, and that the coming together of Brazil, Russia, India, China and South Africa was hailed as the most sought after trans-national dependency of the future. However, BRICS, rather than becoming an elixir for the global economy, quite contrarily has come onto become 'a dependent' on the world. More than a workshop of intensified growth that the world can look up to it has become *via regia* of daunting possibilities. The conspicuous attempt to expose the fissures in BRICS was made by a UK-based senior economist Francesca Beausang (2012) in her book *Globalization and BRICs: Why the BRICs Will Not Rule the World for Long*. It does not take a prodigal insight to understand for a student of International Relations that Beausang's central argument focused on the paradoxes within the supra-continental conglomeration that exist among five nations. The lack of a solid layout for the future and the internal clash of interests among these nations have been quite the talk of the town among the internationalists. In the decade in which we are witnessing the colossal end, many experts have prophesied an abysmal end of the future of BRICS as well (Weitz 2011; Aayush Mohanty 2020; Nivedita Kapoor 2020). As a trained economic historian and a student of diplomacy, I beg to differ from all the pundits who think BRICS is almost drawing its final straw, and her siècle would end soon enough. The foundation of BRICS was primarily to bring about five fastest-growing economies together, and *economics never goes out of business*. Immaculate structures don't exist in the world, and so is true for BRICS, but

DOI: 10.4324/9781003148074-5

reshuffling, revisiting and realising same goals with a different approach may be the answer to the question that many are even scared to ask. The task of this article, thus, is *not* to showcase how ignorant are we of our past nor is the intention to prove that 'nothing is new' but to indicate that 'not everything is as new as contemporary internationalists believe'.

Writing more than half a century ago, Marc Bloch maintained that of all the possible ways of revealing the movement of economy, the analysis of monetary phenomena is without doubt the most sensitive (Bloch 1967: 186). Now add the movement of money through the interconnected maritime world of the three oceanic zones and the *problematique* turns exponentially complicated; to further make it near impossible for a non-inter-disciplinary approach to analyse is when the movement of diaspora is conjoined with the *meta*-problem. The sustenance of BRICS is linked with the maritime oceanic trade, commerce and enterprise, thus making the history lessons part of the problem-solving tool for the solution the world dearly anticipates.

The *fiduciary* money holds a promised upon value against the metal reserves of gold by the national banks across the globe. That makes money a commodity after all, and the metal becomes the intrinsic value of the economy upon which the business enterprise is founded. The agent of the commercial enterprise becomes the merchant and together they all form what we may refer to as meta-trade model of mercantilism. That's the world of money, metallism and mercantilism that one needs to delve into to understand the vitality of maritime linkages among BRICS nations. It is a common error made by scholars across the globe because of the stereotyping that land is the true imagery of territoriality and that is reflected through a plethora of researches on the taxation system, agrarian relations and overland trade routes. Not much heed was paid by the nations until the rise of the 'Second Enlightenment' when collectivism triumphed over individualism; rise of industrialism, the middle class and imperialism; great powers were anxious to redefine politics and nationalism in the name of protecting the people and bring peace and stability in the region (Wagar 1967: 1–11). In other words, science and romanticism were shaking their hands in unison – which defined the *fin-de-siècle* Europe in particular, and its effect was to be felt in Eurasia crossing the three oceans to 'Re-Orient' South Asia. The term 'Re-Orient' is borrowed from Andre Gunder Frank (1998), who has written a book by the same title. He argues very rightly that the centre of world trade, commerce and enterprise was the Orient and not Europe, as it is always presumed. The idea of using the term 'Re-Orient' is to showcase the same paradox where Europe was charting out utilitarian and materialist theorisations to advance imperialism that was not due to their civilisational superiority but because of the rise of the idea of unification and establishment of conglomerates like EIC, the supra-national Joint-Stock Company. What utilitarianism was to EIC, sustainable development is for BRICS! But there are times when the confidence in a system or an organisation like BRICS is weakened. That is not to intend that there exists no inherent problem in the system, only that more than the 'fiduciary' money it is a problem of 'political' money. One causal is precisely the strength of the respective economies of these nations that depends on the strength of their banking and financial institutions that in turn depend on the gold reserves they have that help maintain a percentage share of the global GDP at PPP in US dollars as of now. But the gold reserves cannot alone maintain the strength of it all; there are other factors that must supplement it – of which natural resources, production output and services play a pivotal role.

The maritime oceanic zone stretches from the cold ports of Russia in the Pacific to reach China that crosses through the South China Sea to finally culminate at the series of archipelagos of South East Asia in the Indian Ocean passing through the Straits of Malacca and circumventing the passage of *Bab-al-Mandeb* to avoid pirate-stricken Gulf waters and moves through the Cape of Good Hope touching the fringes of the Cape of Verde of Africa's southern points to enter into the Atlantic Ocean, where it finally touches the shores of South America at Brazil. It is this maritime world of confluence among five nations, that is BRICS, that makes this association one of the mightiest in terms of economic control and percentage share of global GDP, and that if its potential is appropriated thoroughly, 'BRICS will rule the world for long!'. The maritime world may seem as many divided worlds to some, and it may also seem as one greater world. It takes rare clarity to see cultural, civilisational and geographical cohesion, and yet divided is the spirit of nation and its territoriality defined in terms of nautical miles and international conventions. To put it in the words of complexity of methodology, it requires a triple analytical foundation of historical logic – time, space and structure – to underline the political economy and maritime potential of BRICS and the problems associated with it. If BRICS has to sustain itself more than a 'clever investment jargon',[1] it has to revamp its historical connects of littoral trans-migrations, maritime enterprises and commerce, and most of all a cohesive cultural and civilisational tie soon (de Coning, Mandrup and Odgaard 2015: 1).

The Indian Ocean has been defined as an axiom of Indian statecraft, and the propounder went on to say, 'if no Naval Force no Trade, if no Fear no Friendship' – it may sound as if it has been said by a diplomat recently, but surprisingly it was highlighted way back in 1718 by the then serving English Governor of Bombay, Charles Boone (Chaudhuri 1985: 3). There have been several South–South security and defence initiatives through IBSA, and the IBASAMAR naval trilateral exercises have ensured trans-oceanic voyages of fleets to the South African coasts. Out of the aforementioned phrase, there is vigour in the presence of naval force, fear and friendship, but trade is missing the same destiny. It would not be an exaggeration to argue that BRICS maritime policy has not shared the same destiny than that of overland or airborne policies since the time of its inception. Unlike the demarcated borders on land that divide the demographics of the world in various imagined communities, the littoral connect provides more than international waterways that bring security and articles of trade. When an expert refers to BRICS as a mere investment jargon where the fastest-growing economies have come closer to spearhead growth in terms of global GDP, the idea is to highlight the role of these nations as cosmopolitan markets for sustaining the already existing financial capital model where the axis remains Eurocentric. By realising the maritime connect to its maxima, these nations would not stand at the penumbra of the Eurocentricism; rather, it would make these nations become the centre of the new global realties with a sense of shared historic, cultural and geographic oneness – completing the transition from being mere shareholders to stakeholders.

Coming back to *fidiciary* money – it is not derived in gold and silver equivalence, particularly since 1971 when silver was enlisted in the usual list of commodities and the international gold standard came to an end (Garber 1993: 464–491). We have come a long way from the world of commerce that was dependent on metallic currency vis-à-vis bullionism. But have silver and gold lost their intrinsic value, or do they no longer hold psychological advantage over other commodities? The last line of economic defence of most of the South Asian households is still the gold and silver jewellery that are either kept in bank lockers or adorn ornamented safes at homes. Have we really qualified to the level of transactional maturity where metallism and money equivalence is too medieval to exist with the modern world of global cosmopolitanism? Undeniably, they are not just commodities; they are more than what production demands (Vigne 2017: 3). In 1905, De Foville, a statistician, made an astounding discovery that all the gold in the world taken by that date could be confined within 10 metre cube, that is 1,000 cubic metres. If the same quantitative analysis is done for the year 1500, it would measure only 2 meters each, that is 8 cubic meters. This tells us two things: first, a very small quantity or transfer of gold could have disrupted the whole global world of commerce and enterprises; second, the quantity of gold could have never equalled the total money in circulation. And that brings us to another underlying truth – the proportionate share of maritime trade in the economy was exponentially higher than the overland trade pre-1971. The absurdity of an egalitarian equality celebrated as the enigma of twenty-first-century world of commerce becomes conspicuous. It is actually as deceptive as the illusion of money that it holds the same value in the pocket of a millionaire and a beggar's bowl, and as the illusion of universal suffrage.

Money and Metallism went hand in glove with each other until the first Great Depression hit the modern world after the first European Civil War. Before that, money was a social reality (Fournier 1994: 289). When two worlds of the occident and orient at different levels of development came into contact, they had a separate conception of money and its value – otherwise why did the Spaniards give gold in exchange for Indian trinkets? The Portuguese seizure of African gold and the discovery of Cape of Good Hope introduced the Atlantic world of commerce to the Indian Ocean. The Spanish moved westwards, discovered the West Indies, and found gold too – with that began the tripartite endeavour of money, metal and mercantilism with the blessings of the Papacy vis-à-vis *Padroado* (Boxer 1969: 65–83, 228–248). The oceanic route had not only brought the continents closer, but it had done something quite extraordinary. The period from 1500 to 1525 and from 1598 to 1630, the European expansion coupled with the 'price revolution' extended the world market (from Americas to the Far East): the circulation of gold and silver (bullionism) and of credit on the one hand; the appearance of expanding national economies (mercantilism) on the other hand (Chaudhuri 1985: 64–71). The period from 1598–1630 to 1680–1725, there was a relative decline

(Chaudhuri 1985: 71–93, 102–141). The volume of silver reaching was less, and it was dearer: gold was dearer still. The period from 1680 to 1725 and from 1812 to 1817 marked the infamous 'eighteenth-century boom' in Europe; the phase that marked the appropriation of Brazilian gold and then of Mexican silver (Garner 1964: 157–185). From 1812–1817 to 1914–1920 Europe celebrated the triumph of industrial capitalism and it also marked the fidelity with the gold standard (the first gold-silver bimetallism and then without). The opening of new mines in California, Australia and South Africa also happened in this phase (Bernstein 2004: 207–225). From 1914–1920 to 1945–1965 was a period of crisis (two European civil wars and the Great Depression of 1929) that was reflected in the monetary affairs. It was this phase when gold appeared to be giving way to the new conception of money and newly found airborne routes of trade, but surprisingly the overland trade didn't lose much of its charm unlike the maritime trade. Perhaps the idea of a non-physical demarcation on waters both confused and impeded the leaders of 'geo'-politics.

The world of maritime trade and commerce stretched from the Atlantic at one end to the warm ports of the Pacific on the other, while the vast expanse of the Indian Ocean laid in between – a wonder that the BRICS shares hitherto. The erstwhile era of mercantilism brought these separate continents together by establishing a common system of money market based on *bullionism*. There were many regional coins that determined the financial exchanges however there was always one mode of transaction that over-determined. That mode was 'barter with gold or silver'. The networks of merchant guilds linked the overland–overseas transactions. The dynamo of this well–laid system of exchange was founded on by maintaining control over gold and silver production across the globe. By the turn of the fifteenth century, the two Iberian countries, namely Portugal and Spain, were ready to establish their control over the mines that produced these metals. The world was cut into two halves, where the West was given to Spain while Portugal was to get east. In 1492, Columbus thus discovered America, while in 1497 Vasco de Gama came to India and in 1500 Alvarez Cabral discovered the Cape Verde islands of Southern Africa before finally discovering Brazil. Until then the North African gold mines of Nubia, Isle of Tibir and finally the mines of Mina were on the verge of complete exhaustion after serving the Egyptians, the Romans, Genoese and then the Portuguese. If it wasn't for the Portuguese and Spanish discovery of the new mines of Southern Africa, and Caribbean, America and Mexico respectively, the Europeans would never have seen the 'Price Revolution' of the sixteenth century.

From Table 4.1, it is clear that the volume of gold that Portugal brought to Europe was no match in front of the Span's contribution. One end of the axis of the world of maritime trade and commerce was thus going to be America. After the 1520s, silver replaced gold in dominance. Although the world was figuratively divided between the Spanish and Portuguese area of control, these two worlds culminated at two places – one was Europe and the other the Indian Oceanic zone.

As the production of Mina gold declined, the Portuguese moved to Monomotopa gold reserves that were exported to India. By one estimate, 573 kg and 716 kg

TABLE 4.1 Comparison of the quantitative difference between Portuguese and Spanish gold production

Portugal (annual average receipts of Gold in kg from Mina)★		*Spain (annual average receipts of Gold in kg from Caribbean alone)#*	
1504–1507	433.368	1503–1510	4,950
1511–1513	413.922	1511–1520	9,153
1517–1519	443.676	1521–1530	4,889
1519–1522	411.864	1533–1535	More than the previous quantity but not specified
1543–1545	371.578	1551–1560★★	42,600

Source: ★ (Vilar 1967: 56); # (Hamilton 1934: 42, 78)

★★ 42,600 kg is the cumulative figure for both gold and silver for the period 1551–1560

of gold reached India in 1583 and 1610 respectively. It was turned into gold coins at Goa and was called the *saotomes* from São Tomé or St. Thomas, modelled as the intrinsic equivalent of *pagoda*, Vijayanagar gold coin in circulation. The dearth of gold and even more so silver made bandits to ransack African jungles for gold, as one can see in Figure 4.3 that by the end of the nineteenth century they were able to locate quite a number of gold mines at the southern region of Africa (now South Africa). The capture of the Malay Peninsula and Malacca brought the militarised navy and gold trading to the doorsteps of the Far East. Sumatra produced 600 kg of gold around 1600, while whatever little they could mine from Java was exchanged with the Gujarati cotton cloths, at 20 per cent profit (Vilar 1967: 95). Borneo and Celebes also had gold, and there were even some in the Philippines. The latter, however, belonged to Spain, and the Spanish fiscal policy and the abundant supply from America made acquiring gold from Philippines less profitably viable. That partly explains why the Spanish *armada* never entered the Indian Ocean zone.

In the Far East, the Ryuku islands, north of Japan, were the main collecting point of gold. This region was a major bone of contention later between Russia and Japan partly because Russia was searching for warm ports and partly because she wanted to expand her maritime phalanges under Peter the Great to juxtapose herself in front of the expansionist might of Britain (Rohan 2018: 8–11).

By the mid-sixteenth century, the Spanish mines were producing 12,000 kg while mines at Japan produced 2,000 kg of silver per annum respectively (Kobata 1965: 245–266). Japan was at the other end of the axis. All this together prepared the backbone of the Atlantic–Indian–Pacific maritime world of trade and commerce (see Tables 4.2. 4.3 and 4.4):

(a) Silver was dearer in America, while gold was cheaper. The ratio of silver to gold was approximately 11 or 12 to 1.
(b) In Spain and Portugal, silver was dearest, since it was the closest to the colonies in both America and North Africa, while gold was cheaper. The ratio of silver to gold was almost 14 to 1.

(c) The situation gradually shifted as one moved towards the interior of Europe. In France, silver was cheap and here gold became dear. The ratio of silver to gold was almost 8 to 1.
(d) Once the movement of caravan crossed through the Saharan desert, a region known for its gold reserves, the ratio of silver to gold dwindled to 5 or 6 to 1 until it finally took a dip after reaching India. India had only one gold mine, and that too produced too little to fill the treasury of so many empires, while there was no silver mine at all. India was therefore a 'bullion sink'. Here both silver and gold were dearest. The ratio of silver to gold was almost 1: 1
(e) If India was cyclone, the stretch from the Strait of Malacca to Java and Sumatra was an anti-cyclone for bullion, thanks to the newly found gold reserves in the South East archipelagos. The ratio began to move slightly up. The ratio of silver to gold was almost 4 to 1.
(f) At the port of Canton, China, the ratio improved slightly up to 5 or 6 to 1.
(g) And finally, in Japan, where there were silver mines, the ratio was exactly equal to the ratio in America, that is 11 or 12 to 1. The cycle of silver circulation thus completed a full circle.

The proportional ratio, therefore, can be represented as America: Europe: Middle East: India: South East Asia: Japan: 11: 8: 4: 1: 4: 6: 11. It was therefore profitable to trade in silver in the maritime oceanic zone. On a closer examination it becomes apparent that a merchant ship that began its voyage with silver from

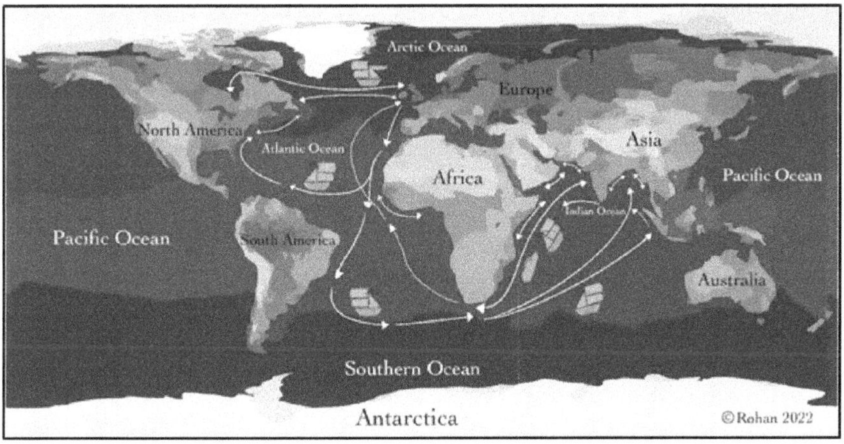

FIGURE 4.1 Trans-Atlantic and Indian Oceanic Maritime Trade Routes

Source: All maps have been created by the author.

Data on metal production is based on the combination of two sources: Historical data from 1850–2011 is sourced from the ClioInfra database. URL: www.clio-infra.eu/

This has been combined with recent data from the USGS Mineral Statistics from 2012 onwards. URL: https://minerals.usgs.gov/minerals/pubs/commodity/aluminum/. The chart is available at URL: https://ourworldindata.org/grapher/gold-production

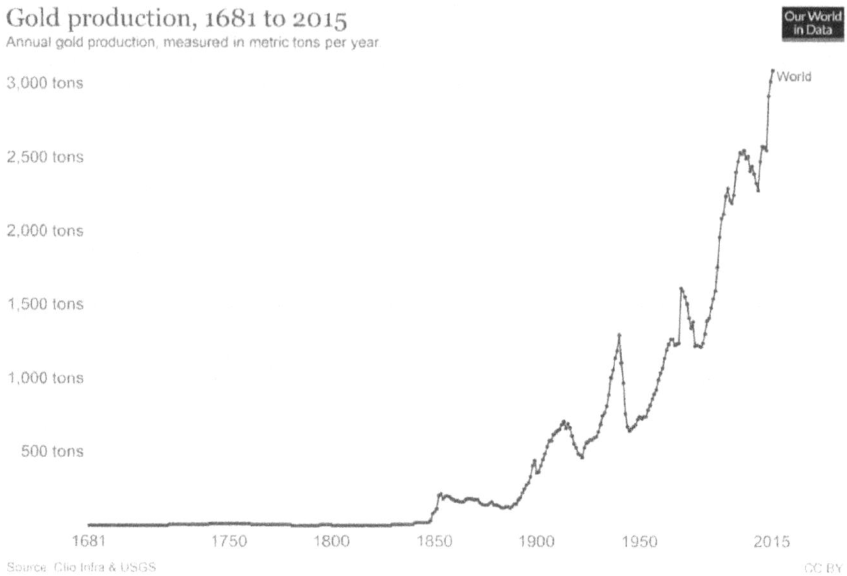

FIGURE 4.2 World gold production in metric tonnes (1681–2015)

Source: Data on metal production is based on the combination of two sources: Historical data from 1850–2011 is sourced from the ClioInfra database. URL: www.clio-infra.eu/

This has been combined with recent data from the USGS Mineral Statistics from 2012 onwards. URL: https://minerals.usgs.gov/minerals/pubs/commodity/aluminum/. The chart is available at URL: https://ourworldindata.org/grapher/gold-production

TABLE 4.2 World supply of gold and silver (1741–1910; unit: 1,000 ounces)

Period	*Gold*	*Silver*
1741–1761	791	17,100
1761–1780	665	21,000
1781–1800	572	28,300
1801–1810	572	28,700
1811–1820	368	17,400
1821–1830	157	14,800
1831–1840	652	19,200
1841–1850	1,762	25,000
1851–1860	6,313	26,500
1861–1870	6,108	39,000
1871–1880	5,472	66,800
1881–1890	5,200	97,200
1891–1900	10,165	161,400
1901–1910	18,279	82,600

Table 4.2 provides the data for a period, that is 1740 to 1850 for which the Figure 4.2 does not provide any figure. When both data are combined, one can see that the maritime trade until 1800 depended mostly on a constant supply of gold and increased demand of silver, and that it was responsible for generating between 400 and 800 per cent profit for the joint stock companies (Vilar 1967: 331).

TABLE 4.3 Silver movement in and out of China (unit: million Mexican dollars)

Year	*Inflow*	*Outflow*
1721–1740	68	150
1752–1800	105	
1814–1850	220	
1850–1866	504	
1868–1886		

The silver movement mentioned in Table 4.3 mostly came from the Japanese mines. After the *Pancarda* system was put in place, the movement of silver happened from the ports outside Japan. Pancarda stopped the European traders to enter Japan, since those traders were accompanied with Jesuits (missionaries) who would come to introduce the faith of the Christ in Japan. Japanese lamented both as it disturbed their businesses as well as religion (Lin 2019: 410).

TABLE 4.4 The net silver outflow from China (1814–1850)

Year	*Net Silver Outflow to India (Liano)*	*Others*	*Outflow of Mexican Dollars*
1814–15	1,324,940	18,873	8,915,042
1815–16	1,068,436	101,465	8,800,000
1816–17	2,021,493	79,762	10,000,000
1817–18	2,549,068	22,929	
1818–19	3,614,671	17,274	
1819–20	985,944	176,022	
1820–21	1,359,661	369,722	
1821–22	1,098,014	330,956	
1822–23	1,045,960	328,373	
1823–24	1,447,722	519,740	
1824–25	1,615,289		
1825–26	3,072,012		
1826–27	2,372,382		
1827–28	2,771,809		
1828–29	1,614,152		
1829–30	1,690,610		
1830–31	3,755,807		
1831–32	3,474,410		
1832–33	3,760,357		
1833–34	3,556,238		
1834–35	4,999,907		
1835–36	6,139,477		
1836–37	816,523		
1837–38	2,630,153		

(*Continued*)

TABLE 4.4 (Continued)

Year	*Net Silver Outflow to India (Liano)*	*Others*	*Outflow of Mexican Dollars*
1838–39	5,677,118		
1839–40	6,233,310		
1840–41	11,648,178		
1841–42			
1842–43			
1843–44			
1844–45			
1845–46			
1846–47			
1847–48			
1848–49			
1849–50			
Total	82,343,641	1,965,116	27,715,042
Total of the aforementioned silver outflow = 149,962,739 (Mexican dollars)			

Table 4.4 is a testimony to the statement of Pliny, the Elder (77 CE), 'India – the sink of world's precious metals'. India was the cyclone that sank all the bullion that arrived at her shores. The thread of economic fulcrum was attached to America's silver mines to one end and Japanese's mines on the other end (Lin 2019: 404–405).

the Iberian Peninsula would have returned back to Europe almost after a couple of years with the same amount of bullion besides all the luxurious items, ranging from silk and ceramics from China, pepper from Java and Sumatra, cinnamon from Sri Lanka, cotton cloths – *calico, chintz and piece goods, zafarkhani, amertees, kimkhab, kalamkari, Madras Red* – and spices from India, and incense and slaves from Africa (Rohan 2014b: 45–78). There was a profit margin of 400 to 800 per cent depending upon from which part of Europe the merchant hailed from. One such fleet, called the *Manila* galleon, started from the Philippines for Spain carrying all the items mentioned here (CMN 1793–1800; fol. no. 41821; RIO 1968; doc. no. 1).[2]

The Portuguese sea-borne empire was expelled from the Indian Ocean circuit at the turn of the seventeenth century, and that compelled them to move to their other discovered colony, that is Brazil, where they set the plantation economy and slave trade. Soon the South African gold reserves (Figure 4.3) and the Brazilian gold reserves (Figure 4.4) were to serve the same purpose that the American or Mexican mines did in the sixteenth century; all thanks to the American war of independence that the transition from the Mediterranean to the Atlantic was finally possible. The stage was the same, only the actors changed. First the Dutch, and then the British and finally the French entered and controlled the Indian Ocean circuit. Power changing hands also marked two significant shifts: first, the early phase of colonisation by the Portuguese that was marked by the militarisation of the maritime trade

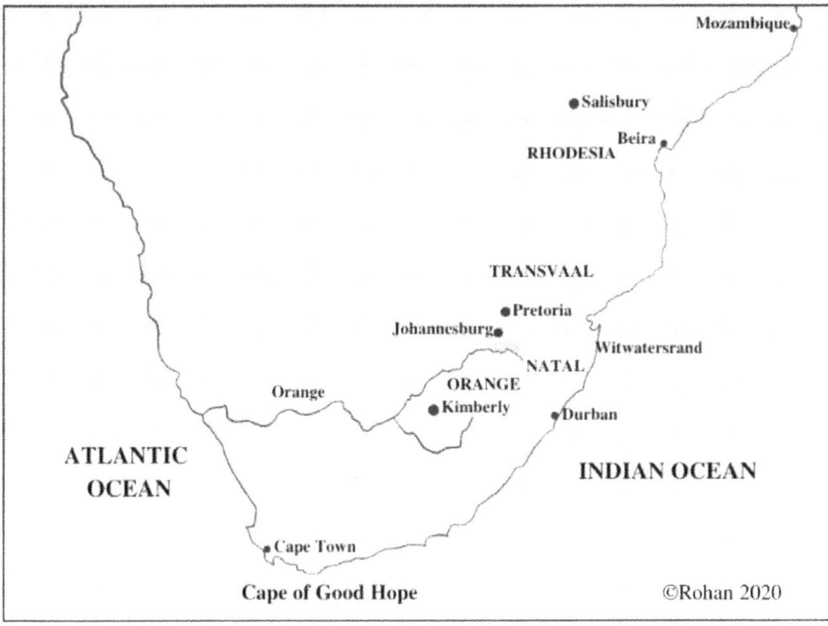

FIGURE 4.3 Gold deposits discovered at the end of the nineteenth century in Southern Africa (1890–1900)

and also the remittance of *conquistadors* financed by privateers was now over. It was replaced by heterogeneous joint stock companies like *VOC* and EIC. Second, the *fiduciary* money was slowly and steadily taking shape, meaning thereby that the transaction through the oceans was to change completely with the growth of new banks and the culmination into financial capitalism, the last phase of imperialism.

Standing at the quarterdeck of *INS Mysore*, on 28 March 1958, the second cruiser that was to be commissioned into the Navy of independent India, Jawaharlal Nehru said, '[H]istory has shown that whatever power controls the Indian Ocean has, in the first instance, India's seaborne trade at her mercy, and in the second, India's very independence itself' (Ganapathi 2015). This was in conformity with the wisdom of a 77-year-old Algerian corsair Khairoddin Barbarossa, who in 1533 said, '[H]e who rules on the sea will shortly rule on the land also' (Stevens and Westcott 2008: 69).

The overarching landed empires, like that of the Mughals, who depended heavily on the revenue from agriculture, could not fully comprehend the collateral advantage of the maritime commerce that was only a handspan away. That is not to say that they did not have a navy of their own but the magnanimity with which the Portuguese, Dutch, French, British, Germans, Danes, Flemish, Armenians and the Jews operated in the vast expanse of the littoral space is incomparable. The *sombuk* (Hornell 1946: 237–238) of the Arabs, *jehazi* (Hornell 1946: 237–238) of East Africa, *bagalla* (Gilbert 2016: 107) of the Gulf, *kotia* (Hornell 1946: 197),

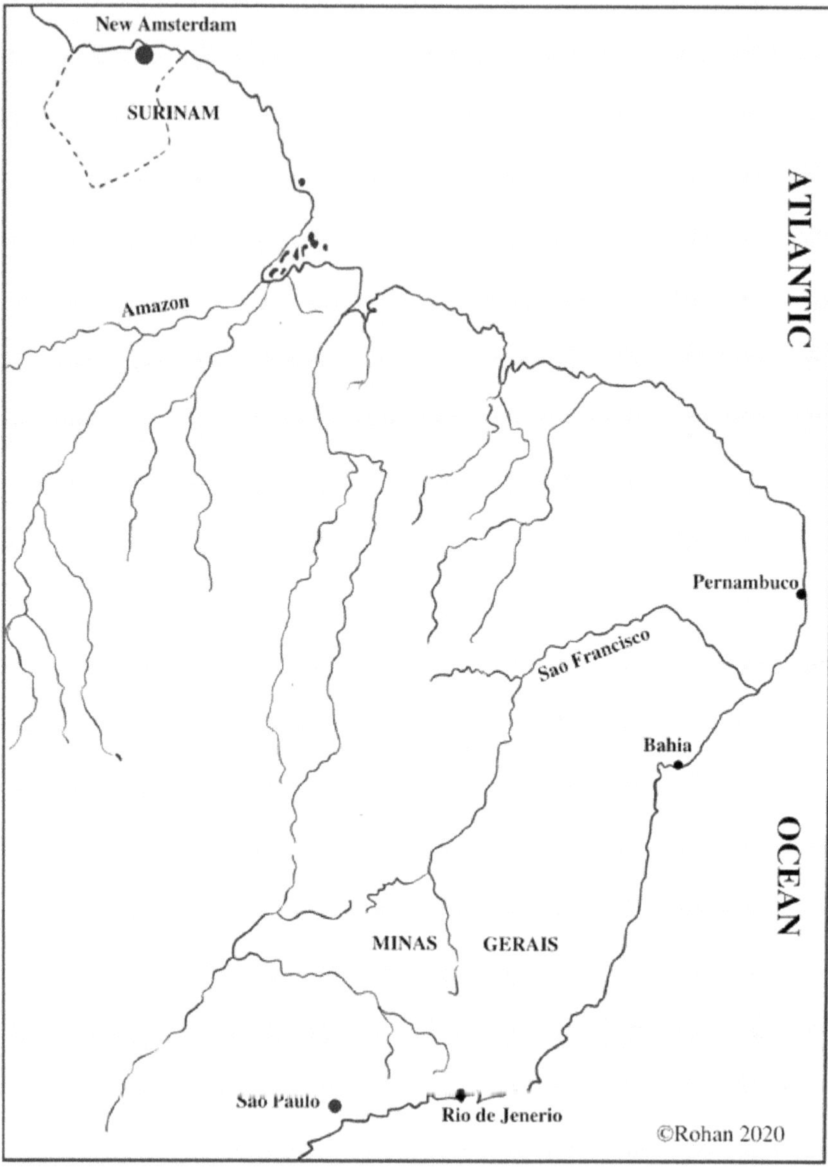

FIGURE 4.4 Gold deposits discovered in eighteenth-century Brazil

odam (Varadarajan 2014: 46–62; Rohan 2014a: 26–35), *grabs* (Singh 1992: 13) and *gullivate* (Singh 1992: 13) of India and the *Fukien junks* (Commercial Reports from Her Majesty's Consuls in Japan 1863–4 1865: 165) of China were the sailing vessels engaged in commerce until the Pope Calixtus III conferred the exclusive right of the Indian Ocean to the Portuguese monarch under the Treaty of Tordesillas vis-à-vis *Padroado* (Boxer 1969: 65–83, 228–248). The coming of the Portuguese also led to establishment of new towns. New monuments changed the urban space in India. As the Indians, particularly merchant and agricultural community, came in contact with them, it affected their relation with each other. Sociologists and anthropologists have studied such changes that were brought by the coming on new architectural changes in colonies. In other words, new spaces articulated themselves for different communities. It had different meanings for different communities at large.

Speaking of Quilon, the Dutch captain Nisuhoff had reported that the Chinese called it 'Coulang China' (Ferroli 1939: 14). Writing in the mid-fifteenth century, Marignolli maintains that Cranganore was known earlier as Cynkali, that is 'Little China' (Yule and Cordier 1964: xiv, 249). In 1563, Garcia de Orta mentions about an inscription on a Chinese stone that was taken by the Zamorins (the Samuthri Raja) from Cochin. It was the same stone that was sent by Yongle that had a poem appended at the end and it was supposed to be written by the emperor himself (Ray 2019: 98). It was a regular site in 1433 to see a Chinese captain Ma Huan, Muslim by faith, to come with a Buddhist Chinese Admiral Zheng Ho to Kozhikode with fleets of ships and stay beside the Hindus Zamorins and the Marakkari Arab merchants who had settled at the Malabar coast of India whose later generations were to become the agrarian-cum-fishing community called the Mopillas of Malabar. Sojourning from the early modern commercial enterprise, the colonial rule transformed the trans-oceanic interaction by imposing *Rex Nullius* (closing of the sea); thus, besides the economy, it threatened the coalescing role of amalgamation of societies through the ocean – a colonial legacy that has impeded a melting pot of various ethnic, religious, political and cultural groups to reconcile and re-emerge as a complete whole.

With the Law of the Sea Convention that inaugurated the new ocean regime on 30 April 1982 – the ocean was divided into national, international and foreign oceans. The newly agreed upon laws of the oceans and the seas were binding upon 160 sovereign states, according to which those states that have coastlines were given territorial rights in order to protect their 'right of innocent passage' over the sea for 12 nautical miles (UN Convention on Law of the Sea, Art. 2, 3–16). The Contiguous Zones extending from 12 to 24 nautical miles authorised the coastal states to 'prevent infringement of its customs, fiscal, immigration or sanitary laws and regulations within its territory or territorial sea and punish infringement of the above laws and regulations committed within its territory or territorial sea' (UN Convention on Law of the Sea, Art. 2 & 33). Under Article 57 of the Convention, the states like India have been given 200 miles under the Exclusive Economic Zone on sea, which adds up to 2.2 million square miles to the total jurisdiction of sovereign India – which accounts for two-thirds of the land area (UN Convention on Law of the Sea, Art. 55–75). That means India is within her rights to establish artificial islands and installations, and she has all the right over the living and non-living littoral resources found in that stretch. Quite paradoxical to what India could have achieved from this, she succumbed to issues of rivalry over seabed resources, narco-terrorism, island grabbing, smuggling (sea cucumber, trees, pearls, etc.), poaching and environmental warfare such as oil fires and oil slick. The neglect of the Indian

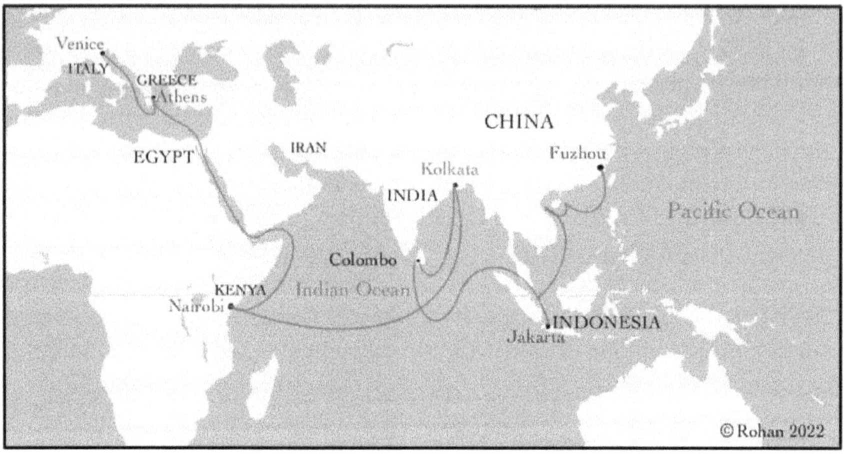

FIGURE 4.5 Twenty-first-century Maritime Silk Road

The twenty-first-century Maritime Silk Road connects China to Southeast Asia, Indonesia, India, the Arabian Peninsula, Somalia, Egypt and Europe, encompassing the South China Sea, Strait of Malacca, Indian Ocean, Gulf of Bengal, Arabian Sea, Persian Gulf and the Red Sea.

Ocean, hitherto, became a breeding ground for 14 out of the 17 enlisted conflict areas the world over by 1990. Revolts at Madagascar, Mayotte; the coup d'état in Comoros, Maldives and Seychelles; and the insurrection in Sri Lanka made the southern part of the ocean a neglected backyard. The international ocean zone mining of seabed resources is regulated by International Seabed Authority (ISA), while the foreign ocean zone can be exploited only by bi-lateral treaties.

Surveys, surveillance and explorations took precedence over the traditional ways of engagement. The advances in the fields of technological exploration have added a new dimension to ocean management, particularly in terms of wind, wave and ocean thermal energy conversion. Data processing, acoustics, computing, mapping and the use of submersibles, and robotics have made oceans a highly technology-intensive region. Post-1950 has seen the growth of various regional cooperation groupings, yet it is in throes of continuing backwardness, internal conflicts, and regional-religious-ethnic fundamentalism. A region that could have drawn together because of a shared socio-cultural tradition and post-colonial history is now divided into several strategic points of dis-engagement. From the building of the Jawaharlal Nehru Port to the newly commissioned Vadhavan port, the 13th major port of India to be built in Maharashtra, India needs to establish a firm National Maritime Policy that can be paralleled to the Maritime Silk Road policy of China on the one hand and can help India continue to connect with Brazil and South Africa towards the East and China and Russia towards the West. If BRICS has to survive, it will have to revisit their maritime endeavours, and India can be the harbinger of this changing image of this cooperation in the long run. It's about time for BRICS to shift from the 'age of ideology' to the 'age of imageology'. Whether trying to integrate the Indian Ocean with the Indo-Pacific region into one vertical (Sanwal 2020) or revamping ties with BIMSTEC and ASEAN countries, BRICS has to find a consolidated integrated approach and not 'One Road One Belt'[3] or the Indian Development Assistance Scheme 'IDEAS' (Devonshire-Ellis 2019), an alternative announced to counter the One Road One Belt Initiative of China by Nirmala Sitharaman, the Finance Minister of India, back in March 2018. More than sustainable development and mutual co-operation, the maritime revamp would require the creation of inter-connected hubs in the Indian Oceanic zone free from the clutches of any nation's geopolitical ambition. To make BRICS be the change one wants to see, we need to create social spaces that are not only cosmopolitan but also commercial cities of global standards. It is about time now that the policy makers ask, 'If the space above the earth can have an International Space Station, Arctic and Antarctica can have research centres that can serve everyone who is part of the endeavour why can't the Indian Oceanic maritime zone?' Without economics, diplomacy will be a conjecture naively filled with political and voluntaristic interpretations.

Notes

1 The BRIC grouping is not a natural, historical, cultural, political or linguistic construct. It has been highlighted by many scholars working on BRICS. This term was used by Cedric de Coning, Thomas Mandrup and Liselotte Odgaard.

2 *Central Museum of the Navy (CMN), manuscripts-documents,* f. No. 41821 dispels a common disbelief that the Russians did not frequent the Indian Ocean during the eighteenth century. (RIO) stands for *Russko-Indiiskie otnoshniya v. XIX v., sbornik arkhivnikh dokumentov e materialov.*

3 The Silk Road Economic Belt is a long-term vision for the infrastructural development, connectivity and economic cooperation of Eurasia and is spanning six development 'corridors', namely:

1. New Eurasian Land Bridge Economic Corridor (NELBEC)
2. China–Mongolia–Russia Economic Corridor (CMREC)
3. China–Central Asia–West Asia Economic Corridor (CCWAEC)
4. China –Indochina Peninsula Economic Corridor (CICPEC)
5. Bangladesh–China–India–Myanmar Economic Corridor (BCIMEC)
6. China–Pakistan Economic Corridor (CPEC)

See, URL: www.beltroad-initiative.com/belt-and-road/

References

'An Unclear Revamp,' 2020. *The Hindu*, 17 February 2020. (Mukul Sanwal), URL: www.thehindu.com/opinion/op-ed/an-unclear-revamp/article30836755.ece (assessed on 20 February 2020).

Beausang, Francesca. 2012. *Globalization and BRICs: Why the BRICs Will Not Rule the World for Long*. Basingstoke: Palgrave Macmilan.

Bernstein, Peter L. 2004. *The Power of Gold: The History of an Obsession.* New York: John Wiley & Sons, 2004.

Bloch, Marc. 1967. *Land and Work in Mediaeval World.* Translated by J.E. Anderson. Berkeley: University of California Press.

Boxer, C.R. 1969. *The Portuguese Sea Borne Empire 1415–1825*. New York: Knopf Books.

'BRICS and its Future: The Challenges of Multilateralism,' 2020. *ORF*, May 13 2020. (Nivedita Kapoor), URL: www.orfonline.org/expert-speak/brics-future-challenges-multilateralism-66053/ (assessed on 19 May 2020).

Central Museum of the Navy, manuscripts-documents, f. No. 41821, *Memoirs of Y.F Lisyanskii, 1793–1800*, l, 51 ob-62 ob. (*Original Handwritten in Russian*).

Chaudhuri, K.N. 1985. *Trade and Civilisation in the Indian Ocean: An Economic History from the Rise of Islam to 1750*. Cambridge: Cambridge University Press.

Commercial Reports from Her Majesty's Consuls in Japan 1863–64. 1865. London: Harrison and Sons.

de Coning, Cedric, Thomas Mandrup and Liselotte Odgaard (eds.). 2015. *The BRICS and Coexistence: An Alternative Vision of World Order*. New York: Routledge.

Ferroli, D. 1939. *The Jesuits in Malabar*, vol. 1. Bangalore: The Bangalore Press.

Frank, Andre Gunder. 1998. *ReOrient: Global Economy in Asian Age*. Berkeley: University of California Press.

Ganapathi, M. 2015. 'Look East – Act East Dimension of India's Foreign Policy,' *Ministry of External Affairs* (GOI), 29 January 2015, URL: www.mea.gov.in/distinguished-lectures-detail.htm?209 (assessed on 3 May 2020).

Garber, P. M. 1993. 'The Collapse of the Bretton Woods Fixed Exchange Rate System,' in M. D. Bordo and B. Eichengreen (eds.), *A Retrospective on the Bretton Woods System: Lessons for International Monetary Reform*, pp. 464–91. Chicago: National Bureau of Economic Research, University of Chicago Press.

Garner, Richard L. 1964. 'Silver Production and Entre-Preneurial Structure in 18th-Century Mexico,' *Jahrbuch für Geschichte Lateinamerikas – Anuario de Historia de America Latina*, vol. 17 (1), Böhlau Verlag: 157–185.

Gilbert, Eric. 2016. 'The "Other" Ships: Dhows and the Colonial Imagination in the Indian Ocean,' in Tricia Cusack (ed.). *Framing the Ocean, 1700 to the Present: Envisaging the Sea as Social Space*, pp. 101–115. New York: Routledge.

Hamilton, Earl J. 1934. *American Treasure and the Price Revolution of Spain (1501–1650)*. Massachusetts: Cambridge University Press.

Hornell, James. 1946. *Water Transport Origin & Early Evolution*. Cambridge: Cambridge University Press.

'Is BRICS a Real Bloc,' 2011. *The Diplomat*, 22 April 2011. (Richard Weitz), URL: https://thediplomat.com/2011/04/is-brics-a-real-bloc/ (assessed on 10 November 2019).

Kobata, A. 1965. 'The Production and Uses of Gold and Silver in the 16th and 17th century Japan,' *Economic History Review* XVIII: 245–266.

Lin, Man-Houng. 2019. 'World Recession, Indian Opium and China's Opium War,' in K. S. Mathew (ed.), *Mariners, Merchants and Oceans*, pp. 385–418. New Delhi: Manohar.

Ray, Haraprasad. 2019. 'An Enquiry into the Presence of the Chinese in South and South-East Asia after the Voyages of Zheng He in Early Fifteenth Century,' in K. S. Mathew (ed.), *Mariners, Merchants and Oceans: Studies in Maritime History*, pp. 98–110. New Delhi: Manohar.

Rohan. 2014a. 'Dynamics of English Trade and Commerce in the Riverine City of Medieval Patna,' *History Today*, No. 15, December 2014: 26–35.

Rohan. 2014b. 'Indian Merchant Diaspora and the Cross-Cultural Trade in Central Asia from 16th to Early 19th Century,' Unpublished Dissertation. New Delhi: Jawaharlal Nehru University.

Rohan. 2018. 'Trade, Territory and the Quest for Empire in Eurasia in the 19th Century,' Unpublished Ph.D Thesis. New Delhi: Jawaharlal Nehru University.

Russko-Indiiskie otnoshniya v. XIX v., sbornik arkhivnikh dokumentov e materialov. 1968. Doc. No. 1. Nauka: Moscow, 1968): 1–16.

Simiand, Francçois. 1994. 'Money, a Social Reality'. Cited in, Marcel Fournier, *Marcel Mauss: A Biography*. Translated by Jane Marie Todd, p. 289. Princeton: Princeton University Press.

Singh, Satyindra. 1992. *Blueprints of Bluewaters, the Indian Navy, 1951–65*. New Delhi: Lancer International.

Stevens, William and Allan Westcott. 2008. *History of Sea Power*. New York: George H. Doran Company.

Varadarajan, Lotika. 2014. 'Odam – The Sewn Boats of Lakshadweep, Pointers of Indian Maritime Traditions,' *History Today*, No. 15, December 2014: 46–62.

Vigne, Samuel Alexandre. 2017. 'As Good as Gold? About the Financial Implications of Gold and Silver,' Unpublished Ph.D Dissertation. Trinity College: University of Dublin.

Vilar, P. 1967. *A History of Gold and Money 1450–1920*. Translated by Judith White. London: NLB.

Wagar, W.W. (ed.). 1967. *European Intellectual History Since Darwin and Marx*. New York: Harper & Row.

'What is India's "IDEAS" Belt & Road Alternative Project?' 2019. *Silk Road Briefing*, 19 July 2019. Chris Devonshire-Ellis, URL: www.silkroadbriefing.com/news/2019/07/17/indias-ideas-belt-road-alternative-project/ (assessed on 3 October 2020).

Yule, H. and H. Cordier. 1964. *Cathay and the Way Thither*, vol. III. London: Hakluyt Society.

5

ECONOMIC GROWTH, TRADE AND INVESTMENT TRENDS IN BRICS

Meeta Keswani Mehra and Sk. Md. Azharuddin

Background

The BRICS (Brazil, Russia, India, China and South Africa) group became the focus of attention through the 2000s because of the significant economic growth in the individual economies of the group amid slower growth or even recession in the developed countries. Since then, BRICS has become a ubiquitous economic entity, often identified by investors, financiers, and policymakers alike as emerging markets (Pant, 2013). This chapter attempts to analyse the origin of BRICS, its evolution as an influential group of emerging economies, and its place in the emerging world order as a means to balance the economic power structures in terms of economic growth, demographics, international trade, global investment flows, and balance of payments. It also includes a discussion of the efforts towards creating new institutional mechanisms, such as the National Development Bank (NDB), and enhancing economic and financial co-operation in the development sectors of the group's members – namely, public health, humanitarian and medical supplies, environmental protection, clean energy, trade and supply networks and technology transfer.

The key takeaways from the analysis in this chapter are as follows.

As is evidenced by the data compiled here, BRICS as a group seems to be moving along the economic pathways visualised by Jim O' Neill (O'Neill, 2021). IMF projects that BRICS could contribute close to 50% of the world GDP by 2030 in comparison with the prevailing 22%. They are economically influential in several specific aspects. China is among the world's biggest industrial and manufacturing hub and is a significant research and innovation centre. India is significantly ahead of other BRICS nations in specific high-tech sectors, namely, information and communication technology and pharmaceuticals. Brazil and South Africa are abundantly endowed with minerals and other natural and ecological resources, while Russia is a large hydrocarbons (oil and natural gas) exporter to rest of the world.

DOI: 10.4324/9781003148074-6

The demographic profiles of BRICS could also support the realisation of economic prospects of the group. Brazil, India and South Africa currently have significant populations below the working age of 0–14 years that could potentially join the workforce by 2030–2040, implying that the dominating position of BRICS in this respect is likely to be sustained over the next two to three decades. Utilising its potential of human capital lies at the core of a robust recovery for the BRICS in the post-COVID-19 era.

As for international trade linkages, intra-BRICS commodity trade patterns hold promise. In the case of specific commodity groups, indicators such as Revealed Comparative Advantage (RCA) and Trade Intensity Index (TII) point to a high comparative advantage and trade intensity within the BRICS countries. These trends are likely to deepen further in case the group endeavours to become a more cohesive global entity and chooses to lower trade barriers to strengthen trade ties. The impressive performance of BRICS in attracting direct investment has been a key driving factor for its economic growth and the internationalisation of financial flows, technology and resources. In fact, inflows of FDI have been steady for most of the BRICS countries in spite of the COVID-19 pandemic.

The next section discusses the evolution of BRICS with a special focus on the institutional mechanisms.

Origin and Institutional Evolution

The acronym BRIC (Brazil, Russia, India and China) was conceptualised in 2001 by Jim O'Neill of Goldman Sachs in a paper titled 'Building Better Global Economic BRICs' (O'Neill, 2001). The key imperative for the modelling of the economic prospects of BRICs and its subsequent recognition was the growing importance of BRICs in the global economy. Goldman Sachs in 2001 observed that towards the end of the first decade of the 2000s, GDP in US$ in purchasing power parity (PPP) terms collectively in Brazil, Russia, India and China was around 23.3% of the aggregate world GDP and 8% on current nominal GDP basis. It predicted that over the next ten years, the share of the BRICs, especially China and India, in the world GDP would grow even bigger, implying that fiscal, monetary and trade policies in the BRICs could affect the global economy.

In a subsequent paper, Dominic Wilson and Roopa Purushothaman of Goldman Sachs (Wilson and Purushothaman, 2003) predicted that if all went well, the BRICs economies could become larger than the G6 in US$ terms over the next couple of decades, from the then prevailing 15% of the world GDP, to account for over half the size of the G6 by 2025.[1] Furthermore, the growth in relative importance of the BRIC as a new demand centre and spending power could be a direct consequence of its higher population growth, associated demographic changes and the rise of the middle class. Faster growth in these economies could also offset the impact of ageing populations and sluggish growth in the advanced economies.

The underlying premise for making these forecasts was that BRICs (and other emerging market economies) could evolve for itself policies and institutions that would help realise this growth potential. The authors contended that despite the challenges encountered by the BRICs to stay on the envisaged development track, the implications for the pattern of global growth and economic activity could be huge if their growth rates came anywhere close to meeting the projections.

BRICs has been perceived to be the vanguard of emerging economies of the Global South. Since 2010, when BRICs invited South Africa to join as a member, BRICS (Brazil, Russia, India, China, and South Africa) has become a political and economic challenge to the Western-dominated global governance architecture.

As a formal grouping of nations, BRIC was launched after the meeting of the state leaders of Russia, India and China in St. Petersburg on the sidelines of the G8 Outreach Summit in July 2006. The grouping was formalised during the first meeting of BRIC foreign ministers on the sidelines of the United Nations General Assembly (UNGA) in New York in September 2006. The first BRIC Summit was held in Yekaterinburg, Russia, on 16 June 2009. Subsequently, BRIC agreed to expand into BRICS with the inclusion of South Africa at the BRIC foreign ministers' meeting in New York in September 2010. Accordingly, South Africa attended the third BRICS Summit in Sanya, China, on 14 April 2011.

Thus far, 12 BRICS Summits have been organised. Russia hosted and chaired the 12th BRICS Summit in November 2020. Despite their individual or bilateral economic and geopolitical challenges, at this Summit, the BRICS leaders reiterated their commitment to deal co-operatively with the complicated and interlinked challenges presented by the COVID-19 pandemic, with its attendant negative consequences for the economy, employment, public health arrangements, financial sector and welfare of the most susceptible groups in the member nations.

Besides the annual Summits, the state heads have also met on the margins of G20 summits. Starting largely with common economic issues, the scope of BRICS meetings has been considerably enlarged over the years to encompass political developments (situation in the Middle East and North Africa region, Afghanistan, Iran and Syria), global governance institutions (UN, International Monetary Fund (IMF), World Bank Group), international terrorism, climate change, food and energy security, public health, the Millennium Development Goals (MDGs), open and inclusive international trade, global supply chains, and the international economic and financial situation. These have entailed the involvement of heads of state and diplomats as well as the ministers of finance, trade, health, science and technology, education, agriculture, communication, labour, and environment to seek co-operation through meetings of working groups and senior official functionaries.

A significant recent institutional development has been the formation of the New Development Bank (NDB) under the aegis of the BRICS. The proposal to create the NDB was first mooted at the fourth BRICS Summit in New Delhi on March 29, 2012, to serve the development sector funding requirements of the five founding countries – namely, Brazil, Russia, India, China, and South Africa – as well as of other emerging and developing economies. It was at the sixth summit in July 2014 at Fortaleza, Brazil, that the member countries signed the articles for the NDB with an authorised capital of US$100 billion. The bank emerged as a formal legal entity, and the first meeting of the Board of Governors was held in July 2015 in Moscow, Russia. Among the important stated goals for establishing the bank has been the need to muster resources for infrastructure and sustainable development projects in BRICS and other emerging economies and developing countries. This is expected to balance the present efforts of multilateral and regional financial institutions for sustaining an inclusive global economic growth and development process. In fact, the NDB was instrumental in channelising an emergency loan assistance of US$1 billion to China to mitigate the impact of COVID-19. Such assistance was also subsequently extended to India, South Africa and Brazil.

In the next section, we discuss the important characteristics of the BRICS economies in the prevailing world economic order.

BRICS in the Emerging World Order

The role of BRICS countries in the global economy has continued to grow in the recent past, in wide-ranging economic and demographic dimensions (see Table 5.1).

In 2019, the BRICS countries as a group accounted for around 3.2 billion people (which is close to 42% of the world population) and their combined GDP had risen from US$5863 billion in 2000 to US$19018 billion in constant 2010 US dollar terms (a significant 22.4% of world GDP). Due to the shock of the COVID-19 pandemic, all economies of the BRICS group have suffered a setback to varying degrees, even as it is reckoned that their share in global output will continue to remain significant.

BRICS countries have become more open, with trade and foreign direct investment (FDI) playing a key role in boosting the growth prospects of the individual countries as well as elsewhere. In 2019, the commodity export and import levels of US$3660 billion and US$3385 billion (both in constant 2010 prices) respectively amounted to world shares of 13–14%, having risen from the low levels of around US$1034 billion and US$799 billion in 2000. A similar increase can also be seen in the case of aggregate trade flows for BRICS, which have registered an increase of nearly US$5212 billion from US$1833 billion to US$7045 billion over 2000–2019, displaying a nearly 6.2%-point gain in world share. The improvement in trade balance has been significant, having risen from US$37 billion in 2000 to US$115 billion in 2019 (in current prices). Furthermore, forex reserves for BRICS as a group rose from US$281.2 billion in 2000 to US$4653.5 billion in 2019 at current prices.

These trends augur well for BRICS as a group, allowing researchers to make encouraging projections of their role in the world economy.

Economic Growth Performance

In terms of economic growth, in aggregate or per capita terms, BRICS countries have been a force to reckon with. Among the group, the GDP growth rates (in constant 2010 US$) for China and India have been especially noteworthy, ranging

TABLE 5.1 Key indicators for BRICS

Member Countries Brazil, Russia, India, China and South Africa	*2000*	*2010*	*2015*	*2019*
GDP at market prices (constant 2005 US$ billion)	5862.81	11871.92	15626.82	19017.51
Share (%) of world GDP	11.74	17.95	20.57	22.41
Population (million persons)	2685.58	2961.77	3085.33	3178.11
Share (%) of world population	43.92	42.79	42.04	41.42
Exports of goods and services (constant 2005 US$ billion)	1034.21	2823.10	3271.61	3660.24
Share (%) of global exports	8.24	14.83	14.21	13.95
Imports of goods and services (constant 2005 US$ billion)	798.99	2570.51	2813.74	3384.97
Share (%) of global imports	6.74	13.92	12.79	13.40
Trade (constant 2005 US$ billion)	1833.20	5393.60	6085.36	7045.21
Share (%) of world trade	7.51	14.38	13.52	13.68
Current account balance (current US$ billion)	36.88	166.24	280.44	115.32
Forex reserves (Includes gold, current US$ billion)	281.20	4025.81	4528.97	4653.49

Source: World Development Indicators database

between 7–11% and 5.5–8.5% annually during 1990–2015, much higher than the world annual average growth rates of 2.3–4.4%. More recently, however, the growth rates in both countries have slowed down, with the annual growth rate having fallen to 6% and 4% in China and India respectively in 2019. The performance in growth terms has been relatively more chequered for other BRICS economies, namely, Brazil, Russia and South Africa, hovering in the range of negative to as high as 10% during 2005–2010. Consequently, the average annual rates of growth for BRICS collectively ranged between 3.5 and 7.3%, much higher than the average world growth rates. These have also translated into raising the shares of the Chinese and Indian GDPs in the world GDP from 2.2% and 1.3% in 1990 to 13.6% and 3.5% respectively in 2019. Brazil's share has fallen marginally, from 3.1% in 1990 to 2.8% in 2019, and that of the Russian Federation more significantly from 3.7% to 2.1% over the same period. In comparison, South Africa remains a small player with a share of 0.5–0.6%. Taken together, however, these trends amount to a near doubling of the share of the BRICS countries in world GDP at market price, from 11% to 22.4%, during 1990–2019. This performance is clearly noteworthy, especially in the face of the global financial crisis of 2007–2008 (see Table 5.2).

In PPP terms, the performance has been even more impressive for some in the BRICS group, with the share for China in world GDP having increased from 3.2% in 1990 to 17.4% in 2019 and for India from 3.1% to 7.1% during the same period. Brazil, Russia and South Africa have registered small to moderate falls (from 3.1% to 2.4%, from 6.2% to 3.1% and from 0.7% to 0.6% respectively) over 1990–2019. The extraordinary economic performance of China and, to some extent, of India have translated into substantial gains in the share of BRICS in world GDP in PPP terms, from 16.3% in 1990 to a whopping 30.4% in 2019 (refer to Table 5.2).

These growth rates have led to substantial gains in GDP per capita, although the rise has been moderated by the population growth in China and India. Even so, the performance in per capita terms is remarkable. China's per capita GDP has increased 11-fold while India's has risen four times during 1990–2019. In absolute terms, these rose from US$730 to US$6500 for China and from US$581 to US$2151 for India in constant 2010 prices. The gains have been relatively lower, in the range of 1.2–1.4 times, in the other BRICS countries, which, nonetheless, have been comparable to those for the world as a whole. Moreover, in absolute terms, Brazil, the Russian Federation and South Africa have had the advantage of much higher GDP per capita, at US$11122, US$12012 and US$7346 respectively in 2019, again closer to the world average level (see Table 5.2).

Consequently, in terms of aggregate GDP rankings, in 2019, China stood at the 2nd position (after the USA) ahead of Japan and Germany, while India was at the 5th position, having surpassed UK and France GDP levels (Data source: World Development Indicators, for the year 2019). The position of India might have changed in the recent past due to a significant decrease in its GDP because of economic setbacks resulting from the COVID-19 pandemic.

TABLE 5.2 Growth of GDP and GDP per capita

Country Name	*GDP at market prices (constant 2010 US$ billion)*	*Rate of growth of GDP at constant 2010 market price (%)*	*GDP per capita (constant 2010 US$)*	*Rate of growth of GDP per capita at constant 2010 market price (%)*	*GDP in PPP terms (constant 2017 US$ billion)*	*GDP per capita in PPP terms (constant 2017 US$ billion)*
Brazil						
1990	1189.60	−3.10	7983.75	−4.84	1567.17	10517.67
2000	1538.71	4.39	8803.15	2.91	2027.07	11597.14
2010	2208.87	7.53	11286.24	6.52	2909.93	14868.33
2015	2337.35	−3.55	11431.15	−4.35	3079.19	15059.23
2019	2347.24	1.14	11121.74	0.38	3092.22	14651.62
China						
1990	827.87	3.92	729.28	2.41	1616.39	1423.90
2000	2232.18	8.49	1767.86	7.64	4358.25	3451.68
2010	6087.16	10.64	4550.45	10.10	11884.96	8884.59
2015	8913.50	7.04	6500.42	6.50	17403.28	12691.82
2019	11537.48	6.11	8254.53	5.73	22526.50	16116.66
India						
1990	507.57	5.53	581.22	3.37	1580.46	1809.80
2000	873.36	3.84	826.59	2.02	2719.47	2573.85
2010	1675.62	8.50	1357.56	7.04	5217.54	4227.19
2015	2294.95	8.00	1751.66	6.80	7146.03	5454.35
2019	2940.16	4.18	2151.73	3.13	9155.08	6700.06
Russian Federation						
1990	1416.19	−3.00	9570.81	−3.16	3188.54	21548.65
2000	951.57	10.00	6491.07	10.46	2142.46	14614.63
2010	1524.92	4.50	10675.00	4.45	3433.35	24034.73
2015	1662.47	−1.97	11355.24	−2.18	3743.06	25566.29
2019	1762.46	1.34	12011.53	1.41	3968.18	27043.94

South Africa						
1990	223.00	−0.32	6059.80	−2.68	378.91	10296.44
2000	267.00	4.20	5937.63	2.74	453.67	10088.85
2010	375.35	3.04	7328.62	1.55	637.77	12452.34
2015	418.54	1.19	7556.79	−0.34	711.16	12840.04
2019	430.17	0.15	7345.96	−1.18	730.91	12481.81
World						
1990	37985.98	2.91	7194.21	1.15	51101.35	9678.15
2000	49948.98	4.39	8169.16	3.02	67770.91	11083.94
2010	66125.92	4.30	9553.18	3.06	96227.26	13901.91
2015	75958.24	2.87	10349.99	1.69	113862.76	15514.83
2019	84865.36	2.36	11059.49	1.28	129789.46	16913.91

Source: World Development Indicators database

According to IMF estimates, the BRICS nations are likely to account for around 50% of world GDP by 2030 in PPP terms. They are influential in a number of significant areas. China boasts of the world's largest industrial and manufacturing capability and is a major R&D hub. India has taken big strides in science and technology, especially in information and communication technology and services, as well as in pharmaceuticals. Brazil and South Africa have large endowments of mineral, water, and other natural and ecological resources, while Russia has emerged as one of largest energy (oil and natural gas) suppliers to the Western countries and others.

The favourable demographic profiles of these countries, with a large proportion of the population in the economically active age group, could be a partial explanation of the impressive growth story of BRICS.

Demographics and Labour Force Participation

BRICS economies continue to have a dominant share of the world population, close to 42%, largely because of the large population sizes of China and India. More significantly, these countries also have a higher share of economically active population (population in the age group of 15–64 years). China had the highest population with the highest share of active population at 71% in 2019, while India follows in terms of population but with a somewhat lower proportion of an economically active population at 67%. However, the size of the economically active category in India is likely to increase given the existing age distribution of the population. Brazil, the Russian Federation, and South Africa also have large shares of economically active populations, at 70%, 67%, and 66% respectively in 2019. These are slightly better than the world average and are much better than that of Japan, the United Kingdom and the United States. Since some countries in the BRICS group such as Brazil, India, and South Africa currently have a major proportion of their population (nearly 20–30%) in the 0–14 years age group that will be joining the workforce by 2030–2040, the high proportion of the economically actively population in the BRICS countries is likely to be sustained over the next decade or so (see Table 5.3).

According to the prediction of Wilson and Purushothaman (2003), within BRICs, demographic impacts vary greatly. Given that changes in demographic profiles take a long time to unfold, the decline in the working-age population is projected to take place later in the BRICS economies than in the developed economies, but these trends will be steeper in Russia and China than in India and Brazil.

The flip side of the favourable demographic profile of the BRICS countries is that, given the structural and technological changes currently taking place, these countries face a huge challenge in terms of skilling and retraining their labour force. Reskilling of younger population (who will migrate to the working age group of 25–64 years) and broad-basing employment opportunities have emerged as a focus area, especially in view of the loss of jobs caused by COVID-19 pandemic.

Since international trade and financial flows between countries offer a channel for growth and development, it is important to recognise the exiting nature

TABLE 5.3 Aggregate and age composition of population

Country	*Year*	*Total population (millions)*	*Percentage of population of each age-group in the total*			
			0 to 14 years	*15 to 64 years*	*65 years and above*	*Total*
Brazil	1990	149.00	35.2	60.6	4.3	100
	2019	211.05	21.0	69.7	9.3	100
China	1990	1135.19	28.6	65.8	5.6	100
	2019	1397.72	17.8	70.7	11.5	100
India	1990	873.28	38.0	58.2	3.8	100
	2019	1366.42	26.6	67.0	6.4	100
Russian Federation	1990	147.97	22.9	66.8	10.3	100
	2019	144.37	18.2	66.8	15.1	100
South Africa	1990	36.80	40.1	55.9	4.0	100
	2019	58.56	29.0	65.6	5.4	100
Japan	1990	123.54	18.5	69.7	11.9	100
	2019	126.26	12.6	59.4	28.0	100
UK	1990	57.25	19.0	65.3	15.7	100
	2019	66.83	17.7	63.8	18.5	100
USA	1990	249.62	21.7	65.7	12.6	100
	2019	328.24	18.5	65.2	16.2	100
World	1990	5280.08	32.9	61.0	6.2	100
	2019	7673.53	25.6	65.3	9.1	100

Source: World Development Indicators database

and potential role that foreign direct investment and international commodity and services trade could play in sustaining economy recovery and future growth of the BRICS. This is discussed in the next few sections.

External Sector Characteristics of BRICS

International merchandise and services trade has played a significant role in bolstering the economic and political status of the BRICS nations. BRICS economies have been relying on trade liberalisation to boost development. As can be seen from the data in Table 5.4, the role of aggregate trade (exports plus imports) as a share of GDP for Brazil, China, Russia and South Africa has increased significantly during 1990–2019, registering a nearly 1.5 to two-fold increase. The increase in India's case has been even more significant with a three-fold increase in trade. In this respect, trade liberalisation trends in the BRICS countries are comparable or slightly more pronounced than for the OECD economies such as Japan, the UK and the USA.

The role of trade in explaining economic growth in and the development performance of BRICS is critical, requiring deeper investigation of its key determinants. This has been dealt with in another chapter, using trade gravity analysis.

Current account balances for Brazil, India and South Africa have been negative, amounting to around −2.77%, −1.04%) and – 3.04% of GDP in 2019 while China and Russia, which are export-oriented countries, have a surplus on the current account. The current account balance refers to the sum of net exports of goods and services, net primary income, and net secondary income. The generally positive balances for China over the years can be attributed to its large share in world exports, while in the case of Russia these are because of large volumes of fuel exports and buoyant global energy prices. Notwithstanding the negative deficits of the former group (which are in themselves not always bad), these have been generally kept under check as a proportion of aggregate GDP, and is similar to those found for the UK (−4%) and the US (−2.2%) (Table 5.4).

All BRICS economies, in general, display comfortable reserves stock positions, amounting to a high of US$3127 billion in China, and between US$350–450 billion in Brazil, India and the Russian Federation. The total reserves comprise holdings of monetary gold,[2] special drawing rights, reserves of IMF members held by the IMF,[3] and holdings of foreign exchange under the control of the monetary authorities. In absolute terms, these amounted to a massive US$4406 billion in 2019, having increased almost 16 times from its 2000 levels and over 100 times in comparison with the level in the 1990s (see Table 5.4).

The external debt stock indicator refers to the total external debt owed to nonresidents repayable in currency, goods, or services. Total external debt is the sum of public, publicly guaranteed, and private non-guaranteed long-term debt, use of IMF credit, and short-term debt. Short-term debt includes all debt having an original maturity of one year or less and interest in arrears on long-term debt. While the numbers tabulated here are large in magnitude, to say the least, the debt servicing ratio, which is defined as the sum of principal repayments and interest actually paid in currency, goods, or services on long-term debt, interest paid on short-term debt, and repayments (repurchases and charges) to the IMF, is found to be comfortable across most of the BRICS economies in most years (see Table 5.4).

Net FDI Inflows

In 2019, the collective FDI of the BRICS group amounted to US$316.53 billion (World Development Indicator data), accounting for a huge 20% of the world net inflows. The rise from 1990 levels is stupendous, from a mere US$4.64 billion (2% of the world level). Here, FDI refers to direct investment equity flows in the reporting economy. It is the sum of equity capital, reinvestment of earnings, and other capital. In 2019, China stands out as the biggest recipient of FDI, at around US$156 billion (9.6% share of world), followed by Brazil (US$73.5 billion), India (US$50.6 billion) and the Russian Federation (US$32 billion). India has surpassed the Russian Federation in terms of FDI inflows after 2010. South Africa is a much smaller player as compared to other BRICS economies with FDI amounting to US$4.6 billion. Moreover, these are generally comparable or sometimes much larger than net FDI inflows into Japan and the UK (see Table 5.5).

TABLE 5.4 External sector features

Country Name	*Trade (% of GDP)**	*Current account balance (% of GDP)*	*Total reserves minus gold (current million US$)*	*Total reserves (% of total external debt)*	*External debt stocks (% of GNI)*	*Debt service (PPG and IMF only, % of exports of goods, services and primary income)*
Brazil						
1990	15.2	−0.83	8239	8.3	26.8	18.6
2000	22.6	−3.70	32434	13.6	38.1	37.0
2010	22.8	−3.58	287056	81.9	16.5	5.9
2015	27.0	−3.02	354175	65.6	30.7	12.7
2019	29.1	−2.77	353588	62.7	31.8	..
China						
1990	24.3	3.32	29586	62.3	15.28	10.6
2000	39.4	1.69	168278	117.7	12.20	7.1
2010	50.7	3.91	2866079	392.3	12.25	0.8
2015	39.6	2.75	3345194	255.3	12.10	1.3
2019	38.2	0.99	3127494	152.4	14.78	..
India						
1990	15.5	−2.19	1521	6.8	26.4	27.2
2000	26.9	−0.98	37902	40.6	21.8	15.4
2010	49.3	−3.25	275277	103.5	17.5	1.7
2015	41.9	−1.07	334311	73.8	23.0	3.1
2019	43.4	−1.04	432378	82.8	19.7	..
Russian Federation						
1990	36.1	..	..	..	..	..
2000	68.1	17.5	24264	18.86	57.98	7.47
2010	50.4	4.4	443586	114.69	28.28	6.61
2015	49.4	5.0	319835	78.69	35.28	10.26
2019	51.5	3.8	443970	113.13	29.80	..
South Africa						
1990	41.7	1.34	1008	..	..	..
2000	51.4	−0.14	6083	29.0	19.9	5.6
2010	56.0	−1.46	38175	40.4	29.5	2.9
2015	61.6	−4.59	41620	36.9	40.1	3.1
2019	59.5	−3.04	48920	29.3	55.1	..
Japan						
1990	19.7	..	78501	..	..	..
2000	19.8	2.7	354902	..	..	..
2010	28.6	3.9	1069985	..	..	..
2015	35.6	3.1	1207019	..	..	..
2019	36.6	3.6	1284974	..	..	..
UK						
1990	48.0	−3.55	35853	..	..	..
2000	52.1	−2.25	46638	..	..	..
2010	58.5	−3.18	84006	..	..	..
2015	56.7	−4.90	137535	..	..	..
2019	61.8	−4.00	158376	..	..	..

(Continued)

TABLE 5.4 (Continued)

Country Name	*Trade (% of GDP)**	*Current account balance (% of GDP)*	*Total reserves minus gold (current million US$)*	*Total reserves (% of total external debt)*	*External debt stocks (% of GNI)*	*Debt service (PPG and IMF only, % of exports of goods, services and primary income)*
US						
1990	19.8	−1.32	72258	..	..	..
2000	25.0	−3.92	56600	..	..	..
2010	28.1	−2.88	121392	..	..	..
2015	27.7	−2.24	106540	..	..	..
2019	27.5	−2.24	118438	..	..	..

* The data listed against 2019 refers to 2018

Source: World Development Indicators and WITS databases.

TABLE 5.5 Foreign direct investment, net inflows (balance of payments, current US$ billion)

Country Name	*1990*	*2000*	*2010*	*2015*	*2019*
Brazil	0.99	32.99	82.39	64.74	73.50
China	3.49	42.10	243.70	242.49	155.82
India	0.24	3.58	27.40	44.01	50.61
Russian Federation		2.68	43.17	6.85	31.97
South Africa	−0.08	0.97	3.69	1.52	4.62
Japan	1.81	10.69	7.44	5.25	37.18
United Kingdom	41.36	164.13	66.73	45.33	20.70
United States	71.23	349.13	264.04	511.43	351.63
World	239.41	1569.12	1916.75	2671.12	1622.00
Country shares in world (%)					
Country Name	*1990*	*2000*	*2010*	*2015*	*2019*
Brazil	0.4	2.1	4.3	2.4	4.5
China	1.5	2.7	12.7	9.1	9.6
India	0.1	0.2	1.4	1.6	3.1
Russian Federation	0.0	0.2	2.3	0.3	2.0
South Africa	0.0	0.1	0.2	0.1	0.3
Japan	0.8	0.7	0.4	0.2	2.3
United Kingdom	17.3	10.5	3.5	1.7	1.3
United States	29.8	22.2	13.8	19.1	21.7
World	100	100	100	100	100

Source: World Development Indicators database

In terms of inflow to outflow ratio, it can be seen from Table 5.6 that for most BRICS countries, it is greater than one. This may be because of the favourable conditions for FDI hosting by BRICS countries in general. BRICS countries are developing in nature and are endowed with rich natural resources and low-cost

TABLE 5.6 FDI inflow/outflow ratios

Country Name	*FDI inflows (US$ billion)*	*FDI outflows (US$ billion)*	*Inflow/ outflow ratio)*
Brazil			
2010	77.69	22.06	3.52
2019	71.99	15.52	4.64
China			
2010	114.73	68.81	1.67
2019	141.23	117.12	1.21
India			
2010	27.42	15.95	1.72
2019	50.55	12.10	4.18
Russian Federation			
2010	31.67	41.12	0.77
2019	31.74	22.53	1.41
South Africa			
2010	3.64	−0.08	−48.05
2019	4.62	3.12	1.48
Japan			
2010	−1.25	56.26	−0.02
2019	14.55	226.65	0.06
UK			
2010	58.20	48.09	1.21
2019	59.14	31.48	1.88
US			
2010	198.05	277.78	0.71
2019	246.22	124.90	1.97
World			
2010	1396.20	1396.03	1.00
2019	1539.88	1313.77	1.17

Source: UNCTAD, FDI-MNE Information System, FDI database (www.unctad.org/fdistatistics)[4]

labour. Further, their market size is considerable, making them attractive as investment destinations.

This impressive performance in attracting direct investment has been a key driving factor for economic growth and the internationalisation of financial flows, technology and resources. FDI into BRICS requires closer scrutiny in terms of its key drivers. This is also attempted by the authors in one of the later chapters that focuses on the determinants of FDI into BRICS countries.

The significant attempts made by BRICS countries to adopt freer trade regimes merits a more detailed discussion of the patterns of trade, which is attempted in the following section.

Explaining International Trade

Aggregate Trade Flows

Evidently, although they have different trade liberalisation policies, the BRICS countries have become much more open to the international movement of goods and services over time, especially over the last two to three decades. Even though trade has increased both within the BRICS group as well as between the group and the rest of the world, the increase in trade among BRICS countries has been found to be much more significant, especially in some important commodity groups.

Within BRICS, aggregate export flows rose from US$17.7 in 2000 to US$355.5 billion in 2019, with the ratio of the group's exports to the rest of the world rising from 0.04 to 0.11 over the period. Similarly, intra-group imports increased from US$28.3 billion in 2000 to US$417.6 billion in 2019, while the ratio of the group's imports from the rest of the world increased from 0.08 to 0.18 (Table 5.7).

At this point, it is also pertinent to analyse the commodity composition of trade of individual BRICS economies, captured by the level of diversity, revealed comparative advantage, and trade intensity indices. The next three sections are devoted to each of these respectively.

Trade Diversity

Trade diversity in the case of commodity trade is most popularly measured by an index such as the Herfindahl-Hirschman (HH) index of product and/or market concentration. It is believed that the more diversified the trade basket of a country – both in terms of the number of products that it is exporting and the number of trading countries it is exporting to – the less vulnerable its export volumes will be to changes in trade policy or sudden market shocks.

The HH product concentration index is a quantitative measure of the diversification of trade value across an exporter's products. A country for which the trade

TABLE 5.7 Merchandise: intra-trade and extra-trade flow of country groups (US$ at current prices in millions)

Year	*2000*	*2000*	*2019*	*2019*
	Intra-group	Rest of the world	Intra-group	Rest of the world
BRICS Exports	17711	458360	355515	3216266
Ratio of Intra group exports to Rest of the World	0.04		0.11	
BRICS Imports	28324	377193	417611	2651462
Ratio of Intra group imports to Rest of the World	0.08		0.16	

Source: WITS and World Bank databases

value is concentrated in very few products will have an index value closer to one. When tracked over time, a fall (rise) in the index may be an indication of diversification (concentration) in the exporter's trade profile. Mathematically, the HH product concentration index is denoted by:

$$\frac{\sum_{k=1}^{n_i}\left(\frac{x_{ik}}{X_i}\right)^2 - \frac{1}{n_i}}{1-\frac{1}{n_i}},$$

where $\boldsymbol{x_i}$ denotes the aggregate value of exports from reporter country i, $\boldsymbol{x_{ik}}$ is the value of exports of product k from country i, and $\boldsymbol{n_i}$ is the number of products exported by country i. Typically, the range of values of this index is 0 to 1. A higher value indicates that exports are concentrated in fewer sectors, whereas a country with a completely diversified portfolio will have an index close to zero.

Similarly, the HH market concentration indicator is a quantitative measure of the dispersion of trade value across an exporter's partners. A country whose destination markets are few will have an index value closer to one. Thus, it is an indicator of the exporter's dependency on its trading partners and the danger it could face should its partners increase trade barriers. Over time, a fall (rise) in the index will be an indication of diversification (concentration) in the exporter's trading relationships. Mathematically, the formula for the calculation of the HH market concentration index is given by:

$$\frac{\sum_{j=1}^{n_i}\left(\frac{x_{ij}}{X_i}\right)^2 - \frac{1}{n_i}}{1-\frac{1}{n_i}},$$

where $\boldsymbol{x_i}$ is the total value of exports from reporter country i, $\boldsymbol{x_{ij}}$ is the value of exports from country i to destination market j, and $\boldsymbol{n_i}$ is the number of partner markets to which country i exports. The value typically ranges between 0 and 1. A higher index value implies that the exports of the country are concentrated across a smaller number of markets, whereas a country trading equally with all partners will have an index close to zero.

The values of these indices for the BRICS countries for the year 2019 are given in Figure 5.1.

A look at Figure 5.1 reveals that the export basket of most countries in the BRICS group is quite diversified, in terms of both products as well as markets, since for most countries, the value of both the indices is less than 0.05. The only exception is Brazil, where exports are relatively concentrated in terms of export markets, and Russia, which has a comparatively lower export diversification in terms of products, as its exports are mainly in the form of hydrocarbon fuels.

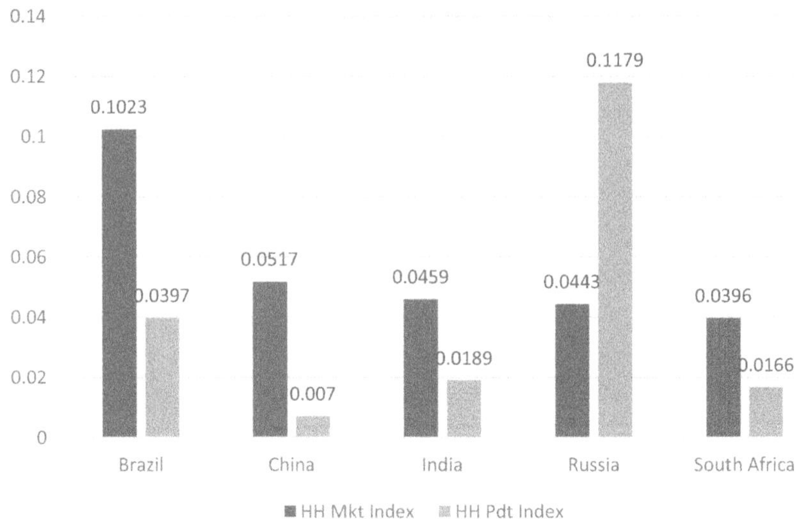

FIGURE 5.1 HH product and market concentration indices in 2019

Source: Authors' estimates from WITS database

Revealed Comparative Advantage

Revealed comparative advantage (RCA) is an indicator of a country's comparative advantage or disadvantage in a specific industry or commodity sector as exhibited by its trade flows. An index above one indicates that a country's share of exports in that sector outstrips the global export share of the same sector. If this is the case, we infer that the country has a comparative advantage in that sector. Specifically, it is calculated as:

$$RCA_{ijk} = \frac{x_{ijk} / X_{ij}}{x_{wjk} / X_{wj}},$$

where $\boldsymbol{x}_{ijk}$ is the value of exports of product group k from country i to destination country j, and $\boldsymbol{x}_{ij}$ is total exports from i to j. With w indicating the world as origin, the denominator is exports from the world to country j of commodity group k. In general, an RCA value between 0 and 1 indicates a comparative disadvantage, while a value above 1 indicates comparative advantage.

The estimates of RCAs for aggregated industry sub-groups for individual BRICS countries for the year 2019 are shown in Figures 5.2–5.6. As can be seen from Figure 5.2, the highest RCAs for Brazil lies in primary products such as animal, vegetable, food, minerals, and wood and wood products and the lowest RCAs are found to be in the case of chemicals, textiles and clothing, machinery and miscellaneous categories.

In the case of China (Figure 5.3), the highest RCAs are in the case of footwear, textiles, hides and skins, and machinery and metals. Further, it has a relative

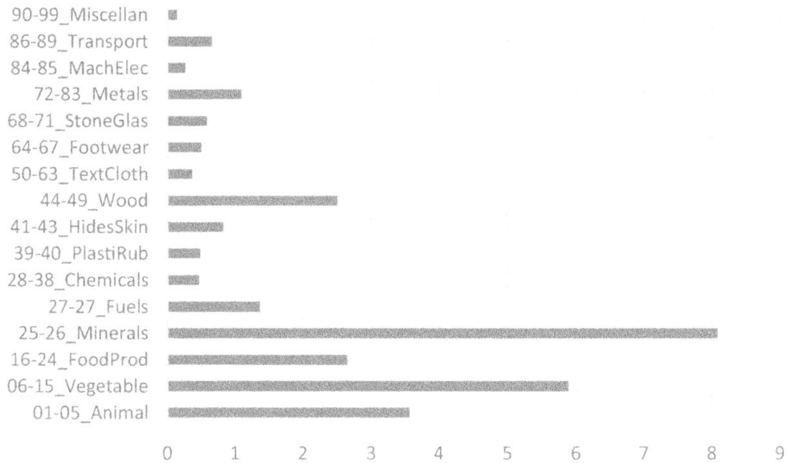

FIGURE 5.2 RCA for Brazil in 2019

Source: Authors' estimates from WITS database

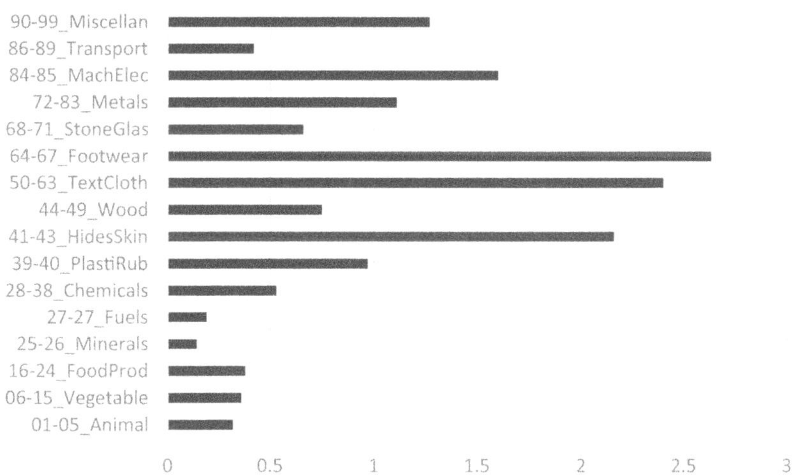

FIGURE 5.3 RCA for China in 2019

Source: Authors' estimates from WITS database

disadvantage in the case of primary sectors such as animal, vegetable and food products, mineral fuels, and transportation.

India's (Figure 5.4) comparative advantage is the highest in the case of stone and glass, textiles and clothing, footwear, hides and skins, animal and vegetable products, chemicals, fuels, minerals and metals, and miscellaneous products. It has a comparative disadvantage in the case of machinery, wood, food products and transport.

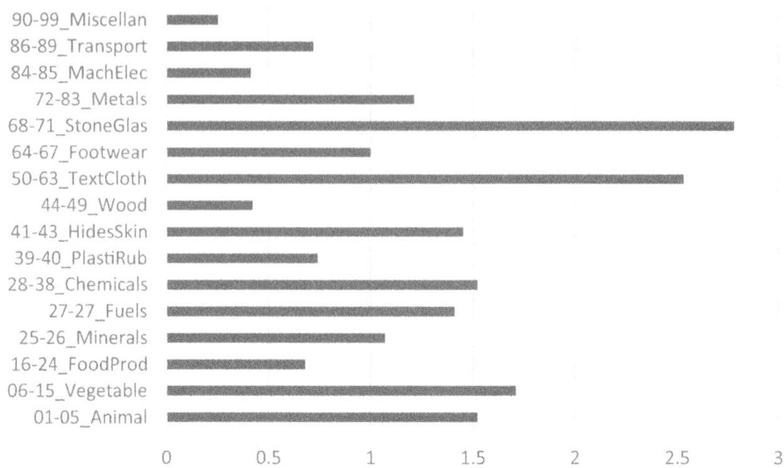

FIGURE 5.4 RCA for India in 2019

Source: Authors' estimates from WITS database

FIGURE 5.5 RCA for Russia in 2019

Source: Authors' estimates from WITS database

Russia (Figure 5.5) has the highest comparative advantage in fuels, followed by miscellaneous products, wood and metals. In most other sectors, Russia has a comparative disadvantage.

For South Africa (Figure 5.6), the highest levels of RCAs in 2019 vis-à-vis the world exist the in case of minerals, followed by stone and glass, vegetable and food products, and metals and transport.

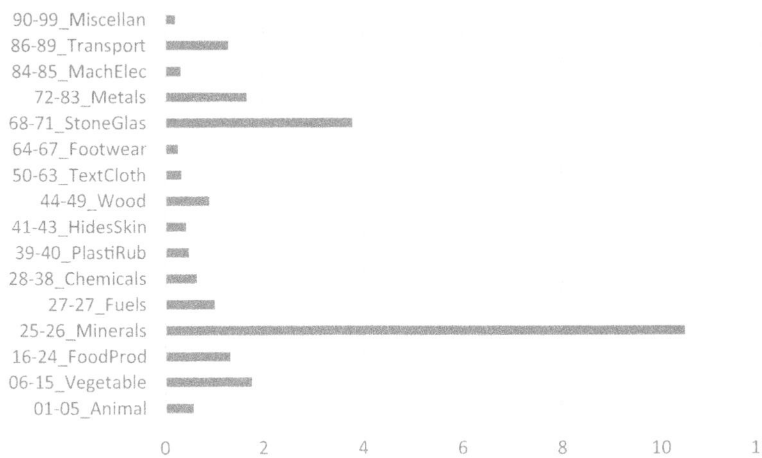

FIGURE 5.6 RCA for South Africa in 2019

Source: Authors' estimates from WITS database

Trade Intensity

The trade intensity index (TII) uses a similar methodology to identify whether a country's exports are concentrated in a few markets. It is a measure of the intensity of trade between two trading partners, measured based on whether a country exports more, as a percentage, to one or a few partners than the world does on average. It is measured as country 's exports to country *j* relative to its total exports divided by the world's exports to country *j* relative to the world's total exports. That is,

$$100 \star \left[\frac{x_{ijk}}{X_{ik}} / \frac{x_{wjk}}{X_{wk}} \right],$$

where $\boldsymbol{x_{ijk}}$ denotes the value of exports of product *k* from origin country *i* to destination *j*, and $\boldsymbol{X_{ik}}$ is total exports from *i* of product *k*. x_{wjk} and x_{wk} indicate global exports of product *k* to country *j* and total world trade in product *k* respectively. In general, the value of this index ranges between 0 and $+\infty$, and a value greater than 100 indicates a relationship more intense than the world average for the partner.

The calculated values of TII for the year 2019 for the individual BRICS countries are shown in Figures 5.7–5.11.

For Brazil (Figure 5.7), the TII in 2019 is generally higher for primary products with BRICS partners – namely, food products with India and China; animal and vegetable products with Russia, China, and South Africa; metals, machinery, and electrical products, transportation of rubber, hides and skins, and wood with South Africa; and hides and skins, wood, and textile and clothing with China and India. Fairly high intensity of trade also exists in the case of minerals with China and fuels with China and India.

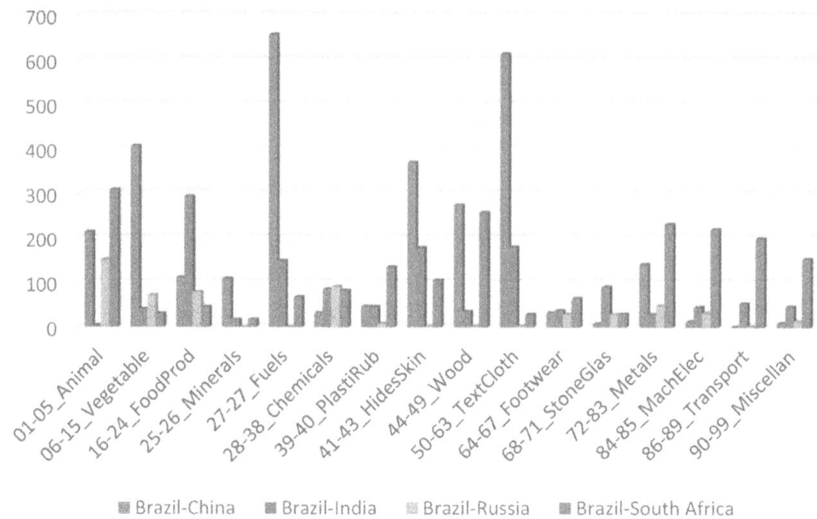

FIGURE 5.7 TII for Brazil in 2019

Source: Authors' estimates from WITS database

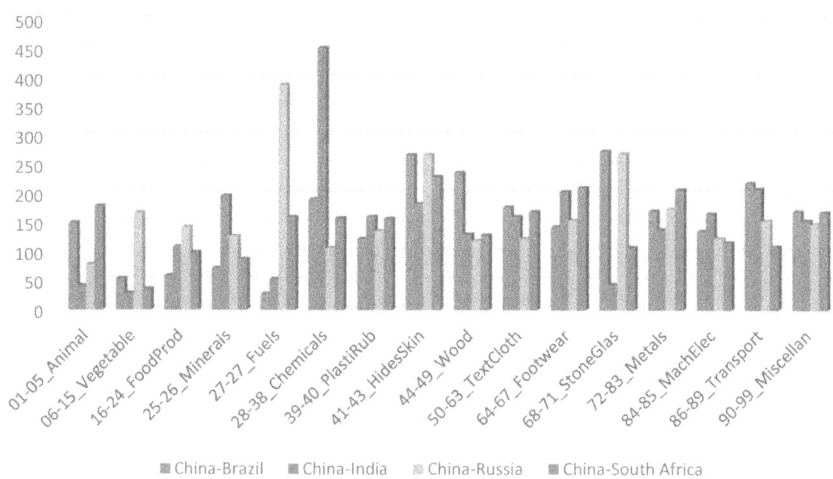

FIGURE 5.8 TII for China in 2019

Source: Authors' estimates from WITS database

China (Figure 5.8) has a high trade intensity in a wide range of commodity groups with almost all the other BRICS partners in 2019. The highest trade intensity is in hides and skins, footwear, textiles and clothing and metals with all its BRICS trading partners, stone and glass with Brazil and Russia, fuels with Russia and South Africa, minerals with India, Russia and South Africa, chemicals with India, and transportation and animal products with Brazil, India and South Africa.

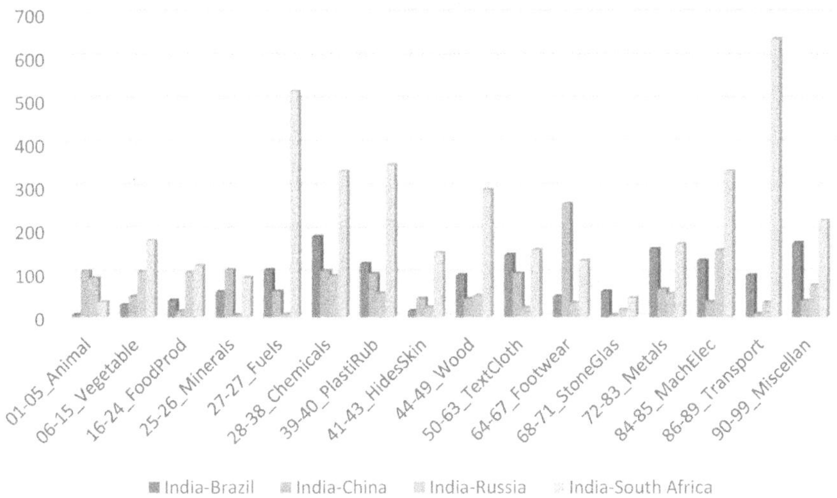

FIGURE 5.9 TII for India in 2019

Source: Authors' estimates from WITS database

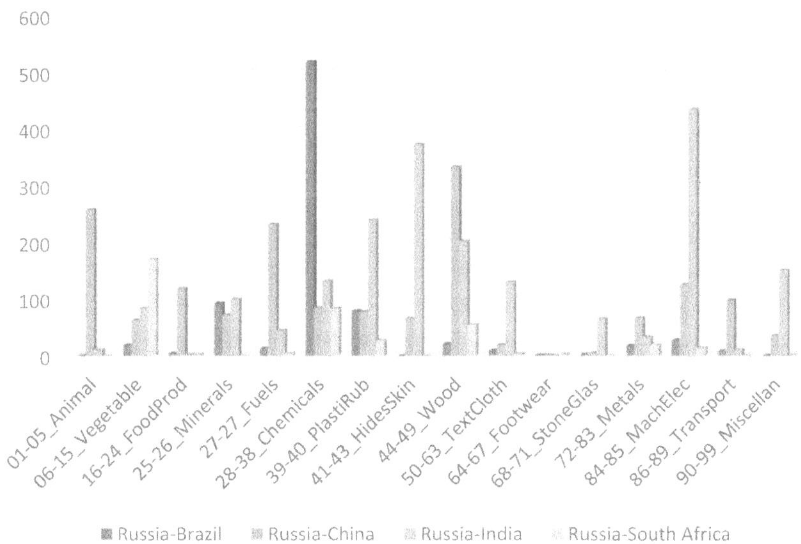

FIGURE 5.10 TII for Russia in 2019

Source: Authors' estimates from WITS database

In 2019, India's trade intensity (Figure 5.9) was generally lower than for other BRICS economies. However, it shows higher trade intensity with South Africa and Brazil. Specifically, there is a high TII for fuels and transportation with Brazil and South Africa, chemicals, plastic and rubber, hides and skins, and wood, metals

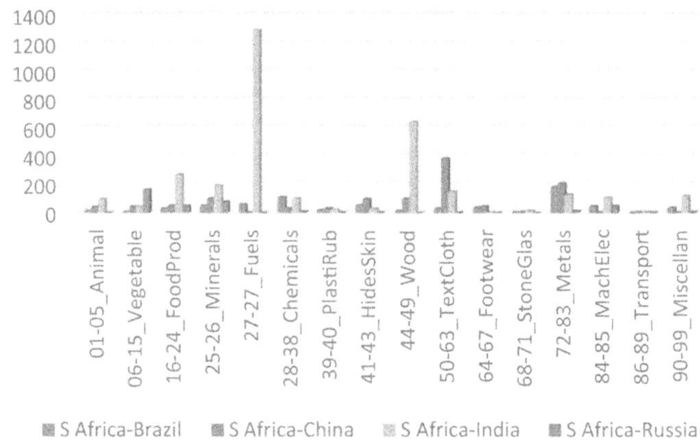

FIGURE 5.11 TII for South Africa in 2019

Source: Authors' estimates from WITS database

and miscellaneous products with South Africa, footwear with China, and chemicals, plastic and rubber, textiles and clothing, metals and mechanical and electrical and miscellaneous products with Brazil.

Like India, Russia (Figure 5.10) also has low trading intensity with rest of the BRICS countries except for select products and destinations. It has high TII for animal and food products, fuels, wood and machinery and electrical products with China, vegetable products with South Africa, chemicals with Brazil, and a range of commodities, such as chemicals, plastic and rubber, wood, hides and skins, textile and clothing, machinery and electrical and miscellaneous commodities with India.

South Africa has a higher intensity of trade with India and China in general (see Figure 5.11). Specifically, its trade intensity is high in the case of food products, minerals, fuels, wood, textile and clothing, metals and machinery and electrical products with India. With Russia, trade intensity is high in the case of hides and skins, wood, textiles and clothing, and metals.

Thus, in the case of specific commodity groups, the RCA and TII point to a higher comparative advantage and trade intensity within the BRICS countries, and the intensity is likely to deepen further as the group strives to become a more cohesive global entity and attempts to strengthen trade linkages. In fact, co-operation towards trade liberalisation could go a long way in enhancing the economic strength of the BRICS group.

In what follows, the chapter alludes to the institutional mechanisms that have been devised by the BRICS member countries as a way to reduce their dependence on the existing multilateral financial institutions such as the World Bank, the IFC and the IMF, often dominated by the Western developed countries.

The New Development Bank

The IMF and the World Bank, created after World War II to overcome the economic slowdown and avoid situations like the Great Depression of the 1930s, served well to meet the economic needs of the West. But these institutions have not been able to adequately cope with two emerging conditions: the growing economic influence of developing countries and cyclical financial crises in the world. Often, their policies and programmes, especially their conditionalities, have been blamed for such crises. The financial crisis of the 1990s, when the economies of the Asian-tigers crumbled, was followed by the crisis in 2008 when the US and the European economies came to a grinding halt. Ironically, the economies of developing countries such as India, China and Brazil showed high resilience to such crises. Further, they continued to grow at a high rate. This engendered confidence among these economies, leading to the clamour for higher stakes in the global order – both financial and political.

The BRICS members represent over 40% of the global population, command more than 22% of the global GDP, have a forex reserve of a little over US$4.4 trillion (2019) and a trade volume (exports plus imports) of US$6.64 trillion (2019), but their role in the financial order is small. For instance, the United States alone has 16.52% of voting share in the IMF while the BRICS together has only 14.18%. China has 6.09% and India 2.64%. This is the situation after an increase in the voting rights for these BRICS countries; the situation was even more skewed against them earlier. Western countries decide on the amount and conditions of loans offered to developing countries. Little has changed despite the growing significance of major developing countries. Consequently, they have been asking for reforms in the existing financial and other multilateral institutions. The inability to restructure and reorient the existing financial institutions pushed these five major developing states to create a new organisation – called the BRICS – in Yekaterinburg in 2009.

After the formation of BRICS in the year 2012, at the 4th BRICS Summit in New Delhi, BRICS leaders (of Brazil, Russia, India, China and South Africa) discussed the possibility of establishing a new financial institution – the NDB – to mobilise resources for projects relevant for their economies, directed towards basic infrastructure and sustainable development in BRICS and in other developing countries. The finance ministers of BRICS countries were given the responsibility to assess the feasibility and viability of establishing the NDB. Further, they were also given the responsibility to form a joint working group to study the proposal in detail and to report the findings during the subsequent 5th Summit in 2013.

At the 5th BRICS Summit in Durban in 2013, analysing the report submitted by the Finance Ministers, the leaders of the BRICS countries decided to establish the NDB. Further, it was agreed by all that the primary contribution to the bank should be adequate to effectively finance infrastructural development.

In Fortaleza during the 6th Summit of BRICS in 2014, an agreement to establish the NDB was signed. In the Fortaleza Declaration, the leaders talked about the role of the NDB to strengthen co-operation among the BRICS countries and its role to provide assistance to BRICS nations to achieve the goal of sustainable and balanced growth. A part of the Fortaleza Declaration reads as follows:

> The Bank shall have an initial authorized capital of US$100 billion. The initial subscribed capital shall be US$50 billion, equally shared among founding members. The first chair of the Board of Governors shall be from Russia. The first chair of the Board of Directors shall be from Brazil. The first President of the Bank shall be from India. The headquarters of the Bank shall be in Shanghai. The New Development Bank Africa Regional Centre shall be established in South Africa concurrently with the headquarters.

Russia chaired the inaugural meeting of the Board of Governors, which was held on the eve of the Ufa Summit (7 July 2015). Following the inaugural meeting, the NDB officially came into existence as a legal entity. Mr. K. V. Kamath was appointed President of the NDB at that meeting and the appointment of four Vice Presidents and the Board of Directors was also completed. The NDB became fully operational on February 27, 2016, after the signing of the Headquarters Agreement with the government of the People's Republic of China and the Memorandum of Understanding (MOU) with the Shanghai Municipal People's Government.

The NDB started with an initial subscribed capital of US$50 billion and an initial authorised capital of US$100 billion. The founding members shared the initial subscribed capital equally amongst themselves. A decision was also taken on providing equal voting rights or shares for each of the members in the subscribed shares of the capital stock of the bank. Further, it was agreed upon that the subscribed capital stock would be divided into two parts – paid-in shares and callable shares. Shares having an aggregate par value of US$10 billion were to be as paid-in shares, and the remaining were to be callable shares. The initial authorised capital of the bank of US$100 billion was divided into 1 million shares, with a par value of US$100,000 each. These shares were available for subscription only by members in accordance with the provisions of the Agreement on the NDB and with specific official protocols.

In 2016, the Board of Directors of the bank approved loans involving financial assistance of over US$1.5 billion for projects in the areas of green and renewable energy, and transportation.

Most recently, the NDB has launched the Emergency Assistance Programme in Combating COVID-19 to deal with the impact of the COVID-19 pandemic, and help member nations in their efforts towards economic and social recovery. The Chinese government has received a loan of RMB7 billion to help local governments finance measures to contain the spread of the virus, to lower financial gaps, render fiscal support, and help finance pandemic-related public health expenditures and for transmission containment in the future. India received a loan assistance of US$1 billion to cover critical healthcare expenses, urgent goods, services and activities that need to be procured and used by the Government of India, including containing transmission of the virus and strengthening social security programmes to mitigate economic and social hardships due to the pandemic. Brazil and South Africa have also been extended loans of US$1 billion each to strengthen their healthcare system to help fight COVID-19 (including detection, diagnosis and protection), minimise the loss of human lives, and reduce social and economic losses through social grants, and protection of jobs.

As part of the efforts to recover from the adverse effects of and the challenges posed by the COVID-19 outbreak and its green development endeavours, co-operation in the domains of fiscal, monetary and trade policies among BRICS members could set the tone for effectual utilisation of the institution of the NDB for future development.

Conclusion

Since the 2000s, BRICS has become an influential entity in the global economic order. Growth rates in the BRICS countries have been impressive, particularly in China and India, during the early 2000s. Even in the face of the global financial crisis and economic slowdown, the BRICS as a group has performed significantly well in terms of economic growth and shown significant resilience against external shocks. BRICS countries account for more than 40% of the global population and have a high proportion of economically active populations, indicating sustained potential for economic growth.

BRICS countries have also performed very well in terms of their external sector, with the group contributing a significant amount to global trade volumes. With a diversified trade composition, intra-BRICS commodity trade patterns holds considerable potential. In the case of specific commodity groups, indicators such as Revealed Comparative Advantage (RCA) and Trade Intensity Index (TII) point to a high comparative advantage and trade intensity within the BRICS countries. These trends are likely to deepen further in case the group endeavours to become a more cohesive global entity and chooses to lower trade barriers to strengthen intra-group trade ties.

Due to favourable domestic market conditions and resource endowments, BRICS countries have also attracted substantial FDIs from the rest of the world. The impressive performance of BRICS in attracting direct investment has been a key driving factor for its economic growth and internationalisation of financial flows, technology and resources. In fact, the inflows of FDI have been steady for most of the BRICS countries in spite of the COVID-19 pandemic.

In the West-dominated global financial order, BRICS took the initiative to set up the NDB to finance infrastructural and sustainable development within the group as well as in other emerging and developing countries. The formation of the NDB provides BRICS a new influential and prominent position in the global financial order. The timely support the NDB rendered to member nations to help cope with the challenges posed by the COVID-19 pandemic has set the tone for enhanced co-operation among them for future development initiatives in spheres such as public health, climate change mitigation, clean energy and urban resilience.

Notes

1 The G-6 represents six governments, namely, France, Germany, Italy, Japan, the United Kingdom, and the United States.
2 Monetary gold refers to gold owned by the government authorities (or by others who are subject to control by the authorities) and held as a reserve asset.
3 These reserves refer to the required quota of currency each member country must provide to the International Monetary Fund (IMF) that can be utilised for its own purposes – without a service fee or any conditions relating to economic reforms.
4 The net inflow and outflow data collected from world development indicators and UNCTAD differs. This is because of the methodological difference followed by the World Bank (BPM6 methodology) and UNCTAD (BPM5 methodology).

Bibliography

"New Development Bank: NDB," accessed 19 June 2020, www.ndb.int/.

O'Neill, Jim. "Building Better Global Economic BRICs. 2001," *Goldman Sachs, Global Economics Paper* 66.

O'Neill, Jim. Is the emerging world still emerging? Two decades on, the BRICs promise lingers. International Monetary Fund: Finance and Development. Summer 2021, accessed 20 September 2021. www.imf.org/external/pubs/ft/fandd/2021/06/jim-oneill-revisits-brics-emerging-markets.htm

Pant, Harsh V. "The BRICS Fallacy," *The Washington Quarterly*, Vol. 36(3) (2013): pp. 91–105.

"Trade Indicators," World Bank, accessed 22 June 2020, https://wits.worldbank.org/wits/wits/witshelp/Content/Utilities/e1.trade_indicators.htm.

"UNCTAD STAT," Data, United Nations Conference on Trade and Development, accessed 10 May 2020, http://unctadstat.unctad.org/wds/ReportFolders/reportFolders.aspx.

"UN COMTRADE," International Trade Statistics Database, accessed during June–July 2016 and again during January–February 15, 2021, https://comtrade.un.org/.

"United Nations Population Division," Department of Economic and Social Affairs, accessed 6 April 2020. https://esa.un.org/unpd/wpp/.

Wilson, Dominic, and Roopa Purushothaman. "Dreaming with BRICs: The Path to 2050. Goldman Sachs, Global Economics Paper no. 99," *Goldman Sachs* (2003): 1–24.

"World Development Indicators," Database, World Bank, accessed 17 February 2020 to 15 January 2021, https://data.worldbank.org/data-catalog/world-development-indicators.

World Integrated Trade Solution (WITS) database, accessed during 2–15 January 2021, https://wits.worldbank.org/.

6

INTER- AND INTRA-BRICS BILATERAL TRADE PATTERN

A Panel Import Gravity Model Approach

Meeta Keswani Mehra and Sk. Md. Azharuddin

Background

The use of gravity models has become popular in a variety of fields, including for understanding international trade patterns between countries. The attractiveness of the gravity approach in international trade analyses can be ascribed to its high intuitive appeal and ease of empirical estimation in explaining patterns of bilateral trade. The underlying logic of the trade gravity model is quite similar to Newton's law of gravity, which states that the gravitational attraction force between two objects is directly proportional to their masses and inversely proportional to the square of the distance between the centres of the masses. Newton's law of gravity can be expressed as:

$$F_{ij} = G\frac{M_i M_j}{R^2},$$

where F_{ij} is the gravitational attraction force between the two objects i and j,
G is the gravitational constant,
M_i and M_j are the masses of the objects i and j respectively, and
R is the distance between the centres of the masses of objects i and j.

Following the work of Newton and using the functional form of Newton's law of gravity, Tinbergen (1962) had proposed that a roughly similar kind of functional form could be used to explain bilateral trade flows between countries. This implies that bilateral trade between any two countries can be expressed as a function where bilateral trade flow is postulated to be directly proportional to the economic size of the trading partners and inversely proportional to the

DOI: 10.4324/9781003148074-7

geographical distance between them. Specifically, Tinbergen's model could be expressed as:

$$X_{ij} = G\frac{Y_i^{\alpha} Y_j^{\beta}}{D_{ij}^{\delta}},$$

where X_{ij} is the bilateral trade between country i and country j,
G is the gravitational constant,
Y_i and Y_j are the size of the economies of country i and country j respectively,
D_{ij} is the geographical distance between the ith and j^{th} countries, and
α, β and δ are the parameters.

In this chapter, we use an import gravity model to test for the key determinants of bilateral commodity trade flows. To achieve this, the import flows between any two countries are related to their economic size and the distance between them, amongst other control variables. To facilitate the econometric estimation, we have used a logarithmic version of Tinbergen's gravity equation, which helps get a log-linearised relationship among the variables as follows:

$$lnX_{ij} = lnG + \alpha lnY_i + \beta lnY_j - \delta lnD_{ij},$$

where, lnG corresponds to the constant intercept term and α, β and δ are the respective elasticities and lnZ represents the natural logarithm of any variable Z.

The model is augmented by incorporating other important factors, which are also expected to influence bilateral import flows, like linguistic proximity (similarity or difference in languages and writing systems between trading countries), gross capital formation in partner countries, tariff rates and the freedom of trade index of the reporting countries. Over time, the trade gravity model has emerged as a powerful tool to explain bilateral trade flows, taking into account the trade complementarities between the two countries and the impact of the formation of trade groups (Lin and Wang, 2004; Liu and Jiang, 2002; Sheng and Liao, 2004). In this chapter, we have augmented the baseline gravity model by considering the effect of the first meeting of the finance ministers of the BRICS countries in 2006 by using a dummy variable to represent this structural change. Moreover, we have included a dummy variable to capture the effects of the global financial crisis of 2007–2009 on trade flows.

Trends in the growth of commodity imports and exports for the BRICS countries over the period 2000 to 2019 indicate that the growth rates of both imports and exports for most of the BRICS countries have been positive. Figures 6.1 and 6.2 show these growth trends.

In 2020, the ongoing Covid-19 pandemic severely affected trade in the BRICS countries. Figures 6.3 and 6.4 show the monthly trends in growth rates in exports and imports respectively for the year 2020. It shows that the pandemic affected both exports and imports of the BRICS countries in most months.

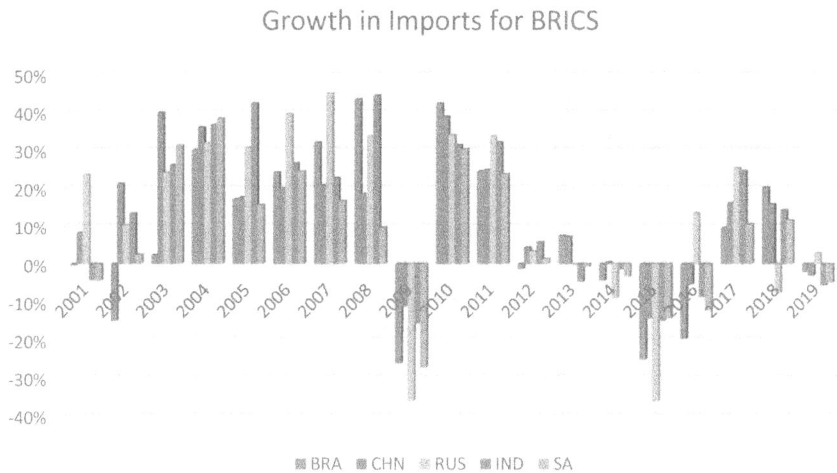

FIGURE 6.1 Trends in commodity imports of the BRICS countries

Source: Calculated by the authors using UNCOMTRADE database

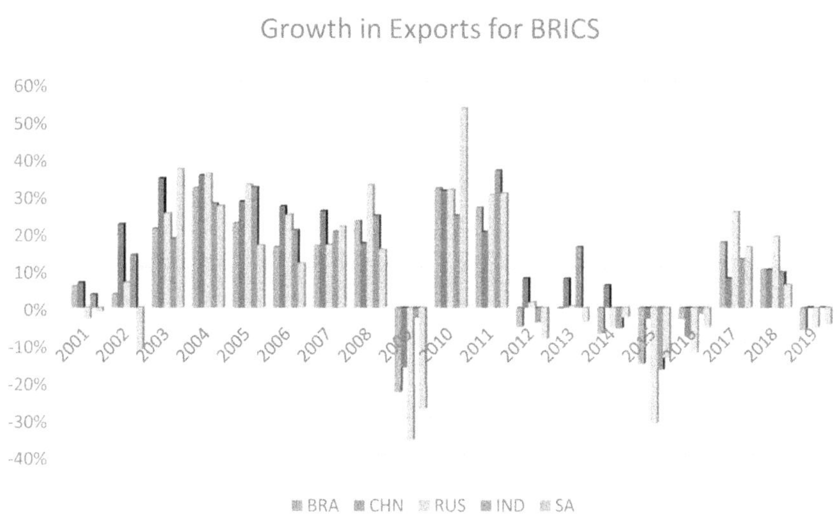

FIGURE 6.2 Trends in commodity exports of BRICS countries

Source: Calculated by the Authors using UNCOMTRADE database

The findings of this research could feed into policy prescriptions for utilising international trade as a driver of economic recovery in the post-pandemic phase of the BRICS' economies.

The rest of the chapter is organised as follows. The next section discusses existing literature on the use of trade gravity models to analyse the determinants of

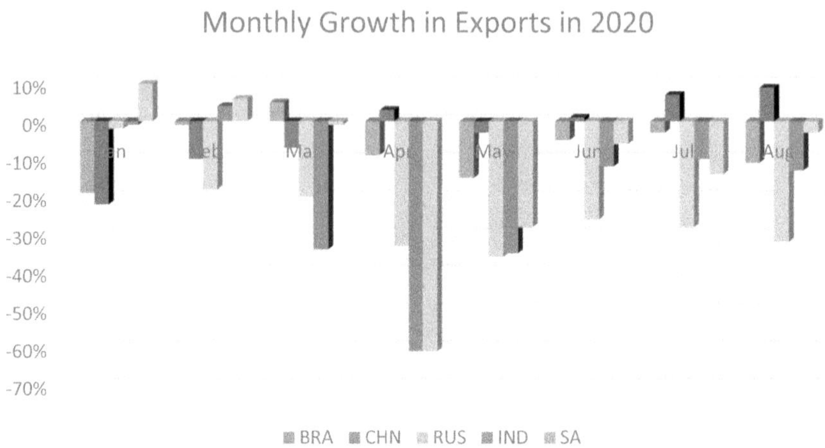

FIGURE 6.3 Monthly growth in exports of the BRICS countries

Source: UNCTAD's global trade update report, October 2020.

FIGURE 6.4 Monthly growth in imports of the BRICS countries

Source: UNCTAD's global trade update report, October 2020.

commodity trade. This is followed by data description, the model specification and the estimation procedure. The next section describes the results of the study followed by the conclusions of the study.

Literature Review

The use of Newton's gravity equation for an empirical analysis of international trade patterns was initiated by Tinbergen (1962), Pöyhönen (1963) and Linnemann (1966). Subsequently, many economists have improved upon this framework and extended it by incorporating newer economic phenomena and factors through the inclusion of additional variables, and attempted to illustrate the role of these variables in explaining international trade flows.

Caves (1981) and Toh (1982) considered geographical distance to be a key factor, determining transportation costs and transaction costs. Bergstrand (1985, 1989) used constant elasticity of substitution (CES)-type preferences and generalised the gravity model by incorporating prices and real exchange rates, whereas Anderson (1979) took the utility functions of both Cobb-Douglas and CES types to obtain a more sophisticated model. A similar approach was followed by Deardorff (1998). Anderson and Van Wincoop (2003) used a monopolistic competition framework, which provided a practical way to estimate augmented gravity coefficients in the context of a cross-sectional dataset. Helpman and Krugman (1985) have estimated the gravity model under the assumption of increasing returns to scale in production. Balassa and Bauwens (1987) found a negative correlation between geographical distance and trade in the context of intra-industry production specialisation and trade in a multi-country and multi-industry framework. Frankel and Wei (1993), in their analysis, found that the level of economic development captured by per capita gross national product (GNP) plays a significant role in determining a nation's trade flows. Arnon et al. (1996) included a new variable – that is, the square of the differences in per capita incomes, to get the possible Linder effect in their study.

Mátyás (1997) mentioned that the conventional cross-sectional approach, without the inclusion of country-specific effects, would be misleading and would lead to biased estimates, whereas Frankel et al. (1997) introduced regional binary variables in their study. Eichengreen and Irwin (1998) and Rauch (1999) suggested that cultural proxies (such as the presence of a common border and common language) should be included in the gravity equation. Frankel and Rose (1998) demonstrated the importance of qualitative variables, which indicate similarities between countries, and improved bilateral trade that led to the formation of regional trading agreements (RTAs). Garman et al. (1998) applied cross-sectional analysis for various years, Liman and Venables (2001) used cross-section analysis over one year and Bougheas et al. (1999) averaged data over time and then applied seemingly uncorrelated regression estimation analysis in the gravity model.

Egger and Pfaffermayr (2003) suggested the use of a three-way model with main effects (in terms of importer, exporter and time) or explicit introduction of time-invariant country pair (importer-by-exporter) bilateral effects to account for country pair heterogeneity. Helpman et al. (2004) first introduced the concept of a heterogeneous firm in the gravity equation.

Haveman and Hummels (2004), Silva and Tenreyro (2006), Helpman et al. (2008) and Eaton et al. (2012) describe how to accommodate zeros in the matrix of bilateral trade flows to estimate the gravity equation. Chaoxing et al. (2005) used dummy variables such as preferential trade agreements and integration or participation in any group or organisation in the gravity model. Kimura and Lee (2006) used a standard-type gravity equation by incorporating a new variable, namely, economic freedom, in their analysis by utilising bilateral trade data for 26 OECD member countries for the years 1999 and 2000.

Cieślik (2007) used the trade gravity model approach using pooled panel data with time-fixed effects and estimated the equation using the heteroscedasticity-adjusted OLS method to find the trade effects of free trade agreements (FTAs) for the period 1992–2004. He found the impact of bilateral and regional trade agreements to be positive and statistically significant and regional agreements to be more trade creating than bilateral agreements. Kepaptsoglou et al. (2010) emphasise the early contribution of gravity models for a ten-year (1999–2009) period for empirical trade analyses and argued that the popularity of the gravity model was because of its extensive empirical robustness and explanatory power.

Natale et al. (2015) used a trade gravity model to analyse the determinants of international seafood trade. Using data on 197 countries and 120 seafood commodities, they explored the influence of primary production, population, food consumption, income, GDP, trade agreements and geographical distance on seafood trade.

Narayan and Nguyen (2016) checked for trade dependency on trading partners between Vietnam and 54 trading partners using a trade gravity model. They have found that trade with richer partners is more sensitive to geographical distance, economic size, trading partner's openness and exchange rate in comparison with lower-income partner countries.

Rasoulinezhad and Wei (2017) utilised a panel gravity trade model to analyse bilateral trade patterns between China and 13 OPEC countries over the period 1998–2014. They have reported that the length of the trade relationship, GDP, per capita GDP, distance, difference in incomes, trade openness, exchange rate and WTO membership are the main determinants of bilateral trade flows between China and OPEC member countries.

Gupta et al. (2019) analysed the effect of geopolitical risks on trade flows among 164 developing and developed countries using a classical gravity model. Using the index of geopolitical risks (GPR index) as an important measure, they found that geopolitical risks affect trade flows negatively. The next section describes the data and methodology used in this analysis.

Data

The study uses annual data on the import flows of individual BRICS countries from their top ten trading partners and on bilateral intra-BRICS import flows. Figure 6.5 shows the countries from which BRICS import the most, including other BRICS nations. Both of these consistently constituted more than 50% of BRICS' total import volumes over the period 2000 to 2016. In addition, the variables considered in the analysis included per capita GDP for both reporter and as well as partner countries (where every BRICS country is the reporter and their partners included other BRICS countries as well as their top ten exporting partners), geographical distance between the reporter and the partner countries (this was expressed in terms of the distance between the capital cities), common language dummy of the reporter and partner countries, trade freedom index of the reporter countries, tariff rates in reporter countries and population levels of the reporting countries.

FIGURE 6.5 Top ten nations (including other BRICS countries) from whom BRICS import the most

There were altogether 1190 observations, 17 time-series components (years) and 14 cross-sectional entities for each of the five BRICS countries (excluding that BRICS country). The data on bilateral trade was collected from the UN COMTRADE database. The data on per capita gross domestic product (GDP) (measured in constant 2010 US dollars) has been obtained from the World Development Indicators (WDI) database of the World Bank. GDP has been used as an indicator of the economic size of a country. Data on tariff rates (weighted mean for all the products), population, and gross capital formation statistics were also taken from the WDI database. The data on geographical distance is taken from the Distancefromto (www.distancefromto.net/) database; the distance between the counties is an indicator of transportation costs. The data on trade freedom and common language were collected from the HERITAGE and CEPII databases respectively. The names of the selected ten major trade partners (in terms of the total import volume of all the BRICS countries put together) in ascending order are listed in Appendix A (also see Figure 6.5).

Model Specification

The estimated gravity model has the following log-linear form:

$$\begin{aligned} lnimport_{ijt} &= \alpha + \beta_1 lnGDP_{it} + \beta_2 lnGDP_{jt} + \beta_3 lnDistance_{ij} + \beta_4 coml_{ij} + \beta_5 tradefreedom_{jt} \\ &+ \beta_6 tariffrate_{it} + \beta_7 GrossCapita_{jt} + \omega_1 BRICS + \omega_2 CRISIS + e_{ijt}, \end{aligned}$$

where

i represents the ten major countries, including other BRICS countries, from whom BRICS imports the most,

j represents any one of the five BRICS countries,
t represents time (year),
coml, *BRICS* and *CRISIS* represent dummy variables indicating whether the two countries share a common language or not, the formation of BRICS and global financial crisis respectively.
α is the intercept term, βs, ω_1 and ω_2 are the parameters, and
e is a random disturbance term having an independent and identical distribution (iid) with mean zero and variance σ_i^2.
Here, $CRISIS = 1$ if $year = 2007, 2008, 2009$
$= 0$ otherwise, and
$BRICS = 1$ if *year is after* 2006
$= 0$ otherwise.

Estimation Procedure

Before proceeding with the econometric analysis, checking for zero values in the matrix of import flows is very crucial. Many solutions have already been proposed in the literature for estimating a model with zero import flows; for example, it has been suggested that either pairs with zero imports should be dropped from the dataset (Johnson and Noguera 2012) or, else, $\ln(1 + import)$ used as a dependent variable (Eichengreen and Irwin 1998). Since, in our dataset, there were no zero values for imports, we have proceeded by using raw data for the analysis with a natural logarithm transformation, as mentioned earlier.

The selection of a proper estimation technique is very essential in the context of the gravity model. Generally, in a panel data framework with dummy variables, either fixed or random effects models are useful when all the variables under consideration are found to be stationary. Thus, the stationarity of all variables should be checked first before going ahead with estimating the regression equation. Furthermore, since our model takes into consideration some time invariant variables, and a fixed effect model is unable to derive the effects of time invariant variables, a fixed effect estimation is not a suitable technique.

In addition, it is possible that we have heteroscedastic disturbances (as each country has its own variance) and/or auto-correlated disturbances (since the error term is dependent upon its own past values for a specific country) in our model. In such circumstances, a Feasible Generalised Least Square (FGLS) and Prais and Winsten (Prais and Winsten 1954) regression with Panel Corrected Standard Errors (PCSE) model are the accepted useful techniques to get robust and unbiased estimates.

Essentially, PCSEs are very similar to White's heteroscedasticity-consistent standard errors for cross-sectional estimators, but are superior as they take advantage of the information provided by the panel structure of the data (Beck and Katz 1995). Using Monte Carlo studies, Beck and Katz (1995) point out that PCSEs provide more reliable standard errors over the FGLS method. In our analysis, we have used the PCSE model but also reported, alongside, the results of the FGLS model for the purpose of comparison.

Results

To estimate our log-linear model specification, stationarity conditions of all variables (endogenous and exogenous, but not dummies) must be established. The results of the stationarity tests are presented here:

From the results presented in Table 6.1, it can be inferred that according to the Levin, Lin and Chu test, the p-values for all variables are found to be less than 0.01, so that at 1% level of significance, one can reject the null hypothesis ($\boldsymbol{H_0}$) that the panel data contain unit-root. That is, it can be concluded that all the variables under consideration are stationary.

We next checked for the presence of auto-correlation and heteroscedasticity in the data by using the Wooldridge test and Friedman's test respectively and found that in our model there is the presence of auto-correlation and heteroscedasticity. These results are presented in Table 6.2.

Given the presence of both auto-correlation and heteroscedasticity, it is most appropriate to do the estimations by relying on the FGLS and PCSE models. Moreover, between these two methods, PCSE provides more reliable results (Beck and Katz 1995).

The results in Table 6.3 suggest that the results from using both the econometric techniques – FGLS and PCSE – are comparable.

In general, the imports of BRICS countries positively depend on the reporter's per capita GDP as well as the partner's per capita GDP, and the elasticities are found to be 1.224 and 0.892 for the reporter's GDP for FGLS and PCSE models respectively, and 0.46 and 0.50 for partner's GDP according to FGLS and PCSE estimations respectively. Moreover, as expected, imports are found to negatively depend on the distance between the countries, and this elasticity

TABLE 6.1 Results of unit-root tests of the variables

Variables	*p-value*	*Remarks*
Imports	0.000	Stationary
Per-capita GDP Reporters	0.000	Stationary
Per-capita GDP Partner	0.000	Stationary
Population Reporter	0.000	Stationary
Trade Freedom Reporter	0.004	Stationary
Gross Capital Formation of Partner	0,00	Stationary

TABLE 6.2 Results of tests for auto-correlation and heteroscedasticity

Test	*Null Hypothesis*	*P-Value*
Wooldridge test of Auto-correlation	Absence of autocorrelation	0.00
Friedman test of heteroscedasticity	Absence of heteroscedasticity	0.00

TABLE 6.3 Result of FGLS and PCSE models

Variables	*Coefficient in FGLS Model*	*P-Value in FGLS*	*Coefficient in PCSE Model*	*P-Value in PCSE*
PGDP Reporter	1.224	0.00	0.892	0.00
PGDP Partner	0.460	0.00	0.50	0.00
Distance	−0.467	0.00	−0.317	0.00
Coml	1.050	0.00	0.864	0.00
CRISIS	0.075	0.17	−0.003	0.97
BRICS	0.131	0.08	0.217	0.12
Tariff of reporter	−0.027	0.00	−0.0366	0.00
Trade Freedom	0.0001	0.96	0.005	0.19
Population Reporter	1.22	0.00	1.14	0.00
Gross Capital Formation Partner	0.130	0.05	0.031	0.00
Constant	−13.02	0.00	−11.08	0.00

is found to be −0.46 and −0.32 for FGLS and PCSE estimations respectively. According to both types of estimations, it is found that the population of the reporter country is a positive determinant of imports, and the elasticity is estimated to be 1.22 and 1.14 respectively for FGLS and PCSE. The presence of a common language has a positive effect on imports, and the formation of BRICS also has a positive effect but the effect of the formation of BRICS is only significant for the FGLS model estimates and at the 8% level. The freedom of trade has a positive impact on imports, but it is insignificant in both models. The population of the reporter country also affects imports positively. The tariff rates of the BRICS countries are found to have a negative and significant effect on their imports (as expected) and the result is consistent for both the models. The coefficients of gross capital formation of the partner countries are found to be positive and significant in the case of both the FGLS and PCSE models. Moreover, the effect of the financial crisis was insignificant under both the econometric techniques, indicating that BRICS nations are generally resilient to external shocks like the financial crisis.

Conclusion

In this study, by utilising a panel import gravity model, we have attempted to determine the principal factors on which the imports of BRICS countries depend. The focus of our analysis is on the top ten countries from which BRICS countries import, besides the other BRICS countries that are also partner countries. Feasible GLS and Panel Corrected Standard Error (PCSE) models have been used to estimate the effect of different variables in determining imports of the BRICS member states. It is found that per capita GDPs of both, the reporter and partner countries positively affect import flows into the BRICS countries, while geographical distance has a negative effect on them. The formation of BRICS and the presence of a common language is found to have a positive influence on imports, while the effect of the global financial crisis is found to be insignificant. Moreover, as the partner countries accumulate more capital over time, their ability to export to BRICS increases. The study also demonstrates that the population level and trade freedom of reporting countries are positive determinants of BRICS imports, while tariff rates in BRICS nations negatively affect import flows.

Going forward, most of these results could be utilised to formulate policies to free commodity trade between countries of the group as well as with the rest of world. That is, judicious policies for more liberalised trade could spur economic growth in the short to medium term in the countries as they attempt to recover from the recessionary situation caused by the pandemic. In the long run, the results of this analysis could feed into decisions on the formation of preferential trading arrangements or regional trading blocs that would offer trade creation benefits for the BRICS group.

Appendix A

Top Ten Partners of the BRICS Countries

USA
Rep. of Korea
Japan
Germany
Australia
Malaysia
Switzerland
Thailand
Saudi Arabia
Viet Nam

Bibliography

Anderson, James E. (1979). "A Theoretical Foundation for the Gravity Equation." *The American Economic Review*, 69(1): 106–116.

Anderson, James E., and Eric Van Wincoop. (2003). "Gravity with Gravitas: A Solution to the Border Puzzle." *The American Economic Review*, 93(1): 170–192.

Arnon, Arie, Avia Spivak, and Jimmy Weinblatt. (1996). "The Potential for Trade between Israel, the Palestinians and Jordan." *The World Economy*, 19(1): 113–134.

Balassa, Bela, and Luc Bauwens. (1987). "Intra-industry Specialization in a Multi-country and Multi-industry Framework." *The Economic Journal*, 97(388): 923–939.

Beck, Nathaniel, and Jonathan N. Katz. (1995). "What to do (and not to do) with Time-series Cross-section Data." *American Political Science Review*, 89(3): 634–647.
Bergstrand, Jeffrey H. (1983). "Measurement and Determinants of Intra-industry International Trade." In *Intra-industry Trade: Empirical and Methodological Aspects*, Tharakan P. K. M. (Ed.). Amsterdam, North-Holland: 201–253.
Bergstrand, Jeffrey H. (1985). "The Gravity Equation in International Trade: Some Microeconomic Foundations and Empirical Evidence." *The Review of Economics and Statistics*, 67(3): 474–481.
Bergstrand, Jeffrey H. (1989). "The Generalized Gravity Equation, Monopolistic Competition, and the Factor-Proportions Theory in International Trade." *The Review of Economics and Statistics*, 71(1): 143–153.
Bougheas, Spiros, Panicos O. Demetriades, and Edgar L. W. Morgenroth. (1999). "Infrastructure, Transport Costs and Trade." *Journal of International Economics*, 47(1): 169–189.
Caves, Richard E. (1981). "Intra-industry Trade and Market Structure in the Industrial Countries." *Oxford Economic Papers*, 33(2): 203–223.
Chaoxing, Shi, Gu Haiying, and Qin Xiangdong. (2005). "A Survey of the Theoretical Basis of Gravity Model used in International Trade." *Nankai Economic Studies*, 2: 39–40.
Cieślik, Andrzej. (2007). "The Impact of Free Trade Agreements on Poland's Foreign Trade in 1992–2004." *Bank i Kredyt*, 6.
Deardorff, Alan. (1998). "Determinants of Bilateral Trade: Does Gravity Work in a Neoclassical World?" In *The Regionalization of the World Economy*, Frankel, Jeffrey A. (Ed.). Chicago, University of Chicago Press: 7–32.
Eaton, Jonathan, Samuel S. Kortum, and Sebastian Sotelo. (2012). *International Trade: Linking Micro and Macro*. No. w17864. Cambridge, MA: National Bureau of Economic Research (NBER).
Egger, Peter, and Michael Pfaffermayr. (2003). "The Proper Panel Econometric Specification of the Gravity Equation: A Three-way Model with Bilateral Interaction Effects." *Empirical Economics*, 28(3): 571–580.
Eichengreen, Barry, and Douglas A. Irwin. (1998). "The Role of History in Bilateral Trade Flows." In *The Regionalization of the World Economy* Frankel, Jeffrey A. (Ed.). Chicago and London, University of Chicago Press: 33–62.
Frankel, Jeffrey A., and Shang-Jin Wei. (1993). *Is there a Currency Bloc in the Pacific?* No. 25. CA: University of California at Berkeley, Department of Economics.
Frankel, Jeffrey A., and Andrew K. Rose. (1998). "The Endogeneity of the Optimum Currency Area Criteria." *The Economic Journal*, 108(449): 1009–1025.
Frankel, Jeffrey A., Ernesto Stein, and Shang-Jin Wei. (1997). *Regional Trading Blocs in the World Economic System*. Washington, DC: Peterson Institute.
Garman, George, Janis Petersen, and Debora Gilliard. (1998). "Economic Integration in the Americas: 1975–1992." *Journal of Applied Business Research*, 14(3): 1–12.
Gupta, Rangan, Giray Gozgor, Huseyin Kaya, and Ender Demir. (2019). "Effects of Geopolitical Risks on Trade Flows: Evidence from the Gravity Model." *Eurasian Economic Review*, 9(4): 515–530.
Haveman, Jon, and David Hummels. (2004). "Alternative Hypotheses and the Volume of Trade: The Gravity Equation and the Extent of Specialization." *Canadian Journal of Economics/Revue canadienne d'économique*, 37(1): 199–218.
Helpman, Elhanan, and Paul R. Krugman. (1985). *Market Structure and Foreign Trade: Increasing Returns, Imperfect Competition, and the International Economy*. Cambridge and London: MIT Press.

Helpman, Elhanan, Marc Melitz, and Yona Rubinstein. (2008). "Estimating Trade Flows: Trading Partners and Trading Volumes." *The Quarterly Journal of Economics*, 123(2): 441–487.

Helpman, Elhanan, Marc J. Melitz, and R. Yeaple Stephen. (2004). "Exports versus FDI with Heterogeneous Firms." *American Economic Review*, 94(1): 300–316.

Johnson, Robert C., and Guillermo Noguera. (2012). *Fragmentation and Trade in Value Added Over Four Decades*. No. w18186. Cambridge, MA: National Bureau of Economic Research (NBER).

Kepaptsoglou, Konstantinos, Matthew G. Karlaftis, and Dimitrios Tsamboulas. (2010). "The Gravity Model Specification for Modeling International Trade Flows and Free Trade Agreement Effects: A 10-Year Review of Empirical Studies." *The Open Economics Journal*, 3(1): 1–13.

Kimura, Fukunari, and Hyun-Hoon Lee. (2006). "The Gravity Equation in International Trade in Services." *Review of World Economics*, 142(1): 92–121.

Liman, Nuno, and Anthony Venables. (2001). "Infrastructure, Geographical Disadvantage, and Transportation Costs, and Trade." *The World Bank Economic Review*, 15(3): 451–479.

Lin, L., and Y. Wang. (2004). "Empirical Test of China's Bilateral Trade with the Trade Gravity Model and Its Policy Implications." *World Economy Study*, 7(5): 56–60.

Linnemann, Hans. (1966). *An Econometric Study of International Trade Flows*. No. 42. Amsterdam: North-Holland.

Liu, Q., and S. Jiang. (2002). "Study on the Chinese Bilateral Trade Arrangement Using the Gravity Model." *Zhejiang Social Sciences*, 6(4): 17–20.

Mátyás, László. (1997). "Proper Econometric Specification of the Gravity Model." *The World Economy*, 20(3): 363–368.

Narayan, Seema, and Tri Tung Nguyen. (2016). "Does the Trade Gravity Model Depend on Trading Partners? Some Evidence from Vietnam and her 54 Trading Partners." *International Review of Economics & Finance*, 41(1): 220–237.

Natale, Fabrizio, Alessandra Borrello, and Arina Motova. (2015). "Analysis of the Determinants of International Seafood Trade Using a Gravity Model." *Marine Policy* 60: 98–106.

Pöyhönen, Pentti. (1963). "A Tentative Model for the Volume of Trade between Countries." *Weltwirtschaftliches Archiv*: 93–100.

Prais, Sigbert J., and Christopher B. Winsten. (2017). *Trend Estimators and Serial Correlation*. Vol. 383. Chicago: Cowles Commission Discussion Paper, 1954.

Rasoulinezhad, Ehsan, and Wei Winston. (2017). "China's Trade with OPEC Member Countries: A Panel-Gravity Model Approach." *The Chinese Economy*, 50(5): 339–355.

Rauch, James E. (1999). "Networks Versus Markets in International Trade." *Journal of International Economics*, 48(1): 7–35.

Sheng, B., and M. Liao. (2004). "China's Trade Flows and Export Potential: The Gravity Model Approach." *World Economy*, 27(2): 4–10.

Silva, JMC Santos, and Silvana Tenreyro. (2006). "The Log of Gravity." *The Review of Economics and Statistics*, 88(4): 641–658.

Tinbergen, Jan. (1962). *Shaping the World Economy: Suggestions for an International Economic Policy*. New York: Twentieth Century Fund.

Toh, Kiertisak. (1982). "A Cross-section Analysis of Intra-industry Trade in US Manufacturing Industries." *Review of World Economics*, 118(2): 281–301.

"UnCOMTRADE. (2021). "International Trade Statistics Database," accessed 21 February 2021, https://comtrade.un.org/.

UNCTAD. (2020). "UNCTAD Global Trade Update Report," October 2020.

"World Development Indicators," Database, World Bank, accessed 17 February 2020 to 15 January 2021, https://data.worldbank.org/data-catalog/world-development-indicators.

7

DETERMINANTS OF FOREIGN DIRECT INVESTMENT INFLOWS IN BRICS COUNTRIES

A panel data analysis

Sk. Md. Azharuddin and Meeta Keswani Mehra

Background

For developing countries, foreign direct investment (FDI) inflows are believed to be a key factor that spurs economic growth and development. FDI inflows are perceived to close the gap between domestic saving and investment, bring in newer technology and managerial skills, and higher employment prospects, while also generating an improved growth outlook. Thus, it is important to ascertain the determinants of FDI inflows into countries.

It has been found that developing countries are attractive destinations for FDI for several reasons. The advantage that many of these economies offer in terms of the size of their domestic markets, their unexploited natural resource endowments and higher population growth rates with a large proportion of the population with education and skills in the economically active age attract multinationals and firms in developed countries to set new plants in these countries.

Figure 7.1 represents the distribution of total world FDI inflows into developing, transition and developed economies for the years from 2010 to 2017. Data consistently show that developing and transition economies have been attracting a significant amount of total world FDI inflows. These trends open up the potential for research focusing on the factors that are primarily responsible for attracting FDI towards developing and transition nations.

According to the UNCTAD World Investment Reports (2017, 2018), in the years 2016 and 2017, among the top 20 FDI (inflows) hosting countries, eight (in 2016) and nine (in 2017) countries were developing and transition economies respectively. This fact is shown in Table 7.1, which lists the top 20 FDI hosting nations of the world in 2016 and 2017.

Among these developing and transition countries, BRICS (Brazil, Russia, India, China and South Africa) are evidently very significant in terms of attracting

DOI: 10.4324/9781003148074-8

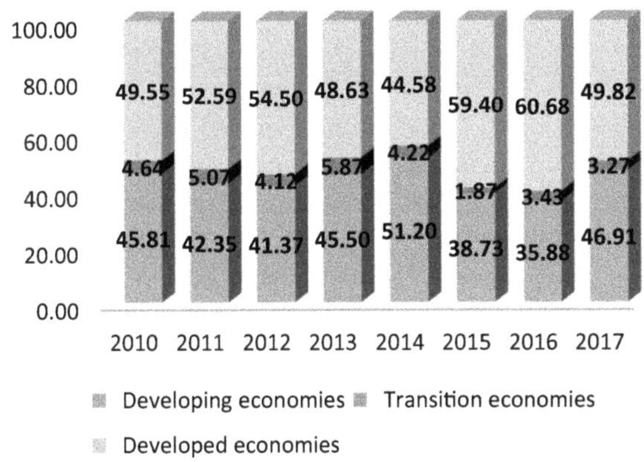

FIGURE 7.1 Share of the developing, transition and developed economies in total world FDI inflows

Source: UNCTAD database

TABLE 7.1 Top 20 FDI hosting countries for 2016 and 2017

Year	*Rank 2016*	*Country*	*Rank 2017*
USA	1	**USA**	1
UK	2	**China**	2
China	3	**Hong Kong**	3
Hong Kong	4	**Brazil**	4
The Netherlands	5	**Singapore**	5
Singapore	6	**The Netherlands**	6
Brazil	7	**France**	7
Australia	8	**Australia**	8
India	9	**Switzerland**	9
Russia	10	**India**	10
Canada	11	**Germany**	11
Belgium	12	**Mexico**	12
Italy	13	**Ireland**	13
France	14	**Russia**	14
Luxembourg	15	**Canada**	15
Mexico	16	**Indonesia**	16
Ireland	17	**Spain**	17
Sweden	18	**Israel**	18
Spain	19	**Italy**	19
Angola	20	**Rep of Korea**	20

Source: World Investment Report, 2017 and 2018.

FDI inflows from developed countries. In fact, of the top developing and transition countries that attract most FDI to the developing and transition world, four belong to the BRICS nations. These four BRICS countries are China (3rd rank in 2016 and 2nd rank in 2017), Brazil (7th rank in 2016 and 6th rank in 2017), India (9th rank in 2016 and 10th rank in 2017) and the Russian Federation (10th rank in 2016 and 14th rank in 2017). Thus, BRICS countries have revealed an edge over other countries in attracting FDI inflows.

In the recent past, due to the Covid-19 pandemic, countries of the BRICS group have observed varied trends in FDI inflows. According to the Investment Trend Monitor of UNCTAD brought out on January 24, 2021, global FDI collapsed by as much as 42% (estimated at US$859 billion from a high of US$1.5 trillion in 2019). A bulk of this decline was concentrated in developed countries, where FDI flows fell by 69%, with the decline in developing countries being relatively moderate, around 12%. In fact, the share of developing countries in global FDI flows was estimated to be at the highest level, around 72%, with China assuming the topmost rank among FDI recipients in 2020.

In relative terms, among the BRICS countries, China experienced a small increase of 4% in FDI inflows during 2020, despite a sharp drop in capital expenditure during the early phases of the pandemic; India displayed the most significant performance of an increase in FDI inflows of around 13%, mainly in the digital sector. Brazil suffered a decline in FDI inflows of around 50%, but the fall in the case of Russia was the most significant – a whopping 96% in inward FDI (UNCTAD, 2021). Going forward, global FDI trends are expected to remain weak throughout 2021, mainly because of investors' uncertainty around fresh waves of the pandemic and lingering economic recession, with major recovery perceived only from 2022 onwards (UNCTAD, 2021).

Despite the sharp fluctuations in FDI flows, this chapter abstracts from these unanticipated short-run shocks to FDI, and instead directs attention to the long-term determinants of inward FDI flows in BRICS. Specifically, the focus is on the BRICS countries' advantage over the other countries in attracting FDI and the attempt to capture the key determinants of inward FDI flows toward BRICS countries through an empirical analysis. The study uses a panel data fixed effect regression model to analyse the effect of important potential determinants of FDI inflows into BRICS countries. Using the data for the period from 1996 to 2016, the study finds that final consumption expenditure, inflation rate, interest rate, availability of natural resources and availability of a larger volume of labour are the main driving factors for inward FDI into the BRICS group. Analysis of this kind could help feed into policies towards FDI flows to improve the growth prospects of BRICS countries.

The rest of the chapter is organised as follows. In the following section, we discuss in brief the existing literature on the determinants of inward FDI. The next section on trends presents a discussion of the pattern of net FDI inflows into BRICS. The subsequent section talks about the potential determinants of these FDI inflows towards BRICS. The section on data and methodology refers to the sources of data and the regression methods used for this research. The next one lays out the key empirical findings of the study, followed by a section that contains a robustness check of the empirical estimates. The final section concludes.

Literature review

A large volume of literature exists on the factors that influence FDI inflows in emerging market economies. Most of these focus on the economic characteristics, availability of resources, and institutional factors that are significant determinants of FDI inflows into the host country. Economics factors are those that relate to the size of the market, labour costs, trade openness, economic stability, and so on. It is generally found that the size of the market is an important determinant of FDI inflows and almost all empirical studies that explain determinants of FDI have accepted this as a key factor. Bhavan et al. (2011), Aw and Tang (2010), Leitão and Faustino (2010), Leitão (2010), Lv et al. (2010), Hailu (2010), Schneider and Matie (2010), Mohamed and Sidiropoulos (2010), Vijayakumar et al. (2010), Jadhav (2012) Aziz and Mishra (2016), Saini and Singhania (2018) and several other studies have used real gross domestic product (GDP) per capita, real gross national product per capita or GDP itself as a measure of the market size of a country. Higher GDP is a proxy for purchasing power and thus, a reflection of market size.

Another important determinant of FDL inflows is large endowments of natural resources in developing and transition countries. Several studies, such as those by Asiedu (2002), and Dupasquier and Osakwe (2006) show that, for African countries, the availability of natural resources is the main factor in attracting FDI. Similarly, Deichmann et al. (2003) suggest that in the case of transition economies, like Eurasian countries, the availability of natural resources plays an important role in attracting FDI flows. Garibaldi et al. (2002) found similar results for 26 transition economies in the case of Eastern Europe, including those that were part of the former Soviet Union. Aziz and Mishra (2016) observe that FDI towards oil-rich Arab countries are resource-seeking in nature. Jadhav (2012) found evidence of resource-seeking FDI for the BRICS countries as well.

FDI inflows may also be to exploit the huge availability of labour in developing countries. Larger population levels and their higher growth rates offer potential for a large supply of labour in the working-age groups in these countries and, hence, lower labour costs as compared to that in developed nations. The higher the percentage of the working age population in total population, the higher is the possibility of FDI inflows to exploit the labour cost advantage. Tsai (1994) tries to capture this exploitation of labour. The huge availability of labour in developing nations makes skilled labour cost-effective for the MNCs of the developed nations.

The work by Nonnenberg and Mendonca (2004) suggests that for 33 developing countries, the main determinants of FDI inflows between 1975 and 2000 were factors such as the market size (measured by GNP), growth rate of product market, availability of skilled labour, receptivity to foreign capital, country risk rating and stock market behaviour. For Latin American countries, Nunes et al. (2006) find that variables such as market size, openness of the economy, infrastructure, macroeconomic stability (inflation), wages, human capital and natural resources were the primary determinants of FDI inflows during the period from 1991 to 1998. The study finds that the size of the market, infrastructure and inflation have some positive influence over FDI inflows, whereas, wage rates in the host country have a negative influence on FDI inflows. Similarly, by using a panel co-integration model, Sahoo (2006) found that market size, labour force growth, infrastructure index, and trade openness are factors that positively affect FDI inflows in South Asian countries.

Employing a panel data model, Vijayakumar et al. (2010) find that variables like market size, labour cost, infrastructure, currency value and gross capital formation are the main determinants of inward FDI towards BRICS countries. Similarly, Jadhav (2012) uses a panel data model for the period 2000–2009 to analyse the significant determinants of FDI into the BRICS countries. He finds that market size, trade openness, availability of natural resources, macroeconomic stability (inflation rate), and potential political and institutional variables as the key drivers of FDI inflows in BRICS countries.

The study by Durán (1999) that uses panel data techniques finds that market size, growth, domestic savings, the country's solvency, trade openness and macroeconomic stability are the main factors that influence FDI inflows. Likewise, Bevan and Estrin (2000) examine the factors affecting FDI inflows to transition economies (Central and Eastern Europe) by considering country risk, labour cost, host market size and gravity. The analysis for the period from 1994 to 1998 found that these factors significant for FDI inflows.

Sánchez-Martín et al. (2014) try to identify the determinants of FDI inflows for Latin American countries during 1990–2010. They found that variables like trade openness and institutional factors such as government stability are among the main determinants of FDI inflows into Latin American nations. Similarly, Aziz and Mishra (2016) find trade openness and institutional variables to be important in attracting FDI.

Saini and Singhania (2018) used the generalised method of moments (GMM) methodology to show that for developing countries, infrastructure (captured by gross fixed capital formation) and trade openness are important variables that determine inward FDI flows.

This paper attempts to capture the factors that are responsible for attracting FDI inflows into BRICS countries. The study considers different economic factors, namely, market seeking, natural resource-seeking and labour-exploiting nature of the FDI, along with existing institutional and governance factors in providing an economic edge in attracting FDI to BRICS countries. Unlike existing literature for BRICS economies that use GDP or GDP per capita as measures of purchasing power and market size, this paper tries to capture the effects of market size and/or purchasing power of a country in attracting FDI by taking final consumption expenditure/ GDP ratio as a measure of market size of that

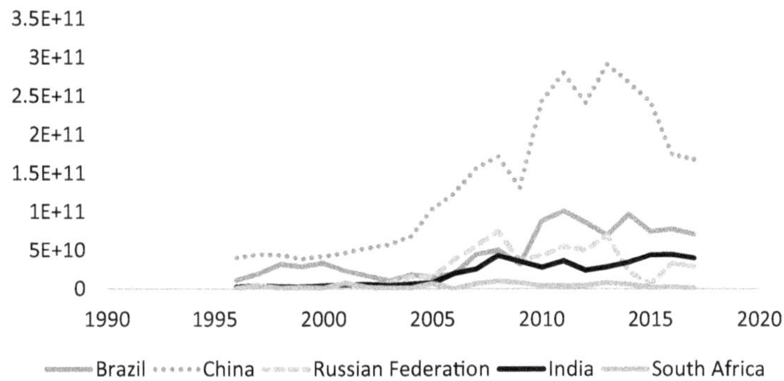

FIGURE 7.2 Trends in net FDI inflows into the BRICS countries

Source: Authors' estimates using data from World Bank Database.

country. Further, the study also focuses on both – the physical (endowment seeking) and price (cost of extraction advantage) seeking nature – of FDI. Thus, the study is an effort towards complementing existing literature on determinants of inward FDI flows.

Trend in net FDI inflows in BRICS

Net FDI inflow trends show that over the last one and a half decades or so, FDI inflows to BRICS countries have increased significantly. Until 1984, Brazil was the most attractive in terms of FDI inflows among the BRICS group, but China has since taken the leading position (Jadhav, 2012). Figure 7.2 shows trends in FDI inflows to BRICS countries over the period 1996 to 2017 in current US$. Evidently, there has been a significant increase in FDI inflows into BRICS countries over the last one and a half decades, although there is a downtrend and fluctuations experienced in the last few years in most BRICS countries. In fact, most recently, in spite of the economic recession created by the pandemic, India and China have emerged as the only two countries in the world that have exhibited positive changes in FDI inflows during 2020.

Potential determinants of FDI inflows to BRICS countries

Several factors influence FDI inflows into BRICS countries.

Market size and purchasing power

Given that BRICS account 40% of the global population and for over 20% of the global GDP, they represent a huge potential market for firms from developed countries. This could act as a major factor in attracting firms from developed countries to set up units to BRICS countries.

Commodity trade

Secondly, trade constraints in the form of high transportation costs or trade policy barriers that make it difficult to access developing country markets that are potentially huge may induce firms to set up plants in these countries to substitute for commodity exports. Thus, FDI inflows also depend on the level of commodity trade between the countries.

Availability of natural resources

Third, access to resources is another major factor that attracts FDI inflows. With large endowments of natural resources, a developing country may offer large potential for FDI inflows, as might be the case for the BRICS countries.

Macroeconomic stability

A stable macroeconomic environment, characterised by low inflation rates and public or external sector deficits is another major attraction for foreign FDI inflows.

Returns on capital

A higher return on capital tends to attract both financial and physical capital. Thus, returns on capital are a significant determinant of FDI inflows/outflows.

Availability of other inputs

Low input costs are another factor that attracts FDI inflows. As BRICS countries are generally categorised as developing ones, and account for around 40% of the world population, labour costs are likely to be lower in these countries; besides, they also offer a demographic advantage in terms of a larger proportion of working-age population. This is particularly true of countries like India and China.

Infrastructure availability

Better infrastructure that acts as a complementary input and facilitates the construction of new plants can facilitate more FDI inflows.

Government effectiveness

Finally, the effectiveness of the host country government may also be a potential determinant for FDI inflows into a country.

Our study postulates that the aforementioned factors are significant potential determinants of FDI inflows into BRICS countries.

Data and methodology

The dataset used in this analysis is annual in nature and covers the period ranging from 1996 to 2016. The variables that the dataset covers pertain to the BRICS countries and include the following:

1. net inflow of foreign direct investment (BOP, constant 2010 US$);[1]
2. final consumption expenditure as a percentage of GDP (a measure of purchasing power and market size);
3. inflation rate (measured using consumer prices indices);
4. trade openness (measured by trade as a percentage of GDP);
5. lending rates;
6. percentage share of the minerals in total exports;
7. availability of natural resources;
8. mineral rents as a percentage of GDP;
9. share of working age population in total population;
10. gross fixed capita formation as a percentage of GDP (which captures the availability of infrastructure);
11. government effectiveness (as an institutional/governance measure).

The variable for net inflow of FDI is subject to logarithmic transformation, while other variables are taken in levels.

The descriptions of the variables used in the empirical analysis are given in Table 7.2.

The data on FDI, FCE, INFLATION, TRADE, MINRENT, LAB and INTEREST are collected from the World Bank Databank database, while data on AVNATRESOURCES is computed using the UN COMTRADE database of UNCTAD-World Bank. Further, the data on GOVEFFECTIVENESS is obtained from World Governance Indicators. The data on the variable INTEREST have

TABLE 7.2 Description of the variables

Variables	*Description*
FDI	Net inflow of foreign direct investment (BOP, constant 2010 US$)
FCE	Final consumption expenditure as a percentage of GDP
INFLATION	Inflation measured using consumer prices
TRADE	Trade openness measured using trade as a percentage of GDP
INTEREST	Lending rates
AVNATRESOURCES	Percentage share of minerals in total exports
MINRENT	Mineral rents as a percentage of GDP
LAB	Share of working age population in total population
GOVEFFECTIVENESS	Government effectiveness
GFCF	Gross fixed capital formation as a percentage of GDP

some missing values (especially for Russia) during the period being considered; these missing values are imputed using interpolation.

The study uses panel data fixed effect methodology to check for the key determinants of FDI inflows to BRICS countries. The panel model used here is an unbalanced one – the data for Brazil and Russia are from 1997 to 2016 while that for India and China cover the period 1996 to 2016, and that for South Africa from 2000 onwards. The results of the Hausman test are the basis of the use of fixed effect over random effect.[2]

The model to test the important determinants of FDI inflows towards BRICS countries is as follows:

$$FDI_{it} = \beta_0 + \beta_1{\star}FCE_{it} + \beta_2{\star}GFCF_{it} + \beta_3{\star}INFLATION_{it} + \beta_4{\star}TRADE_{it} + \beta_5{\star}INTEREST_{it} + \beta_6{\star}AVNATRESOURCES_{it} + \beta_7{\star}MINRENT_{it} + \beta_8{\star}LAB_{it} + \beta_9{\star}GOVEFFECTIVENES_{it} + \beta_{10}{\star}BRICS + U_{it},$$

where all the β's are parameters to be estimated, BRICS is the dummy representing the formation of BRICS and U_{it} is the error term. The dummy variable BRICS takes the value '0' if the year considered is before 2009 and takes the value '1' elsewhere.

Result

Table 7.3 shows the result of the model in a tabulated form.

The results show that that the coefficient for FCE, which indicates the market potential of BRICS, has a positive and significant effect in terms of attracting FDI towards these countries. The coefficient for the inflation rate is negative and significant, which indicates that any kind of macroeconomic instability in an economy

TABLE 7.3 Results of panel data fixed effect model

Variables	*Coefficients*	*T-Statistics*	*P-Values*
FCE	0.045	2.15	0.09**
INFLATION	−0.0042	−2.44	0.07**
TRADE	−0.0035	−0.33	0.76
INTEREST	0.024	3.10	0.03*
AVNATRESOURCES	0.051	3.86	0.01*
MINRENT	−0.14	−1.31	0.26
LAB	0.23	3.59	0.02*
GOVEFFECTIVENESS	1.08	1.53	0.20
GFCF	0.037	0.73	0.50
BRICS	0.202	0.20	0.85
CONSTANT	2.88	0.47	0.62

** and * represents significant at 10% and 5% levels respectively.

discourages MNCs from investing in it. The coefficient of interest rate is positive and significant, which is consistent with the flow of capital theory, that is capital will move to locations where it earns higher returns. The result also suggests that availability of natural resources in the BRICS countries has an important role in attracting FDI; thus, it can be said that FDI towards BRICS is also resource-seeking. Further, the coefficient of LAB is positive and significant suggesting that the abundant availability of labour in the BRICS members states is a factor attracting FDI inflows. The coefficients for other variables, namely, TRADE, MINRENT, GOVEFFECTIVENESS, GFCF and BRICS are also of the expected sign but are not statistically significant.

Robustness check

The results reported in Table 7.3 are found to be robust. The robustness check has been done using control of corruption variable in the existing fixed effect model for the BRICS countries. Table 7.4 gives the robustness check results.

As can be seen in Table 7.4, coefficients of the earlier variables are of similar magnitude and sign as in Table 7.3. Thus, it can be said that the result reported in the Table 7.3 are robust. Additionally, the inclusion of the variable CONTROLOFCORRUP has the expected sign but is not very significant.

Conclusion

The BRICS countries have been attracting a significant amount of global FDI inflows, by virtue of their large market size and input availability. This is also corroborated by the data published by UNCTAD, which indicates that developing

TABLE 7.4 Results of the robustness check

Variables	*Coefficients*	*T-Statistics*	*P-Values*
FCE	0.052	3.74	0.02*
INFLATION	−0.0043	−2.38	0.07**
TRADE	−0.0021	−0.20	0.85
INTEREST	0.025	3.07	0.03*
AVNATRESOURCES	0.049	3.69	0.02*
MINRENT	−0.11	−0.87	0.43
LAB	0.24	5.67	0.00*
GOVEFFECTIVENESS	0.95	1.16	0.30
CONTROLOFCORRUP	0.36	0.57	0.59
GFCF	0.038	0.78	0.48
BRICS	0.17	0.17	0.87
CONSTANT	1.32	0.31	0.77

** and * represents significant at 10% and 5% levels respectively.

countries have exhibited an edge over developed and transition economies in attracting FDI, and among developing countries, BRICS have succeeding in attracting a large part of such FDI.

This paper discusses the factors that constitute the main drivers of net FDI inflows towards BRICS countries and making these countries top destinations for MNCs. The study makes use of a fixed effect panel data model to ascertain the unit significance of select factors that drive FDI inflows. Among these, the ones considered are final consumption expenditure as a percentage of GDP, inflation rate, lending rate, availability of natural resources, and labour force availability. A positive and significant coefficient associated with FCE points towards the market seeking behaviour of MNCs. The coefficient of lending rates has a positive effect on FDI inflows, which ties in well with capital market theory. Further, a positive and significant coefficient of availability of natural resources represents the resource-seeking nature of FDI. FDI inflows into BRICS also tend to exploit the abundant availability of labour in BRICS countries, indicated by the positive and statistically significant coefficient for LAB. The results of the fixed effect panel data model are found to be robust in respect of inclusion of additional variables.

The key takeaways from this research are that, in their attempt to attract FDI inflows, especially in the aftermath of the Covid-19 pandemic, BRICS countries should focus on both fiscal and monetary policy tools that would encourage steady inflows of foreign capital, especially in sectors where they have competitiveness and offer prospects for high rates of technological progress. Higher inflows of capital could supplement domestic investments in host countries and ensure faster and more robust recovery in the post-pandemic period, in terms of growth as well as jobs creation. In this respect, it is reckoned that this research could constitute a useful policy input.

Notes

1 The collected data is in current US $, which is converted into constant 2010 US $ using the GDP deflator.
2 Result of Hausman test is available on request.

References

Asiedu, E. (2002). On the determinants of foreign direct investment in developing countries: Is Africa different? *World Development*, 30(1), 107–119.

Aw, T. Y., and Tang, T. C. (2010). The determinants of inward foreign direct investment: The case of Malaysia. *International Journal of Business and Society*, 11(1), 59.

Aziz, O. G., and Mishra, A. V. (2016). Determinants of FDI inflows to Arab economies. *The Journal of International Trade & Economic Development*, 25(3), 325–356.

Bevan, A. A., and Estrin, S. (2000). Patterns of foreign direct investment and trade in Central and Eastern Europe. William Davidson Institute Working Paper No. 342, October 2000.

Bhavan, T., Xu, Changsheng, and Zhong, C. (2011). Determinants and growth effect of FDI in South Asian economies: Evidence from a panel data analysis. *International Business Research*, 4(1), 43–50.

Deichmann, J. I., Eshghi, A., Haughton, D. M., Sayek, S., and Teebagey, N. C. (2003). Foreign direct investment in the Eurasian transition states. *Eastern European Economics*, 41(1), 5–34.

Dupasquier, C., and Osakwe, P. N. (2006). Foreign direct investment in Africa: Performance. *Challenges, and Responsibilities*, 17(2), 241–260.

Durán, J. E. (1999). Los determinantes de la ied en los países de américa latina y el caribe: su impacto sobre el comercio y la integración regional. ECLAC, Mimeo.

Garibaldi, P., Mora. N., Sahay. R., and Zettelmeyer. J. (2002). What moves capital to transition economies? IMF working paper WP/02/64.

Hailu, Z. A. (2010). Impact of foreign direct investment on trade of African Countries. *International Journal of Economics and Finance*, 2(3), 122–133.

Jadhav, P. (2012). Determinants of foreign direct investment in BRICS economies: Analysis of economic, institutional and political factor. *Procedia – Social and Behavioral Sciences*, 37, 5–14.

Leitão, N. C. (2010). Foreign direct investment: The Canadian experience. *International Journal of Economics and Finance*, 2(4), 82–88.

Leitão, N. C., and Faustino, H. C. (2010). Determinants of foreign direct investment in portugal. *Journal of Applied Business and Economics*, 11(3). http://m.www.na-businesspress.com/JABE/LeitaoWeb.pdf. Accessed on 15 December 2020.

Lv, L., Wen, S., and Xiong, Q. (2010). Determinants and performance index of foreign direct investment in China's agriculture. *China Agricultural Economic Review*, 2(1), 36–48.

Mohamed, S. E., and Sidiropoulos, M. G. (2010). Another look at the determinants of Foreign direct investment in MENA countries: An empirical investigation. *Journal of Economic Development*, 35(2), 75–95.

Nonnenberg and Mendonça. (2004). The determinants of direct foreign investment in developing countries. IPEA Working paper.

Nunes, C. L., Oscategui, J., and Peschiera, J. (2006). Determinants of FDI in Latin America. Documento De Trabajo 252. Working Paper from Departamento de Economía – Pontificia Universidad Católica del Perú, Peru.

Saini, N., and Singhania, M. (2018). Determinants of FDI in developed and developing countries: A quantitative analysis using GMM. *Journal of Economic Studies*, 45(2), 348–382.

Sánchez-Martín, M. E., De Arce, R., and Escribano, G. (2014). Do changes in the rules of the game affect FDI flows in Latin America? A look at the macroeconomic, institutional and regional integration determinants of FDI. *European Journal of Political Economy*, 34(C), 279–299.

Sahoo, P. (2006). Foreign direct investment in South Asia: Policy, trends, impact and determinants. ADB Institute Discussion paper No. 56.

Schneider, K. H., and Matie, I. (2010). Business climate, political risk and FDI in developing countries: Evidence from panel data. *International Journal of Economics and Finance*, 2(5), 54–65.

Tsai, P. (1994). Determinants of foreign direct investment and its impact on economic growth. *Journal of Economic Development*, 19(1), 137–163.

UNCTAD. (2017). *World Investment Report 2017 (WIR17): Investment and the Digital Economy*. New York and Geneva: United Nations.

UNCTAD. (2018). *World Investment Report 2018 (WIR18): Investment and New Industrial Policies*. New York and Geneva: United Nations.

UNCTAD. (2021). Investment trends monitor, 24 January 2021. https://unctad.org/system/files/official-document/diaeiainf2021d1_en.pdf. Accessed on 15 January 2021.

Vijayakumar, Narayanamurthy, Sridharan, P., and Sekhara Rao, K. C. (2010). Determinants of FDI in BRICS countries: A panel analysis. *International Journal of Business Science & Applied Management*, 5(3), 1–13.

8

TOWARDS AN AESTHESIS OF BRICS

Meenakshi Sundriyal

Introduction

In what might seem to be a rather stretched but uncanny resemblance to the BRICS grouping, one is reminded of the reference to a certain 'Chinese Encyclopaedia' inserted by Jorge Luis Borges, the Argentinian writer, as a fictional intertext in his essay *Analytical Language of John Wilkins* (Borges, 1952). The irony of the fact that Borges chooses that the cited encyclopaedia be Chinese, the eternal enigmatic 'other' to the Western world, is not lost on us in the context of BRICS. The taxonomy proposed[1] in the encyclopaedia brings to the fore the unease and destabilisation of scale that can be produced with simple subversions of the hitherto running order of things. It asserts that the present ways of seeing and ordering, however stable they may seem, are prone to undoing and redoing. The Borgesian text has fascinated many a thinker, including Michel Foucault, with its classification of animals within the 'encyclopaedia' who are brought together abnormally in a 'non place' as there cannot be any common meeting ground among the categories (Foucault, 1971 in 1994). The 'emplacement' of the BRICS, much like the Borgesian idea, is a question fraught with complexity given the lack of homogeneity of the constituents and necessitates an exploration of approaches to deal with its elusive locus. Further, while trying to have a general perspective on how to read the interface between BRICS and culture, it becomes imperative to underscore the complexity of the term 'culture'.

Culture as social practice reproducing dominance and contestation

Culture seemingly is one of the most complicated of words to define. In its large trajectory, it has referred to a variety of nuances relating to what have been called

DOI: 10.4324/9781003148074-9

civilisational values, ideas, ways of being and organising societies. With these emerged the corollary as to whose ideas, ways of being and organising does 'culture' reflect. As the idea of a singular universalising nature of these categories was met with serious challenges in twentieth-century theoretical formulations new emphases emerged, but culture as something intrinsic to humankind was recognised.

> Our 'species being' brings with it a structural gap or absence where culture of some kind must be implanted if we are to survive and flourish; and though what kind of culture is highly variable, the necessity of culture is not.
>
> *(Eagleton in Eagleton and Milne, eds., 2005, p. 8)*

The category of culture, however, presents itself as a semiotic challenge owing to the vast multivalence involved in an equally vast number of contexts and frames that the user applies it in. The idea that perhaps 'cultures' instead of singular culture was more appropriate emerged as it increasingly began to be seen in relation with power and ideology. Dominance and subjugation in society led to a dominant culture often with a contestation on the margins. The constituents of culture are as much the concrete material production as the symbolic system that includes language but is not limited to it, as we can see in the numerous ways in which it has proliferated in the present times. Culture is ultimately a social practice that carries a part of the past as selective tradition (Raymond Williams in John Storey ed., 1998) but is also constantly being reworked in accordance with power and its contestation. Notwithstanding the organic relationship of culture with economy, the former's complex ontology makes its scope of influence wider than what it is usually given credit for. The late capitalist world with its ever-proliferating sites of culture creates the conditions for the re-emergence of the sensory mode as a driver of aesthesis, understood as a process of making meaning or judgement that involves the senses. The process itself does not function in a vacuum but is specific to synchronic and diachronic material conditions and is always sought to be appropriated by power. It is with this overview of culture as a point of departure that I attempt to look at BRICS, especially in the light of spatiality, more specifically southernity. I propose a description of the constituents of this southernity using spatial imagination, in particular, heterotopia.

As the advent of 'modernity' propelled by the epistemological inferences of the European renaissance and enlightenment ran parallel with nation state and colonialism it historically led to the development of a cartographic language of power that still survives to a large extent. The spatial directions do not just point to the position on the map but to a position in the hierarchy of nations. The constructs of East/West and later North/South came to represent not just the physical locus of people and nations on the globe but one of their standing and heft in exercising control over earth's resources too. It is observed that, even after the formal cessation of colonisation, the question of coloniality of power remains (Quijano, 1992). The once colonised people have to face the twin challenges of internal decolonisation on the one hand and external prejudice on the other. Physical spaces symbolise hierarchised states of being. Edward Said's seminal work 'Orientalism' (Said, 1978) was one of the earliest texts to theorise the spatial metaphor as a topos on which the 'other' is represented. Another set of spatial binaries frequently utilised in the context of power is the centre/periphery or metropolis/satellite (Frank, 1978) where the powerful centre/metropolis is serviced by the exploited periphery/satellite. Spatial metaphors dominate in the articulation of the unevenness of the world. Since the second half of the twentieth century, there has been a considerable body of work that has gone on to develop the idea of spatiality (Harvey, 1990; Massey, 2005). The appraisals of these writings looked into the construct of space as a product of social relations and its concrete as well as abstract dimensions that place it in the cultural sphere. The element of space was eventually added to the hitherto practiced primacy of time.

The idea of BRICS in terms of its aesthesis can be 'located' in the South, according to the current *mappa mundi* of power. As a matter of fact, cartography itself developed within a social context and the world map is the way it is now for the same reasons. It is more than an interesting fact that the *Tabula Rogeriana*, the world map made by Al Idrisi in the twelfth century showed the 'South' on the top (Talib et al., 2012). The many seemingly empirical facts therefore have more to do with the dominant aesthesis and its conversion into social practice rather than an objective statement of fact.

The narrative war

In recent scholarship, there has been an emphasis on 'narratives' in the context of BRICS. The so-called 'narrative turn' in social sciences is underlined and BRICS is conceived as a space that builds its own particular narrative and puts it out there for people to get attracted to its appeal. Narratives are often divided into three categories: namely strategic narrative, identity narrative and issue narrative (Roselle et al., 2014). Carolidjn van Noort identifies all three in the case of BRICS, based on the official documents issued by BRICS from time to time and finds that BRICS do not precisely follow the grammar of such a narrative, and hence, people might not be attracted to it in that measure (Noort, 2017). While it is true that BRICS form their narrative in official statements, which are usually very carefully considered enunciations that reflect the common minimum agreement of all BRICS members, the narrative of BRICS is not contained in its entirety in official statements only. It is also contained in its gaps, in visual symbols and a variety of other things that might be spaces from which the BRICS narrative might emanate, create its own *istoria*[2] and get picked by the media and the other groupings, and inform the aesthesis of people at large. These, in turn, will interact with the narrative, consume it on their own terms and may further communicate it.

BRICS with its location in the Global South is a subtle contestation of the present order. The power cartograph displaying a powerful West/North and subservient East/South is contested by BRICS, which seeks to create a new one by empowering the Global South. The old order is rendered subverted, however partially, through the very existence of BRICS and the signs that it emanates in international politics. This particularly points out that the study of official 'narratives' could be better understood in relation with the overall system of signs, which could include this narrative. As a case in point, one can see that in spite of the non-threatening, collaborative tone of the BRICS official narrative, it evoked the kind of affective response from the North that it did.

While the idea of BRICS as a contestation from the Global South in the macro view of the current global order is upheld, it is recognised as a heterogeneous space in itself with its own 'centres and peripheries', in terms of both within each country as well as in terms of each other. In spite of the stark dissimilarities impeding any truly homologous parameter of comparison among the BRICS countries, much like the Borgesian encyclopaedia, they nonetheless come together and, by registering their presence, upset the current order of things. It must be acknowledged though that this upsetting is at the level of IR and there remain numerous 'peripheries' within these countries that are in an unequal relationship with their 'cores'.

The year 2021 marks 20 years of the coinage of the term BRIC by the Goldman Sachs economist Jim O'Neil (O' Niell, 2001). BRICS has come a long way from being a potential investment space in corporate imagination to a loose counter club like a group of nations in search of better bargains vis-à-vis the dominant order, to a grouping that has not only stayed its course but also managed to establish financial and other institutions for closer collaboration between members.

Art and culture, and the process of aesthesis in the contemporary world

Human subjectivity allows social milieus to function as sites for the perpetuation of structures as well as the processes that could alter them. These cultural sites are dominated by the image and the narrative, and, with the arrival of the Internet, they have proliferated like never before. This has led to a manifold increase in the complexity of the act of 'seeing'. The process of creating as well as cutting through the subterfuge is a bigger and more complex task now as the democratising capacity of the internet could not escape being tied to the social relations of its production. The virtual world soon enough started mirroring the real world.

As the sites of narrative making grew with new technology, BRICS also put forth, through explicit narratives or implicit ones, a vision of alterity[3] backed by concrete institution-building. Its salience also lies in its being a group that breaks the ceiling of neutrality that alliances of 'regional co-operation' might connote. The inclusion of South Africa just after the formation of BRIC made the intent of representing an inclusive southernity clear. It is a space of unity for the South, a non-hierarchic space in contraposition to the current dominant order. How far would this alterity in IR translate into making BRICS countries more equitable spaces is a far more elusive issue. At the level of IR and in a figurative sense, the space that BRICS seeks to establish could be seen as a heterotopia

(Vidler et al., 2014) of sorts, an 'other' space, a counter space, which contests the long-existing order of things.

The image and visual culture has come to rule the roost in today's world in more ways than one (Panja et al eds., 2009). Walter Benjamin, in the beginning of the twentieth century, had underlined the distinction between the earlier concept of art and the fundamental change that mechanical reproducibility made to it as the society became more and more mechanised (Benjamin in Hannah Arendt ed., 1969). Benjamin's premise has only become more acute as we transit through a technologically advanced world. The act of seeing is even more complex now as sensory perception comes back in the twenty-first century to combine into a potent mix with technology, which finds ready use in mass media (Campbell, 2001). Baudrillard's concepts of hyper reality and simulacra gave an innovative framework of analysis positing that in contemporary times, the sign is becoming devoid of any real referent (Poster, 2001). Our understanding of the cultural in the context of BRICS has to be rooted in the historicity of our times in general even as the world gets heavily influenced and negotiated under the system of the sign, which under late capitalism becomes a commodity in itself, as underscored by Baudrillard (Poster, 2001). It could be further considered then that when such cultural production takes place at the behest of the powerful, what could the viability of its counter-sign be. It is precisely to look into the question of how we can perceive the BRICS phenomenon that we need to locate it well within the framework of spatiality.

BRICS culture or culture of the BRICS

To begin to understand the BRICS phenomenon, especially from the vantage point of culture, is a task that begets a lot of questions of premise affirmation. I seek to emplace BRICS culturally while seeing culture as a varied praxis of ideas in any historical site. The idea of the historical site also gets hugely expanded with its interface with a digitally connected world. In today's world, contesting cultures compete in an unequal eyeball-grabbing game through processes of aesthesis forming a 'sensus communis', the prevailing perception in a society (Dillon, 2016, pp. 367, 369). There is a possibility of shaping this 'sensus communis' as much as getting shaped by it. On the other hand, the question of art having its origin in ritual comes to haunt again as it runs the danger of getting co-opted in a new ritualistic rendition, albeit of a different kind. There is a need to wrest art from the ritual of sanitised 'cultural programmes' in official auditoriums where it has as a sign lost the referents. The reference to the lived lives of people is seldom made and the pretence of art as a neutral, modern ritual is rampant, although such status of neutrality is often not accorded to the art of contrarian visions in authoritarian spaces. Given this context then, do we begin to engage with the idea of 'BRICS culture' or 'Culture of the BRICS'? The answer perhaps is both of these and more. The vast physical space that is the area under the five BRICS countries comprises roughly 26 per cent of the total land mass of the earth and about 42 per cent of the world's population. The huge area that the BRICS countries occupy has been populated for millennia, much before the emergence of the concept of nation states, to state the obvious. This particular space occupied by each of these five countries has seen not a singular culture but cultures that have shaped and, in turn, have been shaped by their respective histories. Centuries of co habitation among particular communities, autochthonous or not, which lived and are living in these areas, have contributed to the acquisition of a diverse range of social practices that is culture. In attempting a cultural reading of BRICS, we must take two perspectives into consideration. One is the perspective of the diverse culture that is already being practised. This forms a continuum from earlier and is the culture of the space, which happens to be in BRICS. The other is the specific set of social practices that has come about or might come in the future owing to the formation and strengthening of the BRICS grouping itself. In other words, we will have to look at an intersecting point between the culture of the BRICS and BRICS culture. One must remember, however, that both these categories are not exclusive to each other after the formation of BRICS but each feeds into the other in a variety of ways.

The opponents of the neoliberal hegemonic order as well as its votaries have seen the formation of BRICS as problematic – the former expressing an acute scepticism and the latter virtually writing its obituary. Carl Meecham of the American think tank Centre for Strategic and International Studies almost exhorts Brazil to come back to accepting US hegemony and abandon its BRICS waywardness as it hardly has a future (Degaut, 2015). It is instructive to note that even after a regime change that has been rather favourable to the United States in recent times, Brazil has not made any effort to abandon the BRICS ship and nor has India.

Notwithstanding the acute scepticism or the total writing off of the BRICS, there is relevance to the idea that has the potential to enact positive change, however small, in the lives of the billions who inhabit the BRICS countries. There are diverse reasons for member nations to remain in BRICS while they may want it to sound more collaborative notes with the North rather than shriller ones.

The idea of BRICS has been located broadly in the postcolonial/decolonial discourse and celebrated as a bypassing of the hegemony and control of the Global North. Its potential to mobilise the Global South was organic as most of these countries have a shared condition of post-coloniality. BRICS could be seen as a form of assertion of the countries that were hitherto denied autonomy and agency, which since long has been in the control of Western powers. Modernity has been critiqued in detail by post-colonial theorists. It has been asserted that the characteristic feature, offsetting the scientific achievements of an 'enlightened' Europe, was its rampant colonial project. Levander and Mignolo say that for some in the Global North,

> the Global South is the location of underdevelopment and emerging nations need 'support' of the Global north (G7, IMF, World Bank and the like). However, from the perspective of the inhabitants, the Global South is the location where new visions of the future are emerging and where the global political and decolonial society is at work.
>
> *(Levander and Mignolo, 2011, p. 3)*

The post-colonial reading of BRICS has found a lot of critical resonance. However, the post-colonial condition by itself might not be sufficient to locate BRICS. The singular salience of the post-colonial condition at the expense of ignoring the political economy of the present and the intra-societal class divisions could be limiting. On the other hand, what needs to be asked is whether the coming together of these vastly diverse cultural spaces meant anything in terms of challenging the dominant international discourse, which seems to pivot around a few hegemonic power centres. Or has it just managed to open yet another conglomeration of the ruling elites of the Global South represented by the governments of these countries trying to bargain within a world economic order that they cannot be bothered to change?

It emerges that there has been no homogeneity of views regarding BRICS since it came into being. The critical assessment of the BRICS experiment has made it controversial in terms of the gap in expectations it generated as a potential challenge to the unequal economic order and the trajectory that it has had so far. BRICS has been seen as not only not providing any challenge to it but conforming and operating within it and, as a result, also perpetuating inequality at home in the BRICS nations (Bond, Garcia eds, 2015, pp. 1–12). The interests of the diverse 'BRICS' within each country identified by these studies as 'BRICS from above' (the governments), 'from the middle' (the civil society) and 'from below' (people at large) are often at loggerheads in spite of some convergences. The 'BRICS from above' itself was supposed to have sprung from an anti-imperialist stance of people sharing the experience of having undergone varying degrees of 'otherization' owing to colonisation, like India, Brazil, and South Africa. The coinage of BRICs resonated with a deep-seated yearning within these nations to 'set right' the injustices of the past and in some, as is the case with Russia, the nostalgia of having been a great power and the aspiration to rebuild made them go for the narrative of South–South co-operation. BRICS, especially BRICS from below, has been already forging alliances and co-operation. The process could be helped if there were more institutionalised mechanisms to facilitate this exchange. There is, for example, a history of world social forums since 2001, where members of the civil society of diverse nations deliberated on forging alliances against neoliberalism. Cultural exchange within BRICS can forge the much-required cohesion and exchange of notes among the people of the BRICS countries. BRICS, thus, can be seen as an open-ended dynamic construct leaving room for a diverse and multifaceted engagement of people instead of a closed and fixed symbolic and material system, only having to do with the ruling powers of these countries. The notion of southernity could be wrested from the abstraction of countries to the lived lives of common people.

The scepticism with which BRICS is seen has its basis in the policies within the BRICS countries themselves. The multiple BRICS within each country, as we see in the three-tiered reading of this construct, could offer precisely the window for a dynamic interaction between the various tiers and act like pressure groups. The potential possibility of BRICS from below pushing the agenda cannot be summarily ruled out. The vertical and lateral interactions among the multiple-tiered BRICS across nations do create a dynamic symbolic and material system, which can produce a new cultural synergy if the BRICS create stronger institutional mechanisms to augment these in this dynamic cultural space. With the signing of the BRICS Agreement on Co-operation in the field of culture, the cultural dimension gets entrenched in BRICS' imagination. This acknowledgement of the importance of the cultural dimension has indeed thrown open an area of immense possibilities. The notion that closer cultural ties are a precondition to foster dialogue has now formally found bearings in BRICS' official discourse.

BRICS through spatiality

The late twentieth century saw a number of studies that opened up the field of the hitherto less explored dimension of spatiality, which has since been constantly renewed by newer insights. The temporal aspect of human experience in this world had been privileged for a long period over the spatial, which is now central to the study of culture in contemporary times. The epistemological tools based on linearity were no longer sufficient to analyse the complex reality of contemporary times marked by the consumer cultures of late capitalism (Soja, 1996). The early precursors of this line of thought, Henri Lefebvre and Michel Foucault, while maintaining the due importance of historicity, tried to bring forth spatiality into the discourse about the 'aesthesis 'of our times. This concept was further developed by Edward Soja who elaborated a theoretical premise of the 'Third Space' (Soja, 1996). Beyond the 'first space', which is the lived space of human beings, comes the 'second space', which is the conceptualisation of the first space. And, apart from these two, there is the 'third space', which is unstable and could encompass a wide variety of meaning formation depending upon a range of factors. Michel Foucault wrote around the same time as Lefebvre came up with new ideas on space. He outlined the conception beyond that of Utopia as an 'other' space, which is contrapuntal to these real and imagined spaces for which he coined the term 'heterotopia', that is the 'other' space.

> 'So there are countries without place and histories without chronology. Whole cities, planets, continents, universes that are impossible to trace on any map or in any sky, quite simply because they do not belong to any space. Without doubt these cities, continents, planets are born, so to speak in the heads of men, or more precisely, in the interstices of their words, in the weft of the tales they tell, or if not there, in the placeless place of their dreams, in the empty well of their hearts; in short, wherever the salve of utopia is sought.' . . . 'of all the spaces which are distinct from one another, there are some that are absolutely different, places that are opposed to all others, they are destined in some way to efface them, to neutralize them or purify them. These are in a sense counterspaces.'
>
> *(Vilder et al., 2014, p. 20)*

The journey of spatiality in recent scholarship intersects space, real or imagined, with concepts like marginality, liminality, hybridity, bordering, and thirding, which allows for a palimpsest of contestation, a subversive space which allows for a radical rewriting of oppressive norms of various kinds. The conceptualisation of the heterotopia or the third/other/counter space allows us its use as a tool to interpret the 'space' created by the idea and discourse of BRICS and the culture that it seeks to establish. When we link the BRICS idea and activities with spatiality, we can observe that it surfaces in a variety of spaces that could be denominated as heterotopic. In the following discussion, a series of spaces are enlisted where the BRICS heterotopia emerges and establishes itself as the counterspace.

The summits

The first and the most important one, at least in terms of what contributes most to the visual emergence of the BRICS idea as heterotopia, albeit curated by mediality of various persuasions, is the space created by the summit meetings of the BRICS leadership. Since BRICS is hugely different from other international groupings associated with the North, the routine activities that it engages in become extraordinary, akin to a declaration of covert defiance. Its summits become then the single biggest point of convergence of the real and the imagined space in which the BRICS idea seeks to carve out a 'deviant' space denoting southernity. The process of holding yearly summits offers a singular big opportunity for the BRICS idea to manifest itself spatially and get etched in the zillion replicated images that this creates. The rhythmic temporality of the process of holding the summits creates a heterotopic space, which intersects its moment and goes much beyond it. Ironically, the various convention centres, foyers of five-star hotels, resorts, and so on as part of specific cityscapes and, more recently, electronic screens in virtual mode got converted into heterotopias: third spaces that go much beyond the space that they originally were. There is an automatic check on the access to the space itself. And this check does not emanate just from formal security concerns but forms part of the very exclusivity inscribed in its formation. The essence of the BRICS in the context of the summits derives from a sense of interpellation which then moves on to performance. However ritualistic and indistinguishable from the counterparts, the summit becomes the theatre where participants perform through their bodies and signal assertion (Ahern, 2003). The spaces themselves are not permanent or static. The constant moving around cityscapes that are themselves symbols of the Global South become doubly so during the summits. This mobility is simultaneously an act of extension of reach and assertion and reiteration of the 'counter-space' of the existing international order. A space allowing mobility is the one from where radical resistance to inequity and discrimination materialises (bell hooks, 1989). The fact that there is no space that is BRICS' headquarters also adds to the dimension of fluidity and mobility of BRICS. Notwithstanding the subtext of the crisscross of power struggles between the BRICS nations, it curates itself, at least as of now, as a space with no centre or peripheries. The absence of a headquarters, by chance or by design, adds to the visual imagery of a non-hierarchical BRICS. It is a lack that is conspicuous by its absence and, by virtue of its 'lack', paradoxically adds value to the message. The flashing of the image of the BRICS leadership holding hands at the summits is powerful. The image that pops out of the newspapers the next morning in sundry places like homes, shops, government offices, seats of power; the moving image that occupies the rectangular space of the television sets installed in myriad spaces throughout the world is reproduced infinitely, simultaneously juxtaposing itself with random things.

The image is the sign that contributes immensely in the process of perception of the BRICS idea, which was being foregrounded in the summit. While at some spaces it would not be perceived as anything more than a bunch of routinely smiling world leaders, at many others, it might be perceived as a deviation and evoke curiosity as such. The summit venue itself, therefore, becomes a heterotopia infinitely replicated and aesthesised in diverse ways.

The NDB and the CRA

The signing of the agreement on the BRICS Development Bank in Fortaleza in 2015 paved the way for the coming into existence of the BRICS Development Bank or the New Development Bank. By 2016, it already became operational, headquartered in the building of the Oriental Financial Centre in Shanghai, China. The idea of the bank is to help in the development and infrastructural work within the BRICS nations. The BRICS states contribute unequal sums of money to the bank but all members have equal say in its affairs. This equality reinforces the notional counterspace of the BRICS, of something that founds itself on the principles of collaboration and absolute equity instead of an artificial relative equity based on the power to pay. The bank, therefore, is at once the physical space that is located in Shanghai as well as the imagined space that resides in 'the heads of men, or more precisely, in the interstices of their words, in the weft of the tales they tell . . .' (Vidler et al., 2014). The space of the bank, real or imagined, is the counterspace to the World Bank, symbolic of Western financial hegemony over the world. Similarly, the other space, which is the Contingent Reserve Arrangement, is a mechanism to help BRICS nations to overcome any problems of balance of payments that they might face. This also could be perceived as a counterspace to the IMF. Although it is the stated position of the BRICS that they do not wish to counter or act in opposition to the financial institutions of the IMF and the World Bank but only collaborate with all for the betterment of all, the establishment of these two financial spaces that are the NDB and the CRA is 'seen' as a counterspace, a heterotopia where resistance to the hegemonic transactions of the IMF and the World Bank is built. The very creation of these two spaces is crucial to the alternate world vision of financial collaboration and security and has the potential of becoming a potent and visible sign of strength of the BRICS.

BRICS network university

The space of higher education represented by the University is one of the crucial areas where the culture is not only practised but also studied. A university is a space like no other. It has the potential to be the ultimate heterotopia through its infinite built-in mechanisms of fostering the widest range of questioning and debate about every idea under the sun so that it can creatively contribute to knowledge production in society. Universities, therefore, can be spaces that can be the spokes in the wheels of any society where young minds are given the space conducive to free engagement with ideas. The BRICS nations took cognisance of the pioneering potential of universities and the positive effect that a collaborating network could have on mutual co-operation in this area although higher education spaces across BRICS countries, especially universities, are crisscrossed with various players and stakeholders and do not usually function in perfect harmony with the government (Schwarzman, Simon et al., eds. 2015). On the other hand, we can observe high handedness from governments, which is not conducive to the idea of a university.

The idea of the BRICS Network University was mooted at the third meeting of the BRICS education ministers held on 18 November 2015 in Moscow (III Meeting of BRICS Education Ministers Moscow Declaration, 2015).[4] Subsequently, a Memorandum of Understanding was signed by the representatives of the BRICS Ministries of Education on the same day, outlining the process of the formation of the BRICS Network University (BRICS University Network MoU). Since then, 12 participant institutions from each BRICS country have been identified by the respective ministries to further the network. The Vice Chancellors of the BRICS NU met in Zengzhau from 1 to 3 July 2017 as also the members of the International Governing Board (IGB) and the International Thematic Group (ITG) of the BRICS NU. The regulations and statutes for the IGB and the ITG respectively were signed (pib.nic.in) moving forward the functioning of the BRICS NU.

The BRICS NU, therefore, is another elevation in the institutional architecture projected by the BRICS towards mutual co-operation in resource sharing. This would be another counter space physically that manifests itself in its numerous centres hosted by 60 odd institutions and universities spread over the BRICS countries and could be seen as an empowering sign for the BRICS idea. The BRICS NU can thus be framed as a heterotopia. It gets projected as a sign of fomenting institutions of intellectual self-sufficiency and exchange of knowledge. It adds another row to the international political power grid and, therefore, just by virtue of coming into existence, is an act of defiance.

Sites of media cultures of BRICS

As culture in contemporary times has undergone fundamental changes in the ambit of both its production and consumption, new sites of mass culture emerge continually. The cultural canon has indeed come a long way from when it was anathema to think about including popular culture. Cultural studies have long discarded the binary of 'high' and 'low' culture although it is not entirely eliminated. The importance of studying kitsch art, pulp fiction and analysing its derogatory or subversive usage or a poem on twitter or a story on Instagram is central to aesthesising the world as it is to study opera or ballet and trace their consideration as 'high' art. In such a scenario, the genres in which popular or mass culture manifests acquire immense importance.

In our age of technological advancement, we are confronted with a proliferation of media of various forms, which through the very nature of their constitution bring about the phenomenon of distinct media 'cultures'. The common perception in the South is that these media cultures usually have their reference point in the Global North rather than the Global South, which is true to a great extent given the dominance of the North. There have been very few studies of the media and the growing relevance of the fast-growing distinct media cultures of the Global South is yet to get amply highlighted. Wendy Willems analyses in depth the study of media cultures of the Global South and finds that it is still very much referenced vis-à-vis the Global North, even if there are definite flows of cultural products from the South to the North also. Willems affirms that

> [i]n addition to work that began to highlight the agency of Third World audiences in media reception, a fourth conceptualisation of the Global South emerged which emphasised the growing role of Asia, Latin America and Africa in the production of news and entertainment. This body of work primarily critiqued the direction and intensity of cultural flows identified by media and cultural imperialism scholars and argued that the global South was not merely a recipient of cultural products but was increasingly gaining a place for itself as part of Global cultural industries. New regional cultural hubs emerged such as India's Bollywood and Latin America's telenovela industry, which for some represented a 'contraflow' to dominant flows of cultural products from the First World to The Third World, from the North to the South.
> *(Willems, 2014, pp. 7–23)*

One of the most important and complex visual medium of our times is perhaps cinema. Right from the time in the late nineteenth century after the invention of photography when the Lumiere brothers started showing their products across continents, cinema began its trajectory of becoming the site where 'modernity' was produced and consumed. It is, therefore, pertinent that one approaches it as the most fertile space to understand the social practice of contemporary culture. Mediality of the cinematic variety possesses the power to engage the masses through deviation from the normative (Jennings and Wilke, 2010).

The BRICS nations are spaces that are seeing fast-growing industries of media cultures (Willems, 2014). In India, for example, the Hindi film industry, popularly known as Bollywood, is one of the largest film industries in the world in terms of the sheer number of films produced and the number of people employed. Cinema in other nations of the BRICS have shown growth and are high in production including transnational productions as in the case of China but then they are low in exhibition (Yingjin Zhang, 2010). Brazilian cinema has been quite acclaimed in international circles as it journeys through the genre of the *chanchadas* with its interface with Hollywood cinema in the early twentieth century to a phase of deeper engagements with human conditions in diverse contexts as part of the 'Cinema Novo' right to the contemporary times (King, 1998).

The Russian cinema industry has had a formidable history and has produced one of the most critically acclaimed films of our times made by renowned filmmakers and which have been internationally recognised. The thematic area, the treatment of the subject in Russian cinema, has been closely tied to the different phases of Russian history and influenced its aesthesis. In the present times, films with a more subjective focus are being produced in Russia, reflective of the times (Strukov, 2016).

South African cinema has to be seen in close conjunction with the colossus of the apartheid and the enormity of the social tasks of the post-apartheid period with which South Africa still grapples, namely, the question of race and extreme social and economic disparity and coming to terms with the process of reconciliation (Kruger, 2011).

Cinema in all five BRICS countries has had its own peculiarity of space in close conjunction with time. This cinematic space has intertextual relations with the rest of the world. The space of cinema and the modes of its production and consumption have been as much sites of perpetuation of inequity and oppression as they have been of subversion of the oppressive discourse. Cinema as a cultural product combines a plethora of artistic media resulting in a very potent delivery system of ideas that are not dependent exclusively on the linguistic sign but instead use a whole lot of other signs that draw from the sensory universe of human beings. The films speak, as it is said, in a 'cinematic language' negotiated through the gaze of that singular innovation of the late nineteenth century, the moving image camera.

It would be still too early to talk of 'BRICS cinema' any differently from the 'cinema of the BRICS countries'. Nonetheless, it could be an important area of future collaboration that could lead to the formation of one. In the formal BRICS architecture of collaboration, there already exists a recently created space called the BRICS film festival where films from the five nations compete and get showcased. The idea of collaboration in the area of cinema and its study can be further boosted by the formation of a BRICS Film Institute in the future. Given the rich legacy of cinematic production in BRICS, it could act as a hub of the best talents in this area in BRICS countries and create a site for technological and creative exchange of ideas in this field of art. It could ultimately boost a look to the South cultural policy that could create a space for these national cinemas to act in synergy and underscore the visual representation of the lived lives of people in the Global South.

Similarly, in other fields of artistic production also, there exist possibilities of synergising the creative space, which would not merely echo the intentions of the various governments but also give voice to the aspirations of people at large, which takes into consideration human stories of dealing with humongous problems that the large majority of populations in these countries face on a daily basis and bring them to the fore. This could happen in the field of literature, performance arts, especially theatre, media, and so on, besides cinema, for it is the pulsating thrust of real people-to-people exchange of experience which will finally underline how we make meaning of the BRICS culture.

Conclusions

Several phases can be observed in the chequered journey of BRICS so far. At the time of its formation and until several years after, BRICS looked formidable and every bit the challenger to the world order. A lot of institution-building was accomplished and there were dreams of fashioning more robust financial instruments to reduce dependency on the Bretton Woods institutions. The regime change in some BRICS countries sent signals of instability about the originally envisaged thrust areas and produced considerable hopelessness among the votaries of the BRICS idea. However, the crisis of the North itself provided reason for BRICS to continue its course together, even in the face of acute incongruences.

The term aesthesis helps us to relate the cultural and the artistic with the realm of perception and the generation of meaning. The contemporary world of late capitalism is a complex space where the symbolic system is frequently subjected to the risk of losing the referent. The intersection of technology, desire, power and inequality is a hallmark of our world where new sites of subjugation and its contestation are constantly being created. The new media cultures create constant and simultaneous linkages between social media, cinema, art and literature. The possibility of each one of them serving as an intertext to each other allows for the creation of the hyper real, or post truth as some might say, to be consumed in a variety of ways. Such a creation of post truth or hyper real is not an organic event but is a carefully designed product of human agency as are the ways of its subversion, utilising similar cultural spaces. It can be observed that there are many layers through which the BRICS idea becomes intelligible. One perspective could be the one that looks at BRICS from the outermost surface, the megascape of BRICS as a formation of nation states from the Global South coming together for mutual benefits in a world witnessing a crisis of credibility on the side of the dominant order. At this particular level, the BRICS project has been able to create a heterotopia, a counter space, which acts contrapuntal to the hegemonic North that has had a history of colonising and plundering territories causing huge parts of the world to be relegated to poverty and want. At another level of perspective, which is more inward-looking, BRICS looks like a space like any other where the BRICS governments themselves seem to favour the elite and do not follow policy that they themselves expect or espouse when they are at the outer/heterotopic level. It is, nonetheless, felt that owing to the heterotopia created by the outer level, an emancipatory vision is engendered, which ultimately enables the creation of institutions that might reduce inequality and discrimination and help people to have better living conditions. The BRICS institutions for collaboration in the field of education and culture could foment a people-to-people exchange that would enable them to learn from each other's experiences and highlight commonalities of struggle against poverty, discrimination and oppression, whether it is within or without. In short, in spite of the obvious limitations of BRICS, the idea of southernity can be a takeaway.

Notes

1 The taxonomy deviates from the 'normal' order of things in that it classifies animals in subsets that are quite impossible to bring together in any parametric unity. Some examples of these mutually incompatible divisions are 'belonging to the emperor', 'embalmed', 'tame',' fabulous', 'etc.', 'mermaids', 'frenzied', 'drawn with a very fine camelhair brush',' having just broken the water pitcher' and so on. The fictional taxonomy in a way upsets the fundamentals of our cognitive system.
2 Rafael Alberti in his work 'On painting' talks about integrating the concept of *istoria* (word of Greek origin essentially meaning story) with painting, underpinning the presence of non-verbal narratives as part of the larger narrative system.
3 Broadly, the conceptualisation of an alternative in opposition to the prevailing/dominant one.

References

Ahern, Mal. 2003. 'Performance/Performativity', in *The Chicago School of Media Theory*. The University of Chicago, lucian.uchicago.edu, accessed on 21 November 2021.

Benjamin, Walter. 1969. Hannah Arendt (eds.), *Illuminations*, translated by Harry Zohn. New York: Schocken Book.

Bond, Patrik and Ana Garcia (eds.). 2015. *BRICS, An Anti-capitalist Critique*. United Kingdom, London: Pluto Press.

Borges, Jorge Luis. 1952. 'Otras Inquisiciones'. https://apuntesliterarios.files.wordpress.com/2013/09/borges_otras_inquisiciones.pdf, accessed on 21 November 2021.

Campbell, Charles. 2001. 'Representation and Unrepresentable', *Journal of Dramatic Theory and Criticism*, 15(2), Spring, pp. 49–67.

Degaut, Marcos. October 2015. *Do the BRICS Still Matter? Foreword by Carl Meacham, A Report of the CSIS Americas Program*. Centre for Strategic and International Studies, csis.org, accessed on 10 December 2020.

Dillon, Elizabeth Maddock. 2016. 'Atlantic Aesthesis: Books and "Sensus Communis" in the New World', *Early American Literature*, 51(2), Special Issue, pp. 367–395 University of North Carolina. www.jstor.org/stable/43946751, accessed on 21 November 2021.

Eagleton, Terry and Drew Milne (eds.). 2005. *Marxist Literary Theory*. United Kingdom, Oxford: Blackwell Publishing.

Foucault, Michel. 1971, 1994. *The Order of Things: An Archaeology of Human Sciences*, Translated from Les Mots et les Choses. New York: Vintage Books.

Frank, Andre Gunder. 1978. *World Accumulation, 1492–1789*. New York: Monthly Review Press.

Harvey, David. 1990. 'Between Space and Time: Reflections on the Geographical Imagination', *Annals of the Association of American Geographers*, 80(3), pp. 418–434. www.jstor.org/stable/2563621, accessed on 7 March 2021.

hooks, bell. 1989. 'Choosing the Margin as a Space for Radical Openness', *Framework: The Journal of Cinema and Media*, 36, pp. 15–23. jstor.org/stable/44111660

III Meeting of the BRICS Education Ministers Moscow Declaration, Moscow, 18 November 2015. www.brics-info.org/%E2%85%A2-meeting-of-the-brics-education-ministers-moscow-declaration/, accessed on 21 November 2021.

Jennings, Michael W. and Tobias Wilke. 2010. 'Editors' Introduction Walter Benjamin's Media Tactics: Optics, Perception, and the Work of Art', *Grey Room*, 39, pp. 6–10. www.jstor.org/stable/27809423, accessed on 21 November 2021.

King, John (reviewed by). 1998. 'Brazilian Cinema by Randal Johnson and Robert Stam', *Journal of Latin American Studies*, 30(2), Cambridge University Press, pp. 451–452. www.jstor.org/stable/15863, accessed on 21 October 2021.

Kruger, L. 2011. 'Media and Identity in Africa, ed. Kimani Njogu and John Middleton, Cinema in a Democratic South Africa, by Lucia Saks', *Research in African Literatures*, 42(1), pp. 192–194.

Levander, Caroline and Walter Mignolo. 2011. 'The Global South and World Dis/Order', *The Global South*, 5(1), Indiana University Press, pp. 1–11. www.jstor.org/stable/10.2979/globalsouth.5.1.1, accessed 21 November 2021.

Massey, Doreen. 2005. *For Space*. London: SAGE Publications.

Noort, Carolijn van. 2017. 'Study of Strategic Narratives: The Case of BRICS', *Politics and Governance*, 5(3), pp 121–129: Cogitatiopress.com, accessed on 21 November 2021.

O'Niell, Jim. 2001. 'Building Better Global Economic BRICs', Goldman Sachs, Global Economics Paper No. 66, goldmansachs.com, accessed on 2 October 2021.

Panja, Shormishtha, Shirshendu Chakrabarti and Christel Devadawson (eds.). 2009. *Word, Image, Text: Studies in Literary and Visual Culture*. New Delhi: Orient Blackswan.

Poster, Mark (ed.). 2001. *Jean Baudrillard, Selected Writings*. Stanford: Stanford University Press.

Quijano, Anibal. 1992. 'Colonialidad y Modernidad/Racionalidad', *Perú Indígena*, 13(29), pp. 11–20.

Roselle, Laura, Alister Miskimmon, and Ben O'Loughlin. March 2014. 'Strategic Narrative: A New Means to Understand Soft Power', *Media War and Conflict*, 7(1), pp. 70–84, SAGE Publications: Reasearchgate.net, accessed on 1 December 2020.

Said, Edward. 1978.1995. *Orientalism*. India: Penguin Books.

Schwarzman, Simon, Romulo Pinheiro and Pundy Pillay (eds.). 2015. *Higher Education in the BRICS Countries, Investigating the Pact between Higher Education and Society*. Dordrecht: Springer.

Soja, Edward W. 1996, *Thirdspace: Journeys to Los Angeles and Other Real-and-Imagined Places*. Oxford: Blackwell.

Storey, John (ed.). 1998. 'Raymond Williams "Analysis of culture"', in *Cultural Theory and Popular Culture, A Reader*, pp. 48–56, University of Georgia Press amherst.edu, accessed on 10 December 2020.

Strukov, Vlad. 2016. *Contemporary Russian Cinema: Symbols of a New Era*. Edinburgh: Edinburgh UP.

Talib, Nurliyana Mohd, Rozia Sidik, and Mat Sidek dan Nabihah Liyana Salan. 2012. 'Innovation of Map Invention in the Islamic civilization', *Journal of Applied Sciences Research*, 8(1), pp. 321–325 researchgate.net, accessed on 10 March 2021.

Vidler, Anthony, Michel Foucault and Pamela Johnston. 2014. 'Heterotopias', *AA Files*, No.69, Architectural Association School of Architecture, pp. 18–22, Stable URL: www.jstor.org/stable/43202545, accessed on 23 March 2021.

Willems, Wendy. 2014. 'Beyond Normative Dewesternization: Examining Media Culture from the Vantage Point of the Global South', *The Global South*, 8(1), pp. 7–23. www.jstor.org/stable/10.2979/globalsouth.8.1.7, accessed on 10 December 2020.

Zhang, Y. 2010. 'Transnationalism and Translocality in Chinese Cinema'. *Cinema Journal*, 49(3), pp. 135–139. www.jstor.org/stable/40800746, accessed on 10 December 2020.

PART II

Member States and Their Interests in BRICS

9

BRAZIL AND BRICS

Bruno De Conti, Édivo de Almeida Oliveira and Júlio Vicente Cateia

Background

All discussions regarding BRICS have necessarily to take into account the role of this group in the world economy, and the role it aims to have in the international arena in the future. These debates have been raised in many chapters in this book.[1] Dealing with the interests of each country in the BRICS, this part of the book allows us to go deeper into each country's history, society and economy. In this sense, it is crucial to start the analysis with a very objective and long-lasting reality: Brazil has been a Portuguese colony for more than three centuries.[2] More than that, its independence in 1822 was the result of a strategy of the Portuguese royal family, which left the King's son (Pedro I) as the Brazilian Emperor.[3] This means that Brazil has been formally subordinated to Portugal for four centuries.[4] Since Portugal in the nineteenth century was heavily under the influence of England, we may state that Brazil was also an informal colony of the British.

Bearing in mind that Brazil was not a unified country in its pre-colonial days, it is important to note that the constitution of a national economy in this territory was made for a very clear reason: the exploitation of the territory for the benefit of the metropolis. This is nothing new for those who are familiar with the history of exploited colonies in the world, but it is an inescapable preamble to properly comprehend the meaning of BRICS for Brazil, which requires discussions about its (current and potential) role in the world economy.

Hence, briefly reviewing its long colonial past is important to understand that the inclusion of Brazil in the world economy was for quite clear purposes. First, it was seen as a supplier of natural resources to Western Europe.[5] Second, it was considered a consumption market for manufactured goods produced in Western Europe. Third, it was seen as a source of high yields for investments made by the Europeans in Brazilian territory. Later on, the United States of America (USA),

DOI: 10.4324/9781003148074-11

after becoming the most important industrial country and the biggest economy in the world, joined the European countries in this asymmetrical relation with Brazil, benefiting from its cheap natural resources, its wide domestic market and its potential to provide high yields for foreign investments.[6] Because of this historical process, the Brazilian economy and society were shaped by what Caio Prado Jr (2011) names a 'sense of colonisation'. After all, the distribution of land (and wealth in general), and the labour market have been profoundly shaped by almost four centuries of slavery.[7] Furthermore, national institutions and economic relations in general – domestic and international – have been shaped by (and for) colonial purposes.[8]

In the twentieth century, there was an effort to transform the Brazilian production structure through an industrialisation process co-ordinated by the federal government. According to existing literature, the so-called development period started with President Getúlio Vargas in 1930 and finished with the 'External Debt Crisis' that hit Latin America in the 1980s. During this period, Brazil did succeed in developing a substantial industrial sector. However, external constraints were never overcome. In fact, the massive participation of foreign capital during the course of this industrialisation process[9] – notably during the military dictatorships from 1964 to 1985 – represented an external vulnerability that exploded with the international liquidity crisis after 1979. More specifically, when Paul Volcker, the head of US Federal Reserve, initiated a very contractionary monetary policy,[10] it resulted in massive capital movements from the peripheral countries[11] to the USA. These capital flights led to Mexico defaulting on its external debts in 1982, followed by many other Latin American countries, including Brazil, leading to the external debt crisis in the region that ended the 'development period'.[12]

Meanwhile, the ascent of neoliberal ideology in the Western Countries led to the recommendation (or almost imposition) of the Washington Consensus for Latin American countries in the 1990s.[13] Like many other countries in the world, Brazil started opening up its economy rapidly, both commercially and financially. Consequently, the industrial sector that had been established in the preceding period started facing a new reality in terms of higher competition from abroad. As a result, many industrial companies went bankrupt, some others were bought by foreign capital and many others started gradually replacing domestic production of intermediate goods with imports. That is, the industrial sector began to lose density and the process of the diversification of the national economy that had continued over a large part of the twentieth century was interrupted.

In the 1980s and 1990s, the external debt crisis and neoliberal policies resulted in very low economic dynamism. Nonetheless, the twenty-first century started with a new reality for Brazil. On the external front, renewed world economic dynamism – driven partly by China's growth – stimulated international trade. More specifically, the boom in commodity prices was very beneficial for the Brazilian economy.[14] Paradoxically, the historical role of Brazil as a supplier of primary commodities allowed it to increase its exports substantively (due to the favourable volumes and prices of exported goods). Internally, the governments of the Workers

Party[15] implemented some policies to foster the internal market, notably through some cash-transfer policies (the 'Bolsa Família' Program) and – more importantly – an increase in the minimum wage.

These developments revived economic growth in the Brazilian economy. While the growth rate was not as robust as it had been in the 1970s or comparable to the growth rates in China and India, it at least reversed the low and unstable growth trend of the previous two decades. Most importantly, this economic growth has been – unprecedentedly – allied to a reduction in income inequalities (the Gini index declined from 0.58 in 2003 to 0.53 in 2011) and an alleviation in the country's poverty levels (from 2003 to 2010, around 30 million persons crossed the poverty line). These good outcomes, associated with the charisma of President Luís Inácio Lula da Silva, contributed to create the image of Brazil as an 'emerging star' in the world economy. In this scenario, the aspirations for a new role in the international arena were quite natural; and the participation in BRICS was one of the important strategies to reach it.

Yet, despite the changes in its image throughout the world, no radical changes were implemented in Brazil's economic structure. The dependence on mineral and agricultural commodities continued to be high (or even higher) and the declining trend in their prices after 2011 reversed the whole situation. Notably from 2013 onwards, the combination of declining terms of exchange for international trade, with more volatility in international finances,[16] and the strengthening of internal political tensions[17] resulted in one of the deepest economic crises in Brazilian history, with adverse economic consequences.[18] Consequently, Brazil's aspirations in the world arena as well as its role within BRICS have dramatically changed in the last few years.

This chapter will focus on these two last periods, that is, the economic boom and the crisis, focusing on the implications of each phenomenon on the participation of Brazil in world economic and geopolitical debates, and especially its role in the construction and development of BRICS. The second section discusses the domestic discourse on BRICS; the third, Brazil's material and normative interests; the fourth, Brazil's economic co-operation with the other BRICS members; and the fifth, the country's politics regarding the Global South. The final section discusses Brazil's concerns regarding BRICS.

Domestic Discourse on BRICS

The discourse on BRICS in Brazil cannot be properly understood if it is not placed in the context of the entire framework of its external policy discourse. In this sense, it is important to highlight the important change in this regard that happened with the transition from Fernando Henrique Cardoso's (1995–2002) to Luís Inácio Lula da Silva's (2003–2010) governments.

Under Cardoso's mandates, the main objective of the external policy was the integration of the country in the so-called 'globalisation era' with the world economy, notably to increase the country's share in global trade and attract foreign capital inflows. Strictly following the recommendations of the 'Washington Consensus', Brazil at that time was moving forward towards the process of opening up its economy, both in the commercial and the financial accounts. In this process, the objective was to deepen the integration of Brazil with the world economy, without any real concern regarding the role Brazil would play. In a certain sense, Cardoso was loyal to his claims as a scholar, that Brazil would have to accept a position of dependency in the world economy – that is, Brazilian economic development should be somehow driven by external forces.[19] As a matter of fact, a project for the creation of an American Free Trade Association (AFTA) was under consideration, but was aborted due to strong domestic opposition, due to the perception that a free trade agreement with the USA would result in the deepening of heterogeneities between the two countries.[20]

When Lula, from the Workers' Party, took office in January 2003, the discourse immediately changed. The general framework within which the discourses for very diverse fields were developed was one of equality. In the internal sphere, this translated into discourses of a struggle to reduce poverty and hunger. In the international sphere, the watchword was the battle for more equal or egalitarian relations among countries.

Due to a very favourable international environment – notably resulting from the extremely high economic growth in China and, in association with it, to the boom in commodity prices – Brazilian economic growth from 2004 to 2010 was quite high (on an average around 4% annually). This economic growth, combined with a significant reduction in poverty levels, engendered in the world a feeling that Brazil was 'taking off'.[21] After decades of social and economic crises, the general belief was that Brazil had set the pace for a very bright future. Obviously, the government took advantage of this good milieu to explore a discourse of success and power. Allied to the charisma of President Lula, it contributed to building an image of Brazil as an 'emerging star' in the international arena, resulting, for instance, in the selection of the country to host the Football World Cup and the Olympic Games.

Utilising this image, the government also explored the idea that Brazil could be one of the leaders of the peripheral countries that were paving the way to development. Within this framework, the official discourse was one of keeping good relation with the rich countries, but most significantly prioritising relationships with the so-called 'Global South'. One of the architects of this appealing discourse was Celso Amorim, the Minister of Foreign Affairs at that time. More than just a discourse, specific policies were designed for Brazil's relations with other peripheral countries, resulting in a considerable increase in international trade relations with many of these countries. Minister Amorim repeatedly stated that Brazil had to embrace an 'active and perky' foreign policy, be a protagonist in the development of co-operation between the peripheral countries and in the construction of a more equal world.[22]

Within this framework, specific discourses were developed for the different regions of the Global South. For Latin America, the watchword was integration, in a rare context in which most of the Southern American countries were under left-wing governments.[23] Lula explored the idea of being close friends with Hugo

Chávez in Venezuela, Evo Morales in Argentina, Rafael Correa in Equador, the Kirchner couple in Argentina, Tabaré Vazques and later José Mujica in Uruguay, and Michelle Bachellet in Chile to create a proper context for integration. In spite of this discourse, Brazil's attitude regarding Latin American integration was quite ambiguous and, with regard to some initiatives, the general perception was that Brazil was hindering the process (e.g. for the Southern Bank, proposed by Chávez).

Regarding the African continent, Brazil also developed a very appealing discourse, stating that over its entire history, its connections with Africa had been very strong. As a matter of fact, for more than three centuries, millions of Africans had been forcefully taken to Brazil as slaves. Consequently, a large part of the Brazilian population has African roots and the country's culture is totally embedded in the African one. In this case, the discourse was followed by some important policies that resulted in the inauguration of new Brazilian Embassies in many African countries and in a sharp increase in commerce with this continent. Yet, among these, the privileged countries were the Portuguese-speaking ones (notably Angola).

In fact, the discourse regarding BRICS and Brazil's role within it have been part of this whole framework of the new discourse on its foreign policy. In this sense, the idea of BRIC – later BRICS – was a total fit in this general picture. First, by appearing besides Russia, India, and China, Brazil was consolidating its image as one of the world's 'emerging stars'. It has been quite suitable for the Brazilian government to take advantage of Brazil having been chosen by Jim O'Neill to take part in a select group of countries that were seen as potentially lucrative economies for financial investments and to integrate into and actively work for this bloc.

Second, in the quest for good partnerships with countries of the 'Global South', developing co-operation with so many large and important countries – and especially with China – was obviously a very beneficial strategy. Following the general discourses of BRIC as a group, Brazilian official posture has never been one of disdain as regards the relationships with the core countries, but rather of diversifying its economic relations.

Third, by adhering to BRIC, Brazil could intensify the discourse of being actively struggling for a new international order. Again, Brazilian discourse – similar to the one of the group as a whole – has never been one of confrontation with the core countries or the Western multilateral institutions. On the contrary, the argument was that the world was changing with the rise of some big economies, and the international order – including the multilateral institutions – should adapt to this new reality, giving more attention to these emerging countries' claims and necessities. This clearly matches the discourse of a 'more equal world'.

Finally, BRICS was also useful for the Brazilian discourse on the beauty of diversity. The pictures of the five heads of state are very illustrative of world diversity, showing people with different phenotypes united for a common cause. During Dilma Rousseff's government, this picture could also show the important presence of a woman among the countries' leaders.

Unfortunately, much of this discourse has changed after the coup d'état in Brazil (2016). Michel Temer, who replaced Rousseff, made a very sharp move backwards with regard to foreign policy, by explicitly stating that Brazil should prioritise relations with the United States of America and Western Europe. Suddenly, the idea of fostering relations with Southern countries was abandoned; official declarations indicated that Brazil would sign a free-trade agreement with the European Zone even if it required the abandonment of the Mercosur (the Southern American common market). Embassies in many African countries were closed; the offices of the Brazilian Development Bank (BNDES) in Johannesburg and Montevideo were also shut down. Brazil's foreign policy entered a new era, with the priority being the adhesion to the Organisation for Economic Co-operation and Development (OECD).

Starting in 2019, Bolsonaro's government has moved in the same direction, with a foreign policy that is even more oriented to gratify the USA. The explicit strategic allies are currently Israel and Japan, besides the USA. During the electoral campaign – and clearly imitating Donald Trump – Bolsonaro has made embarrassing declarations against China. Once in office, he obviously had to change his attitude to keep good relations with Brazil's most important partner in international trade.[24] For the same reason, the discourse regarding BRICS has been rather diplomatic. The discourses on equality, diversity and the ascent of the Global South, and the creation of a new international order, therefore, have been abandoned in favour of a discourse that focused on trade and investments with select countries. This topic will be further discussed later, but it is worthwhile alluding to it before a discussion on the material and normative interests of Brazil in BRICS.

Material and Normative Interests

The discussions on government discourses about BRICS may already indicate that from the moment of its implementation to the current situation, Brazilian interests in BRICS have been quite diversified. The period in which these interests were widest and most intense was during Dilma Rousseff's government (2011–2016).

In fact, the foreign policy in Lula and Dilma's governments had elements of continuity[25] as well as differences, in a process called by Stuenkel (2016) as 'containment in continuity'. In the Lula administration, Brazil assumed a greater political role in debates related to international conflicts and even in conciliation efforts[26] that also reflected its views on the role that BRICS should play in the world arena. In Dilma's government, the prevailing perspective was that the BRICS should not give great centrality to discussions related to security crises, since it would be in matters of this nature that the greatest conflicts of positions and interests among its members would be observed. It felt that the group should focus on economic and technological issues that would be of mutual interest. This in no way meant a conflict with the view that BRICS could be an important forum for a gradual change in the international geopolitical framework – as would be the case with Temer and Bolsonaro, which are discussed subsequently. However, there was a pragmatic attitude to prioritising economic and technological interests, the results of which could be more immediate but which could contribute in the long run to the goals of building a new global order.

Hence, bilateral relations between Brazil and the other members of BRICS – as well as with other blocs formed by the peripheral countries – have advanced significantly during the Dilma Rousseff government. Particularly noteworthy are the results achieved from the agreements that Brazil signed at the 5th Durban Summit in South Africa in 2013, as well as at the 6th Fortaleza Summit the following year. This resulted in 56 new bilateral acts and partnerships between Brazil and China, as well as two initiatives of profound importance for the future of the BRICS coalition: the Contingent Reserve Arrangement (CRA), with US$100 billion, and the New Development Bank (NDB), with a starting capital of US$100 billion (Becard, Barros-Platiau, and Oliveira, 2015).

Simultaneously, the Dilma Government felt that the most viable strategy for the mutual development of the BRICS countries would be to formulate jointly long-term strategies, encouraging each member country to share with the others its strategies in terms of markets, sectors and product types that would be prioritised. The purpose was to optimise and enable the development of medium- and long-term strategies in a multilateral manner, by increasing the capacity for adaptability of each member to the strategic interests of the other partners, rather than simply competing in the same markets (Becard, Barros-Platiau, and Oliveira, 2015).[27]

From the Brazilian perspective, for example, it would be interesting to develop partnerships through which other BRICS members could benefit from the know-how of its institutions and companies in areas such as biofuels, sustainable development, biotechnology and the treatment of tropical diseases. According to the Brazilian government, these partnerships could promote relevant results, both in the productive and social dimensions.[28]

At BRICS Summit meetings, Brazil had also been resolutely asking for the expansion of direct investments among the participants, provided such investment is compliant with the principles of sustainable development, arguing that this would generate greater productivity and quality of life for the population (IPEA, 2014). Throughout the Workers Party governments, the Brazilian authorities have made efforts to establish co-operative standards that help increase productivity and technological progress and incorporation. More specifically, it was understood that it would be important for the Brazilian economy to establish partnerships with other BRICS that would result in investments in infrastructure, logistics, energy and high-tech sectors.

The widely accepted diagnosis among authorities and policy makers – particularly during the Dilma Government – was that Brazilian actions in the BRICS should prioritise a vigorous move towards higher value-added segments in global chains, enabling the country to reduce its dependence on commodity exports and reverse the ongoing deindustrialisation process.[29] From this unfolds the Brazilian interest in prioritising the establishment of agreements with other BRICS partners based on the development of higher value added industrial and primary productive activities, based on greater technological content through co-operative projects, which improve the organisational and technical capacities of some important national players in strategic productive segments.

In parallel, the Dilma administration defended the need for China to assume the responsibility of providing this kind of co-operation, not only within BRICS, but also with other countries. Of course, such a transformation would require a paradigm shift from China in its relationship with the peripheral countries and, consequently, with the Brazilian economy.

Large Chinese corporations have been pursuing an aggressive strategy of expanding their international investments in the peripheral countries, Brazil being an important destination for these business networks. At the same time, the Brazilian economy has not succeeded in entering new international markets, particularly China, for non-resource intensive exports. Consequently, Brazil is increasing not only its technological dependence on other countries, but also its dependence on exports of agriculture and mineral goods. During the Dilma government, this difficulty was a source of great dissatisfaction, with concern about the ongoing deindustrialisation process in the country.

Brazilian manufactured goods, being unable to compete with Chinese-made products, have eventually been displaced in Brazilian markets. In addition, there is a gradual but perceptibly significant shift in the profile of Chinese exports to Brazil towards an increasingly sophisticated commodity range, including aircraft, electronics, biotechnology and nanotechnology products, among others (Shambaugh, 2013).

During the preparatory meetings for the 2014 bilateral summit between Brazil and China, Brazil put forward a series of demands to deepen the complementarity in Sino-Brazilian trade. The Brazilian representatives indicated some areas that they understood to be strategic for the country, but which would also serve Chinese interests, namely, wind energy, photovoltaic technology, technology for the reduction of carbon emission and the use of charcoal in the production of iron and steel ore, auto parts, productive investments in the Manaus Free Zone, and automation of financial services. In addition, Brazil also put pressure on Chinese representatives to further open their markets to some Brazilian primary products such as beef and corn sugar (Becard, Barros-Platiau, and Oliveira, 2015).

Some of these demands were met, especially on the occasion of the visit of Chinese President Xi Jinping to Brazil for bilateral meetings and the BRICS Summit in Fortaleza in 2014. Various acts were signed, in several areas and China committed to the acquisition of 60 Brazilian EMB 190 jets (MRE, 2014). In addition, it agreed to a significant reduction in tariffs on Brazilian soybean oil, suspension of the embargo on Brazilian beef, and the implementation of the partnership between Eletrobrás and Furnas with Chinese companies China Three Gorges Corporation, CWEI and the State Grid Corporation of China (SGCC).

Moreover, partnerships between the Brazilian group Schahin and ICBC Reasing were implemented for the construction of oilrigs and a memorandum of understanding and other agreements were signed to allow credit operations between the Brazilian company Vale, the Bank of China and the Chinese Eximbank. In addition, Brazil took the opportunity to show its interest in implementing joint operations to build 'smart power distribution grids', and in the development of wind and solar energy technologies (Becard, Barros-Platiau, and Oliveira, 2015).

The Dilma government had also shown deep interest in substantially expanding the satellite launching programme held between the two nations through the joint development of Sino-Brazilian remote sensing satellites, coupled with the China-Brazil Earth Resources Satellites (CBERS)' technical co-operation. Between 1990 and 2000, this programme had already launched two satellites (CBERS – 1 in 1999 and CBERS – 2B launched in 2007), with a 70:30 division of responsibilities between China and Brazil. From 2013, the responsibilities for the initiatives undertaken were revised to 50% to be assumed by each country, enabling the launch of the CBERS – 3 satellite, whose failure precipitated the launch of the satellite called CBERS – 4 in the following year. These satellite launches were considered as a case of success in high-tech co-operation between peripheral countries, representing one of the most successful initiatives on state-of-the-art technological development among undeveloped economies (Pires, Paulino, and Cunha, 2015).

With the impeachment of President Dilma Rousseff, everything changed.[30] In the Temer and Bolsonaro governments, there is, in fact, an abandonment of Brazilian interests in building a less heterogeneous world or in contributing to the rise of the Global South. As discussed in the second section, the foreign policy objective has rather moved towards deepening relations with the USA.

It would not be frivolous to say that the entire economic and foreign policy strategy conceived of and implemented during the Lula and Dilma governments, whose efforts were fundamental for the creation and expansion of the bloc, finds no resonance in the Bolsonaro government. The signals given by the minister of economy and the minister of foreign affairs – Paulo Guedes and Ernesto Araújo, respectively – suggest the deliberate intention of neglecting Brazil's relations and participation within the economic blocs formed by peripheral countries and of deepening the integration of the Brazilian economy with the central countries, especially the USA.

Regarding BRICS, there remain only the most immediate economic interests: an increase in trade flows and in investments into Brazil (apart from collaborating in the process of privatisation of public companies, which is an important part of the current economic programme). In either case, there is no clear concern articulated about the type of trade or the sectors to which investments are to be directed. In line with the principles of comparative advantage, these governments consider it natural and beneficial for Brazil to continue to specialise in natural resources, importing high technology and value-added goods. There exists no interest in changing the current framework of trade relations (which will be shown in the next section); the focus is entirely on increasing trading volumes.

Brazil's Economic Co-operation with the Other Members

In the twentieth century, Brazil's economic co-operation with the other BRICS members was not very significant. Trade flows with these countries were at low levels not just due to the geographic distance but also on account of the type of exported goods. Similarly, investments from and in Russia, India, China and South Africa were negligible, especially in the last century.

Thus, the inclusion of Brazil in the BRICS posed, among others, the challenge of making Brazil more commercially and productively integrated with the Chinese, Indian, Russian and South African economies. However, since its inception, the BRICS coalition has resulted in very positive advances in terms of deepening Brazil's trade relations with other members of the bloc. This may be attributed to the efforts of the Lula (2003–2010) and Dilma (2011–2016) governments in bringing the Brazilian economy closer to other peripheral economies, but one may not ignore that part of this success is just the result of the impressive growth of the Chinese economy and its foreign trade.

The magnitude of the progress made in Brazil's trade integration with the other members of BRICS can be seen by comparing the trade flows established between the Brazilian economy and the various economic blocs relevant to its trade balance. Table 9.1 shows that Brazilian exports and imports in relation to the BRICS countries grew at an unprecedented pace in the beginning of this century. From 2000 to 2018, Brazil's trade flow with other BRICS members grew from US$4.31 billion to an impressive US$113.56 billion. This means that in Brazil's total international trade in goods, only 3.9% was with the BRICS in 2000, while it had risen to 27.0% in 2018. For trade balance vis-à-vis the BRICS countries too, the figures are impressive, rising from a negative trade balance of US$ −0.27 billion in 2000 to US$28.7 billion in 2018; this means that in 2018, 49.5% of Brazil's total trade surplus was due to trade with BRICS countries.

Such growth is mainly attributable to China's rapid growth and the consolidation of Brazil's role as a natural resource provider for that country. Table 9.2 shows the evolution of China's importance for Brazilian international trade from 2000 to 2017. In fact, since the 1930s, the USA had been Brazil's main trading partner, but it has been displaced by China since 2009. In the most recent period, Russia and

TABLE 9.1 Brazilian international trade (US$ billion), 2000 and 2018

Economic bloc	*Exp. 2000*	*Imp. 2000*	*Exp + Imp*	*Exp – Imp*	*Exp. 2018*	*Imp. 2018*	*Exp + Imp*	*Exp – Imp*
USA	13.16	12.91	26.07	0.25	28.7	28.97	57.67	−0.27
European Union	15.34	14.52	29.86	0.82	42.11	34.76	76.87	7.35
Latin America and Caribbean	14.1	11.97	26.07	2.13	40.83	28.21	69.04	12.62
Asia (excluding the Middle East)	6.33	8.65	14.98	-2.32	93.18	59.26	152.44	33.92
Middle East	1.33	1.56	2.89	-0.23	9.87	5.18	15.05	4.69
Africa	1.34	2.9	4.24	-1.56	8.1	6.6	14.7	1.5
BRICS	2.02	2.29	4.31	-0.27	71.13	42.43	113.56	28.7
MERCOSUR	7.73	7.81	15.54	-0.08	20.83	13.37	34.2	7.46
World	55.02	55.89	110.91	0.87	239.26	181.23	420.49	58.03

Source: Comtrade. Authors' elaboration.

TABLE 9.2 Brazilian exports, by destinations (2000 and 2017)

2000			*2017*		
Destination	*US$ Billion*	*Share (%)*	*Destination*	*US$ Billion*	*Share (%)*
1° USA	13.19	23.9	1° China	48	22
2° Argentina	6.27	11.3	2° USA	25.1	11
3° The Netherlands	2.79	5.1	3° Argentina	17.8	8.1
4° Germany	2.52	4.6	4° The Netherlands	7.57	3.5
5° Japan	2.47	4.5	5° Germany	6.18	2.8
6° Italy	2.15	3.9	6° Japan	6.72	2.6
7° Belgium	1.79	3.2	7° Chile	5.32	2.4
8° France	1.73	3.1	8° India	4.88	2.2
9° Mexico	1.71	3.1	9° Mexico	4.81	2.2
10° UK	1.50	2.7	10° Spain	4.13	1.9
11° Chile	1.25	2.3	11° Italy	3.62	1.7
12° China	1.09	2	12° South Korea	3.25	1.5
13° Spain	1.01	1.8	13° Belgium	3.15	1.4
14° Provision for Airplanes	0.94	1.7	14° UK	3.02	1.4
15° Paraguay	0.83	1.5	15° Russia	3.01	1.4
16° Venezuela	0.75	1.4	16° France	2.8	1.3
17° Uruguay	0.67	1.2	17° Egypt	2.73	1.2
18° South Korea	0.58	1.1	18° Saudi Arabia	2.66	1.2
19° Canada	0.57	0.9	19° Hong Kong	2.64	1.2
20° Colombia	0.51	0.9	20° Canada	2.61	1.2
Subtotal – Top 20	**44.3**	**80**	**Subtotal – Top 20**	**160**	**72.2**
Total	**55.1**	**100**	**Total**	**219**	**100**

Source: Ministério do Desenvolvimento, Indústria e Comércio Exterior (MDIC). Authors' elaboration.

India have also come to rank among the top 15 destinations for Brazilian exports. South Africa's absence on this list signals the still existing space for further trade integration between these two economies.

Between 2000 and 2015, with the exception of only two years (2000 and 2008), Brazil's trade balance with the other BRICS members was considerably positive, notably due to the impressive increase in the international demand for agricultural and mineral commodities (Table 9.3). This denotes the significant importance acquired by the bloc for the performance and sustainability of Brazil's external accounts over the period considered.

Nevertheless, the benefits to Brazil of this scenario should not be exaggerated. After all, it is important to highlight the significant discrepancy between the degree of technology embedded in the goods exported and imported by the Brazilian economy in intra-BRICS trade (Table 9.4). Between 2000 and 2016, at least 80% of Brazilian annual imports from these economies corresponded to products considered to be of medium or high degree of technology. However, 70 per cent of Brazilian annual sales to these economies consisted of primary or low technology products.

TABLE 9.3 Brazilian trade balance with BRICS (US$ bi)

Year	*Exports*	*Imports*	*Balance*
2000	2.02	2.29	−0.26
2001	3.71	2.62	1.09
2002	4.9	2.74	2.17
2003	7.32	3.39	3.93
2004	8.79	5.34	3.45
2005	12.26	7.62	4.64
2006	14.25	10.84	3.4
2007	17.2	17.02	0.18
2008	24.03	27.71	−3.68
2009	28.55	19.95	8.6
2010	39.74	32.5	7.24
2011	53.41	42.73	10.68
2012	51.71	42.93	8.78
2013	53.97	47.06	6.9
2014	50.5	47.5	3
2015	43.03	36.54	6.49
2016	41.99	28.20	13.79
2017	56.39	33.40	22.99
2018	71.13	42.43	28.70

Source: Ministério do Desenvolvimento, Indústria e Comércio Exterior (MDIC). Authors' elaboration.

TABLE 9.4A Brazilian exports to BRICS countries, by the degree of technological intensity (% of total)

Degree of technology	*2000*	*2002*	*2004*	*2006*	*2008*	*2010*	*2012*	*2014*	*2016*
Primary goods	38.9	41.3	39.6	47.8	56.5	70.0	73.9	73.8	68.1
Low	34.5	38.6	38.2	33.3	28.8	21.4	16.6	18.2	21.7
Middle-Low	5.6	5.3	7.5	4.2	3.7	3.1	2.9	3.7	4.0
Middle-High	17.5	13.3	13.0	13.1	9.0	4.0	4.0	3.4	5.0
High	3.5	1.6	1.7	1.7	1.9	1.5	2.5	0.9	1.2

TABLE 9.4B Brazilian imports from BRICS, by the degree of technological intensity (% of total)

Degree of technology	*2000*	*2002*	*2004*	*2006*	*2008*	*2010*	*2012*	*2014*	*2016*
Primary goods	4.3	7.1	2.7	1.8	2.7	2.2	2.2	1.2	2.5
Low	11.2	9.7	9.7	11.0	10.8	13.1	14.4	13.7	13.0
Middle-Low	19.8	24.2	19.2	19.1	22.2	21.3	18.8	23.1	16.8
Middle-High	42.7	35.5	37.0	32.3	36.8	35.9	39.6	39.2	43.4
High	22.0	23.4	31.4	35.8	27.6	27.5	24.9	22.7	24.4

Source: Tamiosso, Massuquetti, and Azevedo (2018).

Table 9.5 shows the share of the ten most important components of Brazilian exports in 2000 and 2018. These data indicate a substantial increase in the degree of concentration of Brazilian exports in a smaller number of the most important products in its trade balance. In addition, it also signals the loss of market share for some important products over time. This denotes a certain movement towards 're-primarisation' of the country's exports during the considered period.

Thus, Brazil has exports highly concentrated in a few commodity groups, largely dominated by resource-intensive ones, revealing a critical concentration on low value-added commodities, and this reality is manifested in its trade relationship with the BRICS countries. In contrast, Brazilian imports from its BRICS partners, despite the low diversification, are characterised by a higher share of more technologically sophisticated commodities (Table 9.6). The only exception is South Africa, with whom Brazil has succeeded in having more homogeneous trade in terms of technological sophistication, but trade volumes between these two countries are still very low.

Hence, from a Brazilian perspective, despite the unquestionable results achieved under the BRICS grouping, there is still a wide range of possibilities for advancing the process of production and trade integration among the bloc's economies. One way of looking at intra-BRICS trade, provided by Schor and Onuki (2015), is through the calculation of the Grubel–Lloyd Index[31] for trade between Brazil, India and South Africa.[32] This index allows the measurement of the degree of intra-industry or inter-industry trade flows established between different economies.

TABLE 9.5 Brazilian exports – main products (2000–2018)

2000		*2018*	
Product	*Share (%)*	*Product*	*Share (%)*
Airplanes	6.2	Soybeans	13.83
Iron ore and similar	5.5	Crude oil	10.47
Soybeans	4	Iron ore	6.96
Passenger cars	3.2	Chemical wood pulp	3.26
Radio receivers and transmitters	3.2	Other sugars	2.24
Soybean meal	3	Oilcake and other solid residues	2.17
Chemical wood pulp	2.9	Boned meat of bovine	1.88
Coffee beans	2.8	Cuts and edible offal of chicken	1.82
Shoes and similar	2.8	Non-roasted coffee	1.81
Semi-manufactured iron and steel	2.5	Maize grains	1.68
Sub Total of Top 10	36.1	**Sub Total of Top 10**	46.12

Source: Ministério do Desenvolvimento, Indústria e Comércio Exterior (MDIC). Authors' elaboration.

TABLE 9.6 Intra BRICS exports composition, 2017 (as percentage of total exports of exporting country to importing country)

Exporting Country	*Product*	*Importing country*				
		Brazil	*China*	*India*	*Russia*	*South Africa*
Brazil	Primary commodities		94%	80%	84%	51%
	Manufactured goods		6%	15%	16%	49%
China	Primary commodities	4%		4%	6%	5%
	Manufactured goods	96%		96%	94%	95%
India	Primary commodities	7%	49%		27%	31%
	Manufactured goods	93%	49%		72%	68%
Russia	Primary commodities	21%	88%	42%		66%
	Manufactured goods	79%	12%	45%		34%
South Africa	Primary commodities	44%	86%	86%	82%	
	Manufactured goods	55%	14%	13%	18%	

Source: Hiratuka (2019)

TABLE 9.7 Grubel–Lloyd Index

2000	*2013*
Brazil-USA (0.24)	Brazil-USA (0.25)
India-USA (0.16)	India-USA (0.21)
South Africa-USA (0.19)	South Africa-USA (0.20)
2013	
Brazil-India (0.11)	
Brazil-South Africa (0.12)	
India-South Africa (0.05)	

Source: Authors' elaboration, based in Schor e Onuki (2015).

The result tends to be zero when the trade is totally dominated by a strictly inter-industry character. Alternatively, the value of the index will be unitary when the analysed trade flow is fully characterised as intra-industrial, that is when it occurs within the same sectors.[33]

The results reported in Table 9.7 demonstrate not only the nature of trade between Brazil, India, and South Africa but also the nature of the trade relationship they establish with a large common trading partner – namely, the US economy. One of the inferences is that there is high potential for intra-industry trade between Brazil, South Africa, and India, which may carve a space for the future deepening of the relationship between these three economies.

Schor and Onuki (2015) also calculated the so-called Export Similarity Indices for South Africa, India, and Brazil. When the index is zero, the exports of the analysed countries are not coincident. However, the closer it is to unity, the more convergent is the foreign sales content of the countries considered.

The results shown in Table 9.7 suggest that the level of similarity in the exports of these countries does not appear to be critically high in either intra-bloc sales or sales to the US market. Thus, if Brazil's trade within BRICS is currently highly concentrated in China, there is potential for expanding these relations with India and South Africa as well.

The relationship between Brazil and China is even more complex and deserves a more detailed analysis. Between 2004 and 2011, the Brazilian economy performed quite favourably by growing, on average, more than 4% per year, combined with moderate levels of inflation, a favourable trade balance, and a substantial reduction in extreme poverty. One cannot deny that Brazil's satisfactory foreign and domestic performance had a profound connection with what was conventionally called the 'China Effect', due to the strong growth in Chinese demand for agricultural and mineral commodities. The importance of the Chinese market in this period was decisive for Brazil's trade balance, which allowed considerable accumulation of international reserves and loosened external constraints on domestic growth (Libânio, 2018).

Between 2003 and 2008, that is, before the outbreak of the global financial crisis, the average annual growth rate of Brazilian exports was 22% and the main determinant of this performance was, unquestionably, the accelerated expansion of Chinese demand for agricultural and mineral commodities, which had positive effects on both the quantum and international prices of these products. In 2004, the trade flow between the two economies was less than US$19 billion; since then it has been between US$60 and US$90 billion a year.

China's trade relations with Brazil have been a decisive factor contributing to Brazil's significant surpluses since 2002 (having been in deficit only in 2007 and 2008). However, it should be noted again that while Brazilian exports to China are mostly primary and resource-intensive manufactured products, China exports to Brazil manufactured and electronic products, with much a higher degree of technological sophistication (see Table 9.10).

Despite the high importance of the Chinese market for Brazil, it is important to realise that the nature of the Brazilian economy's commercial relationship with China corresponds to a process of 're-primarisation', or regressive specialisation,[34] of Brazil's export. That is, manufactured products were displaced in terms of importance in Brazilian exports by products intensive in natural resources. The strong penetration of and competition from Chinese products in Brazil aggravated this trend. Moreover, the trade surpluses reinforced the tendency of overvaluation of the national currency, which contributed even more to the deterioration of the external competitiveness of Brazil's industrial products. This appreciation of the Brazilian real was driven by strong foreign exchange inflows, catalysed by this relationship with China.[35] In other words, the trade relationship with China has contributed to the weakening of Brazilian industry directly through competition with local products and indirectly through its effect on the exchange rate.

Therefore, if the pattern of Sino-Brazilian trade interactions promotes dynamism, trade surpluses and accumulation of international reserves, it is important to understand that it also brings some challenges for the Brazilian economy. The key concerns pertain to the productive structure of Brazil, since trade occurs quite asymmetrically with China buying low value-added agricultural and mineral goods and selling manufactured goods, with a higher technological component and higher value added. It, therefore, is a relationship that is unfavourable for Brazil in terms of industrial dynamism, diversification and technological development. Changes in global trade due to Covid-19 theoretically could bring an opportunity for a reconfiguration of the Brazilian production structure, and a diversification of trading partners, but the negligent attitude of the Bolsonaro government towards all challenges imposed by the pandemic makes the future very uncertain.[36]

Finally, it is important to discuss Brazil's relationships within BRICS through foreign direct investments. As in trade, China is by far the most important source of FDI for Brazil. After the outbreak of the global financial crisis in particular, Chinese investments have increased significantly worldwide as well as in Brazil (Figure 9.1). Between 2004 and 2018, Chinese companies had invested in 104 projects worth US$60 billion in Brazil, with the expectation of implementing another 164 investment projects worth US$70 billion in the coming years (Libânio, 2018).[37]

Chinese investments in Brazil have been concentrated in resource-intensive sectors, which reinforces the dominance of primary goods in Brazilian exports. In the most recent period, there has been an increase in investments in industry[38] and services,[39] but from the point of view of the volume of investment, minerals or the infrastructure sector – notably electricity and water – still predominate (Table 9.8).

Another striking characteristic of Chinese investments in Brazil is the absolute preponderance of mergers and acquisitions. From 2003 to 2017, about 90% of the volumes were accounted for by mergers and acquisitions of Brazilian companies;

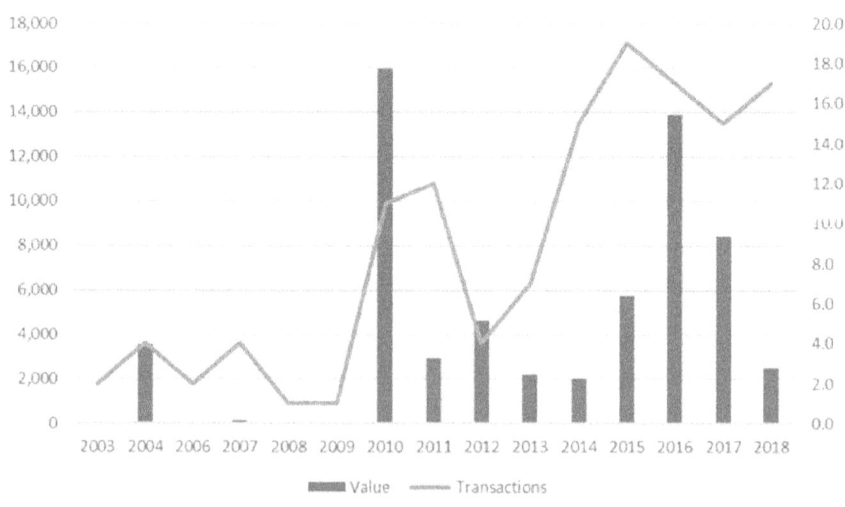

FIGURE 9.1 Chinese FDI in Brazil (US$ million, left axe; %, right axe), 2003–2018

Source: OFDI Monitor of China in Latin America/LAC-China Network. Authors' elaboration.

only 10% were greenfield investments (Hiratuka, 2019). Even if these merger and acquisition operations happen to result in business modernisation, they generally have a more limited effect on new job creation.[40]

From the point of view of Brazilian investments in the BRICS countries, there are unfortunately no recent data, but Table 9.9 shows that these are still negligible; for instance, in 2012, these amounted to a mere 0.10% of the total stock of Brazilian direct investments abroad.

As far as subsidiaries of Brazilian companies in BRICS countries is concerned, only China is relevant, ranking eighth in 2017 (Table 9.10). Given that at the beginning of the century, Brazilian investments in China were negligible, this result can be understood as progress towards greater integration between the countries, which is the result not just of Chinese dynamism, but also of the opening up of the Chinese market to Brazilian capital due to the agreements reached during the Lula and Dilma governments.[41] However, it is clear that the main destinations for Brazilian outward foreign direct investments (OFDI) are still the USA, Europe and Latin America.

TABLE 9.8 Chinese investments announced in Brazil, by sector

Sector	*Value (US$ million)*		
	2003–2009	*2010–2013*	*2014–2017*
Agriculture	0.0	59.5	400.0
Mining	3,960.0	21,630.0	9,564.0
Manufacturing	166.0	2,593.8	1,330.4
Infrastructure	257.7	3,318.4	16,728.0
Electricity and Water	0.0	3,087.4	14,754.0
Telecommunication	18.7	1.0	0.0
Construction	239.0	0.0	0.0
Transport/Storage	0.0	230.0	1,974.0
Financial Services	85.0	1,904.0	842.5
Trade	0.0	120.0	218.7
Other services	0.0	2.8	453.5
Total	4,468.7	29,628.5	29,537.1

Source: Hiratuka (2019)

TABLE 9.9 Intra BRICS FDI stock, 2012 (in US$ million)

Outward	*Total*	*BRICS*	*BRICS/Total*
Brazil	266.252	364	0.10%
China	531.941	12.282	2.30%
India	79.857	2.384	3.00%
Russia	406.295	1.524	0.40%
South Africa	111.780	24.639	22.00%
Total BRICS	1,396,125	41.193	3.00%

Source: De Conti and Hiratuka (2017)

TABLE 9.10 Countries with Brazilian companies (2017)

Position	*Country*	*Number of companies*
1	USA	44
2	Argentina	31
3	Mexico	24
4	Chile	21
4	Colombia	21
4	Peru	21
7	Uruguay	20
8	China	18
9	UK	15
10	Paraguay	14

Source: FDC Ranking. Authors' elaboration.

The top ranking Brazilian companies that established a branch in China are Embraer (aeronautics), Vale (mining), BR Foods and Marfrig (food), Marcopolo, Fras-be (auto parts) and Votorantin (cement). Among the smaller companies are Gerdau (steel industry), Suzano (pulp and paper), Riachuelo (clothing), Tramontina (household utilities), Soprano (hydraulic metallurgy), Oxiteno (solvent), Caloi (bicycles), and financial institutions such as Banco do Brasil, Banco Itaú-BBA and BTG Pactual (Pires, Paulino, and Cunha, 2015).

In sum, the data presented throughout this section suggest a greater integration of Brazilian economy with the other BRICS countries, but with a concentration of its exports on resource-intensive products, contrasting with the larger volumes of value-added goods it imports from these same partners. Thus, the space for the expansion of Brazil's trade integration with the other BRICS countries is definitely a front to be explored, especially expansion that is targeted at establishing an intra-BRICS trade relationship that stimulates the industrial and technological development of the participants, in particular the Brazilian economy itself.[42] A joint strategy of complementarity and technological development could generate advances both in the commercial and productive dimensions, the fruits of which may result in benefits not only for the Brazilian economy but for all members of the bloc.

Therefore, despite the substantial progress made in terms of trade integration between Brazil and the other BRICS countries, there exists a large spectrum of possibilities for deepening this relationship. The low level of similarity between Brazilian exports in relation to the Indian, Russian and South African exports is indicative of the viability of this greater integration. Hence, there is great potential for deepening Brazil's trade relations with Russia, India and South Africa.

Brazil and the Politics of the Global South

Since the 1990s, Brazil has adopted a foreign policy that may be conceptually defined as a 'pragmatic institutionalism', characterised by prioritising the establishment of national entities that work in partnership with international organisations to facilitate institutional co-operation with other nations (Leal and Moares, 2016). In the Lula government, contrary to what was observed in Fernando Henrique Cardoso government (1995–2002), foreign policy was based on four fundamental pillars, namely: i) search to be a protagonist country in geopolitical discussions, ii) defence of general reforms in multilateral organisations, iii) adoption of a regional leadership role in Latin America, and iv) huge efforts to foster the south-south relationship (Engstrom, 2012; Vigevani and Cepaluni, 2007).

These principles guided the Lula Government's actions in the international arena, and they is worth highlighting: (a) the deepening of the South American Community of Nations, (b) the prominent Brazilian action in the WTO negotiations in Doha, (c) the maintenance of a friendly relationship with advanced economies, including the USA, (d) the pressure for general reforms in the Security Council of the United Nations (UN), (e) the consolidation of a strong rapprochement with African countries, (f) the emphasis on social agendas within international governance bodies, and (g) the deepening of political and trade relations with other important emerging economies (Leal and Moraes, 2016).

The success achieved in reducing extreme poverty in Brazil – achieved through the 'Zero Hunger Programme' and other income transfer policies, coupled with a consistent policy of raising the minimum wage – was considered one of the most successful socio-economic development initiatives in the world. These results gave President Lula a prestigious international status, especially in forums dedicated to the reduction of misery in the world.

Because it has no territorial or border disputes, has abdicated the exploitation of nuclear technologies for military purposes,[43] and has a respected and recognised diplomatic corps, Brazil has been entrusted the task of peaceful resolution of conflicts (e.g. the UN Task Force in Haiti in 2004) by the UN.

At that time, Brazil began to claim a seat on the UN Security Council, now occupied by China and Russia, in addition to the USA, the United Kingdom and France (Fernandes and Cardoso, 2015). Especially in conjunction with South Africa and India, Brazil has been exerting constant international pressure to achieve greater participation not only in the UN but also in other multilateral institutions. It is no coincidence that these same countries were part of the IBSA (India, Brazil and South Africa) dialogue forum, which preceded BRICS in mobilising co-ordinated efforts to promote co-operation strategies (Stuenkel and India-Brazil-South Africa Dialogue Forum, 2014).

In fact, South–South technical co-operation[44] acquired great centrality in Brazilian foreign policy during the Lula Government (2003–2010).[45] During this period, the Brazilian government developed a strategy to strengthen trade and co-operation relations with African countries, and many bilateral agreements were established with sub-Saharan African countries, especially the Portuguese-speaking ones (BURGES, 2012).

During the Lula and Dilma governments, at least 19 ministries and national agencies were directly or indirectly involved in activities associated with South–South co-operation. Of these, about 80% of the programmes developed was concentrated in five ministries, namely, foreign affairs, education, health, agriculture, and science and technology. Among the institutions and executing agencies, it is important to highlight the works of EMBRAPA in terms of agricultural research, FIOCRUZ in health research and SENAI in the field of technical and industrial training (BURGES, 2012).

Finally, another important dimension of Dilma Rousseff's foreign policy was the commitment and aspiration to becoming an international reference with regard to environmental sustainability. Brazil hosted the RIO +20 in June 2012, being one of the main voices in defence of sustainable development in conjunction with the fight against poverty; as a matter of fact, Brazilian government declared to the international community its commitment to rigorously control deforestation of the Amazon Forest[46] (Silva, 2016).

Consequently, during the Dilma Government, there were great advances in the deepening of trade and technological co-operation, both with the other BRICS members and with other peripheral economies. Nevertheless, this has not provoked detachment from the central countries.

However, the progress under earlier governments, unfortunately, has suffered accelerated reversal with the Jair Bolsonaro government. The current Brazilian president has repeatedly and explicitly demonstrated since the election campaign his obsession with aligning Brazil's foreign policy and economic agenda with US interests. In his first post-election speech, Bolsonaro publicly stated that one of the main priorities to be pursued by his government would be 'to liberate Brazil . . . from the ideological bias that had guided its foreign policy in the recent years', by referring to a supposed 'communist' orientation prevailing in foreign and trade policy implemented during the Lula and Dilma governments (Libânio, 2018).

The seriousness and future implications of these categorical and obscure statements arise also from the fact that they occur during a period in which the country had the opportunity to assume the temporary presidency of three of the most important multilateral bodies and blocs it belongs to. In March 2019, Brazil assumed the BRICS presidency for a rotating one-year term; as a result, the 2019 BRICS Summit held in Brasilia was the most hollow and ineffective since the bloc's inception. In the second semester of the same year, Brazil held the presidency of MERCOSUR for a six-month term, but its agenda for the Common Market consisted only of signing an agreement with the European Union. In the third and most dramatic case, the Bolsonaro government formalised, in April 2019, Brazil's exit from the Union of South American Nations (UNASUR) by denouncing its Constitutive Treaty, exactly in the same month in which the country assumed the presidency of the organisation for a one-year term. The reason for this decision – taken with no discussions with Brazilian society – was allegedly the deep ideological differences between the Bolsonaro team and the values defended by the organisation, founded in 2008 under the leadership of Lula and Hugo Chávez (Venezuelan president at that time).

There is, therefore, a drastic change in the foreign policy that Brazil had in place since the 2000s. The current government systematically demonstrates its intention to subordinate its interests to those of the USA (and also Israel, Japan and Australia), to the detriment of a foreign policy based on trade, political and technological integration with other countries of the Global South.

Brazil's Concerns at the BRICS

The analysis here indicates that there are three main concerns for Brazil in its relation with BRICS: two external and one internal.

The first external concern the heterogeneities within BRICS. It is quite clear that among the five countries, there is one that is by far the most important in the current world arena, both economically and politically, namely, China. Hence, in spite of all rhetoric in favour of a horizontal relation among all countries, the risk of asymmetries in the relations with China is real. Unlike the Western multilateral institutions, BRICS has so far succeeded in creating for its institutions (e.g. New Development Bank) a governance structure that respects the principle of equal votes. Nevertheless, it is undeniable that beyond the votes, the *real politik* of the group may suffer a disequilibrium in favour of China.[47]

The second external concern for Brazil is related to another heterogeneity, the one between the economic structures of the five countries, and notably between Brazil and China. On the one hand, it is interesting to see that these countries have complementary productive structures, potentially allowing very voluminous international trade flows, which is already the case between Brazil and China. On the other hand, it is clear the there is an asymmetry in the commerce between Brazil and the other BRICS countries as regards the quality of traded goods. As pointed out earlier, Brazilian exports to Russia, India and China are almost exclusively composed of agricultural and mineral commodities; and its imports comprise goods with higher value-added (notably manufactured goods). The only exception is South Africa, which also imports industrial goods from Brazil. This situation reflects the general picture of Brazilian international trade. Nevertheless, it shows that the possibility of Brazil changing the structure of its external trade in favour of higher valued-added goods will probably not be reached within BRICS. To the contrary, trade with BRICS countries tends to reinforce Brazil's position in the international division of labour, as a supplier of mineral and agricultural commodities.

Finally, the internal concern regarding BRICS comes from the attitude of the Brazilian government towards BRICS after the coup d'état (2016) and notably after Bolsonaro took office. After all, having a president whose foreign policy is totally oriented to the USA is undoubtedly very harmful to Brazilian participation in BRICS. As discussed in this chapter, Brazil has no reason to abandon the group, mainly due to its dependency on China's trade and investments. Nonetheless, it is quite clear that since 2016, BRICS has not been a priority in the foreign policy agenda. The Brasília summit in 2019 made this evident, because Brazil organised it, respecting the commitments of the rotating presidency, but did nothing relevant for the group. In other words, Brazil keeps a pragmatic posture of maintaining its position within the group, but has seemingly abandoned the pro-active attitude it had under the Lula and Rousseff governments. Moreover, Brazil is currently using BRICS to promote trade and attract investments, but not anymore as a group that could collectively struggle for a new economic order.

In this regard, we can raise a question: does this new attitude arise from an autonomous decision of the Temer and Bolsonaro's governments? Or are there international forces behind it? Over the recent past, the way the United States of America intervened in Latin America to defend its own interests has been quite evident. As a matter of fact, the declassification of secret documents from the White House make it now clear that the USA actively participated in the promotion of the military coups in Brazil and many other Latin American countries (Argentina, Chili, Uruguay, etc.) during the 1960s and 1970s. Coming back to the current situation, many analysts raise the possibility of another hidden intervention by the USA in the recent coup d'état against Dilma Rousseff. More than that, some claim that one of the reasons behind the possible participation of the USA in the coup in Brazil is its participation in BRICS. After all, this increasing proximity to China and Russia is harmful to the long lasting economic and political insubordination of Brazil in relation to the USA. So far, we can neither prove, nor deny these statements. In any case, it is already clear that at least the private sector in the USA has an important influence over the sudden change in the political scenario in Brazil, through lobbies and massive investments in pro-USA and anti-China think tanks.[48]

We see, therefore, that Brazil has important concerns regarding the BRICS, both external and internal. Nevertheless, the potential benefits, discussed in the chapter, tend to be much larger. Hence, in spite of the ambiguous posture of the Bolsonaro government, Brazilian participation in the group will certainly be maintained. The main doubt is whether this participation will be restricted to the quest of economic benefits for Brazil – that at the end may be seem as economic benefits for only some economic groups – or will be open to (and pro-active in) the effort of constructing a new international order. If it depends only on the Bolsonaro government, the first possibility is more likely. We hope, however, that the next governments will shift its focus to wider and nobler purposes.

Notes

1 See for instance chapters 1 and 3.
2 From 1500, when the Portuguese navy arrived in America, to 1822, the Independence of Brazil.
3 Later, he was replaced by his son, Pedro II.
4 Only in 1889 did Brazil become a Republic, having a president who was not a member of the Portuguese royal family.
5 Even the name of the country is the name of a commodity, 'pau-brasil', the first tree whose wood was exploited by Portugal in the territory. Later on, gold, sugar cane, rubber and coffee have been the most important commodities explored in Brazil.
6 This has been case not only in Brazil but in almost all Latin American countries.

7 Brazil was the last country to abolish slavery in the world, in 1888.
8 For brilliant research on the economic formation of Brazil, see Furtado (1976).
9 Foreign capital in both formats: external loans and foreign direct investments.
10 The so-called 'strong dollar policy' (Tavares, 1985).
11 According to the 'core-periphery' framework, the world economy is composed of 'core countries' (the developed ones) and 'peripheral countries'. The peripheral countries are suppliers of commodities and/or low-cost labour to global production networks, as well as markets for the high value-added goods produced in developed countries. That is, the peripheral countries' position in the international division of labour is totally subordinated to the economic dynamism of the core countries. For details, see Bielschowsky (2016).
12 Deeper discussions about this 'developmentalist period' in Brazil are beyond the scope of this chapter, but it is important to state that in spite of some progress in terms of industrialisation, the social results were totally unsatisfactory. Mainly during the military dictatorship, worsening income distribution, destruction of the public educational system and violent political repression were some of the terrible social outcomes of the period.
13 For details, see Williamson (1990)
14 Beneficial in the short term. In the long term, the historical fragilities appeared again, as we will argue below.
15 The Workers Party governed the country from 2003 to 2016, when a coup d'état interrupted Dilma Rousseff's second term (President Lula, from 2003 to 2010; Dilma, from 2011 to 2016).
16 In May 2013, Ben Bernanke, the head of the US Federal Reserve, announced the 'tapering', i.e., the reversal, of the expansionary monetary policy implemented in the USA with 'quantitative easing'.
17 In June 2013, mass demonstrations in the country started destabilising Dilma Rousseff's government. Even though she was re-elected in 2014, the opposition parties immediately started looking for an excuse to interrupt her second term. Through a parliamentary and juridical manoeuvre, a coup d'état was implemented in 2016, with the impeachment of President Dilma.
18 For a deeper analysis on the reversal of economic dynamism in Brazil, from a boom to a crisis, see De Conti, Noije, and Welle (2020).
19 Cardoso is a former scholar of the University of São Paulo. With Enzo Faletto, he developed a stream of the 'Dependency theory' (Cardoso and Faletto, 1979).
20 A good example of the result of a free trade agreement between such heterogeneous countries is currently provided by the European Zone, in which the divergences between the core and the peripheral countries of the European Union have sharply deepened in the last few decades.
21 This expression was used in the cover of 'The Economist' in November 2009.
22 Further details about the Brazilian policy for the Global South will be discussed in the fifth section.
23 Some analysts name this context as the Latin American 'pink tide', due to the combination of left-wing governments that – in general – were not radical, being more 'pink' than 'red'.
24 Moreover, the agribusiness sector is an important group supporting Bolsonaro and given this sector's dependency on the trade with China, the president had to moderate his declarations.
25 In her inaugural speech, Dilma Rousseff publicly stated her desire to maintain the Brazilian position in defence of the reformulation of international governance bodies, particularly the United Nations Security Council.
26 For instance, in 2010, Brazil (with Turkey) tried to mediate the conflicts involving the Iranian nuclear project (CID, 2017).
27 Some important advances in terms of joint technology development projects and programmes, and trade agreements have already been made between Brazil and other BRICS economies, particularly with China, and are reported in the fifth section, which deals with Brazilian strategies and plans in relation to peripheral and developing countries.

28 For details, see Becard, Barros-Platiau, and Oliveira (2015).
29 Ibid.
30 The impeachment of Dilma Rousseff is considered by many analysts and by an important part of the Brazilian population as a coup d'état.
31 The Grubel-Lloyd Index is calculated through the following equation: $GL = 1 - [(X-M) / (X + M)]$, where X is exports and M is imports (Mikic and Gilbert, 2009).
32 China will be treated in more detail below.
33 It is important to highlight that this index was calculated for the global economy aggregated in three categories, namely: high-income countries, middle-income countries and low-income countries. The results pointed to a value of 0.324 for the former; a value of 0.2 for middle-income economies and only 0.067 for low-income ones (Brülhart, 2008).
34 Expression by Coutinho (1997).
35 As stated by the 'Dutch disease' debate, the massive inflows of foreign capital flows associated with the abundance of natural resources put an upward pressure on the Brazilian currency. It is important to highlight that these inflows were not only the result of trade surpluses, but also of capital entering through the financial account (FDI and portfolio investment). Nevertheless, a large share of these financial flows was in sectors related to natural resources.
36 In the first six months of 2020, China's participation in the Brazilian foreign trade became even higher.
37 An important part of the Chinese investments is made via Hong Kong, which makes it difficult to accurately measure FDI in Brazil, resulting in some differences in data presented by different surveys. However, there is some consensus on the approximate level of these investments.
38 E.g. Electric vehicle and solar panels.
39 E.g. Financial sector.
40 Post-COVID-19, the concentration of Chinese investments in the so-called 'brownfield' units will be probably higher, because the deep crisis in Brazil, the associated devaluation of the Brazilian currency and the government's plan to privatise many public companies will result in a wide array of very cheap assets for international investors.
41 Some of these agreements will be presented in Section 8.5.
42 Especially in a post-COVID-19 scenario, this could be an interesting policy for the BRICS countries.
43 Among the members of the BRICS, only Brazil and South Africa have abandoned their efforts to gain international respect via military and nuclear rule, preferring to implement a soft power foreign policy strategy.
44 According to the United Nations Development Program (UNDP)'s Special South-South Cooperation Unit, the concept of South-South co-operation essentially refers to a process whereby two or more countries are organised and combine synergies for capacity building through the exchange of skills, knowledge and technologies (UNDP, 2004). According to the UNDP Special Unit, South-South co-operation unfolds into two main axes of collaboration between the developing and underdeveloped economies involved, namely: economic co-operation between countries; or development and technical co-operation between developing countries (Santos and Cerqueira, 2016).
45 Between 2005 and 2009, Brazil spent a total of US$1.42 billion on South-South co-operation programmes, the highest volume of resources going to international organisations and programmes providing scholarships and technical co-operation. At the end of Lula's two terms, at least 400 projects with these goals were implemented by the national government with 58 different countries (IPEA, 2010).
46 A commitment that has been completely broken from 2019 onwards with the Bolsonaro government, as we will discuss below.
47 Depending on how Brazil, India, Russia and South Africa face the so-called 'corona crises', this disequilibrium may become even more pronounced in the post-COVID-19 scenario.
48 In our opinion, adopting an anti-China policy may be very harmful for Brazil, notably due to the strong economic dependency it currently has in regard to this country. The most convenient posture would thus be to maintain good relationships with both the USA and China.

References

Becard, D.R.; Barros-Platiau, A.F.; Oliveira, C.C. O Brasil, a China e a VI Cúpula do BRICS. ***Contexto Internacional. Rio de Janeiro***, Vol. 37(1), janeiro/abril, pp. 81–112, 2015.

Bielschowsky, R. ***ECLAC Thinking, Selected Texts (1948–1998)***. Santiago de Chile: ECLAC, 2016.

Brülhart, M. An Account of **Global Intraindustry Trade, 1962 – 2006. Background paper, World** Development Report 2009, UNCTAD, 2008.

Burges, S. Desenvolvendo a partir do sul: cooperação sul-sul no jogo de desenvolvime3nto global. ***Revista Brasileira de Estratégia e Relações internacionais***, Vol.1(2), jul–dez, pp. 237–263, 2012.

Cardoso, F. H.; Faletto, E. ***Dependency and Development in Latin America***. Berkeley: University of California Press, 1979.

CID, M. A estratégia brasileira no Oriente Médio: uma visão histórica no século XX. ***Conjuntura Internacional,*** Vol. 14(1), April, pp. 39–53, 2017.

Coutinho, L. A especialização regressiva: um balanço do desemprego industrial pós-estabilização. In: Velloso, J. P. R. (Org.). ***Brasil: desafios de um país em transformação. IX Fórum Nacional***. Rio de Janeiro: José Olympio, 1997.

De Conti, B.; Hiratuka, C. Le dialogue économique chez les BRICS: potentiel et défis. ***HERMÈS (PARIS)***, Vol.3, p. 114, 2017.

De Conti, B.; Noije, P.; Welle, A. Brazilian economy: from euphoria to crisis. In: Ipek, V.; Akarçay, E. (org.), ***To democratize or not? Trials and tribulations in the post-colonial world***. Cambridge: Cambridge Scholars Publishing, 2020.

Engstrom, P. Brazilian Foreign Policy and Human Rights: Change and Continuity under Dilma. ***Critical Sociology***, Vol. 38(6), pp. 835–849, 2012.

Fernandes, I. F. A. L.; Cardoso, L. F. P. B. A política externa brasileira e o grupo dos BRICS. ***Leviathan/Caderno de Pesquisa Política***, Vol. 11, pp. 121–144, 2015.

Furtado, C. ***Formação econômica do Brasil***. São Paulo: Nacional, 1976.

Hiratuka, C. Chinese OFDI in Brazil: trends and impacts, 2000–2017. In: Dussel-Peters, E. (ed.). ***China's Foreign Direct Investment in Latin America and the Caribbean.*** Mexico, DF: UNAM, 2019.

IPEA – Instituto de Pesquisa Econômica Aplicada. ***Cooperação Brasileira Para o Desenvolvimento Internacional 2005–2009***. Brasília: IPEA/ABC, 2010.

IPEA – Instituto de Pesquisa Econômica Aplicada. **6° Fórum Acadêmico do BRICS. 2014.** Disponível em: <www.ipea.gov.br/forumbrics/pt-BR/o-forum.html> Accessed on 15 May. 2019.

Leal, F. G.; Moraes, M. C. B. Política externa brasileira, cooperação sul-sul e educação superior: uma perspectiva do PEC-G. In: ***XVI Colóquio Internacional de Gestión Univesitaria (CIGU):*** Gestión de la investigación y compromisso social de la universidad. Arequipa – Peru, 23–24/November, 2016.

Libânio, G. Mr. Bolsonaro e os chineses: uma sugestão de interpretação. ***Brazilian Keynesian Review***, Vol.4(2), pp. 300–312, 2018.

Mikic, M.; Gilbert, J. ***Trade Statistics in Policy Making: A Handbook of Commonly Used Trade Indices and Indicators***. New York: United Nations, 2009.

MRE – Ministério das Relações Exteriores. ***Declaração conjunta entre Brasil e China por ocasião da visita de Estado do presidente Xi Jinping***. Brasília, 17 July 2014.

Pires, M. C.; Paulino, L. A.; Cunha, A. T. Brasil, China e a cooperação sul-sul. In: Ramanzini Júnior, H; Ayerbe, L. F. (eds.). ***Política externa brasileira, cooperação sul-sul e negociações internacionais***. 1ª ed. São Paulo: Cultura Acadêmica, 2015.

Prado Jr, C. ***Formação do Brasil Contemporâneo***. São Paulo: Companhia das Letras, 2011.

Santos, R. F.; Cerqueira, M. R. Cooperação Sul-Sul: Experiências brasileiras na América do Sul e na África. ***História, Ciência, Saúde – Manguinhos, Rio de janeiro***, Vol. 22(1), pp. 23–47, 2016.

Schor, A.; Onuki, J. Política externa brasileira e a coalizão IBAS: comércio e inserção internacional. In: Ramanzini Júnior, H; Ayerbe, L. F. (eds.), ***Política externa brasileira, cooperação sul-sul e negociações internacionais***. 1ª ed. São Paulo: Cultura Acadêmica, 2015.

Shambaugh, D. ***China Goes Global: The Partial Power***. Oxford: Oxford University Press, 2013.

Silva, A. L. R. O Brasil, a Argentina e os BRICS: convergências e interesses em perspectiva comparada. ***Relaciones Internacionales***, Vol. 25(50), pp. 101–116, 2016.

Stuenkel, O. ***Post-Western World: How Are Emerging Powers Changing the World***. Malden: Polity Press, 2016.

Stuenkel, O.; India-Brazil-South Africa Dialogue Forum (IBSA). ***Rise of the Global South***. London and New York: Routledge Global Institutions, p. 198, 2014.

Tamiosso, R. F. L.; Massuquetti, A.; Azevedo, A. Z. Análise do impacto da integração do BRICS, do TICKS e do MINT para o Brasil por meio de um Modelo de Equilíbrio Geral. ***XXI Encontro de Economia da Região Sul***, 2018.

Tavares, Maria da Conceição. A Retomada Da Hegemonia Norte-Americana. ***Brazilian Journal of Political Economy***, Vol.5(2), pp. 5–15, 1985.

Vigevani, T.; Cepaluni, G. A política externa de Lula da Silva: a estratégia da autonomia pela diversificação. ***Contexto Internacional***, Vol. 29(2), pp. 273–335, 2007.

Williamson, J. ***Latin American Adjustment: How Much Has Happened?*** Washington: Institute for International Economics, 1990.

10

RUSSIA AND ITS INTERESTS IN BRICS

Oxana Kharitonova

Background

The disintegration of the socialist camp resulted in the transition to a unipolar world. The United States, supported by the EU and Japan, dominated the world order. Initially, Russia sought to integrate with the West, and its relationships were built on mutual consensus and close co-operation. In its efforts to be recognised by the West, Russia joined various Western institutions and mechanisms, including the EU–Russia partnership and co-operation agreement (1994), the Council of Europe (1996) and the G7 (which became G8 after Russia's participation from 1997 to 2014). It also ratified the European Convention on Human Rights (1998). The political elite, in the early years following the break-up of the Soviet Union, was oriented towards the West, at the cost of the rest of the world. Some would claim that although Russia

> never completely sacrificed its national interests, it nevertheless demonstrated its readiness to give up some of them up for the sake of co-operation with the 'civilized world', which it wished to join (Lukin, 2016, p. 98). But the 'civilized world', despite its encouraging rhetoric, continued to view its relations with other countries in Cold War terms, sincerely regarding itself as the victor of that conflict.

In the mid-1990s, the notion of universal fraternity weathered away, and Russia started to assert its interests as a re-emerging power which did not want to put up with its subordinate status vis-à-vis the West (Panova, 2012).

At least rhetorically, Russia has always played an active role in the 'BRICSization'[1] process. The BRICS has its roots, first, in the axis of strategic partnership between Moscow and Beijing based on shared geopolitical interests and,

DOI: 10.4324/9781003148074-12

second, in Yevgeny Primakov's (Foreign Minister of Russia at that time) idea of the Russia–India–China (RIC) triangle. The interaction within the triangle was seen as a process to diversify Russian foreign policy from obsession towards the West and produce a counterweight to US dominance. The RIC forum, which formally still exists, became the prototype of the BRICS. In the words of Sergei Lavrov, the foreign minister of Russia, 'the principles of foreign policy formulated by Primakov and the multipolarity concept now form the basis of the Russian Foreign policy concepts in all its editions' ("Lavrov rasskazal ob idee Primakova", 2019). Russia's Foreign Policy Concept of 2008 stated that the 'strategic stability issue cannot anymore be addressed exclusively within the framework of Russia-US relations' (Foreign Policy Concept of the Russian Federation, 2008).

Withdrawal from the G8 group, the introduction of Western sanctions and the consequent confrontation with the West reduced Russia's international standing to a peripheral one. As a result, 'Russia lost faith in the US and Europe as political and economic partners and . . . began a real, not just rhetorical, political and economic turn to the non-Western world' (Lukin, 2016, p. 98). The Russia–West deadlock brought the idea of the triangle into the implementation phase. Russia turned to the East and became 'more reliant on non-Western countries and the BRICS' (Toloraya and Chukov, 2016, p. 73).

Today, the BRICS is seen in Russia as the most important geopolitical event after the start of the twenty-first century. It seeks to create a polycentric arrangement with a collective leadership of five regional powers. According to Vyacheslav Nikonov, the Chairman of the Board of the Russian World Foundation, 'the formation of BRICS is an expression of the will of these five countries to change the world, not to the detriment of anyone else but rather for the sake of a more equitable system of global governance' (Nikonov, 2019).

Russia's former superpower status, its important geostrategic position in the Eurasian region and imperial legacies of two successive empires (the Russian Empire and the USSR) encouraged the 'rex quondam, rexque futurus' (once and future kings)[2] political behaviour and the alteration of its foreign policy vector towards the East through the formation of and participation in BRICS. The group, which was originally seen as a non-Western economic alliance of emerging powers aimed at limiting Western economic hegemony, gradually became the group that resists the unipolarity of the world system and strives to build a more just polycentric global order. Vadim Lukov, the ambassador of the Russian Ministry of Foreign Affairs and Russia's BRICS Sous-Sherpa, clearly states that

> BRICS is an alliance of reformers in international relations grounded on the strategic interests which include an independent course in foreign affairs, the affirmation of international law as the main norm in international affairs, and the affirmation of the central role of the United Nations in international affairs.
>
> *(Rossiiskii Sous-sherpa, 2015)*

Domestic Discourses on BRICS

Domestic discourses on BRICS and Russia's place in them can be classified according to their research focus and disciplinary matrices, that is economics, international relations and political science. As Richard Sakwa puts it, 'the Brexiteer slogan is "Take back control"' (Sakwa, 2019b, p. 19) either in the sphere of economic or political global governance or in international relations depending on the researcher's focus. Within each of the three fields of study, it is possible to distinguish between transformationalists and sceptics. Transformationalists believe that the BRICS is destined to transform the world, stress Russia's pivotal role in this process and forecast that Russia will become one of the regional centres in the new polycentric world. Sceptics tend to underestimate the global role of the BRICS as an alliance, stress the inferior status of Russia in the group and question its membership regardless of the fact that it initiated its formation.

Economic Perspective

The economic research of BRICS is the most common in Russia. The economists follow the perspective of Goldman Sachs and study the individual and joint economic potential of BRICS countries, their impact on global and regional economic and financial processes, and co-operation between BRICS in the spheres of economy, finance and trade.

The economic perspective stresses the BRICS' objective to reform the dated international financial and economic system, which does not consider the economic power of developing countries. Russia's participation in BRICS is justified by economic interaction within the group.

Alekseenko (2015, p. 61) claims that in the near future, BRICS countries will become centres of world economic growth and the collective stances of BRICS will secure profitable conditions for member states.

BRICS, at the moment, is viewed as a group of states aiming to reform the system of international economic relations. From the economic perspective, it is possible due to the rising cumulative potential of the five states resulting from structural factors, including territories, population and rates of growth. BRICS attracts large amounts of foreign direct investment.

According to a Goldman Sachs paper published in 2003, by the middle of this century, 'the BRICs economies together could be larger than that of the G6 in US dollar terms' and GDP forecasts for 2050 predicted growth in all BRICs economies – 'roughly 2% for Russia, 3–4% for Brazil, 3–4% for China, 5–6% for India' (Purushothaman and Wilson, 2003, p. 4, 8). As projected, 'out of the current G6 (US, Japan, Germany, France, Italy, UK) only the US and Japan may be among the six largest economies in US dollar terms in 2050' (ibid, p. 4).

Sceptics who regard economic factors as the main preconditions for the emerging power status argue that Russia is an outsider in BRICS. But the assessment of belonging depends on the characteristics and differences. In reality, BRICS countries differ according to various indicators, and Russia is often characterised as the weakest link in the group. Four of the BRICS countries are developing economies, while Russia regressed for nearly 20 years after the collapse of the USSR due to declining economic development and high rates of corruption. Russia returned to the development track only in the twenty-first century. Compared to other BRICS states, Russia has the largest territory with a low population density. Russia's population is almost one-tenth the population of the two BRICS giants – India and China.

Russia has a better rank in human development and has the highest ratio of a university-educated population though this relative strength is mostly due to the USSR legacy, which had a well-developed educational system. Overall, the population is ageing and declining, and thus the labour force is shrinking, while all other BRICS countries face only decreasing rates of population growth (Figure 10.1, Table 10.1).

According to a 2020 report on BRICS, the cumulative growth of the group was 32.83 per cent since 2015, while the growth of the G7 was less than half this, that is 15.35 per cent. India had the highest growth rates (41.10 per cent), China was second (38.35 per cent), Russia third (12.99 per cent), South Africa fourth place (10.97 per cent) and Brazil fifth (7.12 per cent). In 2019, cumulative GDP in terms of purchasing power parity (PPP) of BRICS states was higher than that of the G7 (US$47.26 trillion compared to US$43.38 trillion) (Meshkova, 2020, p. 66).

Russia's GDP per capita is so far the highest among BRICS (Figure 10.2), although the average ten-year growth rates are very modest compared to China

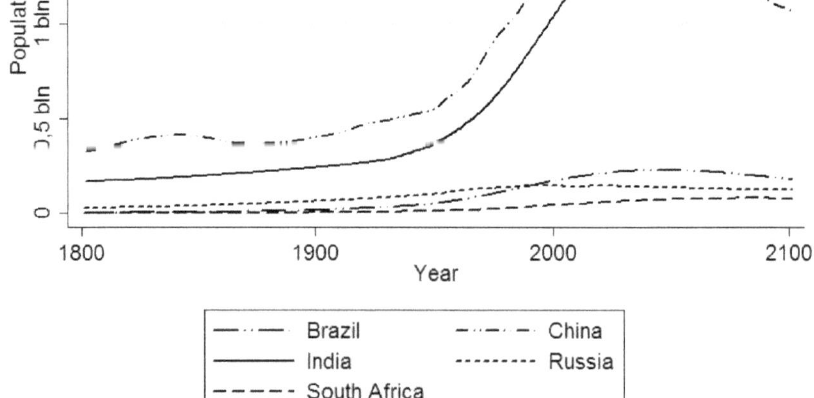

FIGURE 10.1 Population projections of the BRICS states

Source: Compiled by the author based on SDG tracker data (Ritchie et al., 2018).

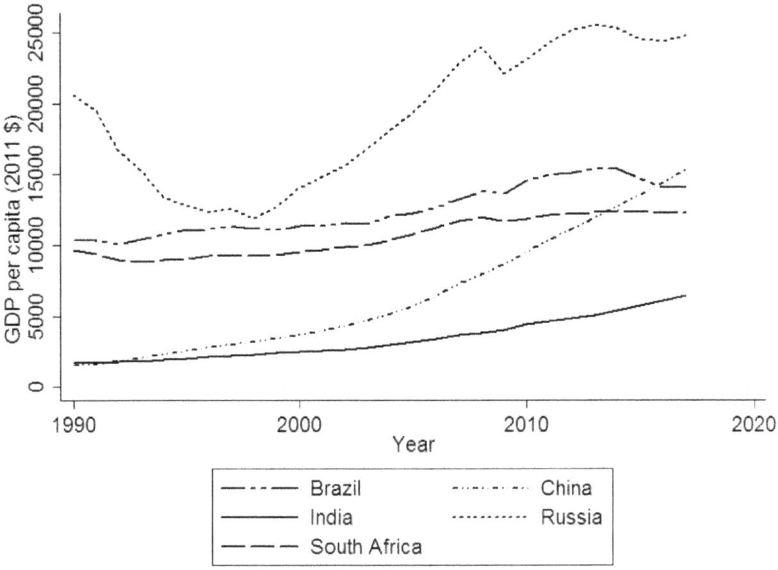

FIGURE 10.2 GDP per capita of the BRICS countries

Source: Compiled by the author based on SDG tracker data (Ritchie et al., 2018).

and India. It was quite comparable to that of Brazil and South Africa. The Gini index reveals that India, China and Russia are much better off than the other two partners are (Table 9.1).

According to the World Economic Forum ranking of global competitiveness, which covered 141 economies in 2019, the best performer among BRICS is China (28th place), then Russia (43rd place), South Africa (60th place), India (68th place) and Brazil (71st place). In 2019, Russia improved its innovation capability on the global competitiveness index by 2.2 points (from 50.7 in 2018 to 52.9 in 2019) due to 'increased quality of its research institutions and constant R&D expenditure (1.1% of GDP)' (Global Competitiveness Report, 2019, p. 18). 'Innovation was also supported by increased ICT adoption (+4.9 points), and rapid diffusion of the internet, which had reached 81% of the population'. The report states that

> 'the skill base of Russia's labour force is eroding (–0.2 points) and while educational attainment remains relatively high in Russia – an average student is expected to stay in school 15.5 years – the quality of education is not keeping up with the needs of a modern economy.
>
> *(ibid., p. 19)*

With regard to the Human Development Index, the best performer is Russia with a very high level of human development, ranking highest in the group (49th place out of 169 countries), ahead of three countries with high human development, that

TABLE 10.1 BRICS comparative data (2019)

	Russia	*China*	*Brazil*	*India*	*South Africa*
Population (million)	144.0	1,395.4	208.3	1,334.2	57.7
Population growth (%, 2018)	0	0.5	0.8	1	1.4
GDP per capita (US$)	11,326.8	9,608.4	8,967.7	2,036.2	6,377.3
Total natural resource rents (% of GDP)	10.7	1.5	3.5	2.1	5.1
Ten-year average annual GDP growth (%)	1.7	6.7	1.2	6.4	1.6
Income Gini	37.7	38.6	53.4	35.7	63.0
Gross enrolment ratio, tertiary education (2013)	78.65	39.39	46.45	23.89	19.66
Global competitiveness index score	66.73	73.9	60.9	61.4	62.4
KOF Globalisation Index	72.6	65.1	60.6	62.3	70.1
Trade openness index (% GDP, 2017)	46.73	37.8	24.12	40.64	58.18
Corruption Perception Index (2018)	28	39	35	41	43
HDI	0.824	0.758	0.761	0.647	0.705

Source: Global Competitiveness Report; Human Development Report; Gygli et al.,2019; Ritchie et al., 2018.

is Brazil (79th place), China (85th place) and South Africa (111th place). The last one of the group is India with medium-level human development (129th place).

The 2019 KOF Globalisation Index measuring economic, social and political dimensions of globalisation shows that Russia and South Africa are the most globalised in the group (Gygli et al., 2019). In terms of the trade openness index calculated as the sum of exports and imports of goods and services divided by GDP, South Africa has the best score followed by Russia and then the rest. But Russia's exports are centred on natural gas and energy products, and the natural resource rents (the total revenue generated from the extraction of the natural resource minus the cost of the extraction) amount to almost 11 per cent of GDP, while other BRICS countries have more diversified economies (Roser and Ortiz-Ospina, 2019a). In this respect, one of the main goals of Russia as constantly declared by the government in the economic sphere is diversification, a switch to new high-technology modes of development and a gradual withdrawal from the dependence on oil and gas. At the same time, although all BRICS countries score badly in terms of corruption, Russia is ranked as the most corrupt among the group according to the Corruption Perception Index (Roser and Ortiz-Ospina, 2019b). The comparison reveals that there are large differences between BRICS states, but the differences are not consistent, and frontrunners in one sphere become strugglers in some others, while Brazil stably occupies a medium position.

Regardless of the economic successes of individual members and, cumulatively, of the group, sceptics say that economic growth and overcoming the gap between BRICS states would not automatically guarantee an increase in their role in global decision-making (Toloraya, 2011). In the view of A. Sergunin and F. Gao (2018), only 'a relatively small amount of research is devoted to the development and prospects of BRICS as a special mechanism of interstate co-operation, including its ability to stimulate changes in the system of global economic governance' (Sergunin and Gao, 2018, p. 56). Other researchers believe that the BRICS grouping resists some aspects of economic globalisation, which negatively influences the situation in developing countries. Although BRICS member states have significant differences in their approaches to regional problems, they stand united in assessing global issues. Such convergence of viewpoints allows them to combine their resources in addressing the challenges and threats of globalisation. The BRICS format can strengthen their positions in the world economic system and facilitate the implementation of various projects, especially ones involving cross-cutting issues for all members (Lunev, 2014).

International Relations Perspective

Multipolarity is the dominant concept of the Ministry of Foreign Affairs of Russia. The concept of multipolarity appeared in Russia's foreign policy discourses after the Cold War and is still one of its main tenets. While speaking about multipolarity in global politics, scholars mention 'power poles' (Toloraya, 2011). 'The terms multipolar and polycentric put emphasis on the power hubs of the modern world (poles and centres) rather than on communication between them as in multilateralism' (Kortunov, 2019, p. 11). As Andrei Kortunov emphasises,

> the advocates of a multipolar world apparently think that the "poles" of a new world order will emerge naturally, and small and medium-sized countries will be joining "centres of power" not by coercion but due to geographical closeness, economic expediency, common history, and cultural similarities.
> *(Ibid., p. 25)*

But neither every state nor a group of strong states can act as a distinct 'pole' in the international system. Some authors believe that only a 'self-sufficient civilisation' can become a pole, since 'a pole is a civilisation and a large space (that is, cultural unity linked to a certain territorial attribute). A pole means culture and power. A pole is identity (cultural originality) and sovereignty (ability to protect originality)' (ibid., p. 23). Multipolarity advocates think that BRICS is one of the few alliances that could become the pole or power centre in a new world order.

BRICS is considered to be the first experience of informal institutionalisation of multipolarity and an example of multilateral diplomacy built on the principle of networking (Meshkova, 2020, p. 29). The main rationale for the BRICS states to form an alliance was to set up a new post-unipolar world order that would be more representative and just and which takes into account all positions, and not only the Western ones. As Richard Sakwa puts it, 'BRICS' fundamental demand is to become accepted co-managers of international affairs and parallel structures created by BRICS like the New Development Bank (NDB) and Contingent Reserve Arrangement (CRA) represent a shift away from dependence on the Western financial system' (Sakwa, 2019b, p. 26). According to the sceptics, 'multipolarity should remain in history as a sensible intellectual and political response to inflated ambitions, arrogance and various excesses demonstrated by unsuccessful architects of the unipolar world' (Kortunov, 2019, p. 34). In Kortunov's view, since 'the unipolar world concept is approaching its decline, so its antipode – the multipolar world concept – will inevitably face a downfall too' (ibid.).

Some analysts go even further, stating that the real ambition of the group members is to replace the traditional world powers. They state that 'BRICS succeeded when both traditional and emerging powers supported the G-20 as the new platform of global policymaking; however, G-7 and BRICS members quickly turned to behaving as factions in the G-20 and then in the world order at large' (Denisov et al., 2019, p. 496). During the last decade, BRICS increased its outreach to very important global and regional non-economic issues which were considered in BRICS annual declarations. 'Since BRICS states were unable to reach compromises with the faction of traditional leaders, they moved towards their own agenda without traditional leaders' (Denisov et al., 2019).

Some scholars stress the security dimension in the gradual formation of the multiple poles. In their view, BRICS countries managed to form 'a viable security agenda and the necessary institutional capacity to form a new international security system and to serve collectively as one of the global security providers' (Bratersky and Kutyrev, 2019, p. 597). They emphasise that 'the BRICS security agenda is remarkably non-ideological as it does not set human rights against collective rights of nations, and that is why it is very attractive' (ibid., 605).

The priority of international law is the main consensus point of the BRICS states. According to V. Kozyrev, 'BRICS countries attempt to offset the hegemonic practices of the Western post-Cold War neo-liberal elites, stepping in as real guardians of the basic tenets of the liberal normative consensus based on inclusiveness, openness, and international law' (Kozyrev, 2019, p. 652).

BRICS countries always emphasise their commitment to the principles of international law, rely on effective co-operation with international and regional organisations, and consider the UN to be the core of international relations architecture. The main BRICS principles include the value of international law against unilateral action and an increase in the role of the UN and the Security Council (Yurtaev and Rogov, 2017). According to Shelepov, the UN is the most frequently mentioned institution in BRICS documents, and the UN's share in the total number of references exceeds 28 per cent, while the next most frequently mentioned institution is the G20 (10.8 per cent of all mentions) (Shelepov, 2015, p. 9). Such content analysis confirms that BRICS countries see the central role of the UN in the international system and of the G20 in the global economic system.

The United States, which had led the development of the liberal international order, is now less committed to preserving that order. Under the Trump administration, the United States withdrew from the UN Human Rights Council and the United Nations Educational, Scientific and Cultural Organization (UNESCO), announced its decision to consider withdrawal from the WTO and to terminate relationship with the World Health Organization. The United States does not offer clear formats for 'stable international cooperation in such areas as trade, security, the environment and climate change' (Novikov and Skriba, 2019, p. 594). BRICS states have the opportunity to step in. Since the instruments of global governance do not work as originally intended, new ones need to be set up, with or without the former leaders. Thus, if the BRICS is viewed only as a group of states strengthening its place in world politics not emphasising historical differences, Russia's former superpower status and a low starting point before rapid growth, then Russia organically blends with the group (Panova, 2012).

Political Science Perspective

Political scientists pay attention to the processes of globalisation and see the role of BRICS states both individually and collectively in global governance and the world market. They operate within the globalisation and regionalisation[3] paradigms; regionalism is considered to go hand in hand and is also a part of globalisation.

Russian scholar S. Lunev (2014) thinks that globalisation and regionalisation are two contradictory processes, though they can proceed simultaneously. In his view, economic and political factors determine that regionalisation and regional integration become dominant in world development, and that is why the world system will become multipolar and multi-civilisational. Regional powers will not only be the part of global economy but also be leaders in their regions. In the present world, only a few states can be called regional powers. BRICS states are regional powers, and they can influence the politics of neighbouring countries through soft power (Lunev, 2014, p. 100).

Higher School of Economics (Moscow) scholars, Batalina, M., Bordachev T. and Bochkova M. state that the concept of trans-regionalisation describes the birth and evolution of BRICS more accurately (Meshkova, 2020). Since globalisation overrode the geographic determinism of the economic networking, it 'erased' the barriers to co-operation between countries of various regions and thus brought an end to geography. BRICS became 'a trans-regional pentagon which represents the global configuration and improves the relations between the vertices, and thus, stabilizes the situation in the world' (Meshkova ed., 2020, p. 29).

Another perspective of political scientists deals with statehood and the role of the state. Globalisation deepens interconnectedness and fosters the openness of the modern states. The role of the state gains importance because only global actors relying on the advantages of national economic and political systems will become competitive in the world market (Busygina and Okunev, 2015, p. 18). Only strong states are able to successfully deal with the challenges of globalisation and create favourable economic and political conditions for national actors, and the BRICS alliance has the potential to strengthen the states of its members.

Sovereignty is an important characteristic of strong states in globalisation; all five states are sovereign, and none of them is tied to any alliance that could limit its free action and hinder independent policy-making. The independent-choice potential of five BRICS states is similar to that of the United States, and they can act at their own discretion (Grishin and Dukhareva, 2017, p. 44). The

> advocates of multipolarity insist that the overwhelming majority of existing nation states are not able to ensure their own security and economic growth. In the current transitional world and in a future multipolar one, only a handful of countries will have 'real sovereignty', while all others will sacrifice their sovereignty one way or another for the sake of security, well-being or just survival.
> *(Kortunov, 2019, p. 24)*

Some researchers name BRICS states 'sovereignty hawks',[4] that is countries defending the sovereignty of other states and promoting non-interference in internal affairs (Panova, 2012).

BRICS is an 'alliance of values, which are sovereignty, respect for national dignity, non-intervention in internal affairs, respect for the interests and traditions of partners, and a desire for peace and harmony' (Meshkova, 2020, p. 19). These values, which disregard violence or hegemony, will allow BRICS states to become regional powers and, as an alliance, BRICS to find its place in the structure of global governance. Sakwa calls such standpoint the model of conservative internationalism, emphasising the importance of sovereign decision-making by nation states, but also understanding the importance of internationalism (Sakwa, 2019a, p. 457).

BRICS states are important members of the UN, the G20 and almost all other formats of global governance. However, the discontent with the existing system of international relations and member states' roles pushed them towards modernisation of global governance. In their vision, such reform should provide a fair redistribution of authoritative power and strengthen the influence of the developing countries in global decision-making. In this respect, they aim at

> a constructive reset of existing institutional pillars of the current system without creating any 'mirror' structures of global governance, but if such mirror structures are created (under the auspices of BRICS), they would be incorporated harmoniously into the existing world order, thereby contributing to the solution of global problems.
>
> *(Novikov and Skriba, 2019, p. 594)*

The BRICS format is thus seen as a geopolitical alternative of the twenty-first century (Toloraya, 2011), as well as a tool helping member states to strengthen their positions in global governance. Another important characteristic of the BRICS format is that it 'differs from other "club" formats due to the lack of a dominant player' and fosters co-operation of equal states since it is based on 'the absolute equality of the members' (Toloraya and Chukov, 2016).

The analysis of various research views shows that Russian academics support the transformationalist point of view. The economic rise of BRICS states becomes the structural precondition for modernising the system of global governance to make it more fair, just and grounded in the values of sovereignty, equality and international law under the guardianship of strong regional powers (poles) aiming to find a solution to global problems. The only question for the transformationalists is whether such transformation of global governance will be comprehensive or gradual, radical or moderate.

Sceptics stress national interests of the member states and assess their potential either individually or in a group. When assessing the present state of affairs, it is stated that 'although BRICS has become one of the key global platforms for dialogue, it has not yet reached its full potential' (Novikov and Skriba, 2019, p. 587). BRICS is mostly oriented at counteraction since all its ideas are reactive and aim to influence the West and strengthen its power while reforming existing international institutions (Panova, 2012). In order to become truly transformationalist, BRICS needs to become more proactive.

Material and Normative Interests of Russia in the BRICS

Russia's interests in BRICS can best be viewed through an analysis of the four consecutive foreign policy concepts of the Russian Federation.

The 2000 Foreign Policy Concept of the Russian Federation stresses the objective to form 'a stable, just and democratic world order, built on the norms of international law, including the goals and principles of the UN Charter, and equitable relations among states'. Russia is concerned about the 'trend towards a unipolar structure with economic and power domination of the US'. The main goal is seen in creating 'a multi-polar system reflecting the diversity of the modern world'. Although the concept stresses the necessity 'to intensify the role of international institutions and mechanisms' in world economics and politics (including the IMF, the WB and the G8 in which Russia participated at that time), the concept stated that regional and sub-regional integration in Europe, Asia-Pacific, Africa and Latin America becomes 'significant factors of regional and sub-regional security and peace making'. It is stated that the crucial direction of the foreign policy in Asia means developing friendly relations with the leading Asian states, primarily China and India. The concurrence of fundamental approaches of Russia and China to key global political issues is one of the basic pillars of regional and global stability. While Russia seeks to develop 'mutually advantageous co-operation with China' in all areas, according to the Concept, the main task is still economic, that is 'to bringing the scale of economic interaction in conformity with the level of political interaction'. The Concept mentions India in the context of South Asia and stresses 'the necessity to strengthen its traditional partnership with India' (Foreign Policy Concept, 2000).

The 2008 Foreign Policy Concept again emphasises 'the supremacy of international law and relations of equal partnership among states with the UN playing a central and co-ordinating role in developing full-fledged inter-civilizational dialogue as an organisation with unique legitimacy'. It states that Russia has acquired 'a full-fledged role in global affairs, based on a solid foundation of its national interests'. The Concept supported the strengthening of the principles of multilateralism and stated that 'the trend to a polycentric world order is growing with the development of regional and sub-regional integration'. World politics requires 'collective leadership by the leading states, which should be representative in geographical and civilizational terms and fully respect the central and co-ordinating role of the UN'. Russia's foreign policy is described as 'a balanced and multi-vector type'. It is the first time that the RIC Troika format (Russia, India and China) and the BRIC Four (Brazil, Russia, India and China) are mentioned among the foreign policy directions (Foreign Policy Concept, 2008).

The 2013 Foreign Policy Concept mentions 'the tendency towards decentralisation of the global system of governance, as regional governance emerges as the basis for a polycentric world model (with the UN being its foundation)', reflecting the world's diversity and variety. The concept describes the regionalisation trend in the form of 'new centres of economic growth and political power increasingly taking responsibility for their regions'. Regional integration is seen as 'an effective means to increase competitiveness of the participating states'. It is stated that 'the ability of the West to dominate the world economy and politics continues to diminish as global power and development potential is becoming more dispersed and is shifting to the East, primarily to the Asia-Pacific region'. The concept emphasised the world cultural and civilisational diversity and stated that 'global competition takes place on a civilisational level, whereby various values and models of development based on the universal principles of democracy and market economy start to clash and compete against each other' (Foreign Policy Concept, 2013).

The 2016 Foreign Policy Concept emphasises that 'the world is currently going through fundamental changes related to the emergence of a multipolar international system'. It stresses that 'the global power is becoming decentralised, and is shifting towards the Asia-Pacific Region, eroding the global economic and political dominance of the traditional western powers'. While 'existing military and political alliances are not capable of countering the full range of challenges and threats the world is currently facing', Russia attaches great importance to 'ensuring the sustainability of global development, which requires collective leadership from the major states that should be representative in geographic and civilization terms and fully respect the central and co-ordinating role of the UN'. It is stated that Russia 'will continue developing a comprehensive, equal, and trust-based partnership and strategic co-operation with the People's Republic of China, and proactively step up co-operation in all areas'. The concept confirmed the commitment to 'further strengthen the special privileged partnership with the Republic of India, based on shared foreign policy priorities, historical friendship and deep mutual trust' (Foreign Policy Concept, 2016).

An analysis of mentions of various organisations and regions (Figure 10.3) confirms Russia's commitment to international law and the UN (99 mentions of the UN in the four concepts). The second place belongs to the CIS as the priority region for Russia (66 mentions). The number of mentions of BRICS/RIC and individual BRICS countries outnumber the mentions of the EU by two to one (51 to 25), demonstrating the diversity of Russian foreign policy and the reorientation of its focus from the North to the South.

The analysis of Russia's Foreign Policy Concepts reveals that Russia aims to resist the political influence of the United States and its Western partners globally and

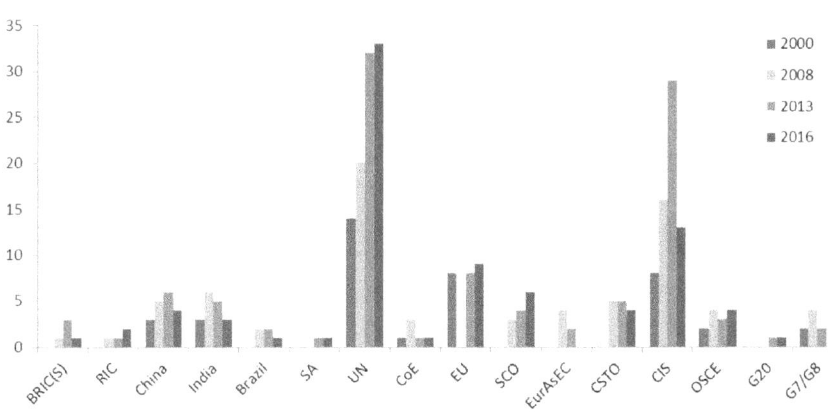

FIGURE 10.3 Analysis of institutions mentioned in Russia's Foreign Policy Concepts

Source: Compiled by the author on the basis of four Foreign Policy Concepts of the Russian Federation

especially in the CIS region, which used to be a traditional zone of Russian influence. It concerns issues of national security and defence of Russia's sovereignty. Multipolarity is viewed as a solution to unilateralism, and all four concepts state that Russia aims to set up a polycentric world order, based on the principles of multilateralism, international law and active co-operation with international and regional organisations, maintaining the UN as the core international institution. Russia's participation in the BRICS group allows it to avoid international isolation backed by the West and re-emerge as an active regional and global player in a new multipolar world system.

In 2013, the Concept of participation of the Russian Federation in BRICS was adopted, dealing only with the BRICS format and Russia's objectives in co-operation with BRICS states. The Concept stated that BRICS is 'one of the most significant geopolitical events in the new century and that the association managed to become an important factor in world politics'. According to the Concept,

> the establishment of BRICS reflects an objective trend in global development towards the formation of a polycentric system of international relations, which is increasingly characterised by the use of non-institutionalised mechanisms of global governance, network-based diplomacy, and growing economic interdependence of states.

The political influence of BRICS 'stems from the fact that the participating states are reputable members of leading international organisations as well as regional associations'. It states that the Russian Federation's relations with its BRICS partners are based on 'the principles of openness, pragmatism, solidarity, non-bloc character and nonaggressive nature with regard to third parties'. The strategic objective of the Russian Federation in BRICS as the key long-term foreign policy vector is 'to enhance the multi-vector character of the foreign policy of the Russian Federation, thus strengthening the country's international position'. The long-term objective of the Russian Federation's participation in BRICS is 'to gradually transform the association from a dialogue forum and a tool to co-ordinate positions on a limited range of issues into a full-fledged mechanism of strategic and ongoing co-operation on key international political and economic issues' (Concept of participation of the Russian Federation in BRICS, 2013).

The aforementioned ideas were included in the Concept of the Russian Federation's Presidency in BRICS in 2015–2016. The Concept also outlined the key objectives of Russia's BRICS presidency, which were as follows: 'first, to strengthen the position of BRICS, second, to diversify Russia's foreign economic ties, third, to strengthen its economic security, and fourth, to reinforce the foundations of the multipolar world order in the economic sphere' (Concept of the Russian Federation's Presidency in BRICS in 2015–2016).

The priorities of the Russian BRICS Chairmanship in 2020 outlined at the end of 2019 included, inter alia, 'the strengthening of multilateral principles in global politics, promoting the shared interests of the BRICS countries in international fora and the expansion of collaboration with partner countries in the "BRICS

Plus" and "Outreach" dialogue formats'. Since the most institutionalised sphere of co-operation between BRICS states is economics and trade, the priorities in the sphere included among other priorities

> the renewal of the strategy for BRICS economic partnership; the facilitation of trade and investments between members; promotion of the NDB and enhancement of the CRA; co-operation in the field of energy, digital economy and innovations; and strengthening ties in healthcare, agriculture, food security.

The ambitious priorities of BRICS at the global level included in the Concept were 'the consolidated collective efforts to respond to global and regional challenges and threats including terrorism, extremism, drug and arms trafficking and cybercrime' (Priorities of the Russian BRICS Chairmanship in 2020).

To conclude, Russia has always considered co-operation within the BRICS format as one of its foreign policy priorities. Russia intends to strengthen the position of BRICS in the international arena and thus the positions of individual member states. It is in Russia's interests to expand the agenda of BRICS and transform it into an impactful actor in world politics. The co-operation within the BRICS format is beneficial for Russia in resisting international economic pressure and all members in overcoming various globalisation challenges in the political, social, economic and information spheres. BRICS for Russia is also an attempt to use the association for the benefit of its own modernisation of the economy and the development of Russian eastern regions such as Siberia and the Far East.

Russia's Economic Co-operation with Other Members

The development of joint trade ties, the struggle against protectionism and the WTO reform have been at the centre of the BRICS group's attention since the first summit. Since that time, BRICS announced 45 commitments in the sphere of international trade (Meshkova, 2020, p. 23). Although each of the BRICS states has its own national interests, which do not necessarily correlate with the national interests of others, it does not hinder economic interaction between them. As Lukin puts it, 'Europe and the United States are seen as unreliable partners, ready to sacrifice economic ties for the sake of political pressure, which is why objective circumstances and economic interests have compelled Russia to shift its attention to other regions' (Lukin, 2016, p. 107). Russia's solid interest in cooperation within the BRICS format started from the sanctions imposed by the West and became its counter-response while seeking to find exporters of agricultural products and food to replace the Europeans.

The total share of BRICS group in the global GDP in 2019 was

> 33% and it is predicted that the growth rate of the BRICS member-states, which is higher than the global rate (4.5% as compared to 2.5% in the coming years) will lead to a further increase in the share of the five countries.

> By 2030, it will exceed that of the USA and European countries combined, reaching 37% of the global economy.
>
> *(BRICS Russian Chairmanship, 2020, pp. 54–55)*

At the moment, BRICS countries jointly produce around one-third of the world industrial commodities and half of agricultural products.

As stated in the Concept of Russia's participation in BRICS, membership in BRICS aims to 'develop privileged bilateral relations with BRICS partners to make a fuller use of advantages emanating from mutually complementary opportunities of co-operation among the participating states in various spheres' (Concept of participation of the Russian Federation in BRICS, 2013).

The trade between BRICS states and Russia is not balanced and China is Russia's largest trading partner (16.6 per cent). Trade with India accounts for less than 2 per cent, while that with Brazil and South Africa jointly accounts for less than 1 per cent (Table 10.2). If considered in USD, the annual growth rate of trade with each country amounts to over 100 per cent, and around 140 per cent for China, but in Russia's overall trade profile during the last decade, only the share of China increased noticeably. Trade with BRICS partners increased 2.8 times from US$45,648 million in 2010 (11.9 per cent of all RF trade) up to US$127,859 million (19.2 per cent) in 2019.

The structure of trade with Russia with each BRICS country varied during the period from January 2013 to June 2019 (Table 10.3).

Russia's main trade partner is China, making up a significant share of trade volume, which increased from US$38,964 million in 2010 (9.5 per cent) to up to US$110,918.6 million (16.6 per cent share) in 2019 with an average annual trade volume increase of over 100 per cent. China is number one importer to Russia (20 per cent) during the period, with Germany being the second (11 per cent). Chinese export to Russia amounted to US$301.1 billion. China mainly exported machinery and mechanical appliances, electrical equipment (49 per cent), and textiles and textile articles (8 per cent). Russia's export to China amounted to US$249 billion. Russia mainly exported mineral products (73 per cent), wood and

TABLE 10.2 Share of trade of individual BRICS states in the overall trade profile of the Russian Federation

	2010	*2011*	*2012*	*2013*	*2014*	*2015*	*2016*	*2017*	*2018*	*2019*
China	12.1	10.13	10.5	10.5	11.3	12.1	14.1	14.9	15.7	16.6
Brazil	0.9	0.85	0.7	0.6	0.8	0.9	0.9	0.9	0.7	0.7
India	1.5	1.01	1.3	1.2	1.2	1.5	1.6	1.6	1.6	1.7
South Africa	0.2	0.07	0.1	0.1	0.1	0.2	0.2	0.1	0.2	0.2
Total	14.7	12.06	12.6	12.4	13.4	14.7	16.8	17.5	18.2	19.2

Source: Compiled by the author from the data from the Russian Federation Federal Customs Service annual reports. URL: http://customs.ru/statistic/vneshn-torg/vneshn-torg-countries

TABLE 10.3 The export/import of products in the foreign trade of Russia with BRICS states in the period from 2013 to 2019

	China		*Brazil*		*India*		*South Africa*	
	Export	*Import*	*Export*	*Import*	*Export*	*Import*	*Export*	*Import*
Animals, Animal products	3	0.6	0	48.4	0	3	0	0
Vegetable products	0.5	2	0	15.7	1	11.3	57.7	33.5
Food, tobacco	0.4	1.2	0.2	18.1	1	7.7	1.1	6.9
Chemical industry	3.4	4.5	75.4	3.3	9.9	29.8	10.9	6.9
Metal	1.4	7.4	4.1	3.6	5.2	6.3	4.9	7.1
Transport	0.4	4.3	0.2	2.7	0.1	4	0.3	14.3
Mineral products	72.4	0.3	14.3	0.2	12.2	0.6	10.4	24.3
Plastics, rubber	1.2	4.6	2.9	0.3	3	3.1	3.8	0.7
Wood	7.5	0.5	0	0.1	0.2	0	0.6	0
Textile	0	8.7	0	0.1	0.3	11.1	0.1	0.1
Paper, books	2.4	0.7	0.5	0.4	4.5	0.2	5.9	0
Pearls and Precious stones	0.2	0.3	0	0	16.2	1.4	0.1	0.1
Machinery, equipment	4.3	49.1	1.1	3.3	17.6	14.4	1.9	5.7
Instruments, apparatus, clocks	0.4	2.2	0.3	0.2	3.8	0.8	2	0.1
Other	2.50	13.60	1.00	3.60	25.00	6.30	0.30	0.30
Total	100	100	100	100	100	100	100	100

Source: Compiled by the author from the Database of export and import of Russia (FEA) URL: https://ru-stat.com/

articles of wood, wood charcoal, and cork and articles of cork (7 per cent). Thus, Russia mostly exports resources and imports industrial products. China is the second-largest importer (9 per cent) from Russia after the Netherlands (12 per cent).

According to the Russian Federation Federal Customs Service reports, the export/import share of trade between Russia and China had changed radically during the research period, and, as of 2018, the exports exceeded imports (Figure 10.4).

India is Russia's second-biggest trade partner among BRICS states, although the gap between China and India is significant. India ranks 19th among Russian import partners and 18th among export partners. Indian exports to Russia amounted to US$18.8 billion. Russia mainly imported products of chemical or allied industries (29 per cent), and machinery, mechanical appliances and electrical equipment (15 per cent). Russia's exports amounted to US$41.6 billion and included machinery, mechanical appliances and electrical equipment (18 per cent), and other unclassified products (24 per cent).

Brazil is Russia's third-largest trading partner, but ranks 37th among all of Russia's trading partners for both import and export. Brazilian exports to Russia amounted to US$19.6 billion. Russia imported mainly live animals and animal products (46 per cent), food, beverages, spirits and vinegar and tobacco (18 per cent). Exports from Russia to Brazil amounted to US$13.6 billion, and Russia

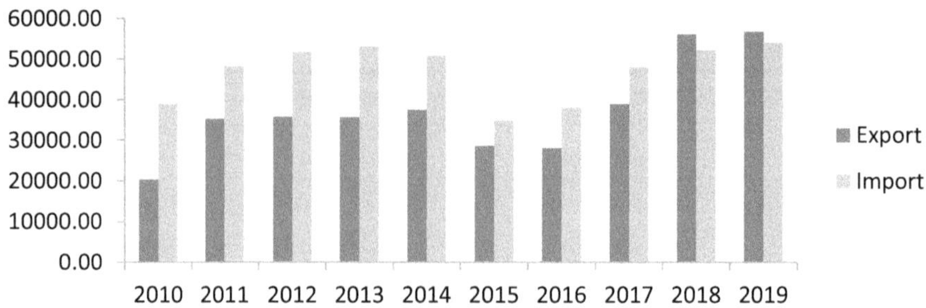

FIGURE 10.4 Export/import share in the trade relations between Russia and China (in millions USD).

Source: Compiled by the author from the database of the Russian Federation Federal Customs Service annual reports. URL: http://customs.ru/statistic/vneshn-torg/vneshn-torg-countries

mainly exported products of chemical or allied industries (75 per cent) and mineral products (14 per cent).

South Africa ranks 48th among import partners and 85th among export partners. During the period, Russia's imports from South Africa amounted to US$4.38 billion. Russia mostly imported vegetable products (34 per cent) and mineral products (24 per cent). Exports from Russia to South Africa were considerably less amounting to US$1.63 billion. Russia exported vegetable products (58 per cent) and products of the chemical or allied industries (11 per cent).

Economic co-operation between BRICS states takes into consideration their uneven resources and is based on the complementarity of the partners. As Vladimir Putin stated at the end of 2019, 'the participants of the "Five" consistently deepen mutually beneficial economic ties, build trade and investment approaches, jointly address the important tasks as modernisation of industry, adoption of innovation technologies and improvement of well-being' (Putin: devizom predsedatelstva RF v BRICS, 2019). Close co-operation in the economic sphere makes BRICS countries more interconnected and stronger in the global economic arena. In 2019, the BRICS states 'account for 19% of global exports, 16% of global imports, 19% of incoming and almost the same amount of outgoing direct investment' (BRICS Russian Chairmanship, 2020, p. 55).

Russian scholars still see untapped trade potential in the sphere of services. Tourist services amount to 20 per cent of imports in all countries, while for China and South Africa these are also the main exports (Sharova, 2016, p. 165). Transport services accounted for almost 40 per cent of imports in India, Russia and South Africa, while other business services including information and communication are an important component of import for all BRICS states with the exception of South Africa. The sphere of services thus provides high potential for co-operation within BRICS. Economic co-operation among BRICS countries could take advantage of their specialisations in various sectors. Brazil specialises in financial services; Russia in transport and constructions services; India in computer and information services; China in construction, transport and tourist services; and South Africa in tourist, financial and insurance services (ibid).

Russia and the Politics of the Global South

BRICS is becoming important for bringing together largest and most influential non-Western states claiming to represent the entire Global South. According to Yurtaev and Rogov, BRICS is 'the quintessence of non-western views and theories of world order in the building of a new multipolar international system' (Yurtaev and Rogov, 2017, p. 479). The group wants its members to rise geopolitically and rejects the hegemony of the North for political, economic and civilisational reasons and aims to make the West consider the positions of the South. BRICS is 'the manifestation of the irreversible tendency of the shift in power centre from the West to the East, from the North to the South, from developed countries to developing countries' (Nikonov, 2013).

The Westernisation of the world is being overridden by easternisation since the countries of the South, having a centuries-long civilisational history, are coming to the forefront of global development, replacing the five-century-long domination of the North (Toloraya, 2011). Scholars attempt to give a foundation for such development. Lunev observes that since the end of the last century, the non-West is experiencing a real religious renaissance with the rise of religion's influence on the state. The process of revival of traditional values and alienation from many values of the European civilisation is the result of many structural factors including the poverty of significant portions of population leading traditional lives, and the erosion of the absolute superiority of the European civilisation (Lunev, 2014, p. 103).

In the Russian political and academic discourse, BRICS is mostly considered in global, non-Western (meaning non-West-centric) or civilisational terms, which is broader than the Global South perspective (Concept of participation of the Russian Federation in BRICS, 2013). The group is understood as an inter-civilisational project to develop the norms of global order. As stated in the Concept of Russia's participation in BRICS, it is 'a new model of global relations, overarching the old dividing lines between East and West, and North and South' (Concept of participation of the Russian Federation in BRICS, 2013).

The vision of the rise of the non-North, non-West or the Rest[5] is supported by the accumulated civilisational potential of the members; that is why the format is not only an inter-state but also an inter-civilisational one. BRICS states are situated on different continents, have different political regimes, vary in the levels of socio-economic development, have diverse historical legacies and cultural traditions and belong to different civilisations. They have fewer similarities than the countries of the West, but they prove that the differences do not prevent them from fruitful co-operation.

The civilisational diversity is thought to be a significant advantage of the BRICS format. BRICS countries belong to the following five civilisations in Samuel Huntington's terms (stressing the role of civilisation in international affairs): Latin

American, Orthodox, Sub-Saharan African, Confucian and Hindu. Moreover, Islam is the second-largest religion in India and Russia and the number of Muslims in India (14.2 per cent of the country's population or approximately 172 million[6]) is more that the population of Russia. This is why BRICS truly represents a miniature non-Western world with civilisations that do not clash but that aim to work together for the common good of the world. Contrary to the clash of civilisations forecast, the BRICS states are considered to be 'the archipelago of stability' (Meshkova, 2020, p. 11).

Civilisations have a lengthy existence, and their influence on the world's historical development is immeasurably bigger and more significant than that of states. For centuries, the civilisations developed in isolation and provided individual inputs to global history, in which some became world centres and others stayed at the periphery. Globalisation gave the periphery the means to change the order, and the necessity arose to develop the principles of inter-civilisational interaction (Vinogradov, 2014, p. 47).

BRICS states are dissatisfied with the current state of events, when a small group of highly developed Western countries dominates the system and establishes the rules for the rest. They would like to transform the current order

> in an evolutionary rather than radical (revolutionary) way, which justifies considering them reformist rather than revisionist powers. BRICS countries are striving to cultivate an image of themselves not as spoilers or revisionists, but as reformers of the existing unfair system.
>
> *(Sergunin and Gao, 2018, p. 57)*

Regional powers usually do not attempt to rise to the global level and cannot successfully act in more than one region (Voskressenski, 2012, p. 52). The alliance of five regional powers makes it possible. And when each of the regional powers represents a distinct civilisation, the alliance can legitimately claim to represent the entire Global South. BRICS has now become the only non-Western alliance that has the potential to become a power pole in the emerging multi-polar system.

Civilisations have the highest measure of identity and more defined responsibility for the world and for the region (Vinogradov, 2014, p. 47). The fact that the historic role of civilisation is bigger than that of the state becomes common justification for BRICS' political aspirations and responsibility for the developing world at large. Countries belonging to the Global South, which entered the political and economic process later, have to co-operate with BRICS in order to maintain their sovereignty and independence from former metropolitan states and other developed nations (Emelianov, 2018, p. 38).

BRICS' rationale originates not only from the economic and political leadership within their respective regions but also from shared geopolitical interests in strengthening South–South solidarity. Without Russia, BRICS would be another alliance of the developing states of the South, and would stay at the regional level (Vinogradov, 2014, p. 50). The membership of Russia moved BRICS to the global level. Moreover, each member of BRICS not only represents the interests of a large geopolitical region but also acts as its leader.

Georgy Toloraya compares BRICS to the only analogous alliance in history – the Non-Aligned Movement – that also promoted South–South solidarity and multilateral assistance to developing nations. After the end of the Cold War, the movement disappeared, but its idea of an alternative development path did not die out (Toloraya, 2011). Toloraya's idea has some conceptual stretching since, in the case of BRICS, the members are the largest and most influential non-Western countries, which try to stand united and not divided like the Non-Aligned Movement. Thus, BRICS is the only historic precedent of the kind, but this project is still under construction.

Russia's Concerns at the BRICS

Within its present borders, Russia is a new sovereign state compared to other BRICS countries, and it needs to consolidate society both culturally and politically, especially considering the post-Soviet reawakening of certain ethnic groups. A common civilisational narrative, success on the international stage and a redefinition of the superpower status have already been proven by the Russian empire and the USSR to be useful tools to foster loyalties to the central authority and overcome societal conflicts. The worsening of relations with the West made Russia seek other alternatives to prove its status in global politics.

Russia's position in the BRICS is ambivalent. On the one hand, historically and culturally it is closer to the North, and the alliance with the South can hurt the national pride of the former Empire and Great Power. But co-operation with developing nations objectively corresponds to Russia's national interests. Participation in BRICS proves

> to be very useful from a reputational/status point of view. Since BRICS partners did not support Western sanctions against Moscow, Russia managed not only to avoid complete international isolation, but also to actively influence international developments, both regionally and globally.
>
> *(Sergunin and Gao, 2018, p. 66)*

BRICS remains a strategic priority for Russia since 'in long-term geopolitical confrontation with the West, Russia has simply no alternative strategy that would enable it to hold its position as one of the world's centres of power' (Toloraya and Chukov, 2016, p. 81).

As Vladimir Putin stated in 2019, 'Russia takes BRICS seriously' (Vladimir Putin otvetil na voprosy, 2019). Russia has global ambitions, but it is possible to restore the great power status only through collaboration with the states having similar views on the threats to and challenges of the world. While India, Brazil and South Africa aim to have a stronger cumulative voice in global affairs, China and Russia try to compete with the United States on equal terms (Alekseenko, 2015, p. 59).

The inter-civilisational narrative of the essence of BRICS seems more significant and promising for Russia because it shows its new role in the world and within BRICS. In this context, one of the dominant discourses redefining Russia's role in the world dwells upon its dual civilisational and geostrategic location as Eurasia or 'Asiopa', making it an important actor transmitting orders and values between the West and the East and connecting them with each other. Since BRICS does not intend to break up with the North, Russia's new role can be that of a bridge, a counterbalance, a mediator between the North and the South. As A. Lukin states,

> the role of Russia in this transitional world is only just beginning to take shape. The country is positioning itself as the linchpin of Eurasian integration. Whether it has enough resources to sustain this project is unclear. What is clear is that Russia cannot afford an open-ended confrontation with other powers because of its heavy economic dependence on the West . . . Moscow should revive its role as a kind of bridge between Europe and Eurasia, allowing for the transmission of certain European political standards to Eurasia while also making clear to Europeans that Eurasian countries, including Russia, have their own traditions, and will not accept the wholesale imposition of Western values where these contradict their own moral principles.
> *(Lukin, 2016, p. 109)*

In 2020, the border conflict between India and China brought about incidents on the line of actual control. Russia's position has always been to support conflict de-escalation through diplomatic means. According to the Russian Foreign Minister Sergei Lavrov, Russia 'welcomed immediate contacts between militaries, which are ongoing. They reached agreements on de-escalating tensions. Their politicians and diplomats also met. We can see that neither India nor China want their relations to get worse' (Foreign Minister Sergey Lavrov's remarks, July 10, 2020). In September 2020, the meeting of the foreign ministers of Russia, China and India was considered an attempt to start a dialogue through diplomatic means. But since Russia is not part of the border conflict, its position is rather cautious, as Russia does not want to interfere unless both partners ask for mediation or facilitation. That is why Russia 'is not participating in the conflict settlement but is playing its role in creating a positive atmosphere' (Moskva miagko podtalkivaet Pekin I Delhi k primireniyu, 2020). This clearly shows that Russia wants to be the bridge between conflicting interests in BRICS.

The economic crisis led to the weakening of ties between the members of BRICS; each of them started to pay more attention to their own interests, which are still more connected with the West. The researchers from the Higher School of Economics (Moscow) state that BRICS by 2020 reached its 'plateau of development' and a reset (*perezagruzka*) of BRICS is needed to develop new unified approaches to solving global problems, which could justify its claim to participate in global governance (Meshkova, 2020, pp. 8–9).

Russia is very interested in BRICS in which it sees the potential that other organisations lack. The BRICS states agree on both the paradigm and the ultimate goal – peaceful reform of the post–Cold War world order. This major goal can become the basis for further developing the political and economic agendas.

From the economic perspective, the economic potential of BRICS needs to be strengthened to turn the informal club into a strong alliance of major developing states (Sharova, 2016, p. 171). Bilateral trade relations are very uneven within BRICS states, with China being the major trading partner for all members. The effectiveness of economic interactions within the group is determined by low competition and the complementarity of the members' economies. That is why some scholars advocate a free trade agreement among the BRICS states. In the conditions of trans-regional integration alliances (Transatlantic and Trans-Pacific Partnerships), only an economically strong BRICS can become another pole in a multipolar global economy. If BRICS becomes a sustainable trade alliance, it will increase the competitiveness and investment appeal of the members and attract other developing nations to co-operate with the group both economically and politically.

In the view of Timofey Bordachev, Member of the BRICS Russia Expert Council,

> the New Russia does not have a stake in the competition of imperial ambitions but it does have a stake in closer international co-operation and in the creation of really effective formats of interaction that can provide an alternative to the growing chaos in the global economy and global politics. It is largely because of this that BRICS is gradually shifting from its original mission of serving as a platform to express the consolidated opinion of new, growing economies in a world dominated by the US and its allies to an agenda that offers the world new solutions that reflect the changes in the international environment.
>
> *(BRICS Russian Chairmanship, 2020, p. 28)*

The Covid-19 pandemic strengthened co-operation within BRICS in the health sphere, although interactions began much earlier in 2015, when the BRICS states established co-operation in combating infectious diseases. Then, in 2018, the initiative was advanced to establish a vaccine development and research centre. In the view of the Russian foreign minister Sergei Lavrov, 'Thanks to the visionary decisions adopted at the earlier summits, the BRICS countries were well prepared and are now able to mobilise their full potential in the face of the coronavirus infection' (Foreign Minister Sergey Lavrov's remarks, September 4, 2020). Russia sees BRICS as one of the leaders capable of taking actions to prevent such pandemics and overcoming the aftereffects. At the time of the pandemic, the world witnessed closer BRICS partnership and an increase in the role of BRICS in world affairs.

For Russia, BRICS is 'the partnership in the interests of global stability, mutual security and innovation growth' (Vladimir Putin prinial uchastiye vo vstreche, 2019). According to the Russian President V. Putin, BRICS 'is not a closed alliance, and its role and significance of BRICS will certainly increase' (Vladimir Putin otvetil na voprosy, 2019).

Notes

1 Term borrowed from G Toloraya (Toloraya, 2011)

2 The original phrase, coined by W. Shakespeare, was used to describe Russian foreign political behavior by M. Iluin (Busygina and Okunev, 2015, chapter 10)

3 Regionalisation means two different things. It can either mean the resurgence of regional powers (type 1) or the formation of regional integrational alliances (type 2), and these two contradictory processes cannot go in parallel in the bipolar world. Regional powers are interested in formalising the status of their relations with neighbouring countries, but the presence of the regional relations of the first type prevents their evolution into the second type because the character of relations between the leading power and dependent states will be violated. Thus, during bipolar period, the presence of the regional power was combined with ineffective regional alliances. After the end of bipolarity, these two types of regionalisation do not contradict each other any longer (Busygina and Okunev, 2015, p. 313).

4 Originally, the term was used by Strobe Talbott, head of the Brookings Institution and former deputy secretary of state who defined India as a sovereignty hawk in the context of the nuclear deal. (Johnson J., & Luce E. Delhi nuclear deal signals US shift. *Financial times*. (2007, August 2) URL:// www.ft.com/content/1ef60d2e-4122-11dc-8f37-0000779fd2ac [Online Resource] (Accessed 1 June 2020)

5 In Samuel Huntington's terms "The West versus the Rest"

6 Data from 2011. CIA Worldbook. India. People and society. URL:// www.cia.gov/the-world-factbook/countries/india/#people-and-society [Online Resource] (Accessed 1 June 2020)

References

Alekseenko, O. (2015). BRICS: The Role of Russia in the Group. *Observer*, Vol. 5, pp. 58–67.

Bratersky, M., and Kutyrev, G. (2019). BRICS and the Evolving Russia-India-China Security Agenda. *Strategic Analysis*, Vol. 43(6), pp. 597–619.

BRICS Russian Chairmanship 2020. (2020). *Mezhdunarodnaya zhizn (International Affairs Special Issue)*. Krasnogorsk Printing Plant. https://eng.brics-russia2020.ru/images/39/54/395496.pdf [Online Resource] (Accessed 1 December 2020).

Busygina, I., and Okunev, I. (Eds.). (2015). *Modernizatsiia i demokratizatsiia v stranakh BRICS. Sravnitel'nyi analiz [Modernization and Democratization in BRICS Countries: Comparative Analysis]*. Aspekt Press.

Concept of Participation of the Russian Federation in BRICS. (2013). http://static.kremlin.ru/media/events/eng/files/41d452b13d9c2624d228.pdf.

Concept of the Russian Federation's Presidency in BRICS in 2015–2016. (2015). http://en.brics2015.ru/russia_and_brics/20150301/19483.html

Denisov, I., Kazantsev, A., Lukyanov, F., and Safranchuk, I. (2019). Shifting Strategic Focus of BRICS and Great Power Competition. *Strategic Analysis*, Vol. 43(6), pp. 487–498.

Emelianov, A. (2018). Features of Interaction with BRICS in Terms of Geopolitical Transformations. Vestnik of Moscow State Linguistic University. *Social Sciences*, pp. 32–39. www.vestnik-mslu.ru/Vest/3_806.pdf [Online Resource] (Accessed 10 June 2020).

Foreign Minister Sergey Lavrov's remarks and answers to media questions at a news conference following an online meeting of the BRICS Foreign Ministers Council, Moscow, September 4, 2020. [Online Resource] www.mid.ru/web/guest/meropriyatiya_s_uchastiem_ministra/-/asset_publisher/xK1BhB2bUjd3/content/id/4318038?p_p_id=101_INSTANCE_xK1BhB2bUjd3&_101_INSTANCE_xK1BhB2bUjd3_languageId=en_GB (Accessed 1 December 2020).

Foreign Minister Sergey Lavrov's remarks and answers to questions during the online session "Russia and the post-COVID World," held as part of the Primakov Readings international forum, Moscow, July 10, 2020. [Online Resource] www.mid.ru/foreign_policy/news/-/asset_publisher/cKNonkJE02Bw/content/id/4217691?p_p_id=101_INSTANCE_cKNonkJE02Bw&_101_INSTANCE_cKNonkJE02Bw_languageId=en_GB (Accessed 1 December 2020).

Foreign Policy Concept of the Russian Federation. (2000). www.fas.org/nuke/guide/russia/doctrine/econcept.htm [Online Resource] (Accessed 1 June 2020).

Foreign Policy Concept of the Russian Federation. (2008). http://en.kremlin.ru/supplement/4116 [Online Resource] (Accessed 1 June 2020).

Foreign Policy Concept of the Russian Federation. (2013). www.mid.ru/en/foreign_policy/official_documents/-/asset_publisher/CptICkB6BZ29/content/id/122186 [Online Resource] (Accessed 1 June 2020).

Foreign Policy Concept of the Russian Federation. (2016). www.mid.ru/en/foreign_policy/official_documents/-/asset_publisher/CptICkB6BZ29/content/id/2542248 [Online Resource] (Accessed 1 June 2020).

Global Competitiveness Report. (2019). World Economic Forum. [Online Resource] http://www3.weforum.org/docs/WEF_TheGlobalCompetitivenessReport2019.pdf (Accessed 1 June 2020).

Grishin, O., and Dukhareva, A. (2017). Rossia i BRICS: nekotoriye tendentsii I perspektivi razvitiia [Russia and BRICS: Several Tendencies and Development Perspectives]. *Post-Soviet Issues*, Vol. 4(1), pp. 41–48.

Gygli, S., Haelg, F., Potrafke, N., and Sturm, J.-E. (2019). The KOF Globalisation Index – Revisited. *Review of International Organizations*, Vol. 14(3), pp. 543–574 https://doi.org/10.1007/s11558-019-09344-2 (Accessed 10 June 2020).

Human Development Report. (2019). UNDP. http://hdr.undp.org/sites/default/files/hdr2019.pdf [Online Resource] (Accessed 10 June 2020).

Kortunov, A. (2019). Between Polycentrism and Bipolarity on Russia's World Order Evolution Narratives. *Russia in Global Affairs*, (1), pp. 10–51.

Kozyrev, V. (2019). Washington's 'America First' Global Strategy and Its Implications for the BRICS. *Strategic Analysis*, Vol. 43(6), pp. 645–656.

Lavrov rasskazal ob idee Primakova sozdat' "treugolnik" Rossiya-India-Kitai [Lavrov told about Primakov's idea to set up the "triangle" Russia-India-China]. (2019, October 29). *RIA News*. https://ria.ru/20191029/1560334084.html [Online Resource] (Accessed 1 June 2020).

Lukin, A. (2016). Russia in a Post-Bipolar World. *Survival*, Vol. 58(1), pp. 91–112.

Lunev, S. (2014). BRICS Countries in Globalization Processes. *Comparative Politics Russia*, Vol. 5(3), pp. 81–108. https://doi.org/10.18611/2221-3279-2014-5-3(17)-81–108. [Online Resource] (Accessed 1 May 2020).

Meshkova, T. (Ed.). (2020). *Strategiia razvitiia BRICS I prioritety Rissii [Development Strategy of BRICS and Priorities for Russia].* HSE expert report. HSE Publishing House.

Moskva miagko podtalkivaet Pekin I Delhi k primireniyu [Moscow softly pushes Beijing and Delhi to reconciliation]. (2020, September 9). www.ng.ru/world/2020-09-10/1_7961_india.html [Online Resource] (Accessed 1 December 2020).

Nikonov, V. (2013). *BRICS: Analyzing the Security Dimension.* BRICS Information Centre. www.brics.utoronto.ca/newsdesk/durban/nikonov.html Online Resource] (Accessed 1 December 2020).

Nikonov, V. (2019). BRICS Reality. *Russkiy mir.* https://russkiymir.ru/en/publications/261425/ Online Resource] (Accessed 1 December 2020).

Novikov, D., and Skriba, A. (2019). The Evolution of Russian Strategy towards BRICS. *Strategic Analysis*, Vol. 43(6), pp. 585–596.

Panova, V. (2012). Mesto Rossiyi v BRICS: videniye i prakticheskiye resultati. Vliyaniye vneshnikh igrokov na protsess vzaimodaistviya v "klube" [Place of Russia in BRICS: influence of external actors on the process of interaction in the "club"]. *All Europe*, pp. 7–8. http://alleuropa.ru/?p=3927 [Online Resource] (Accessed 1 May 2020).

Putin: devizom predsedatelstva RF v BRICS stanut partnerstvo, bezopasnost i innovatsii [Putin: the motto of Russian chairmanship in BRICS will be partnership, security and innovations]. (2019, November 14). TASS. https://tass.ru/politika/7119969 [Online Resource] (Accessed 1 May 2020).

Priorities of the Russian BRICS Chairmanship in 2020. (2019). https://eng.brics-russia2020.ru/russia_in_brics/20191226/1469/Priorities-for-the-Russian-Federations-presidency-of-BRICS.html [Online Resource] (Accessed 1 June 2020).

Purushothaman, R., Wilson, D. (2003) *Dreaming with BRICs: The Path to 2050.* Global Economics Paper N 99. Goldman Sachs. http://globaltrends.thedialogue.org/publication/dreaming-with-brics-the-path-to-2050/ [Online Resource] (Accessed 15 May 2020).

Ritchie, H., Roser, M., and Ortiz-Ospina, E. (2018). Measuring Progress Towards the Sustainable Development Goals. *SDG-Tracker.org, website.* https://sdg-tracker.org/ [Online Resource] (Accessed 15 May 2020).

Roser, M., and Ortiz-Ospina, E. (2019a). Trade Openness. Published online at OurWorldInData.org. https://ourworldindata.org/global-rise-of-education [Online Resource] (Accessed 15 May 2020).

Roser, M., and Ortiz-Ospina, E. (2019b). Corruption Perception Index. Published online at OurWorldInData.org. https://ourworldindata.org/global-rise-of-education [Online Resource] (Accessed 15 May 2020).

Rossiiskii Sous-sherpa: BRICS – eto alians reformatorov v mezhdunarodnykh otnosheniyakh [Russian Sous-Sherpa: BRICS is an Alliance of Reformers in the International Relations] (2015, March 30). http://brics2015.ru/transcripts/20150330/29159-print.html [Online Resource] (Accessed 1 May 2020).

Sakwa, R. (2019a). BRICS and Sovereign Internationalism. *Strategic Analysis*, Vol. 43(6), pp. 456–468.

Sakwa, R. (2019b). The International System and Models of Global Order. *Russia in Global Affairs*, Vol. 17(3), pp. 8–31.

Sergunin, A., and Gao, F. (2018). BRICS as the Subject of Study of International Relations Theory. *International Organizations Research Journal*, Vol. 13(4), pp. 55–73.

Sharova, E. (2016). Vzaimnaya torgovlia stran BRICS na sovremennom etape [Trade Among BRICS States at the Present Stage]. *Problems of National Strategy*, Vol. 35(2), pp. 150–174.

Shelepov, A. (2015). BRICS and International Institutions: Models of Engagement in Multilateral Governance. *International Organizations Research Journal*, Vol. 10(4), pp. 7–24.

Toloraya, G. (2011). Rossiia I BRICS: strategiia vzaimodeistviya. [Russia and BRICS: Strategy f Interaction]. *Strategiia Rossii [Strategy of Russia].* http://sr.fondedin.ru/new/fullnews_arch_to.php?subaction=showfull&id=1314789648&archive=1314876917&start_from=&ucat=14& [Online Resource] (Accessed 1 May 2020).

Toloraya, G., and Chukov, R. (2016). BRICS to Be Considered? *International Organizations Research Journal*, Vol. 11(2), pp. 70–81.

Vinogradov, A. (2014). Dialogue format of BRICS and its Role in the Shaping of a Multipolar World. *Comparative Politics Russia.* Vol. 5(1), pp. 47–52.

Vladimir Putin otvetil na voprosy rossiiskikh zhurnalistov [Vladimir Putin answered to the questions of Russian journalists]. (2019, November 14). http://kremlin.ru/catalog/keywords/13/events/62047 [Online Resource] (Accessed 1 June 2020).

Vladimir Putin prinial uchastiye vo vstreche glav gosudarstv i pravitelstv stran-uchastnits BRICS [Vladimir Putin took part in the meeting of heads of states and heads of governments of BRICS]. (2019, November 14). http://kremlin.ru/events/president/news/62045 [Online Resource] (Accessed 1 June 2020).

Voskressenski, A. (2012). Concepts of Regionalization, Regional Subsystems, Regional Complexes and Regional Transformations in Contemporary IR. *Comparative Politics Russia*, Vol. 3(2), pp. 30–58.

Yurtaev, V., and Rogov, A. (2017). BRICS and SCO: Particular Qualities of Formation and Activities. *Vestnik RUDN. International Relations*, Vol. 17(3), pp. 469–482.

11

MULTILATERALISM IN RUSSIA'S FOREIGN POLICY AND BRICS

Surbhi Choudhary

Introduction

Why is multilateralism important from the practical as well as research standpoints? The world has avoided another war of the scale of the World Wars, and states' interdependence has increased, particularly after the end of the Cold War. Despite persistent conflicts in separate pockets, nations have joined hands in a multilateral co-operative spirit to promote global trade, connectivity and people-to-people exchange. What this shared spirit did to the world was to glue it together even in the face of disagreements, lack of common worldviews and sometimes even conflicts. The most prominent examples in this regard emerge from great power relations. The changing relations among countries with major powers as well as among the major powers themselves are perhaps the most prominent paradigms to understand the rapidly changing interdependence in global relations. The expansion of globalisation contributed to intensified multilateral efforts since the 1980s.

For a long time, the United Nations and its various ancillary organisations have been the nodal bodies for steering global multilateralism. The unprecedented loss of lives and physical destruction caused at the end of World War II created the need for global governance. For the Allied powers, it underlined the need for a global institution that represented most of the world, which could act as a nodal decision-making body and decide against war. The establishment of the UN was a manifestation of the Allied powers' conviction regarding the need for such a world body. Despite substantive grounds for the criticism of its role (read as inability) in preventing global conflicts from happening, the UN helped in not just deepening the world's faith in the spirit of multilateralism but also helped consolidate it. Peace through dialogue became a means to avoid conflict, and international institutions helped in creating a platform for multilateral co-operation.

DOI: 10.4324/9781003148074-13

Evolution of Russian Multilateralism

At the end of the Second World War, the Soviet Union, of which Russia was a part, found itself with the Allied Powers, having agreed to the structural modalities and institutions that would govern the world. However, until the end of the Cold War, the Soviet Union viewed multilateralism with scepticism and preferred bilateral means to conduct its foreign relations. Despite this, multilateralism continued to flourish.

The collapse of the Soviet Union left a unipolar world that lasted for about a decade. It constrained Russia's foreign relations, co-operative bids and multilateral engagements. The decade that preceded the collapse of the Soviet Union was perhaps the toughest phase for Russia's multilateralism. It was struggling with the economic and political turmoil created by *Glasnost* and *Perestroika*. The internal outlook certainly limited how Russia came to view, engage and co-operate with the outside world. The geopolitical and geostrategic shocks that came with the end of the Cold War for Russia forced it to align broadly with the multilateral choices that Western-dominated multilateral institutions made. Makarychev and Morozov (2011) argue that to do so was in Russia's long-term interests. Some decisions by Russia supporting Western decisions like German unification and the Gulf War may not have found support had it concerned solely Russian interests and Russian decision-making. However, the decade of the 1990s proved very decisive in shaping Russian multilateralism. Russia became a part of various European or global multilateral institutions, paving the way for a renewed multilateral era for Russia. It was during this period that Russia participated in the Council of Europe in 1996 and the Group of 8 (G8) in the following year, and went on to sign comprehensive agreements with the EU and NATO in 1994 and 1997 respectively.

However, Russia's alliance with Western multilateral institutions was brief because of the West's disinterest in accepting Russia as an equal member of its organisations. For instance, after the USSR's disintegration, NATO expanded to the East and admitted new members but it did not include Russia. This exclusion made the Russian Foreign Minister Primakov change the foreign policy priorities for Russia to enhance its focus on re-establishing influence in the post-Soviet region as well as to establish better relations with the Third World. Russia's domestic stability and foreign policy interests felt threatened when NATO's expansion reached close to Russian border. The pro-American colour revolutions in Georgia, Ukraine and Kyrgyzstan made Russia change its strategy and it adopted a multi-vector and assertive foreign policy.

According to Russia, the multilateral system in place after the Second World War is lopsided and gives power and authority to the US and its Western allies. The great powers need exceptionalism despite being part of multilateral institutions, to sustain influence. The Western quest for power garbed in multilateralism has often run counter to Russia's interests on the global stage. Russia is critical of the Western understanding of multilateralism and of West-led multilateral institutions as they favour the interests of the Western bloc and does not give equal say to the rest of the members. Russia advocates multilateralism that upholds the principles of sovereignty, non-intervention and consensual decision-making.

It is the difference in worldview, together with differences in the priorities of great powers, that has led to the great debate between multilateralism and multipolarity. Multipolarity has been defined as a system of power dissemination, which gives influence to several countries. Multilateralism, on the other hand, refers to several countries working in tandem with interdependence where more powerful countries wield greater influence. Russian foreign policy perhaps offers the best insight into the tussle between multipolarity and multilateralism. Makarychev and Viatcheslav Morozov (2011) argue that the conception of the Russian doctrine of multipolarity, particularly in the backdrop of Russia's competitive, and sometimes hostile, relations with the West, offers an insight into the evolution of its multilateralism.

Lavrov (2021) clearly stated that multilateral organisations should not be used to interfere 'in the domestic affairs of other countries'. For Russia, the West-based multilateral order and liberal values and norms are not the only way to arrange the world order. Russia now focuses on re-arranging the architecture of global governance that is not controlled by the 'elite club'. It aims to introduce a multilateral order, which includes more diverse countries of the world on an equal footing under the larger aegis of the UN system. Russia has become the co-founder of multiple multilateral organisations that keeps the West in check by establishing relations with fast-growing countries like India, China and Brazil. One of its best examples is BRICS.

In recent decades, Russia has become aware of its own weaknesses and vulnerabilities as well as the weaknesses and vulnerabilities of its opponents, and this is a major step towards a good foreign policy. Russia now has its own plan and commitment to multilateralism with its own unique characteristics. If the three great Eurasian powers – Russia, China and India – co-ordinate their foreign strategies and uphold a common approach to core global problems together with the help of international institutions, they will gain wider legitimacy, and then the meaning of multilateralism in the world will change dramatically. These countries have come together on platforms like SCO and BRICS and are propagating the Eurasian form of multilateralism, which upholds the principles of sovereignty, non-intervention and consensual decision-making.

However, there are also challenges that stand in the way of Russia. In many ways, Russia continues to be guided by Western institutions of multilateralism. In the words of Makarychev and Morozov (2011) 'a careful analysis of the origins of Russian multipolarity, particularly in the context of Russia's uneasy relationship with the West, will reveal that various approaches to multilateralism coexist in Russian foreign policy'. First, Russia's vision of multipolarity rests on its policy shift away from a US dominated unipolar order. Second, the Eurasian landmass lies at the centre of Russia's multipolar outlook. Third, Russia looks at the EAEU, the SCO and the BRICS as mechanisms to manage the West's competitive multilateralism.

Fourth, China's unprecedented rise has complicated Russia's position in multilateral organisations like BRICS and the SCO. And finally, the on-going shift of focus that Russian has adopted in the Indo-Pacific, opposing the US, along with its cautious approach to China, is likely to redefine its approach to multilateralism (Makarychev and Morozov 2011).

Russia's Changing Approach to Multilateralism

The Russian approach to multilateralism began to change from the Kosovo War in the late 1990s – primarily owing to a difference in opinion between the West and Russia over the West's approach to the war (Hughes 2013). Hughes contends that

> the Kosovo crisis beginning in 1999 could be seen as the first major crisis of multilateralism in the international system after the end of the Cold War. Russia, however, saw its multilateral engagement over Kosovo as a strategic interaction to counterbalance and compensate for its weakness vis-à-vis NATO.

What marked a significant break for Russia from the West-dominated institutional multilateralism was Russia's eviction from the G8 in 2014 over its annexation of Crimea (Makarychev and Morozov 2011). In March 2014, the G8 leaders made a decision to terminate Russia's role in the group of leading industrialised nations (CNN 2014). Russia was a member of the G8 forum from 1997 through 2014. Besides the Crimean issue, Russia also disagreed with other G8 members on trade and climate policies, and the importance of the bigger Group of Twenty (G20) as an alternative framework (The G7 and the Future of Multilateralism, CFR 2019). There were growing differences between Russia and the West on other issues of global importance such as Russia's own embargos against European officials, Russia's support to Syria against the West and the supposed Russian interference in the US elections. These incidents created a deep mistrust between Russia and the West and charted a new path for Russian multilateralism. Since 2014, Russia's focus was to engage with other countries without pressure or restrictions from the West (Ambalkina 2014).

Jordan (2010) argues that during the period 2000–2008, as the Russian economy recovered and Russia became a net creditor on the back of enhanced revenues from high oil and gas prices, it began to exercise more multilateral choices. For instance, Russia started to contribute in debt relief and other multilateral development-aid programmes, predominantly in Africa. This helped Russia revise its great power status. Even in Russia's multilateral approach, its focus on geopolitics and balance-of-power have been evident. As such, Russian leaders go on to employ great power perception in its multilateralism, which is more 'instrumental than principled' (Pamela 2010). In this regard, the Russian President Vladimir Putin stated in 2000 that 'Russia shall seek to achieve a multi-polar system of international relations that really reflects the diversity of the modem [*rn*] world with its great variety of interest' (The Foreign Policy Concept of the Russian Federation 2000).

The year 2007 is again significant with regard to Russia's policy enunciations. In one of the most powerful policy enunciations by Putin, in his 2007 speech at the Munich Conference on Security Policy, criticised the 'unipolar' world propounded by the West as being dictatorial and the actions taken by the US-led multilateral system as being adversarial to global security as they perpetuate conflicts and wars. In his diatribe against the unipolar worldview being pushed by the US, the Russian President launched his most fierce defence of the multipolar order (Speech at the Munich Conference on Security Policy 2007).

Is the character of Russia's multilateralism changing? Russia's association with multilateral organisations and the nature of its multilateral engagements seem to have changed considerably since the end of the World War II, and then again at the end of the Cold War. Multilateralism did exist in Russia, but it differed from the values of the West. Russia's membership in international organisations projected a certain worldview. While during the Cold War, the prime goal of Russian multilateralism was to gain one-upmanship apropos the US, post-Cold War multilateral engagements have reflected a broadening of the agenda for Russia, especially in its engagements with groups like the G8 that included the US, which was unthinkable during the Cold War. This is also reflected in Russia's membership in the Collectively Security Treaty Organization, an intergovernmental military alliance in Eurasia among selected states of the erstwhile Soviet Union. The year 2014 proved critical in redefining Russia's approach and response to multilateral organisations because of Western sanctions. Due to increasing international sanctions, Russia's embrace of alternative multilateral platforms such as the SCO and BRICS has become firmer.

Russia and the BRICS

In order to understand Russian multilateralism, the evolution of the Russian strategy on the road to BRICS is very crucial. The West has dominated most multilateral organisations, including those that Russia has been a part of. Faced with a choice between ignoring the organisations dominated by the West and participating in them, Russia's clear choice for the latter has been evident, particularly through its participation in the G20. While the G20 provided the right platform for Russia to engage with the largest economies and the developing world, BRICS allowed it an alternative platform that did not include Western countries as members and provided Russia its space in South–South co-operation.

BRICS has become an important organisation in world politics today and its role is likely to expand in the future. It has the potential to play a larger economic and strategic role, especially with the involvement of three large economies like India, Russia and China. The gradual retreat of the US from the global space under Trump administration further allowed BRICS to increase its international influence. China's increasing international heft has further added to BRICS' image as a prominent organisation.

For Russia, BRICS remains a key organisation to shape international response, particularly on non-Western issues. The importance of BRICS has been enhanced by the fact that Russia has ceased to be a member of the G8 since 2014 and the agenda of the G20 continues to be decided by the West, with limited Russian role. The changing international role of the US has deeply affected the functioning of multilateral institutions and the rise of the collective BRICS economy has created the lateral space for Russia's multilateral engagement. BRICS' tacit opposition to Western hegemony has also given Russia more reasons to consolidate its footing in the organisation. While the lack of domination by one single country was certainly a factor in BRICS, the ideological space provided by the spirit of South–South co-operation was an added advantage for Russia. As such, BRICS remains a critical mechanism to propagate Russia's foreign policy. With regard to BRICS, the Russian foreign policy says:

> Russia attaches great importance to ensuring the sustainable manageability of global development, which requires collective leadership from the major States that should be representative in geographic and civilization terms and fully respect the central and coordinating role of the UN. To these ends, Russia has been expanding its ties with its partners within the Group of Twenty, the BRICS (Brazil, Russia, India, China and the Republic of South Africa), the SCO (Shanghai Cooperation Organization), the RIC (Russia, India and China) alongside other organizations and dialogue platforms.
>
> *(The Foreign Policy Concept of Russian Federation 2016)*

Going through the literature on Russia's changing role in BRICS reveals that the year 2014 marked a decisive turn, to the extent that Russia's engagement with this multilateral organisation can be divided into the pre and post-2014 eras. The 2014 sanctions on Russia by the West ensured that Russia was more steadfast in its embrace of BRICS and the organisation became a 'tool' to subdue Russia's international isolation (The Foreign Policy Concept of Russian Federation 2016).

Co-operation within BRICS is among Russia's long-term foreign policy goals as its participation in the grouping helps it achieve certain objectives like a common approach to reforming the international monetary and financial system to create a more representative and equitable system for Russia and other BRICS states; to enhance the foreign policy co-operation with BRICS participants with due respect for sovereignty and non-interference in their domestic affairs; using BRICS to strengthen Russia's international standing; to co-ordinate proposals based on common interests of all BRICS states in the UN and other international forums; to prevent use of force and the imposition of unilateral solutions to conflicts; to jointly oppose the politicisation of human rights via multilateral institutions; collaboration on maintenance of regional stability by developing similar approaches towards non-proliferation of weapons of mass destruction, combating terrorism and so on (Concept of participation of the Russian Federation in BRICS).

Some of the other strategic objectives of Russia in the BRICS are using BRICS to enrich the multi-vector disposition of Russian foreign policy; to consolidate Russia's status as a global power pole in international relations; to boost Russia's cultural presence in the world and to use RBICS to promote better bilateral relations with other member states. For Russia, BRICS is a prime tool to balance against the US hegemony in the global system, especially in the face of Western sanctions to alienate the country after the Ukraine crisis, to uphold the UN Charter and other international laws and counter the Western efforts to circumvent these laws. Overall, Russia promotes BRICS as a new exemplar of international relations that can overcome the longstanding dividing lines between the West and the East and the North and the South.

By the end of the last century, Russia had begun making efforts to promote the idea of trilateral co-operation with China and India. In this new multilateral formation, Russia saw the potential for non-Western co-operation and engagement in the economic and military spheres as well as in the field of space. These factors pushed Russia to take one of the first steps to co-operate with the other members of the grouping. The trilateral co-operation formed the basic mechanism of co-operation, which matured into BRICS later on. The initiative for trilateral co-operation between the Russian Federation, India and the PRC is often attributed to Yevgeny Primakov, Russia's Foreign Minister in 1996–1998 (Russia-India-China: RIC Format 2019). Later, the foreign ministers of the three countries met at a sideline event to the UNGA session of 2002. The ordinal meeting of the leaders of the three countries took place in St. Petersburg in 2006 along with the G20 summit. This was preceded by the interaction of foreign ministers of BRIC countries in 2006 on the sidelines of the UN General Assembly in New York. From the following year, various efforts started to set up a mechanism for interaction and co-operation among BRICS members, with Russia as an active participant. The first BRIC summit was held at Yekaterinburg in 2009 by the Kremlin's support (Russia-India-China: RIC Format 2019). South Africa officially became a member nation of BRICS in 2010.

Gradually, Russia also began to look at BRICS to strengthen its financial situation by keeping its exports and financial co-operation afloat through intra-organisational co-operation. In the June 2009 BRIC meet in Yekaterinburg, Russian President Dmitry Medvedev said, 'it is very likely that this kind of coordination would help clarify each other's positions and help us develop new innovative ways to address international financial problems and reform international financial relations' (Opening Address at Restricted Format Meeting of BRIC Leaders 2009). Russia's economic focus in BRICS began after the 2008 financial crisis. Prior to the financial crisis, Russia saw BRICS as a mechanism of a middle-great power organisation that could shape great power behaviour but hardly engaged in any concrete co-operation. Russia's economic focus in BRICS became sharper in the years since 2009. In the BRICS leaders' summit of 2010, Russian President Dmitry Medvedev put out his views on co-operation within BRICS in a paper. Among other things, the paper had a clear economic focus:

> Our key task is to achieve sustainable economic growth and an increase in the income of citizens based on a diversified economy, technological

> modernization and innovative development. We increasingly invest in further space exploration, energy efficiency, development of nuclear and alternative energy, information, telecommunications and new medical technologies, and development of drugs. We attach great importance to processing of mineral resources our country is rich in, as well as to agricultural production growth. I am convinced that our BRIC partners will find these Russian achievements useful.
>
> *(Medvedev 2010)*

Over time, BRICS moved from economic to political issues. The BRICS meeting in New Delhi in 2012 discussed political issues like Syria and Iran. Russia also took the lead in framing an initiative to provide aid to Syria. Russia's intention to broaden the BRICS agenda, which was evident during the 2012 summit, became clearer after 2014. This was most clearly spelt out in an article titled, 'BRICS: Towards new horizons of strategic partnership', that President Putin wrote in 2017 as a run-up to the ninth BRICS Summit, Xiamen, China:

> Russia highly values the multifaceted cooperation that has developed within the BRICS. Our countries' constructive cooperation on the international arena is aimed at creating a fair multipolar world and equal development conditions for all . . . Russia stands for closer coordination of the BRICS countries' foreign policies, primarily at the UN and G20, as well as other international organisations. It is clear that only the combined efforts of all countries can help bring about global stability and find solutions to many acute conflicts, including those in the Middle East. I would like to say that it was largely thanks to the efforts of Russia and other concerned countries that conditions have been created to improve the situation in Syria. We have delivered a powerful blow to the terrorists and laid the groundwork for launching the movement towards a political settlement and the return of the Syrian people to peace.
>
> *(Putin 2017)*

A constant assertion of power and influence, along with a persistent effort to change its negotiating position in a new world order has been the underlying theme of Russian multilateralism. The ongoing pandemic has exacerbated these trends with the United States looking inwards and China scrambling to fill in the gap. This space has also allowed further consolidation of the Sino-Russian relationship and is playing out in a nuanced way in various strategic domains such as Central Asia, Europe and even in the Arctic (Stronski and Nicole 2018).

Despite pessimism associated with the proposal made at the 2012 BRICS Summit held at Delhi to establish a new financial institution, BRICS went on the establish the New Development Bank (NDB) and the Contingent Reserve Arrangement (CRA) in July 2014. The CRA has a capital of $100 billion, which is meant to extend support to the members to face any short-term liquidity and balance of payment pressures. NDB has also expanded its strategic co-operation by signing an MOU with the Asian Development Bank and the World Bank in 2016 and is exploring ways to co-operate with the Asian Infrastructure Investment Bank. With the opening of new regional offices in São Paulo (The New Development Bank Opens Its Indian Regional Office 2022) and Moscow (The New Development Bank Opens Its Indian Regional Office 2022), the NDB has expanded its presence and is consolidating its pathway to success.

Russia, which has been ardent in pursuing the idea of NDB, has been steadily involved in its functioning as well as in obtaining loans from it. It has been allocating the funds to its infrastructure, environmental, sanitation and flood management projects. Russia also wants to free trade from dependence on the US dollar and wants 'de-dollarisation' of trade. In this pursuit, the BRICS has already created the Local Currency Bond Fund, which allows utilising local currencies for trade among BRICS' members although the progress has been below expectations. Russia has been backing the idea of currency-swap in bilateral trade between the members and the development of an International Payments System, an idea that was put forward in the 2019 Brasilia Declaration. The current international payments are largely routed through the Society for Worldwide Interbank Financial Telecommunications (SWIFT), which is under the Western control. Russia was also threatened with being cut off from the SWIFT system as a part of the Western sanctions, which resulted in the establishment of the System for the Transfer of Financial Messages (SFPS) that ensures bank-to-bank transfers since 2017. How the BRICS system will turn out to be is yet to be known.

Multilateral forums like BRICS and SCO that were already critical for Russia have gained further prominence in its foreign policy in the backdrop of Western sanctions. Through these forums, Russia tries to assert its global aspirations in a concerted manner, avoiding any confrontational issues with the West. Russia has been postulating the idea of focusing on global political issues and to co-ordinate on global strategic issues within BRICS. However, BRICS as an institution does not want to be tagged as an anti-Western forum and thus, other members have pursued their bilateral alliances with the Western powers, sometimes even gaining closer partnership. Even though BRICS members do not want to include global political events in its agenda, they did not shy away from backing Russia when there was a threat to restrain it from entering the G20 summit. The BRICS members issued a joint communique stating that 'the custodianship of the G20 belongs to all member-states equally and no one member-state can unilaterally determine its nature and character', thus displaying its political astuteness (The Economic Times 2014). Further, Brazil, China and India refrained from voting on a UN General Assembly resolution, which censured the Russian policy in Ukraine. They also abstained from the UN General Assembly resolution criticising the Crimea referendum. Thus, displaying solidarity with Russia and backing it up with action.

Bipolar competitiveness has given way to competitive multilateralism, despite growing Chinese relative gains vis-à-vis the US. This is backed not just by the growing relative power and influence of major countries across the world but also the realisation that giving increasing space and importance to global multilateralism is the way forward. In this regard, Belo and Carment (2020) argue that, 'since great powers are the most sensitive of all states to the relative gains made by their opponents and allies, the alliances they form are a kind of competitive multilateralism'. Russia's active participation in BRICS, especially the trends in its relationship with other BRICS partners like India and China, is testimony to a form of hedging strategy that seeks to enhance Russia's international leverage through multilateral engagements.

Conclusion

Over the years, Russia's role in BRICS has matured and changed a lot. Besides, Russia has played a principal role in shaping the BRICS agenda. Russia has come to perceive BRICS as one of the prime multilateral non-Western organisations that is useful in shaping the global order. This importance will be asserted further in the aftermath of the Covid-19 pandemic, where the influence of the US recedes and China gains prominence. Moreover, the rise of a middle power coalition that includes India will only further strengthen the BRICS mechanism. Russia's own role vis-à-vis China is one factor that is likely to shape how BRICS evolves. The fact that India and China share a relationship that can at best be described as working but not cordial, along with Russia's own careful balancing with China, points to the difficulties and limitations of the BRICS grouping as a multilateral forum. BRICS' inner tensions are likely to increase as India becomes a power that is increasingly drawn towards the US. Besides, the economic agenda of BRICS is likely to take a backseat in the post-pandemic phase with each country looking inwards. India's intermittent border tensions with China, and China's growing dominance and assertiveness are likely to create fissures in BRICS. For Russia, China's unprecedented rise has eaten into its strategic space. Ceding space to China on the international stage may be complicated for Russia's grand design and may impinge on the intra-organisational mechanism of the BRICS, going forward. The new conditions in the world now require a reformed role for BRICS and Russia's engagement with the multilateral organisation will have to be seen in that light (Novikov and Skriba 2019).

Russia's association with BRICS will depend on how it can work with other partners in the organisation. BRICS offers an opportunity to consolidate non-Western multilateralism and sustain governance in an era where leadership is fast vanishing from the international order. However, China's assertiveness may complicate the Russian agenda of making BRICS an effective 'non-Western' multilateral organisation.

Finally, it is also argued that heterogeneity has impeded BRICS' progress (Yaroslav and Vinokurov 2019). Will a more compact, more inclusive group deliver better? The answer is contingent upon how the economic and security agendas of BRICS play out in the short to medium term, even as the world seeks to recover from a broken security agenda at the multilateral level and recuperates economically.

How these factors will affect Russia's position in other multilateral organisations such as the SCO and the nature of its ties with other BRICS members remains to be seen. However, Rewizorski (2015) argues that BRICS marked a fundamental change in the growing role of non-Western countries clustered in institutions, led by BRICS. BRICS differs significantly in comparison to groups such as G7 or the G77, which preceded it, in words of Marek Rewizorski (2015), in terms of 'its growing economic power, its demography, natural resources, combined gross domestic product (GDP), its participation in leading international organisations, and its common principles of openness, pragmatism, solidarity, and mutual assistance'. BRICS appears united on some of the issues where non-Western and non-normative components are concerned (Rewizorski 2015).

The future trends of Russian multilateralism may emerge from a comparative assessment of some of the major decisions supported/not supported by Russia over the past few years in multilateral organisations. To arrive at a more affirmative prediction of Russia's future role in BRICS, a cross-comparison with other multilateral institutions like the SCO and the G20 would be a good exercise. Are there a set of 'best practices' that could emerge from Russia's role in these multilateral institutions? What can BRICS do to incorporate Russia's best practices in multilateralism within its framework in order to learn from Russia's external multilateralism? Here it is important to mention that Duggan (2015) has presented a cross-institutional comparison between the EU and BRICS. There is a degree of variance in the Russian attitude towards BRICS. For instance, in the ascendance of the BRICS as an economically resurgent group, Russia kept itself aligned with the agenda of the group but on the issue of climate change, particularly in the Copenhagen Climate Conference in 2009, Russia maintained a gap with the other members of BRICS.

Russia's security agenda is another factor that will define and shape Russian multilateralism in the future, inside BRICS or outside. To that end, a few questions vis-à-vis evolving Russian multilateralism become very critical: What has been the position of BRICS countries in Russian security endeavours in Eastern Europe, Syria or other places? Did Russia's involvement and its aggressive foreign policy lead to a tacit 'securitisation of BRICS'? Finally, has Russia's participation in the BRICS changed its organisational purpose or has the BRICS itself modified Russian multilateralism? Perhaps, answers to these complex questions will provide the future roadmap of Russian multilateralism.

References

Ambalkina, A. 2014. 'Russia's Multilateral Aid Practice'. Available at: www.unescap.org/sites/default/files/2014-S3-4_Abalkina.pdf (Accessed 2 May 2020).

Belo, D. and Carment, D. 2020. 'Unilateralism and Competitive Multilateralism in Gray-zone Conflict: A Comparison of Russia and the United States', *Air University*. Available at: www.airuniversity.af.edu/Wild-Blue-Yonder/Article-Display/Article/2292990/unilateralism-and-competitive-multilateralism-in-gray-zone-conflict-a-compariso/ (Accessed on 18 December 2020).

'BRIC countries oppose ban on Putin attending G20 Summit', *The Economic Times*, March 25 2014. Available at: https://economictimes.indiatimes.com/news/economy/policy/bric-countries-oppose-ban-on-putin-attending-g20-summit/articleshow/32616450.cms (Accessed 13 June 2020).

'BRICS Summit', *President of Russia*, March 29, 2012. Available at: http://kremlin.ru/events/president/news/14868 (Accessed on 5 May 2020).

'Concept of participation of the Russian Federation in BRICS', Kremlin Website. Available at: http://static.kremlin.ru/media/events/eng/files/41d452b13d9c2624d228.pdf. (Accessed 11 October 2020).

Duggan, N. 2015. 'BRICS and the Evolution of a New Agenda within Global Governance', in Marek Rewizorski (ed.), *The European Union and the BRICS Complex Relations in the Era of Global Governance*, p. 16. Poland: Springer.

'The Foreign Policy Concept of the Russian Federation, Approved by President of the Russian Federation Vladimir Putin', November 30, 2016. Available at: www.rusemb.org.uk/rp_insight/ (Accessed 4 May 2020).

'The Foreign Policy Concept of the Russian Federation, Approved by President of the Russian Federation Vladimir Putin', 28 June 2000. Available at: www.fas.org/nuke/guide/russia/doctrine/econcept.htm (Accessed 6 May 2020).

Hughes, J. 2013. 'Russia and the Secession of Kosovo: Power, Norms and the Failure of Multilateralism', *Europe-Asia Studies*, 65(5), 992–1016. Doi: 10.1080/09668136.2013.792448 (Accessed 11 November 2020).

Jordan, Pamela A. 2010. 'A Bridge between the Global North and Africa? Putin's Russia and G8 Development Commitments', *African Studies Quarterly*, 11(4), 83–115.

Lavrov, S. V. 2021. 'On Law, Rights and Rules', *Russia in Global Affairs*, 19(3), 228–240. https://doi.org/10.31278/1810-6374-2021-19-3-228-240 (Accessed 04 April 2020).

Makarychev, A. and Morozov, V. 2011. 'Multilateralism, Multipolarity, and Beyond: A Menu of Russia's Policy Strategies', *Global Governance*, 17(3), 353–373. Available at: www.jstor.org/stable/23033752 (Accessed 18 December 2020).

Medvedev, D. 2010. 'Dmitry Medvedev's Article, BRIC Countries: Common Goals- Common Actions Has Been Published', *President of Russia*, April 13. Available at: http://en.kremlin.ru/events/president/news/7443 (Accessed 5 May 2020).

Novikov, D. and Skriba, A. 2019. 'The Evolution of Russian Strategy towards BRICS', *Strategic Analysis*, 43(6), 585–596. https://doi.org/10.1080/09700161.2019.1672129.

'Opening Address at Restricted Format Meeting of BRIC Leaders', *President of Russia*, June 16, 2009. Available at: http://en.kremlin.ru/events/president/transcripts/4474 (Accessed 4 May 2020).

Putin, V. 2017. 'BRICS: Towards New Horizons of Strategic Partnership', *The Times of India*. September 1. Available at: https://timesofindia.indiatimes.com/blogs/toi-edit-page/brics-towards-new-horizons-of-strategic-partnership/ (Accessed 5 May 2020).

Rewizorski, M. 2015. 'Participation of the European Union and the BRICS in the G20', in Marek Rewizorski (ed.), *The European Union and the BRICS Complex Relations in the Era of Global Governance*, p. 59. Poland: Springer.

'Russia-India-China: RIC Format Receives New Impetus/Valeria Gorbacheva'. 2019. July 07. Available at: www.nkibrics.ru/posts/show/5cfa52836272692ee0170000 (Accessed 5 May 2020).

'Speech and the Following Discussion at the Munich Conference on Security Policy', *President of Russia,* February 10, 2007. Available at: http://en.kremlin.ru/events/president/transcripts/24034 (Accessed 3 May 2020).

Stronski, P. and Nicole, N. G. 2018. 'Competition: Russia and China in Central Asia, the Russian Far East, and the Arctic', *Carnegie Endowment for International Peace*, February 28.

Available at: https://carnegieendowment.org/2018/02/28/cooperation-and-competition-russia-and-china-in-central-asia-russian-far-east-and-arctic-pub-75673 (Accessed 20 December 2020).

'The New Development Bank Opens Its Indian Regional Office', *BRICS Website*, May 26, 2022. Available at: http://infobrics.org/post/35789/ (Accessed 30 May 2022).

'U.S., other powers kick Russia out of G8', *CNN*, March 25, 2014. Available at: https://edition.cnn.com/2014/03/24/politics/obama-europe-trip/index.html (Accessed 2 May 2020).

Yaroslav, L. and Vinokurov, E. 2019. 'Extending BRICS to BRICS+: The Potential for Development Finance, Connectivity and Financial Stability', *Area Development and Policy*, 4(2).

12

INDIA AND BRICS

Rajan Kumar

India's economic growth has expanded its global footprints necessitating a web of multilateral networks. Its strategy is to align with powerful states that matter to its economic and security interests. Essentially, it is a non-ideological, pragmatic and a flexible strategy to navigate securely in a multipolar world. The emphasis is on retaining the core of the liberal international order, seeking multilateral reforms, forging close ties with the US and Russia, and, to the extent possible, restraining China from threatening its interests.

The complexity of India's multilateralism springs from the paradox of its vocal commitment to a liberal international order coexisting simultaneously with a geopolitical compulsion to deal with the regional security dilemma created by a strategic nexus between Islamabad and Beijing. In the regional security architecture, Russia becomes a vital player due its influence over Eurasia, West Asia and China. India's larger geopolitical strategy is to keep Russia neutral and the US on its side to overcome the visible military asymmetry that it has with China. This strategy features prominently in India's foreign policy and its multilateralism.

In its dealings with global powers, especially the US, Russia and China, it pursues a 'straddle strategy' – a risk-averse strategy that offers flexible choices to its diplomacy. In the last two decades, it has joined organisations that are diametrically opposed to each other in their orientations. For instance, it has embraced the Quadrilateral Security Dialogue (QUAD), but it is also a founding member of BRICS, and recently joined the Shanghai Cooperation Organization (SCO). It also participates in Russia, India and China (RIC) trilateral forum. One may find it paradoxical, but New Delhi considers this as the best option available in the present circumstances. In the local jargon of Indian policy makers, it is widely known as a policy of 'multi-alignment'. It presupposes partnerships with all the world's powers short of a military alliance. BRICS is clearly a subset of India's 'multi-alignment strategy'.

DOI: 10.4324/9781003148074-14

Recent developments validate the claim that India is more inclined to joining multilateral institutions than in earlier times. Among several other organisations that India embraced in the last two decades, BRICS stands out as the most unique and consequential one. In a short span, it has succeeded in creating a formidable institutional structure, has learnt how to build a consensus, and has endured a fratricidal conflict between its two prime members. Although it is a highly heterogeneous organisation with far more divergences than convergences, it would be naïve to dismiss it as an inconsequential chatterbox. New Delhi views it as a work-in-progress and a useful platform on which to engage with the regional powers of the Global South. It uplifts India's status somewhat by placing it in the club of a former and an emerging superpower.

India has largely been consistent in its support to BRICS. The change of regimes has not resulted in any significant shift in New Delhi's orientation towards this organisation. Its engagement with BRICS can better be understood by answering three critical questions: how does this organisation fit into New Delhi's scheme of geopolitical balancing? What are the major objectives pursued through this organisation? And finally, what are India's concerns and dilemmas at BRICS?

India and the origin of BRICS

In its formative years, BRICS appeared to be an ideal forum for emerging countries. The latter shared a sense of historical discrimination and fretted over the dominance of the West. Their frictions with the institutions of the North contributed to the emergence of a collective alternative forum. As regional hegemons, these states sought to extend their influence beyond their respective regions. They resented their exclusion from the centre of power in global politics (Zakaria 2008).

BRICS owes its origin to the idea of a strategic triangle involving Russia, China and India (RIC), proposed by Yevgeny Primakov, the then prime minister of Russia in 1998. India embraced RIC, anticipating a close collaboration with China and Russia at a time when its relations with the US were unsteady. RIC held regular meetings on the sidelines of other multilateral summits but it never really took off as a viable forum. It remained a 'discussion-forum' of three dissatisfied powers – lamenting the hegemonic policies of the US and issuing grand statements on possibilities of collaboration. Almost a decade later, however, the idea of the triangular co-operation extended further to constitute BRICS as an organisation of the Global South.

BRICS turned out to be the first serious attempt at counter-institutionalisation or regime shifting in the post-Cold War years. India carries a long grudge against the prevailing world order. The period of the Cold War was particularly disadvantageous to India. Most security regimes excluded India because of its proximity to the USSR. India survived the rigid politics of the bipolar world through its non-alignment strategy. But with the end of the Cold War, this strategy became obsolete and irrelevant. Most of the non-aligned countries rushed to embrace the US and India was left in the lurch in the unipolar world of the 1990s. It desperately needed new partners to protect itself from the hegemonic thrust of the US. It flirted with RIC and India, Brazil and South Africa (IBSA) Dialogue Forum during this period.

BRICS was foreseen as a useful forum to expand its co-operation with the powerhouse economies of the South, and give a collective push to its long pending demands of reforming the key global institutions, viz., the International Monetary Fund (IMF), the World Bank (WB), the World Trade Organization (WTO) and the United Nations Security Council (UNSC). New Delhi genuinely believed that BRICS would lend a sympathetic ear to its grudges and help in reforming international institutions. At the time of BRICS' inception, India was not as hostile to China as it became following the border skirmishes at Doklam (2017) and East Ladakh (2020).

Throughout the 1990s, although the Indian economy opened up to the West, the mutual suspicion between India and the US remained strong. Russia refused to give cryogenic engines to India under Western pressure. The US and many countries of the West sanctioned India for its nuclear test in 1998. It was not until 2008 that a dramatic shift in its relationship occurred, owing primarily to the famous Indo-US civil nuclear deal between the two countries. By that time, however, India was already in the process of formalising BRICS, the meetings for which had been taking place since 2006. India did not see any contradiction in engaging with Russia and the US at the same time. It was possible also because the strains between Russia and the US were not yet pronounced.

BRICS for strategic autonomy and geopolitical balancing

In assessing India's external strategy, two of its perceptions are particularly relevant. The first concerns its sense of vulnerability emanating from its colonial past and Cold War politics, and the second, its consequent policy of neutrality over alignment. Two hundred years of colonial subjugation and Cold War politics created a deep sense of suspicion towards the West. In the initial years of the Cold War, it feared subordination by the Cold War titans. As a consequence, it projected the notion of 'sovereignty and autonomy' as the key objectives of its foreign policy. Ever since independence, it never locked itself out in an exclusive relationship with any power. It turned abhorrent to the politics of alliance and sought neutrality in its external engagements. That historical anxiety persists in the minds of policy makers and intelligentsia even today. In the bipolar Cold War period, the quest for strategic autonomy led India to adopt a policy of non-alignment and brought it closer to the USSR; in the unipolar 1990s, it toyed with the idea of fomenting ties with Russia and China; and with the rise of China today, it is inching towards the US (Mohan 2020a). Its so-called policy of multi-alignment can be seen as an extension of its non-alignment approach. It has rejected the 'universalism of the weak', as in the NAM, to embrace the pragmatism of the strong (Mohan 2013). Hence, we see India seeking to forge closer ties with all friendly powers.

The dominant view in India is that it should shed its colonial and post-colonial hangover and forge close ties with the West. It endorses the idea of an alliance with the US to check the rise of China in the Indo-Pacific. This syncs well with the 'pivot to Asia' policy of the US started by the Obama administration and pursued by succeeding administrations (Mohan 2020a). A large number of scholars and policy-makers in India, however, advocate caution and underline the relevance of strategic autonomy in its foreign policy (Mehta 2020; Menon 2020; Tharoor 2020). They suspect that an alliance with the US will escalate tensions with China (Mehta 2020). As a growing economy, India should exercise caution and not get ensnared in the technological and geopolitical conflicts of the US with China. A border conflict will hold India back for a decade from the path of development. A stronger economy will place India in an advantageous position even in its border negotiations with China. Therefore, building multiple coalitions without playing second fiddle to the US serves the best interest of India (Menon 2020). BRICS is considered a significant step in that direction.

The strategy of 'multi-alignment' is stressed as a policy superior to the policy of alignment. It is essentially a risk-averse strategy, a hedging, to protect itself in an uncertain world. It presupposes partnerships with multiple powers in the world (Tharoor 2012; Sidhu et al. 2013). India's Minister of External Affairs, S. Jaishankar (2019), a scholar and an experienced diplomat, noted, 'the independent mindset that drove non-alignment and then protected our strategic equities can today be better expressed in multiple partnerships . . . it is having many balls up in the air at the same time and displaying the confidence and dexterity to drop none'. He further argues that India's foremost priority is to create a multipolar Asia that can lead to multipolar world. Such arguments have widespread appeal and adherents in India. Two successive regimes in New Delhi in the last two decades have dismissed the idea of a military alliance with the US. The Modi administration, with its overwhelming majority, has the best political and ideological orientation to forge an alliance. But as the statement of the minister here shows, New Delhi remains cautious in crossing the Rubicon. It is wary of alienating Russia, and the level of trust required to take such a leap is absent. Washington is still viewed as an unreliable partner compared to Moscow. Desh and Gramer contend that Modi is gradually shedding the legacy of non-alignment, but the US is still viewed with a degree of scepticism. Madan (2021) also notes a lingering scepticism in ties with the US despite all the progress in the last two decades. In fact, the sudden withdrawal of the US forces from Afghanistan without informing its alliance partners, and the way US cornered France in its submarine deal with Australia, have reinforced the notion of the US as an unreliable partner. If it can betray its NATO partners, it can do the same to any country.

India's act of engaging with multiple powers is essentially hierarchical and consists of two layers: a 'dominant policy' sitting aside a 'subordinate policy'. The two trends are meant to counterbalance each other. The goal is to avoid being sucked into an emerging bipolar rivalry. In the Cold War period, the dominant policy was the non-alignment movement (NAM), but it was supplemented by a subordinate policy of forging ties with the USSR. Often, observers have focused more on the dominant policy, ignoring the subordinate trends. At present, BRICS appears to be its 'subordinate policy' meant to complement the dominant pro-US orientation.

In the last two decades, India has moved very close to the US. The successive regimes of the United Progressive Alliance (UPA) and the National Democratic Alliance (NDA) vigorously pursued this policy of rebooting ties. India signed a number of logistics and information sharing agreements and has become one of the closest non-NATO security partners of the US. The US has also emerged as one of the biggest suppliers of arms and weapons to India in the last 15 years. Yet it is unlikely that India will go the Australia way and join a security alliance such as AUKUS (Australia, UK and US), which was announced in September 2021. S Jaishankar, India's External Affairs Minister, has reiterated time and again that India would never be the part of an alliance system, and the US must 'look beyond traditional alliances' to more 'plurilateral' coalitions (Haidar 2020). An alliance will adversely impact its ties with Russia, China, Iran, Pakistan, Afghanistan and countries in Central and West Asia. Therefore, it seeks to create a new balance by forging ties with multiple powers bilaterally and multilaterally. It can be a part of the Quadrilateral Dialogue (QUAD) against Chinese adventurism, while maintaining trade and multilateral ties with China (Shashi Tharoor, the former Minister of State for External Affairs (Quoted by Suhasini Haidar, 9 August 2020)). The two statements here of consecutive ministers testify to a bipartisan consensus on the politics of balancing articulated through its policy of multi-alignment. India joined BRICS when a centrist-coalition led by the Congress Party was in power, but the change of regime under a right-wing coalition did not lead to any notable shift in its approach towards this organisation. The withdrawal of American forces from Afghanistan will enhance the relevance of organisations such as BRICS and the SCO.

The chronology of BRICS and the QUAD reveals India's dilemma and strategy. India joined BRICS (2009) immediately after the famous civil nuclear deal (2008), and almost at the time of the inception of the QUAD (2007). It cannot be a coincidence that the two negotiations were underway simultaneously. Instead, these instances reinforce the notion that the quest for a balance pushed India to forge close ties with both Russia and the US. One may find it paradoxical, but New Delhi has mastered the art of cementing ties with hostile actors. BRICS enabled a new balance in India's otherwise pro-US orientation.

BRICS for reformed multilateralism

Since the early 2000s, all projections hinted towards the emergence of a multipolar economic order in which China, India, Russia and Brazil would play pivotal roles. Asia, led primarily by China, was to become the hub of production, and India would replace Japan to become the second most powerful economy in Asia. In the words of Mohan and Kapur (2015), an epochal change in terms of shift of economic activity is underway. The fulcrum of economic activity is shifting gradually from the North Atlantic to the continent of Asia. This can be understood in terms of the ratio of per capita income of the US to Asia, which changed from 13:1 in 1950 to 5:1 in 2015. India's growth rate averaged 6 per cent and China's 10 per cent during 1980–2014. The share of the G7 in the global economy was 46 per cent in 2017, down from 52 per cent in 2009. The share of BRICS increased to 23 per cent in 2017 from 16 per cent in 2009, according to the IMF (Goodrich 2018). In terms of PPP, the share of the BRICS was 32 per cent compared to 30 per cent of the G7 in 2017 (ibid). The US' share was 22 per cent and the European Union's 24 per cent in 2017. By 2060, the GDP of the BRICS is likely to increase to roughly 50 per cent, compared to the G7's 30 per cent. This shift should have led to a default re-configuration of international institutions. Since that is not happening, the reform of these institutions became the foremost priority of BRICS.

India with the second highest population in the world, a robust economy, and a functioning democracy has remained peripheral in global politics. In the four decades of the Cold War, the West constituted regimes that were discriminatory to developing states. India's grudge is economic as well as status centric as it finds itself excluded from the 'political or economic high tables' (Varadarajan 2009). For instance, India is not a member of the Nuclear Supply Group. The Security Council of the United Nations has the UK and France as permanent members but not India. The Biden administration is trying to revive the G7, but India is not a member. It was invited as an external member at the Cornwall Summit of the G7 in 2021, but it has little role in decision making there.

Along with other states, India demands quick reform of the IMF and the World Bank. Each member of the IMF is assigned a quota, which affects its voting right and its capacity to borrow. The West has controlled these institutions through a voting system that is disproportionate and unbalanced (Babb 2013; Kaya 2018). The US has the highest quota of 17.44 per cent and a vote share of 16.51 per cent. This allows the US to have effective veto in cases where a super majority of 85 per cent is needed. The bias in the IMF emanates from three sources: inequalities inherent in the design of this institution, disparity in staff representation and asymmetry in geopolitical influence (Heinzel et al. 2020). It is headquartered in Washington DC, the centre of American power, and the power deal takes place between the US and Europe. The gap between the economic clout of emerging countries and their share in quota is growing. Therefore, BRICS demands an increase in quota size and redistribution of their votes and shares.

BRICS was constituted to act as a counterweight to existing financial institutions. These countries claim to represent the voices of the countries in the Global South. The New Development Bank (NDB) and the Contingent Reserve Arrangement (CRA) are two finance related institutions that do not discriminate among members on the basis of their capital contribution (Liao 2015). Through these institutions, BRICS intends to escape the domination of the Western financial institutions (Parízek and Matthew 2017). The formation of the Asian Infrastructure Investment Bank (AIIB), the NDB and the CRA demonstrate an attempt at counter-institutionalisation by BRICS (Zurn 2018). New Delhi played a leading role in creating the NDB (Saran 2016). At the World Trade Organization, India formed greenroom coalitions with other members of BRICS. On the issues of terrorism, international trade, climate change and maritime security, it co-ordinates its policy with other members.

India as a rule-maker at BRICS

In recent years, India has shown greater interest in taking on responsibilities on several issues of global governance. India was traditionally seen as a 'rule taker' – seeking to adapt to existing norms (Sidhu et al. 2013, p. 6). As a rule taker, it complied with the values of international liberalism, and supported the cause of UN peacekeeping operations without questioning its efficacy. India's role in the G20, climate negotiations, maritime security and even health co-operation during the pandemic is widely acknowledged. There are a few cases, nonetheless, where it is viewed as a 'rule-breaker' as in disarmament and climate change (Sidhu et al. 2013). For instance, the testing of nuclear weapons in 1998 despite international pressure, and its role in the collapse of the Doha round of WTO negotiations round and later in Bali on trade liberalisation are instances of its being a 'rule-breaker'. On the issue of food subsidy at the Bali Round of the WTO, The Guardian criticised India as 'intransigent about its food subsidy measures, which are illegal under the agreement on agriculture. India stands isolated in the global community but still threatens to bring the multilateral trade negotiations to a grinding halt again' (The Guardian, 1 August 2014). India is yet to acquire the status of a rule-maker, but on the issues of food security and disarmament, it has strongly defended its interests. India is often criticised as being either a rule-taker or a rule-breaker, but at BRICS, it is definitely a rule-maker.

India supports non-intervention

An area where India distances itself from the West is the issue of democracy and human rights. India does not support the cause of promoting democracy in another country's territory (Sidhu et al. 2013). Respect for sovereignty and non-interference are the two core features of its foreign policy. In this regard, it is closer to BRICS than to the West. Recently, India abstained from voting against Sri Lanka in the United Nations Human Rights Council (The Print, 23 March 2021) and against Myanmar at the United Nations General Assembly Resolutions. Interestingly, China and Russia also abstained from voting against the military junta of Myanmar (Raj 2021). This resolution was brought by the Western bloc, especially the US, UK, France and Germany. India considers Western attempts to promote democracy as hypocritical, inconsistent and ineffective. It supported Russia on the issue of the annexation of Crimea by saying that Russia had legitimate interests there. New Delhi participated in the Biden administration's 'Democracy Summit' in December 2021, but its reservations about the promotion of democracy remain intact. There are two other critical issues of terrorism and climate change where India is trying to evolve a consensus among the BRICS states.

India spearheads BRICS on terrorism

Ever since the NDA government came to power in 2014, cross-border terrorism has become a core issue of India at international forums. India and Russia are victims of cross-border terrorism. Prime Minister Narendra Modi has flagged the issue of terrorism at every multilateral forum. At a United Nations General Assembly speech, he exhorted the members to develop a consensus on the definition of terrorism, and make a concerted effort to counter the menace of global terrorism (Lakshman 2019). Most terrorist attacks in India have roots in Pakistan. As an all-weather friend, China has taken it upon itself to defend Pakistan at any cost. Whenever India tries to name a terrorist leader or an organisation from Pakistan, China raises objections. It seeks to protect Pakistan from diplomatic embarrassment and consequent repercussions.

BRICS states have no disagreements over identifying other terrorist organisations such as the Haqqani network, Islamic State/Daesh, the Islamic Movement of Uzbekistan, Tehrik-i-Taliban Pakistan (TTP), Eastern Turkistan Islamic Movement, and Hizb-ut-Tahrir (Kumar 2017). But it was almost after a decade that China agreed to lift its objection, and allowed the United Nations to designate Masood Azhar, the chief of Jaish-e-Mohammed, a "global terrorist" in May 2019. Earlier, China used to block the UNSC 1267 resolution on banning him. At the Goa BRICS Summit in 2016, when India tried to raise this issue, it was censured by China. Hua Chunying, the Chinese spokesperson said, "I don't think this is an appropriate topic to be discussed at the BRICS summit" (Roche 2017). China warned of a possible discord at the summit if its 'all-weather friend' – Pakistan was targeted (Kumar 2017). New Delhi succeeded in convincing Beijing to name Lashkar-e-Taiba and Jaish-e-Mohammed as terrorist organisations in the Xiamen official declaration of 2017. To this declaration, Khwaja Asif, the foreign minister of Pakistan, responded: "We need to bring our house in order to prevent facing embarrassment at the international level" (The Indian Express, 7 September 2017). India put forward the issue of terrorism strongly at the Goa (2016), Xiamen (2017) and Moscow Virtual Summit (2020). Due to the persistent efforts of India and Russia, the Moscow Declaration included a call to a convention on terrorism within the UN framework (BRICS Summit Moscow Declaration 2020). New Delhi holds that it has taken the lead in galvanising BRICS to stand tough against the menace of terrorism (Roy 2019). India is largely responsible for terrorism becoming a part of BRICS' key agenda items.

India closer to BRICS on climate change

The other major issue on which India has been attempting to forge a consensus within BRICS is climate change. Climate change has become a serious concern for both developed and emerging countries. It is not possible to mitigate the adverse impact of climate change without the active participation of developing countries such as China, Brazil, India and Russia. China account for around 30 per cent of global greenhouse gases (GHGs), while the US, Europe and India account for 15 per cent, 10 per cent, and 7 per cent respectively (Puri 2020). India's per capita GHG emission is still less than half the global average.

Proactive participation by the BRICS countries is fundamental to negotiations on climate change. BRICS countries are some of the highest emitters of carbon as they depend heavily on coal-based industries (Basso and Viola 2016). In a positive development, these states have begun to acknowledge the necessity of investing in sustainable energy resources (Baker 2019). BRICS states have underlined the importance of urgent negotiations on climate change and actively promote and participate in international regimes on climate change (Rinaldi and Martuscelli 2016). The NDB began to allocate huge sums for alternative sources of energy from 2016 (Mattos and Rosa 2016). In contrast, the US under the Trump administration turned its back on climate agreements and decided to encourage fossil-fuel projects. The Paris Agreement would have become redundant had China, India, Japan and other European countries not stood behind it.

In a significant departure from its earlier positions on GHGs, China announced that it would seek to achieve carbon neutrality by 2060, and India by 2070. In the words of Kevin Rudd, the former prime minister of Australia, climate change has become a key Chinese priority, and it shows China's willingness to assume climate leadership (Rudd 2021). China's move encouraged India to announce a date at the Glasgow Summit of COP-26. In earlier stances, both China and India would insist on the principle of 'Common but Differentiated Responsibility' (CBDR) of the United Nations Framework Convention on Climate Change (UNFCCC) where developed and developing states held distinct responsibilities because of non-uniformity in the levels of development. BRICS states insist on transfer of resources and technology from developed to developing nations as articulated by India at the COP26 meeting at Glasgow. In the words of seasoned commentator C Raja Mohan (2020b), "Delhi is no longer defensive on climate change and is actively engaged in shaping the international debate". Fortunately, India is willing to work with other BRICS members to evolve a consensus on this issue. The leadership of BRICS on climate change will go a long way in shaming the West and encouraging the rest to adopt similar measures.

India's hesitations and concerns at BRICS

India is committed but cautious in its commitments to BRICS. For Russia and China, BRICS has the potential to emerge as a viable alternative institution to chip away the influence of the West. India does not carry any revisionist intentions (Kumar 2017). It is simply responding to the emerging global uncertainty caused by the shift from unipolarity to multipolarity. From India's perspective, it is necessary to maintain ties with other "poles". BRICS offers the most convenient multilateral forum to discuss issues of common concern.

A persistent puzzle for policy makers, however, is the extent of India's engagements with BRICS. New Delhi would not like to be seen as a part of a forum constituted to counter the liberal influence of the West. The biggest dilemma for India is to cement its ties with the West, without antagonising the other BRICS members and the *vice versa*. Strengthening defence ties with the US has become a strategic necessity, but this cannot come at the cost of alienating Russia.

India finds itself constrained by its territorial requirements. For the US, China is an adversary located far away from its territory. But for India, China is not only an adversary but also a neighbour. Strong defence ties with the US may send the wrong signal to both China and Russia – the reason India hesitates to develop a formal alliance with the US. It seeks the support of non-Western countries in pushing its agenda of multilateral reforms, have better economic ties with members, and develop a consensus on issues of terrorism and climate change. In the words of Sidhu et al. (2013: 9), 'India is not seeking to destroy or even replace the existing international governance institutions with alternative or new institutions; it is merely knocking on the door to gain entry or have a bigger say or protect its interests'. India seeks reforms in global governance without having an anti-West agenda.

BRICS is regarded as a 'hedging strategy' in a transitional and uncertain world (Kumar 2017). 'Status seeking' and 'hedging' constitute two prime interests of China and India at BRICS (Cooper and Farooq 2016:73). Beijing seeks to hedge against Washington, while New Delhi is doing the same against Beijing (Cooper and Farooq 2016:73). As an exclusive club of powerful states, BRICS certainly raises the prestige of India, and provides a platform to voice its concern at the global level (Kumar 2017). No other country is South Asia has a similar privilege.

Many Indian experts question the relevance of BRICS. The political and cultural heterogeneity, asymmetry of powers, differences in political regimes, demography, and developmental disparities are often cited as reasons for the unviability of this grouping. According to Brahma Chellaney (2016), a seasoned security expert, BRICS is just an 'acronym without substance'. It is not a 'viable multi-country economic grouping' (Pant 2016). 'The lack of a binding ideology, bilateral differences, diversity in terms of socio-cultural and political systems, and China's overwhelming presence' diminishes the space for other members in the forum (Pant and Sharma 2019). In contrast to these views, successive governments have responded favourably to this grouping. With the change of regime in 2014, it was widely speculated that India may change its strategy. That, however, did not happen in any perceptible manner.

Another dilemma that worries India is the preponderance of China at this forum. There is concern that China may try to control this organisation given the existing power asymmetry. Russia is already under the influence of China due to its economic and strategic vulnerabilities. South Africa is too small to sustain China's thrust. Brazil, facing economic recession and political instability, may not be in a position to defy China. India objected to China's proposal to include other countries in the 'BRICS Plus' model. It may tilt the balance of this organisation in China's favour. South Africa and Brazil are also against expanding the organisation, fearing a loss of their privileged status in their respective regions.

China wants to integrate BRICS with its flagship project, the 'Belt and Road Initiative'. This may not be possible as India abstained from the BRI because of the China-Pakistan Economic Corridor (CPEC). A section of this corridor falls in the disputed area of Jammu and Kashmir, which is claimed by India but is currently under Pakistan's occupation. Moscow insists on India joining the BRI. Sergei Lavrov (2017), the foreign minister of Russia, urged that the 'specific problem in this regard should not make everything else conditional for resolving political differences'. Under the present circumstances, especially after the onset of a standoff between the Indian and Chinese armies at the Ladakh border, it would be unrealistic to expect that India would review its decision on the BRI. There is high trust deficit between the two countries.

The biggest threat to the viability of BRICS is the possible border conflict between China and India (Kumar 2017). We have witnessed this at the Doklam in August 2017 and at the Ladakh border in 2020. The relationship between the two countries is far from cordial (Saran 2017). M.K. Narayanan, the former National Security Advisor of India, stated, 'While professing friendship, both sides nurse a mutual suspicion of each other – at times prompting several degrees of alienation' (Narayanan 2017). The two countries remain cautious and suspicious of each other's motives.

The border situation has deteriorated in the last few years. In the previous standoff at Doklam in 2017, the two armies were kept on high alert but there were no casualties. The two countries also managed to restore the status quo through existing bilateral mechanisms. At the Ladakh border standoff in 2020, however, there were military casualties on both sides. Nearly 50,000 army personnel were deployed from each side and dialogues remained inconclusive for several months. The possible disruption of the BRICS Summit to be hosted by Russia did not act as a deterrent. The stances of the two countries have become rigid and they accuse each other of disregarding bilateral agreements on resolving border disputes amicably. All indications hint towards a further escalation of border disputes between the two countries. BRICS may not remain untouched if border conflict persists.

Conclusion

BRICS is a subset of India's multilateral strategy aimed at forging close ties with non-Western states. From its perspective, it is not an anti-West organisation, nor does it intend to overturn the rules of the liberal international order. Its limited purpose is to enhance co-operation with BRICS members, and work together in areas of global governance such as institutional reforms, maritime security, terrorism, education, culture, pandemic control and climate change. On issues of sovereignty, democracy and human rights, it supports the BRICS' policy of non-intervention. It considers the Western policy of regime change as hypocritical and ineffective.

India has remained consistent in its engagements with BRICS. The change of regimes has not led to any perceptible shift in its orientation towards this organisation. The withdrawal of NATO forces from Afghanistan has enhanced the significance of non-Western organisations such as BRICS and the SCO. The importance of Russia has increased, while the US is treated as an important but unreliable strategic partner. China is viewed as an assertive and a non-placatable hegemon in Asia. New Delhi's stand against Beijing is likely to be rigid and hard in the coming years. It would cooperate with China, but it cannot be seen as ceding grounds to Beijing. The preponderance of China at BRICS is a serious concern for India, comforted partly by the presence of Russia.

Finally, an escalation of border conflicts between China and India has the potential to disrupt the functioning of this organisation. BRICS needs to develop mechanisms to de-escalate such tension and rebuild mutual trust.

References

Babb, S. 2013. 'The washington consensus as transnational policy paradigm: Its origins, trajectory and likely successor', *Review of International Political Economy*, 20(2), 268–297. doi:10.1080/09692290.2011.640435.

Baker, D. 2019. 'The green New Deal is happening in China', *Centre for Economic and Policy Research*. http://cepr.net/publications/op-eds-columns/the-green- new-deal-is-happening-in-china (accessed 15 January 2019).

Basso, L., and E. Viola. 2016. 'Wandering decarbonization: The BRIC countries as conservative climate powers', *Revista Brasileira de Política Internacional*, 59(1), 1–22. doi:10.1590/0034- 7329201600101.

BRICS Summit Moscow Declaration. 2020. November 17. www.brics.utoronto.ca/docs/201117-moscow-declaration.html (accessed 18 July 2021).

Chellaney, Brahma. 2016. 'Has BRICS been reduced to a talking shop?' *Hindustan Times*, October 19. www.hindustantimes.com/analysis/has-brics-been-reduced-to-a-talking-shop/story-fuwLqfVDJDOPyiaJ0roLIO.html (accessed 8 July 2020).

Cooper A. F. and Asif B. Farooq. 2016. 'The role of China and India in the G20 and BRICS: Commonalities and competitive behaviour?' *Journal of Current Chinese Affairs*, 45(3), 90. https://journals.sagepub.com/doi/10.1177/186810261604500303.

Goodrich, John. 2018. 'Decoding BRICS: How do BRICS and the G7 match up?' July 23, *CGTN*. https://news.cgtn.com/news/3d3d674d3367544f78457a6333566d54/share_p.html (accessed 15 July 2020).

The Guardian. 2014. 'World Trade Organization's future in doubt after India blocks trade deal', August 1. www.theguardian.com/world/2014/aug/01/wto-future-doubt-india-blocks-deal (accessed 14 October 2020).

Haidar, Suhasini. 2020. 'China's aggression pushing India closer to U.S. but alliance unlikely at present: Experts', *The Hindu*, August 9.

Heinzel, Mirko, Jonas Richter, Per Olof Busch, Hauke Feil, Jana Herold, and Andrea Liese. 2020. 'Birds of a feather? The determinants of impartiality perceptions of the IMF and the World Bank', *Review of International Political Economy*, 28(5), 1249–1273. doi:10.1080/09692290.2020.1749711.

Jaishankar, S. 2019. 'How do you reconcile Howdy Modi and Mamallapuram? Look beyond dogma', *RNG Lecture. The Indian Express*, November 16. https://indianexpress.com/article/india/full-text-how-do-you-reconcile-howdy-modi-and-mamallapuram-look-beyond-dogma-says-s-jaishankar-6122001/ (accessed 18 December 2020).

Kaya, A. 2018. 'BRICS and the international financial institutions: Voice and exit', in K. S. Yeon (ed.), *BRICS and the Global Economy*, 1–28. Singapore: World Scientific.

Kumar, Rajan. 2017. 'India and the BRICS: A cautious and limited engagement', *International Studies*, 54(1–4), 162–179. https://doi.org/10.1177/0020881718777348.

Lakshman, Sriram. 2019. 'At UN General Assembly, Narendra Modi calls for unity against terror', *The Hindu*, September 28. www.thehindu.com/news/national/at-un-general-assembly-narendra-modi-calls-for-unity-against-terror/article29533551.ece (accessed 25 July 2020).

Lavrov, S. 2017. 'In Sanjeev Miglani's Russia urges India to line up behind China's Belt and Road initiative', *Reuters*, December 11. www.reuters.com/article/us-india-china-russia/russia-urges-india-to-line-up-behind-chinas-belt-and-road-initiative-idUSKBN1E51EX (accessed 20 October 2021).

Liao, R. 2015. 'Out of the Bretton Woods: How the AIIB is different', *Foreign Affairs*, July 27. www.foreignaffairs.com/articles/asia/2015-07-27/out-bretton-woods?cid=soc-tw-rdr (accessed 10 February 2019).

Madan, Tanvi quoted by Detsch, Jack and Robby Gramer. 2021. 'Russian arms sale clouds u.S.-India Ties', *Foreign Policy*, March 19.

Manjeev Singh Puri. 2020. 'India must forge coalition with like-minded nations on climate change', *The Indian Express*, December 7. https://indianexpress.com/article/opinion/columns/climate-change-india-us-china-7094360/ (accessed 3 January 2021).

Mattos, B., and J. Rosa. 2016. 'Novo Banco de Desenvolvimento', *Radar Socioambiental N.* 4 July. Rio de Janeiro: BPC. http://bricspolicycenter.org/homolog/publicacoes/interna/7150? tipo=Radar (accessed 18 August 2021).

Mehta, Pratap Bhanu quoted by Suhasini Haidar. 2020. 'China's aggression pushing India closer to U.S. but alliance unlikely at present: Experts', *The Hindu*, August 9.

Menon, S. quoted by Suhasini Haidar. 2020. 'China's aggression pushing India closer to U.S. but alliance unlikely at present: Experts', *The Hindu*, August 9.

Mohan, C Raja. 2013. 'A hesitant rule shaper', in Waheguru Pal Singh Sidhu, Pratap Bhanu Mehta and Bruce Jones (eds.), *Shaping the Emerging World: India and the Multilateral Order*. Washington, DC: Brookings Institution Press.

Mohan, C Raja. 2020a. 'India's Pivot to the United States', *East Asia Forum*, May 19. www.eastasiaforum.org/2020/05/19/indias-pivot-to-the-united-states/.

Mohan, C. Raja. 2020b. 'Delhi's real test on climate change is on building political consensus to adapt to changed reality', *The Indian Express*, December 8. https://indianexpress.com/article/opinion/columns/india-climate-change-global-warming-modi-govt-7095665/.

Mohan, Rakesh, and Muneesh Kapur. 2015. 'Emerging powers and global governance: Whither the IMF?' *IMF Working Paper*. www.imf.org/external/pubs/ft/wp/2015/wp15219.pdf.

Narayanan, M. K. 2017. 'Understanding the Chinese mind', *The Hindu*, September 1. www.thehindu.com/opinion/lead/understanding-the-chinese-mind/article19595813.ece (accessed 14 September 2021).

Pant, Harsh V., and Raj Kumar Sharma. 2019. 'India and its BRICS dilemmas', *Observer Research Foundation*, November 18. www.orfonline.org/research/india-and-its-brics-dilemmas-57891/ (accessed 18 July 2019).

Pant, Manoj. 2016. 'Using BRICS to isolate Pakistan makes no sense. Here's why', *Catch News*, October 18. www.catchnews.com/india-news/using-brics-to-isolate-pakistan-makes-no-sense-here-s-why-1476727047.html (accessed 23 October 2020).

Parízek, M., and S. Matthew. 2017. 'The representation of BRICS in global economic governance: Reform and fragmentation of multilateral institutions', in K. S. Yeon (ed.), *BRICS and the Global Economy*, 1–34. Singapore: World Scientific Publishing.

The Print. 2021. 'India abstains from voting on Sri Lanka resolution at UNHRC', March 23. https://theprint.in/diplomacy/india-abstains-from-voting-on-sri-lanka-resolution-at-unhrc/627137/ (accessed 12 October 2021).

Raj, Yahswant. 2021. 'India abstains from vote on UNGA's Myanmar resolution', *Hindustan Times*, June 20. www.hindustantimes.com/india-news/india-abstains-from-vote-on-unga-s-myanmar-resolution-101624129552897.html (accessed 13 September 2021).

Rinaldi, Augusto, and Patricia Martuscelli. 2016. 'The BRICS on climate change global governance', *Meridano 47 Journal of Global Studies*, 17. http://dx.doi.org/10.20889/M47e17020. www.academia.edu/33846614/The_BRICS_on_climate_change_global_governance (accessed 8 July 2021).

Roche, Elizabeth. 2017. 'Donald Trump seeks India's role in Afghanistan, warns Pakistan for terror support', *Livemint*, August 22. www.livemint.com/Politics/OTlT1rlfAPFNycp-ZLlblYP/Donald-Trump-seeks-Indias-role-in-Afghanistan-warns-Pakist.html (accessed 18 July 2020).

Roy, Subhajit. 2019. 'BRICS Summit: What it means for India in the global order', *The Indian Express*, November 15. https://indianexpress.com/article/explained/explained-why-brics-matters-for-india-6116737/ (accessed 13 July 2021).

Rudd, Kevin. 2021. 'Modern diplomacy, The new geopolitics of China's climate leadership', *Modern Diplomacy*, January 2. https://moderndiplomacy.eu/2021/01/02/the-new-geopolitics-of-chinas-climate-leadership/ (accessed 8 March 2021).

Saran, Samir. 2016. 'BRICS remains on course for bigger, more effective projects in the years to come', *ORF Commentaries*, October 18. www.orfonline.org/research/brics-remains-on-course-bigger/ (accessed December 1, 2017).

Saran, Samir. 2017. 'After Doklam, India and China must begin anew at the Xiamen BRICS meet', *Hindustan Times*, September 3.

Sidhu, Waheguru Pal Singh, Pratap Bhanu Mehta, and Bruce Jones. 2013. *Shaping the Emerging World: India and the Multilateral Order*. Washington, DC: Brookings Institution Press.

Tharoor, Shashi. 2012. *Pax Indica: India and the World of the 21st Century*. New Delhi: Allen Lane.

Tharoor, Shashi quoted by Suhasini Haidar. 2020. 'China's aggression pushing India closer to U.S. but alliance unlikely at present: Experts', *The Hindu*, August 9.

The Indian Express, September 7, 2017. Foreign minister Khwaja Asif accepts terror groups like LeT and JeM are an 'embarrasment' for Pakistan'. https://indianexpress.com/article/pakistan/pakistan-foreign-minister-khawaja-asif-need-to-rein-in-terror-groups-to-avoid-embarrassment-4832381/ (accessed on July 29, 2022).

Varadarajan, Siddharth. 2009. 'BRIC is not a bloc but a soft balancer', *The Hindu*, June 13.

Zakaria, Fareed. 2008. *The Post-American World*. New York: Norton.

Zurn, M. 2018. 'Contested global governance', *Global Policy*, 9(1), 138–144. doi:10.1111/1758-5899.12521.

13

CHINA AND BRICS

Liu Zongyi

At the end of 2001, Jim O'Neill, the chief economist of the Goldman Sachs Group, first proposed 'BRIC' (Brazil, Russia, India and China) as an investment market concept. In 2006, the BRIC foreign ministers held their first meeting during the UN General Assembly, marking the beginning of the BRIC mechanism as an international political and economic group. In May 2008, Brazilian Foreign Minister Amorin, Russian Foreign Minister Sergey Lavrov, Indian Foreign Minister Mukherjee and Chinese Foreign Minister Yang Jiechi held talks in Yekaterinburg, Russia, and decided to co-operate on the international stage. This was the first BRIC meeting of the four foreign ministers held outside multilateral forums such as the UN General Assembly. The four foreign ministers also decided to hold regular ministerial meetings to showcase the achievement of the BRIC countries. After the outbreak of the international financial crisis in 2008, the BRICs countries held the Yekaterinburg summit in Russia in 2009 when the BRICs co-operation mechanism was formally formed. Vyacheslav Nikonov and John J. Kirton regard BRICS as a broader developing country coalition seeking to shift the balance of global political influence from the West towards the developing world as a whole (Nikonov 2014; Kirton 2015:3). In December 2010, South Africa joined the BRICS as a full member. As of today, the BRICS co-operation mechanism is only over a decade old.

The BRICS countries account for 30% of the world's land area, and nearly 42% of the world's population. As Economy Daily (2017) said, between 2008 and September 2017 when the Xiamen Summit was held, the contribution of the BRICS countries to the global economy had risen from 12% to 23%, their share in international trade from 11% to 16% and the proportion of foreign investment from 7% to 12%. The proportion of foreign investment inflows as a percentage of global foreign investment inflows into BRICS countries reached 16% in 2016. The BRICS countries also accounted for 50 per cent of the growth in the global economy.

DOI: 10.4324/9781003148074-15

Although the concept of BRIC is said to have been coined by Jim O'Neill (2001), the BRICS co-operation mechanism today is quite different from the concept coined by him in 2001. The BRIC countries in 2001 was only an investment market concept; the BRICS co-operation mechanism today is an important global political and economic group that is comparable to the G7. The BRICS co-operation mechanism has evolved over the years. At the 2009 Yekaterinburg Summit, the BRIC members focused on how to promote the reform of the international financial system. With the establishment of the New Development Bank and the BRICS foreign exchange reserve, the BRICS co-operation mechanism has become an important global governance platform that can provide global public goods.

BRICS is still an evolving concept, and it may not remain limited to five members. At present, each member of the BRICS countries has three identities at the same time: They are all emerging economies and developing countries, and major powers in their respective regions. Therefore, BRICS is not a small group of emerging economies, but a new South–South co-operation mechanism, composed of representatives of developing countries, which is making its voice increasingly heard.

Starting from the 2013 Durban Summit in South Africa, it has become a convention to invite countries from the region to participate in the BRICS Summit. This was the case at the 2014 Fortaleza Summit in Brazil, the Ufa Summit in Russia in 2015 and the Goa Summit in India in 2016. In 2017, China hosted the BRICS Xiamen Summit. At the summit, China invited representatives from emerging economies and developing countries around the world to participate in the 'BRICS+' mechanism. The BRICS co-operation mechanism continues to expand its relationship with a wide range of emerging markets and developing countries through the 'BRICS+' model. The Johannesburg Summit in South Africa in 2018 continued with the concept of the 'BRICS+' co-operation model and invited the chair countries of international organisations in Africa and other developing countries to participate in it. The 'BRICS+' co-operation model lays the foundation for co-operation between BRICS members and developing countries and the possible expansion of the BRICS co-operation mechanism in the future.

China is an important member of the BRICS co-operation mechanism. The rise of emerging economies has become an important driving force for the transformation of the international political and economic system. China has played an important strategic role in promoting co-operation among BRICS countries. BRICS co-operation not only marks the realisation of the importance accorded in China's diplomacy to developing countries but also constitutes a vital part of its multilateral diplomacy (Zhao 2014:44). Although China did not establish the BRICS co-operation mechanism, its establishment and development are in line with China's strategic interests.

Western countries, especially the United States, dominate the international system today. If China and other emerging economies want to join the international systems, they must go through a process of persuading Western countries to accept them as an equal partner, as well as a process of constantly learning, adapting and abiding by international norms. Western dominance of the international institutional system limits the role of China in the governance of these institutions. China's influence is small in the formulation and revision of institutional rules and the distribution of rights and obligations within the organisation. This dilemma not only is incompatible with China's growing status as a major power but also greatly limits further development in China (Gao 2015:58–59).

Following the global financial crisis, industrialised countries, contrary to their advocacy of the 'free market' and 'trade without borders', have moved to setting up barriers to investment and towards increasing protectionism. In order to protect themselves, the United States, Europe, and Japan continue to use their dominance and rulemaking rights in the current system, such as the IMF/World Bank, to benefit themselves at others' expense, such as passing on financial risks through quantitative easing, which makes emerging economies, including China, increasingly feel that it is too risky to blindly 'attach' their economic prosperity to the old order and old model.

Therefore, China must take a different approach, co-operate with other emerging economies, and construct new international organisations to offset the deficiencies of the existing system. The international environment is an important factor in promoting China's establishment of the BRICS mechanism. China is convinced that the BRICS co-operation mechanism can increase its social power – leverage and a certain kind of acceptance – in international relations, implement a 'networking strategy', and pursue the status of a global power through the establishment of a parallel network of states rather than by competing for hierarchical rights (Gao 2015:59–60).

In fact, China's promotion of the establishment of the BRICS mechanism reflects the tradition of establishing an international united front in China's diplomacy. Since the 1950s, China has strengthened its solidarity and co-operation with third world countries. Chinese leaders like Mao Zedong, Deng Xiaoping, Jiang Zemin, and Hu Jintao all have attached importance to strengthening diplomatic relations with a vast number of developing countries.

China's driving and leading role is not only reflected in the establishment of the BRICS co-operation mechanism but also backed by her economic strength. First, China is the country with the largest population and accounted for about 45% of the GDP of the BRICS countries in 2006; its share increased to two-thirds by 2016 (Kong 2017). China's economic weight is of great significance in enhancing the importance of BRICS as a whole on the international stage. Second, trade between China and other BRICS members accounts for a large part of trade among the BRICS members, and is actually at the core of BRICS' economic co-operation. As compared to China's trade with other BRICS countries, the development of trade among the remaining members is at an early stage (Sun 2015:27). This situation is not conducive to co-operation among BRICS countries, and will take time to change. Finally, China has made a major contribution to the institutionalisation of BRICS co-operation, and the establishment of the New Development Bank (headquartered in Shanghai, China.) and the BRICS foreign exchange reserve. In terms of emergency reserve arrangements, China promised to invest the most (at US$41 billion), so that it gets the highest voting share (at 39.95%) (BRICS Economic Think-Tank 2015).

China attaches great importance to co-operation among the BRICS members. In the report of the 18th Congress of the Communist Party of China in 2013, the BRICS co-operation mechanism, together with the United Nations, the G20 and the Shanghai Cooperation Organization, is mentioned as an example of China's active participation in multilateral affairs and active role in international affairs, and its efforts to make the international order and system more just and equitable (Hu 2012). In the report of the 19th National Congress of the Communist Party of China, although the BRICS countries are not listed separately as in the 18th report, the BRICS members are covered in the following statement:

> 'China will promote co-ordination and co-operation with other major countries and work to build a framework for major country relations featuring overall stability and balanced development. China will deepen relations with its neighbours in accordance with the principle of amity, sincerity, mutual benefit, and inclusiveness and the policy of forging friendship and partnership with its neighbours. China will, guided by the principle of upholding justice while pursuing shared interests and the principle of sincerity, real results, affinity, and good faith, work to strengthen solidarity and co-operation with other developing countries.' 'China . . . supports the efforts of other developing countries to increase their representation and strengthen their voice in international affairs.'
>
> *(Xi 2017)*

In terms of the orientation of Chinese foreign policy, 'big powers are the key; the periphery is the priority; developing countries are the foundation; multilateral platforms are the stage' (Su 2017). The BRICS co-operation mechanism encompasses all these objectives.

Whether it is the 'handle' of China's relations with developing countries, or the bridge between China and other emerging economies in their dialogue with the West, or as the main multilateral diplomatic strategy platform for promoting global governance, the BRICS co-operation mechanism is an important pillar of China's international strategy in the new era. Therefore, the co-operation of the BRICS countries has an extraordinary strategic significance for China's diplomacy. The progress of the BRICS' co-operation mechanism will determine the success or failure of major country diplomacy with distinctive Chinese features (Zhao 2014:51–52). Emphasising the importance of BRICS' co-operation to China's international strategy does not mean that China must 'start another stove' or build another international system outside the existing international system. What China needs to do is to consolidate and enhance unity and co-operation with developing countries through the platform of BRICS co-operation, and jointly promote the development of the international system in a fair and reasonable direction (Zhao 2014:52–53).

The Development of the BRICS Co-operation Mechanism and the Role of China

In 2009, when the BRICS co-operation mechanism was just established, there were only 15 joint statements by the leaders of the BRIC countries in Yekaterinburg. In 2017, there were as many as 71 statements by the leaders in Xiamen. The essence of the BRICS co-operation mechanism is inter-regionalism. It is generally believed that inter-regionalism can have seven functions: regional (national) checks and balances, bandwagon, construction of an international mechanism, rationalisation of global issues, setting and controlling the narratives around global issues, developing a regional identity, and ensuring the stability and development of international relations (Liu 2008:44). A review of the BRICS co-operation mechanism indicates that it has become a constructive force to promote world economic growth, improve global governance, and promote the democratisation of international relations.

So far, the BRICS co-operation mechanism has formed a wide-area, multi-level structure for pragmatic co-operation led by leaders' summits and supported by a series of institutional arrangements. Such arrangements include the meeting of senior representatives of the National Security Councils, the foreign ministers' meeting, the meeting of foreign ministers during the UN General Assembly, the BRICS permanent missions to UN branches at New York, Geneva and Vienna, and other multilateral institutions, as well as the working groups – the Business Council, the Think Tank Council, and the Youth Leadership Forum. The co-operation covers dozens of fields such as trade, finance, agriculture, education, health, science and technology, culture, drug control, statistics, tourism, think tanks, friendship cities, local government co-operation, global security environment, counter-terrorism, cybersecurity, major international or regional hotspot issues, transnational organised crime, peacekeeping operations, demilitarisation of outer space, and relationship between national security and development.

The establishment of the BRICS Leaders' Summit Mechanism has provided political guidance and a strong impetus for co-operation and development among the BRICS countries. The regular meetings of BRICS leaders provides a platform for BRICS to increase understanding, strengthen co-operation and ease some bilateral contradictions and conflicts. For more than 10 years, the BRICS countries have assumed the responsibility of developing countries and actively co-operated on multilateral platforms such as the G20, the United Nations, the World Bank, the International Monetary Fund and the World Trade Organization. They jointly set agendas and work hard to formulate international rules, promote the process of global economic governance reform, and jointly voice major international and regional issues, all of which greatly enhance the representation and voice of emerging economies and developing countries.

Recently, BRICS co-operation has formed a 'three-wheel drive' structure for economic, trade and finance, politics and security, and people-to-people and cultural exchanges. Firstly, economic and financial co-operation is the fundamental driving force and core area for BRICS co-operation. Co-operation in the financial sector is the most striking aspect of the achievements of BRICS co-operation in the past 10 years. The original intention of the establishment of the BRICS co-operation mechanism was to promote the reform of the international economic and financial system. In 2011, the Sanya Declaration emphasised the establishment of a BRICS co-operation mechanism focusing on economy and finance, based on the principle of benefit sharing. In March 2012, during the fourth meeting of BRICS leaders, the initiative to establish a BRICS Development Bank was formally proposed. In March 2013, the leaders of the BRICS countries explicitly agreed to establish a 'New Development Bank' and an emergency reserve fund during the Durban meeting. In July 2014, the leaders of the BRICS countries announced the signing of the New Development Bank Agreement during the meeting in Brazil. In July 2015, the New Development Bank was officially opened in Shanghai. In August 2017, the New Development Bank African Branch was officially unveiled in Johannesburg, South Africa. In just a few years, the New Development Bank has turned from vision to reality and from concept to practice. It demonstrates that BRICS countries are not satisfied with the limited concessions given by Europe and the United States within the framework of the IMF/World Bank, It also indicates the desire to 'break fresh ground' and build a parallel international financial architecture. This is the first time since the establishment of the Bretton Woods system that the international financial architecture has faced competition from an equal and will become a milestone in the history of international finance (BRICS Development Bank 2014).

The establishment of the New Development Bank is a milestone in the institutionalisation of BRICS co-operation. The BRICS co-operation mechanism has effectively promoted the reform of the governance structure of international monetary and financial institutions such as the IMF and the World Bank. The US Congress passed the 2010 version of the IMF reform programme at the end of 2015 under pressure from the New Development Bank and the Asian Infrastructure Investment Bank initiated by China. This project has enabled the BRICS countries to make themselves heard in the international financial system. The voting shares of the BRICS countries in the World Bank rose to 13.24% and that in the IMF to 14.91% (Lin 2017).

In 2016, the New Development Bank issued US$1.5 billion in loans for seven projects (Lin 2017). In 2017, it provided US$2.5 billion to US$3 billion in loans for more than 10 projects and in 2018, it planned to complete its goal of providing US$8 billion in loans for 35 projects (Lin 2017). According to the *Bank's General Strategy document for 2017–2021*, the number of projects approved by the bank will reach 50–75 by 2021 (Lin 2017). Besides, the BRICS co-operation mechanism has also carried out fruitful co-operation in currency swaps, local currency settlement, crisis relief, and the capital markets. In the US$100 billion emergency reserve arrangements, China has invested US$41 billion.

The BRICS also tries to promote trade co-operation and interconnectivity. The Ufa Summit in 2015 laid the blueprint for long-term economic and trade co-operation among the BRICS countries and promoted their advance towards the goal of 'integrated markets, multi-tiered network, connectivity by land, air and sea, and greater cultural exchanges'. At the 2017 Xiamen Summit, the 'Belt and Road Initiative' and development issues were listed as core issues. President Xi Jinping announced a series of pragmatic measures to strengthen co-operation with emerging economies and developing countries, demonstrating China's commitment to the cause of sustainable global development, which have been widely acclaimed internationally. In the first decade, the BRICS countries closely focused on the theme of development, which not only promoted economic and social development but also provided a good solution for the world to solve security and development problems.

Secondly, the BRICS countries are also strengthening the mechanism of political and security co-operation. In fact, at the first BRICS Summit in 2009, Russia hoped to promote the political and security co-operation of the BRICS countries and established a meeting mechanism for BRICS security representatives. At the 2011 Sanya Summit, the security concerns of the BRICS countries began to expand to include regional conflicts including the Middle East issue and Libya and reform of the UN Security Council. At the Durban Summit in 2013, the position of political and security co-operation in BRICS was clearly defined. Co-operation on security and economic and financial co-operation together constitute the two pillars of BRICS co-operation. After 2014, the BRICS countries' willingness to increase the influence of the co-operation mechanism on political and security issues has risen remarkably, and they have more actively co-ordinated their positions on international security matters. In the 2014 Fortaleza Summit Declaration, the 2015 Ufa Summit Declaration, and the 2016 Goa Summit Declaration, international and regional security issues have taken up a lot of space.

At the 2017 Xiamen Summit, China, as the host country, has significantly increased its willingness and ability to lead the BRICS security agenda. First, China has led the BRICS countries to form a strategic consensus on understanding the current global governance structure and response on international security affairs. Second, China has called on emerging economies and developing countries to play a greater role in international security affairs. Third, China emphasises pragmatically promoting security co-operation among the BRICS member countries.

In 2009, the BRICS countries held the first meeting of BRICS High Representatives for Security Issues to discuss the impact of the financial crisis on security. Then, the meetings of BRICS High Representatives for Security Issues regularly focused on strengthening communication on the overall international security situation. At the Xiamen Summit, China, as the chair of the National Security Affairs High Representative Meeting, for the first time reported the outcome of the meeting to the leaders' summit. In addition to the regular meetings of the BRICS foreign ministers during the UN General Assembly, a separate meeting of the BRICS foreign ministers was held before the Xiamen Summit, and a *Media Note of the Meeting of the BRICS Ministers of Foreign Affairs/International Relations* was released. In addition to the BRICS Counterterrorism Working Group, South

Africa recommended establishing a BRICS Peacekeeping Working Group. The BRICS also expressed support for the role of the African Union in strengthening the peace and security system in Africa.

After nearly a decade of development, the BRICS countries have strengthened their consensus and co-ordination on a series of issues, including the global security environment, anti-terrorism, cybersecurity, major international and regional hotspot issues, transnational organised crime, peacekeeping operations, and demilitarisation of outer space, and so on. The BRICS countries have begun to actively express their concerns on international, regional and national security issues, and their collective positions on relevant issues have become more and more clear. At the same time, there is room for in-depth co-operation among BRICS countries in areas and topics such as establishing the authority of the United Nations, promoting the reform of the United Nations Security Council, opposing unilateral interventionism, supporting developing countries to dominate their own political security process, strengthening BRICS co-operation in peacekeeping affairs and dealing with non-traditional security threats.

Thirdly, people-to-people exchanges and co-operation among BRICS countries are also of great significance to promoting exchanges, mutual learning, harmonious coexistence and common progress among different civilisations. At present, the BRICS countries have signed intergovernmental agreements on cultural co-operation, and have established film festivals, games, educational co-operation frameworks, media exchange and youth exchange mechanisms. Since 2017, various cultural exchanges such as the forum of BRICS political parties, think tanks and civil society organisations, and BRIC countries' high-end media forum have been established, and the first BRICS games and second BRICS film festival have been held. In future, the BRICS countries should work together to continue to enrich the cultural exchange and co-operation mechanism and promote in-depth co-operation in culture, arts, sports, media, think tanks, traditional medicine, and youth (Lin 2017). In particular, it is necessary to strengthen exchanges between young people in various countries, and help the youth of all countries recognise and understand the BRICS mechanism. The BRICS multilateral people-to-people exchange mechanism provides a good platform for promoting exchanges among BRICS countries.

Fourthly, consultative democracy and the 'BRICS spirit' are the key reason that the BRICS co-operation mechanism has made significant progress. In the past 10 years, the member states have constantly put forward new co-operation concepts and formed a 'BRICs spirit'. In this process, China played an important role. At the first BRICS Summit, Chinese President Hu Jintao proposed transforming the BRICS mechanism into a model of mutual respect and equal consultation in international society through dialogues and exchanges. At the Fourth BRICS Summit, Hu Jintao put forward the principle of 'persisting on equal consultations', which was widely welcomed by the BRICS countries. It has become the basic model for all BRICS meetings and talks at all levels (Gao 2015:61–62). After taking office, President Xi Jinping put forward a series of important proposals on co-operation among the BRICS countries, actively promoted such co-operation, and continuously pointed out the direction for the development of the BRICS mechanism. In 2013, when President Xi Jinping attended the BRICS Leaders' Summit in Durban, South Africa, he proposed four major goals that BRICS should strive to achieve – integrated markets, multi-tiered network, connectivity by land, air and sea, and greater people-to-people exchanges. In Fortaleza, Brazil, 2014, President Xi Jinping advocated the spirit of 'openness, inclusiveness, and win-win co-operation'. In Ufa, Russia, 2015, President Xi Jinping proposed building partnerships in the four key areas of safeguarding world peace, promoting common development, promoting pluralistic civilisation, and strengthening global economic governance. In 2016, in Goa, India, President Xi Jinping emphasised the need to expand and consolidate the 'friends' circle' of the BRICS countries.

Progress and Deficiency of the Relationship Between China and BRICS Members After the Establishment of the BRICS Mechanism

Through the establishment and development of the BRICS co-operation mechanism, China and other BRICS members have formed a new type of development partnership. The reason why the BRICS co-operation mechanism could be established was that all members faced common development tasks and were in a similar position in the international economic and political system. They all faced and continue to face the constraints of the international political and economic system established by Western developed countries. They all hope to see progressive reform of the existing international political and economic system and play a greater role in global governance. Playing a greater role in global governance or taking on greater responsibilities is not only the general aspiration of emerging economies represented by BRICS but also the urgent need of the international community, including Western developed countries, for global economic governance. This is the reason why Western countries have established 'G8 + 5' and other dialogue arrangements. It is for these reasons that the BRICS quickly progressed from being an investment concept to a highly influential international political and economic group (Liu 2017).

However, due to the different strategic intentions of BRICS members, it is difficult for the BRICS co-operation mechanism to develop further like the EU, NAFTA and NATO. Because different countries have different goals on different issues, BRICS co-operation can only establish a coalition of issues (Zhao 2014:48–49), which is in the nature of a partnership, not an alliance or an international organisation. Unlike the co-operation mechanisms of developed countries such as the G7, BRICS is neither a new major power group nor a political alliance, but a development partnership. Focusing on the economy, finance and development, the mechanism is an active advocate and practitioner of a new global development partnership and a bridge between the North and South (Zhao 2014:48–49). Although it is a coalition of issues, the fulfilment rate of promises made in BRICS

Summits is almost the highest in the existing international mechanisms: the fulfilment rate of the 2014 summit is 70%; of the 2015 summit 78%; of the 2016 summit 89% (Kong 2017).

In the Xiamen summit, President Xi Jinping pointed out three important practices for the development of BRICS: treating each other as equals and seeking common ground while shelving differences, taking a results-oriented innovative approach to make co-operation benefit all, and developing themselves to help others keeping in mind the well-being of the world. Xi pointed out that in terms of BRICS co-operation, decisions are made through consultation among all members, not by one country alone. BRICS is not a talking shop, but a task force that gets things done. Since the very beginning, the five countries have been guided by the principle of dialogue without confrontation, partnership without alliance, which has become a positive energy in international society. These messages integrated traditional Chinese philosophy, contemporary diplomatic theory and diplomatic practices in the new era, which reflects the core of co-operation among the BRICS countries and the BRICS spirit. It symbolises the pursuit of common values during 10 years' co-operation by the five members, providing new models of international relations with win-win co-operation as the core (Wang 2017).

After the establishment of BRICS co-operation, China has made the largest progress in economic co-operation with other BRICS countries. As the biggest economy in the BRICS, the total GDP of China is approximately twice as much as the sum of the GDP of the other BRICS countries. Since the establishment of the BRICS mechanism, trade volumes between China and other BRICS countries have increased substantially. Bilateral trade between China and Russia, India and Brazil was around US$50 billion in 2010 and now, it is almost over US$100 billion (DuoWei News 2019). According to the data released by the Russian customs, the trade volume between China and Russia in 2018 was about US$1082.84, an increase of 24.5% over 2017; Russia had a surplus of nearly US$4 billion with China that year (DuoWei News 2019). In 2018, the bilateral trade volume between China and India was US$95.54 billion, a year-on-year increase of 13.2%. China exported US$76.71 billion to India, an increase of 12.7% as compared to the previous year; and imported US$18.83 billion from India, up 15.2% year-on-year (Ministry of Commerce of China 2019a). Brazil continued to remain China's largest trading partner, with a bilateral trade volume of over US$100 billion in 2018. Brazil's exports to China increased by more than 32% from the previous year. In 2018, the bilateral trade volume between China and South Africa was US$43.55 billion, a year-on-year increase of 11.18%, of which China's exports were US$16.251 billion, an increase of 9.62%, and imports were US$27.299 billion, an increase of 12.13% (Ministry of Commerce of China 2019b).

China's investment in the BRICS countries has also grown rapidly. According to data from the Skolkovo School of Management in Moscow, Russia, China's investment in the Russian economy in 2011–2017 amounted to US$36 billion (China-Russia Info 2018). Liu Xuesong, Deputy Director-General of the Department of European-Central Asian Affairs of the Ministry of Commerce of China, revealed at the press conference of the Fifth China-Russia Expo held by the Ministry of Commerce that China's direct investment in 2017 in Russia was US$2.22 billion, a year-on-year increase of 72% (Sputnik news agency 2018). In terms of investment in India, statistics show that by the end of 2017, China's accumulated direct investment in India was US$4.74 billion. By the end of 2018, India's actual investment in China was US$900 million (Ministry of Commerce of China 2019a). But according to insiders, China's investment in India may be at least five times as much as the official figure. According to the foreign investment briefing released by the Brazilian Ministry of Economic Affairs, from 2003 to March 2019, China's investment in Brazil totalled US$71.3 billion, surpassing the US's US$58.3 billion, making it the largest source of investment in Brazil. For nine consecutive years, China has become South Africa's largest trading partner and a major source of investment and tourists. As of the end of 2017, the Chinese stock of direct investment in South Africa was US$7.473 billion. In 2018, Chinese direct investment in South Africa was US$272 million. By the end of 2018, South Africa's enterprises had accumulated direct investment in China of US$774 million (Ministry of Commerce of China 2019b).

However, China's rapid economic and trade exchanges with other BRICS countries are not due to the BRICS co-operation mechanism. India and Brazil are among the countries that have implemented the most 'anti-dumping' actions against China. There is no doubt that after the launch of the BRICS New Development Bank, countries such as India have received a large number of loans and benefited a lot. The BRICS co-operation mechanism has indeed provided a degree of mutual recognition for people among the BRICS countries, and provided some convenience for promoting economic and trade exchanges between China and other BRICS countries. The economic co-operation among the BRICS countries is centred on China. The trade growth between other BRICS countries is not as much as that between them and China, which has made it difficult for BRICS countries to deepen their economic co-operation further. In fact, from the perspective of the global value chain and supply chain, the close economic and trade relations between other BRICS countries and China are only a reflection of China's current key position in global value and supply chains. Because Russia, India and other countries have not been deeply integrated into the global economy, their economic co-operation with China is mainly limited to traditional trade, and there is no whole industry chain co-operation between China and other BRICS countries like China's co-operation with developed countries such as the United States, Europe and Japan (Feng 2019). However, obstacles and challenges still exist in co-operation between China and India, Brazil and other BRICS countries.

There are considerable gaps among BRICS countries in terms of political systems, economic development, and cultural background. Therefore, there are indeed many challenges to further co-operation. In recent years, China and Russia have been building a closer relationship with each other, and the China-Russia comprehensive strategic partnership of co-ordination is at its best in history through bilateral efforts and co-operation under the BRICS mechanism, Shanghai Cooperation

Organization and other multilateral frameworks. This is closely related to the serious egoism and bullying ideology of the United States, increasing unilateralism, multiple shocks suffered by multilateralism, the evident rise of uncertainty and instability and the fact that people's eager expectations of peace and development are at stake. At the same time, it shows the charm of China's political and economic pattern. Politically, Russia has praised China's governing experience more frequently. In the economic field, Russia's interest in China's economic development model is expanding. In the financial field, the growth of China's financial system makes the Russian elite realise the unique value of co-operation with China.

On June 5, 2019, Chinese President Xi Jinping, together with the Russian President Vladimir Putin signed the *Joint Statement Between the People's Republic of China and the Russian Federation on developing a comprehensive strategic partnership of co-ordination for the new era*, which enhances the bilateral relationship to a whole new level. It declares that the two countries will take larger and more important historical responsibility for the future of the world. However, developing a comprehensive strategic partnership of co-ordination for the new era between China and Russia has nothing to do with an alliance. China and Russia have become partners in pursuing development and progress. This closer relationship should not be interpreted as allying. Actually, there is no alliance between China and Russia, in form or connotation; there is also no need for such an alliance. The document regards the two countries as the ballast on the ships of peace, stability and development. It is of great significance for the two countries and the world. Therefore, it has aroused tremendous repercussions and praise in the international community (Xu 2019).

Although South Africa has complained a lot about China's economic activities in Africa in the past, and former President Thabo Mbeki even accused China of implementing 'neo-colonialism' in Africa, China's relations with South Africa developed fast since it joined the BRICS mechanism at China's suggestion and invitation. During President Zuma's visit to China in August 2010, the two heads of state jointly signed the *Beijing Declaration of the People's Republic of China and the Republic of South Africa on the establishment of a comprehensive strategic partnership*, elevating the bilateral relations to a comprehensive strategic partnership. In March 2013, President Xi Jinping visited South Africa and a joint communique was issued, marking a new stage in the China-South Africa comprehensive strategic partnership. In December 2014, President Zuma visited China and the two sides signed a *Strategic plan for 5–10 years co-operation between the People's Republic of China and The Republic of South Africa 2015–2024*, promoting the further development of China-South Africa relations. In 2017, China and South Africa officially launched a high-level people-to-people and cultural exchange mechanism. In July 2018, President Xi visited South Africa and attended the 10th BRICS Summit. In September 2018, President Ramaphosa visited China and attended the China-Africa Cooperation Forum Beijing Summit. However, China's relation with India and Brazil, especially Sino-Indian relations, have posed challenges to BRICS co-operation.

First, the strategic mutual trust between China and India needs to be strengthened, and the BRICS mechanism cannot resolve the geopolitical differences between them. The contradictions between China and India, as well as the differences in their overall national strength, results in lack of mutual trust. It has hindered political and security co-operation among BRICS countries greatly. Historical border conflicts made the Indian elite view China as an enemy, a view that has been reinforced constantly. China-Pakistan relations, the lingering boundary issue between China and India, and China's economic co-operation with South Asia and Indian Ocean countries have been regarded as China's offensive actions to encircle India and squeeze India's strategic space by India's elites. India would like to be on an equal footing with China on the world stage or the Asian region, believing that it truly pursues a multipolar world and multipolar Asia while China pursues a bipolar world and unipolar Asia. They believe the conflict between China and India is structural at the regional level, which is difficult to resolve. Western countries are keen to sow discord on these issues. At the same time, India also hopes to play the role of the so-called 'swing state' or 'linchpin' in the international system and often takes cues from Western countries. It has affected BRICS co-operation and joint voice on some international or regional hotspot issues greatly.

Before the 2017 Xiamen Summit, the Dong Lang (Doklam) standoff took place between China and India. Although the two countries resolved the crisis peacefully and set a good example for the solidarity of BRICS countries and co-operation among developing countries, the Dong Lang standoff cast its shadow on the Xiamen Summit. C. Uday Bhaskar has contended that India deftly managed the crisis, using its potential boycott of the 2017 BRICS Summit as a means to bring about a mutual stand-down (Bhaskar 2020). In fact, compared with China, India needs the BRICS organisation more. In 2018, Modi government reviewed and adjusted its foreign policy based on changes in the international and domestic situation as well as its needs for the next election. Leaders of China, India and Russia held informal meetings in Wuhan and Sochi respectively and reached consensus on a range of international issues. The solidarity of BRICS countries has laid a solid foundation for the success of the Johannesburg Summit. However, India remains jealous of China's leadership in BRICS co-operation. India is against the expansion of BRICS, China's proposal of building a human community of shared destiny, and the belt and road initiative. In particular, India hopes to play the role of 'swing state' or 'balancer' in the international system when China and Russia are faced with great geopolitical pressure. Some Indian think tanks even hope to reset the trilateral dialogue forum among India, Brazil and South Africa. Therefore, co-operation among the BRICS countries is seriously affected.

In recent years, India-US relations have improved constantly. India has merged with the United States on its 'Indo-Pacific' strategy, and India is actively promoting the quadrilateral security dialogue (Quad) among the United States, Japan, India and Australia. The close relationship between India and the United States will inevitably damage its traditional relationship with Russia. Judging from the current trend, it is difficult to reverse the momentum of further rapprochement between India and the United States, which will have a serious impact on BRICS co-operation.

Secondly, in terms of politics, unlike China and Russia, Brazil, India and South Africa adopt a Western democratic system. The significant difference in political systems, social systems, cultural traditions, and international status lead to a lack of unanimity among these countries. This situation is obvious when it comes to the relationship between China and Brazil. As a major country in Latin America, Brazil is influenced greatly by the United States. Its foreign policy and global strategy show certain uncertainty, and whether it will or will not play the role of a great power depends on its leaders to a large extent. The relationship between China and Brazil had developed successfully during the presidencies of Lula, Rousseff and Temer. In 2012, the bilateral relationship was upgraded to a comprehensive strategic partnership. Nevertheless, since the inauguration of the new president Bolsonaro on January 1, 2019, he declared the pro-US stance, changing the neutral tradition of Brazilian diplomacy for many years, and attacked China for buying Brazil's key energy resource, agriculture, minerals and other core industries, and even land. Although in May 2019, Brazil's vice president Moran visited China to save the bilateral relationship between China and Brazil damaged by Bolsonaro's anti-China speeches and to find a balance between Brazil's desire to shift its focus to the United States and the practical consideration of China's economic importance to Brazil (Reference News 2019), the BRICS co-operation mechanism seems unable to eliminate the disagreement in values and ideologies between China and some members of the BRICS.

Finally, the diversity of the BRICS members is evident and their pursuit of political, security and economic benefits are not the same. As permanent members of the UN Security Council, China and Russia are vested beneficiaries of the international system. However, India, Brazil and South Africa are looking forward to promoting reforms of the UN and the Security Council and become permanent members of the Security Council. China, Russia and India are all countries with nuclear weapons; South Africa conducted nuclear tests but later announced the abandonment of nuclear weapons. India has so far refused to sign the NPT. Owing to economic structural problems, China and other BRICS countries including India and Brazil ran into trade imbalances, about which India, Brazil and other countries have many complaints. With the rise in China's economic strength and international status, China and other countries including India and Brazil will have greater disagreements on WTO and issues like climate change, which will affect BRICS co-operation adversely.

References

Bhaskar, C. Uday (2020). "India-China Relations Post-Galwan," China-India Brief #162, https://lkyspp.nus.edu.sg/cag/publications/details/china-india-brief-162#guest (accessed on July 7, 2020).

"BRICS Development Bank: A Milestone in the History of International Finance", *Qian Jiang Evening News*, http: //finance.china.com.cn/roll/20140714/2536152.shtml (accessed on July 13, 2015).

"BRICS Share of the Global Economy Rose to 23%, and its Contribution to World Economic Growth Reached 50%", *Economy Daily* (2017), http: //www.ce.cn/xwzx/gnsz/gdxw/201708/29/t20170829_25458089.shtml (accessed on August 30, 2017).

Feng, Yujun (2019). "Speech on Seminar Series on'70 Years of China's Diplomacy' of Shanghai Institutes for International Studies – Review and Prospect of China-Russian (Soviet) Relations," March 22, 2019.

Gao, Shangtao (2015). "The Practice Theory and the Practice Pattern: An Analysis of the process of China Participating the BRIC Cooperation Mechanism", *Foreign Affairs Review*, 2015(1):14.

Hu Jintao(2012). "Full text of Hu Jintao's Report at 18th Party Congress", www.china-embassy.org/eng/zt/18th_CPC_National_Congress_Eng/t992917.htm (accessed on July 13, 2015).

Kirton, John J. (2015). "Explaining the BRICS Summit Solid, Strengthening Success", *International Organisations Research Journal*, 10(2).

Kong Weizhuo: "former Chinese counsellor to the United States: the proportion of GDP of the BRICS countries in the world is driven by China and India", Phoenix International iMarkets, http://finance.ifeng.com/a/20170904/15647114_0.shtml (accessed on October 13, 2017).

Lin Yongliang (2017). "Go through the Golden Decade", *Outlook*, 2017(36).

Liu Zongyi (2008). "The Development of Inter-regionalism and its Significance to China", *Forum of World Economics & Politics*, 2008(4).

Liu Zongyi (2017). "The BRICS Summit Will Lay the Foundation for the Next Decade", *China Review*, www.crntt.com/doc/1047/9/6/1/104796176.html?coluid=137&kindid=7730&docid=104796176&mdate=0902000136 (accessed on September 13, 2017).

Ministry of Commerce of China (2019a). "A Brief Introduction to China-India Economic and Trade Cooperation", http://yzs.mofcom.gov.cn/article/t/201902/20190202836075.shtml (accessed on February 20, 2019).

Ministry of Commerce of China (2019b). "Brief Introduction to China-South Africa Economic and Trade Cooperation", http: //xyf.mofcom.gov.cn/article/tj/hz/201903/20190302839325.shtml (accessed on February 20, 2019).

"Ministry of Commerce: China's Direct Investment in Russia Increased 72 percent Year on Year to US $2.22 Billion in 2017", *Sputnik News Agency* (2018), www.ccpit.org/Contents/Channel_3974/2018/0427/995332/content_995332.htm(accessed on April 27, 2018).

Nikonov V. (2014) "BRICS Represents a Challenge to Western Domination", *Russkiy Mir Foundation*, www.russkiymir.ru/en/publications/140423/ (accessed on April 28, 2015)

O'Neill, Jim (2001). "Building Better Global Economic BRICs", November 2001, www.goldmansachs.com/insights/archive/building-better.html (accessed on May 20, 2020).

"Remarks by Foreign Media: Brazilian Vice President Visits China to Repair Bilateral Relations", *Reference News* (2019), http: //www.cankaoxiaoxi.com/china/20190520/2380583.shtml (accessed on May 20, 2020).

"Russian Economic Development Minister: The Trade Volume Between Russia and China Can Break the 200 billion USD Mark", *DuoWei News* (2019), http: //economics.dwnews.com/news/2019–06–06/60136537.html (accessed on June 6, 2019).

Su Ge (2017). "General Secretary Xi Jinping's Diplomatic Thoughts Lead China's Major Power Diplomacy", www.ciis.org.cn/chinese/2017-09/28/content_40031024.htm (accessed on July 13, 2018).

Sun Mingcan (2015). "Problems Existing in BRICS Trade Cooperation Mechanism and China's Countermeasures", *Prices Monthly*, 2015(6).

Wang Yi (2017). "Carry Forward Our Cause into the Future and Write a New Chapter in the History of BRICS Cooperation – further study on the important speech of President Xi Jinping at the BRICS summit in Xiamen", *People's Daily*, http: //opinion.people.com.cn/n1/2017/0912/c1003–29528871.html (accessed on September 13, 2017).

Xi Jinping (2017). "Full text of Xi Jinping's Report at 19th CPC National Congress", www.xinhuanet.com/english/special/2017-11/03/c_136725942.htm (accessed on July 13, 2018).

Xu Yicong (2019), "China-Russia Comprehensive Strategic Partnership of Coordination in the New Era is of Far-reaching Significance", *Xinhuanet*, http: //www.xinhuanet.com/world/2019-06/09/c_1210154013.htm (accessed on June 9, 2019).

Zhao Kejin (2014). "The Cooperation of BRICS in China's Global Strategy", *International Review*, 2014(3).

14

CHINA, GLOBAL GOVERNANCE AND BRICS

G. Venkat Raman

Introduction

China has grown as a serious economic and military power in the past two decades, and its ambitions have risen correspondingly. This rise in its influence has translated into a desire to transform global governance rules and norms to suit its interests. The collapse of the infallible American financial system and its consequent dent in the Washington Consensus's credibility fuelled China's ambitions to rewrite the rules of global governance. China's expansive role in the BRICS platform is part of this plan, particularly in the aftermath of the global financial crisis of 2008. The growing relevance of emerging markets and Russia's re-emergence as a power to reckon with coincided with their grievances with the liberal order established by the US-led West. China wanted to encash on the clamour by emerging powers like India, Russia and Brazil and explore possibilities of new alliances. It suited Beijing's national interests to be part of a coalition of emerging powers rather than directly antagonising the US. It continued to reap rich economic dividends from its participation in the liberal order. To be precise, China's goals in joining the 'accidental allies' (Brütsch and Papa 2013, p. 303) of the BRICS group of nations served two purposes. First, it enabled it to deal with the international hostility it was likely to face in the US-led hegemonic order as a prospective revisionist power. Second, a political formation like BRICS legitimised its demand to 'reform' the international system's status quo to suit its interests. It is debatable how far the BRICS group has advanced these objectives, particularly after the Covid pandemic's disastrous effect on its global reputation.

In this chapter, I examine China's motivations to invest in a political project like BRICS. I firmly believe that appreciating China's investment in BRICS as a by-product of its global governance stance and its emergence as a global power. The first section deals with China's political posturing on the question of global

DOI: 10.4324/9781003148074-16

governance. In the second section of the chapter, I try to summarise briefly the historical evolution of China's policy towards multilateralism in its foreign policy. In the third section, I examine the various unit and system-level factors that influenced China's growing interest in the BRICS as one of its political projects. In the final section, I conclude that China's position on BRICS reflects its changing stance on various aspects of global governance and is a well-crafted combination of a certain level of dogmatism laced with anti-Western rhetoric and an unmistakable emphasis on pragmatism to preserve its own core interests.

China's Emergence as a Global Power: Background

When the Cold War ended in 1989, China was facing multiple crises. The Tiananmen students' unrest and Chinese leadership's ruthless determination to crush the movement strengthened the conservative faction in the Communist party. The subsequent international outcry against China's open defiance of human rights seriously hampered its 'economic modernisation' project. Additionally, it affected its onward march to further integrate with the international economic and trade order. Its leaders were also extremely wary of the likelihood of a unipolar international system, with the US at its helm. They were aware that China was shorn of the capacity and intent to don the developing world's leadership. Deng Xiaoping, the architect of China's reforms launched in 1978 as part of the now famous 'reforms and opening up' policy to fuel China's 'economic modernisation' drive, fundamentally transformed its interactions with the world. Laying the ground rules of this cautious integration with the international system to overcome the economic backwardness caused by Chairman Mao Zedong's isolationist policies in the name of self-reliance, Deng outlined four principles on which China's domestic and foreign policy would be based: 'Observe and analyse calmly, Strengthen your position, Undertake change with confidence, Conceal your true potential, Contribute your part, never become the leader' (Bergsten, Freeman, Lardy, and Mitchell 2008, p. 209).

Not many international observers of China were surprised by Deng Xiaoping's reticence (Gu, Humphrey, and Messner 2008). As recently as 2004, influential voices derisively called China a developing country. However, within a few years, the disjuncture between China's limited influence in setting the global governance agenda and the vast improvements in its material conditions made such disparaging characterisations untenable. China abandoned the 'lying low' strategy and replaced it with striving for achievement (henceforth SFA). Challenging and rewriting global governance rules in its favour through a 'mixture of victimology and aggrandisement' was a vital element of this shift in China's strategy (Mitter 2003, p. 221).

Ever since China's liberation in 1949, its foreign policy has evolved through different phases. In the initial years, China's ideological affinity with the erstwhile Soviet Union and its economic backwardness left it with no other option than to join the Soviets. Khrushchev's destalinisation speech marked the beginning of the Sino-Soviet split formalised with Nixon's landmark visit in 1972. Its ideological affiliation with socialist ideals led to China's mistrust of the US-led West. This trust deficit impelled it to support the politics of alienation and non-alignment among the developing world nations within the superpower-dominated bipolar world order. The 1955 Afro-Asian relations Bandung conference was a significant event in this regard (Wang and Rosenau 2009, p. 7). This narrative continued in the 1960s to influence their foreign policy, with Beijing consistently voicing its opposition against imperialism, revisionism, and reactionaries (*fandui di xiu fan*). In the 1970s, China adopted what came to be known as the three worlds approach (*san ge shijie*), comprising the superpowers, developing countries, and those in between (second world). After exiting the socialist bloc, China replaced the Republic of China (Taiwan) as one of the five permanent members in the UN Security Council in 1971, marking another signpost in China's elevation as a significant power within the international system. The post-Mao reforms and its 'four modernisation' programmes paved the way for the initial phase of China's integration with the world economy from 1978 onwards.

According to scholars like Nicholas Lardy (1994), China's initial foreign direct investment (FDI) policies during the earlier phases of its economic modernisation drive exemplified its leadership's eagerness to overcome its economic backwardness caused by the calamitous years of the Cultural Revolution. Although China was inspired by the export promotion growth strategy adopted by the so-called East Asian tigers (Hong Kong, Singapore, Taiwan, and South Korea), it was far bolder and liberal in some of its experiments during the earlier phase of modernisation. Scholarship related to China's trade and foreign direct investment (FDI) policies highlight that Chinese policies were far more liberal than those of Japan and South Korea at a comparable development stage (Lardy 1994). China joined key international economic organisations, including the Bretton Woods Institutions (International Monetary Fund and the World Bank), in April 1980. In the mid-1980s, the Chinese government began to negotiate membership in the General Agreement on Tariffs and Trade that would later transform into the World Trade Organization (WTO) (Jacobson, Karan, and Oksenberg 1990). By the second half of the 1990s, China was perceived as a benign power and at ease with liberal order norms. China's signing and ratifying the UN human rights covenants and the Kyoto Protocol on climate change were cited as examples in this regard. Furthermore, it has been frequently cited that China had also made sincere commitments to gain membership in the WTO that became formalised in 2001.

China's stance on global governance issues has been based on a shrewd mixture of dogmatism and pragmatism. On the one hand, it has consistently voiced its opposition to imperialist designs and hegemonic practices. On the other hand, it has been practical in terms of its discretion to form need-based alliances. It has also been very cautious in crafting its stance towards global governance to suit its national interests. For instance, China is very keen to demand changes in global governance. Still, it has not been willing to discuss the expansion of the UN Security Council's permanent membership. It also demanded a prominent role in the international financial system by advocating reforms in the Bretton Woods

Institutions. Simultaneously, it resorted to creating alternative institutions like the Asian Investment Infrastructure Bank and the New Development Bank. Similarly, China has never expressed any qualms with the post-World War II international order that had given it specific privileges such as freedom from interference in its internal affairs. On the contrary, it has been very taciturn about the UN Security Council's powers that can impinge on sovereignty privileges. Further, in the last decade or so, China is desirous of an ambitious role that would enable safeguarding its national interests and advocating a different set of values by which international politics and global governance are discussed. These values emanated from its identity as a 'civilizational-state' (Jacques 2009, p. 26).

China and Global Governance

Chinese official discourses on global governance (*quanjiu zhili*) is more of a recent development. One can see internal discussions and debates on this concept as late as the beginning of the twenty-first century (Chan, Pak, and Chan 2008, pp. 4–5). Since 1996, Chinese leaders have advanced a 'new security concept'.[1] The new security concept's central goal was to counter American hegemony with a 'multilateral approach to participating' in foreign affairs. The mainland domestic discourse on global governance comprises two divergent schools of thought. The first school accepts the existing framework of global governance while the other does not. The proponents of the first school aver that there are several governance challenges that cannot be categorised along national boundaries. These include environmental degradation, transnational crime, pandemics, and financial crises. This group of scholars draws a clear distinction between the national government and global governance. While national governments apply hierarchical structures to implement policies and manage their internal affairs, negotiation and co-ordination among national representatives is the mechanism by which global governance is executed (Wang and Rosenau 2009, pp. 11–15).

The roots of the scepticism of existing notions of global governance among other Chinese scholars come from their broader suspicion of the liberal values of 'democracy', 'human rights' and 'free markets', propagated by the US-led West. They believe that institutional mechanisms like the Bretton Woods institutions are a fig leaf for advancing the geo-strategic and the geo-economic agenda of the US and its allies, based on neoliberal economic policies. In contrast, a 'civilizational-state' like China, based on a rich cultural legacy of Confucianism and Daoism, can offer an alternate vision of international order. Drawing upon this legacy, China can lead the developing world to find different solutions to their problems by tapping into their own cultural and political tradition rather than presuming the Western framework as the default. These analysts believe that the approach to 'global governance' and the institutions that regulate them should reflect these emerging countries' values and reflect the power shifts in the twenty-first century. Some variant of both these perspectives represents the Chinese view of multilateralism and guides its investment in BRICS.

China, Multilateralism and BRICS

China has put its weight behind BRICS to advance its multilateralism version in an international forum. It views the current order as being characterised by 'one superpower, many great powers' (*yi chao duo qiang*). China's economic integration with the global economy compelled the Chinese leadership to conceptualise its version of multilateralism. In the early 1990s, when China came up with the peaceful rise (*heping jueqi*) proposition, many countries, especially in the West, were suspicious of China's aspirations to become a revisionist power. These concerns prompted the leadership to replace the 'peaceful rise' with the 'peaceful development' thesis. The latter was invoked to align its discourse with assuaging international concerns and adding a certain legitimacy to its stance on multilateralism. The boycott of China by several major powers following the Tiananmen crackdown until the early 1990s forced a change in China's approach to multilateral institutions. Consequently, multilateralism became a vital ingredient of China's 'foreign economic and security policy' in the 1990s.

The growing relevance of multilateralism was indicative of an increasingly confident China as its economy began showing desirous results. China's grievances against the US-led liberal international order in the post-2008 world led to increasingly vocal concerns about the adverse impact of economic liberalisation on developing countries. Instead of the 'one size fits all' orientation of the Washington Consensus,[2] China advocated a 'horses for courses' economic development policy for low and middle-income countries. China also wanted the liberal order to expand the consensus decision-making zone that respected emerging powers' wishes. Hughes (2005) argued that despite China's qualified support for multilateralism, power balancing with the US-led West remained a significant motivator for Chinese investment in regional organisations like the Shanghai Cooperation Organization (SCO) and political coalitions like BRICS.

Following the 2008 sub-prime crisis, emerging powers like China and India were given greater recognition in the G20. The Chinese were quick to notice the potential of BRIC[3] as a partnership of states interested in a global governance regime that represented their interests. It also helped prevent China being singled out as a defiant state against the US liberal order and reinforce suspicions of those critics who alleged that China harboured ambitions of being a revisionist state. However, the 2008 financial crisis put a dent in the unipolar international order. It led to China aspiring to become a 'peer competitor' of the US (Goldstein 2008, pp. 55–86). The 2008 sub-prime crisis led some influential Chinese observers like Li Hongmei, the then editor of People's Daily,[4] to predict an 'unambiguous end to the US unipolar system after the global financial era'. This kind of thinking motivated China's enhanced participation in the BRICS coalition.

In its policy level statements, China ensured that it projected its perception of the BRICS being more than a mere pressure group that negotiated favours for emerging powers within the framework of the US-led liberal international order. The official Chinese view of BRICS in 2010, represented by Wu Hailong,

Director-General of the International Department at the Ministry of Foreign affairs at the time, was that it was an 'evolution from hypothetical (*xuni*) into a realistic platform for international co-operation' and was a 'logical choice' (*shunli cheng-zhang*) (Glosny 2010, p. 108). They also perceived BRICS as a platform for 'sharing experiences, and exchanging lessons learned' (*fenxiang jingyan, jiaoliu xin de*) (Glosny 2010, p. 108). China's overall interest in BRICS has stemmed from a combination of idealism and hard-core realpolitik in addition to some unit and system-level factors. Although one cannot distinguish the various unit and system-level elements in shaping China's official policy towards BRICS, I would endeavour to delineate the various domestic and external factors that help us understand and appreciate China's motivations to make substantial investments in BRICS.

China's Motivations Behind Investment in BRICS

The Chinese leadership felt that a political coalition comprising of leading developing states can be a formidable one to fight common problems confronting them in areas related to poverty alleviation, disaster management and infrastructure modernisation. Since the other member states of the group were also facing similar challenges in their respective socio-economic development, exchanging ideas on policies to tackle such non-traditional security threats was beneficial for two important reasons. One, it helped China project its identity as a developing country facing common challenges like other developing countries. Second, it enabled the launching of BRICS as a political alliance forging a formidable partnership to effect global governance changes emanating from non-Western models based on different hybrids of state-market relations due to their unique historical, cultural, social, and political factors. For instance, China was critical of some aspects of the 'rule-based' liberal international economic order that have impeded poverty eradication. The Washington Consensus rules, it contended, have created distortions across the global economic system, whose ill effects have been recurring inside various national economies, including some of the advanced ones. The idea was to project non-Western development models as equally or perhaps more effective in tackling problems like poverty.

BRICS as a Platform to Discuss Non-traditional Security Issues

China's aim to establish a moderately prosperous society can be cited as an instance in this regard. Although leaders like Deng Xiaoping and Jing Zemin spoke of the concept of the 'moderately prosperous' society (*xiaokang shehui*) in the post-Mao era, it gained political currency in later years. In recent times, the slogan started featuring more regularly in the party leadership's discourse since Hu Jintao, the then President and General Secretary of the party defined it in 2012, 'Completing the Building of a Moderately Prosperous Society in All Respects' in his report to the 18th party national congress. On the one hand, it helped China project itself

as a developing country faced with similar challenges confronting other developing countries. On the other hand, it enabled it to showcase that non-Western models like its unique developmental model of 'socialism with Chinese characteristics' are equally or maybe even more effective in tackling poverty eradication issues. Chinese leaders have been keen to stress that the BRICS platform is a handy tool to exchange ideas on various non-traditional security threats.

As part of its multilateralist approach in foreign policy, China has shown keen interest in exploring various options to build new coalitions to tackle non-traditional security threats (Li 2009). For instance, in 2003, China and ASEAN had a high-level summit exclusively devoted to combating the SARS pandemic and discussing various possible joint initiatives to address public health's co-operation issues. To cite another instance, China forged an understanding with Japan and South Korea to exchange seismic information, and information on technology and counterterrorism. In a similar vein, via the SCO, China seeks to tackle the banes of separatism, religious extremism, and terrorism.

Even in the 2020 BRICS annual meeting in Moscow, the Chinese statement endorsed the calls for a 'partnership for global stability, shared security, and innovative growth'.[5] Speaking on this occasion, President Xi Jinping stated:

> We remain convinced that the theme of our times, peace and development, has not changed, and that the trend toward multipolarity and economic globalization cannot be turned around. We must keep people's welfare close to heart and pursue the vision of a community with a shared future for mankind. Through concrete actions, we will contribute our share to making the world a better place for everyone.[6]

Influence of Nationalism on Foreign Policy

China's growing international stature following the 2008 crash triggered a spike in Chinese national pride. Prosperity gave a large segment of the Chinese population the confidence to desire that their country be viewed as a global power. The Chinese Communist Party (CCP) recognised that its domestic legitimacy had increasingly become a function of substantial foreign policy initiatives to advance this agenda. The BRICS was seen as one instrument among many to do this. Chinese nationalism has been traditionally studied in binary opposites such as affirmative versus assertive, 'us versus them' (Whiting 1983), top-down/political or state-centred nationalism, and bottom-up and cultural nationalism (Guo 2004) or as merely aggressive (Zhao 2005). In the mid-1990s, nationalist works like 'China can say no' (*Zhong Guo keyi shuo bu*) and 'Unhappy China' (*Zhong Guo bu gao xing*) became best sellers. Chinese confidence was boosted by the spectacular success of the Beijing Olympics. The World Expo Forum in Shanghai in 2010 further solidified this self-image as a country whose moment in the sun had arrived.

As a consequence of these mega events of global significance, the CCP was able to fan nationalist emotions. It cited China's 'century of national humiliation' and propagated slogans like 'never forget national humiliation' (*wu wang guochi*). As is the case in most authoritarian systems, the CCP leadership has successfully channelised nationalist sentiments to consolidate their power in the past decade. A section of international relations scholars has theorised that the political leadership in a country resorts to warmongering to distract the various internal constituencies from domestic strife. Better known as diversionary war theorists, scholars like Haynes (2017), Levy (1989), Richards (1993), and Theiler (2018) have argued that leadership in certain countries instigate external conflicts to shore up their positions within the public and the military establishment during such times. Following the outbreak of the corona epidemic, the political manifestations of Chinese nationalism have become more visible. The adoption of 'wolf-warrior diplomacy' has served to counter the intense criticism it has faced for its lapses that allegedly set off the coronavirus in Wuhan.

The current leadership presided by the incumbent President of the PRC, and the General Secretary of the communist party, Xi Jinping, is pursuing the path of 'national rejuvenation' (*fuxing zhilu*) to construct a new narrative of realising the 'China dream'.[7] This policy goal necessitates a broader scope of international responsibilities. There is talk of being part of a 'community of shared future of mankind' (*goujian renlei mingyun gong tongti)* (Nathan and Zhang 2021, p. 1). This policy has prompted Beijing to shift its foreign policy from 'strategic prudence' to 'active engagement' (*fenfa youwei*) with other emerging powers. The BRICS project has the added advantage of camouflaging China's political ambitions in the garb of pursuing the cause of a just international political and economic order.

The Narrative of China as a 'Responsible Power'

A section of influential commentators in the mainland responded to the US calls to China to become a 'responsible power'. Certain Chinese commentators became critical of the then US Department of Security, Robert Zoellick, when he called upon China to become a 'responsible stakeholder'. For such analysts, the 'responsible stakeholder' tag implied that the onus of international responsibility lies solely with China. At the same time, the US can get away with its whimsical conduct. Some influential Chinese policy sections have interpreted the responsible stakeholder tag as equivalent to blaming China for contributing to global economic imbalances by manipulating the RMB exchange rate to its alleged attempts to manipulate the RMB exchange rate and in the process contributing to global economic imbalances. Furthermore, these analysts argued that China should be extremely cautious of getting trapped in the net cast by the US-led West. The arguments put forward were as follows. First, 'responsible China' calls were attempts to impose international responsibilities to overburden it with tasks that it cannot afford, given its domestic compulsions. Second, such calls would jeopardise China's flexibility to pose as a 'developing country', enabling it to draw concessions relevant to its national interests. Third, some scholars like Yuan Peng stated, 'China, for its part, does not base its notion of international responsibility on US expectations' (Hachigian and Peng 2010, p. 82). Yuan Peng and others questioned the US's *locus standi* regarding their *fairness and authority* (emphasised by me) to make international demands on a developing country like China. Such scholars argued that, given the US system's dubious role that led to the 2008 financial crisis and the Washington Consensus's glaring shortcomings, the US had no moral legitimacy to preach to others (Hachigian & Peng p 124). Finally, the narrative of 'responsible power' was perceived as an attempt to contain China and a part of Western endeavours to sermonise China. Such a scathing rebuke of the 'responsible stakeholder' proposals led to the emergence of revisionism in the conservative sections of the party leadership, prompting calls for a China that is 'less willing to obey but more willing to command' (Deng 2014, p. 124). This new China also necessitated a reorientation of what constitutes China's 'interests'. As Deng Yong put it succinctly, China set a new strategy (that) places a premium on 'interests and interest binding' (2014, p. 125).

In this new diplomatic policy, China sought to manipulate its interpretation of national interests. Sometimes, it construed interests as its readiness to adopt any means to defend what it calls 'core interests'. On other occasions, its pronouncements of interests were an end-purpose in the form of orchestrating new collaborations in the form of 'interest binding' with like-minded states to influence and shape the contours of global governance in the twenty-first century. BRICS was one such platform that China could not afford to ignore given its new foreign policy priorities. Given China's deep integration in the process of economic globalisation, its foreign policy was bound to be moulded by its responses to the various developments in the international arena. In the following section, I will try to highlight some of the significant changes in China's foreign policy owing to changes in the international system. In other words, what were the various system level factors that led to a clear departure from its earlier foreign policy goals?

China's foreign policy in the latter part of the first decade of the 2000s metamorphosed into a more assertive one. China became more assertive of its territorial claims and national interests in a very overt shift from the foreign policy based on the 'peaceful rise' thesis (Johnston 2013, p. 19). More recently, under President Xi Jinping, one is increasingly witnessing widening of the gulf between China's verbal pronouncements and *praxis*. This gulf is manifesting itself in the form of wolf warrior diplomacy, bearing a streak of aggression and assertiveness hitherto unseen. This growing assertiveness has led to its pronouncements being more 'confrontational towards regional and global affairs' (Liao 2018, p. 288). For instance, since 2009, China came up with the idea of 'core interests' (*hexin liyi*) against 'national interests'. Under Xi's leadership, it has shed the earlier, lying low approach advocated by one of its paramount leaders, Deng Xiaoping, and replaced it with the ambitious SFA approach (Liao 2018). Following the new policy, China has sought to develop and support new institutions like the Asian Investment Infrastructural Bank and the New Development Bank.

BRICS' importance for China is reflected in the work report of the eighteenth Communist party congress. In the report, the party laid out its foreign policy strategy for the coming years. Within this vital document, apart from the UN, G 20, SCO, BRICS finds special mention as far as China's institutional priorities are concerned. To ensure that its investments in the BRICS are not jeopardised, it has consciously avoided posturing that could be considered dominating.

Challenging the US by Allying with Emerging Powers

China's liberal international order experiences following its accession to the WTO have been predominantly rewarding. However, conservative leaders adopting a hard-line stance have expressed reservations about the possible political and ideological ramifications arising from China's growing integration in the liberal economic order. A significant part of Beijing's grouse with the liberal order was the US's perceived hegemonic influence and its impact on the operational aspects of the liberal order. Chinese leaders at the highest level have touched upon China's opposition to Western domination. In one of his speeches, Jiang Zemin, the former President of China, declared that China is keen to promote the development of economic globalisation but is firmly opposed to all forms of 'hegemonism' in world politics (Jiang Zemin 2002). On another occasion, Jiang's successor Hu Jintao in one of his speeches stated that China desired to take an 'active part in global economic governance to promote, [and] facilitate free trade and investment, and oppose protectionism in all its forms' (Hu Jintao 2007). The concerns of emerging powers like India and China about the unjust exploitation of the developing world arising out of the inappropriate free trade policies by the Washington Consensus driven by the Bretton Woods Institutions are well known. India and China have also protested Western attempts to impose similar exacting standards to curb environmental pollution in various climate change talks for them and the developed world. After 2008, China sensed an opportunity to address such injustices by allying with other BRICS member states. In the words of one of its top officials Wang Yi, China sought to 'improve the international system and order and meet the wishes of the developing countries in the process' (as quoted in Beeson and Li 2016, p. 493).

The BRICS platform provides a convenient tool for China to avoid a confrontation with the US and serves another critical purpose. It enables China to engage and deepen ties with other member-states in the grouping. One can account for China's pro-active efforts to bring South Africa within the BRICS fold, reflecting its growing interests in engaging Africa. China perceives its alliance with other BRICS countries as a very potent weapon to strengthen the chorus clamouring for greater diversity and 'institutional pluralism' in international affairs (Öniş and Kutlay 2020, p. 2). The BRICS member-states have been advocating the ushering in of global governance mechanisms that are more representative and enable negotiating 'interest intermediate structures' (Öniş and Kutlay 2020, p. 2).

Through the BRICS grouping, China believes that it can explore possible alliances with other states more appreciative of the developmental models stemming from hybrid state-market relations (Acharya 2016; Flockhart 2016; Bremmer 2010;

McNally 2012). In the case of the BRICS countries, their unique historical, political, and social circumstances have inspired unique models of development with varying degrees of success, and they have felt that the Washington Consensus's homogenising tendencies were detrimental to their interests. The 2008 financial crisis was an unprecedented opportunity for China to draw an alliance and encash on such sentiments. Furthermore, China's recent initiatives like the Belt and Road Initiative, Shanghai Cooperation Organization, and the AIIB and its ardent advocacy of BRICS is an endeavour to carve out spaces for 'developing countries with minimalist conditions, a kind of 'no-strings attached' approach (Öniş and Kutlay 2020, p. 3). By pushing this agenda, China seeks to don the mantle of leadership championing the cause of the developing world and claim some bragging rights as a power that believes in a just international order.

One of China's foreign policy-making rhetoric has been its advocacy of developing countries' inclusiveness in the international economic order. Beijing has very adroitly balanced its foreign policymaking by preserving its interests in those areas in which it tends to benefit by maintaining the status quo. However, from time to time, it has sought to claim some moral legitimacy by calling for changes in the norms governing international development and committing itself to the cause of inclusiveness for the developing world (Abdenur 2014, p. 90).

This policy gets reflected in official discourse at the highest levels. For instance, in 2012, in a speech, the then Chinese President Hu Jintao stated:

> In their co-operation, BRICS countries have committed to promoting South–South co-operation and North-South dialogue, endeavouring to implement the United Nations Millennium Development Goals, working for early realisation of the goals set out in the mandate for the Doha development round negotiations, striving to secure a greater say for developing countries in global economic governance, and fighting all forms of protectionism.[8]

The invitation for South Africa to join the BRICs and the invitation for a broader range of African countries to be part of the BRICS meeting this year bears testimony regarding the group's orientation for expanding and deepening co-operation with other developing countries. Therefore, it is not a coincidence that in the various BRICS Summits, the Chinese president's address has always been laced with words like 'justice', 'greater co-ordination among BRICS countries', 'political trust', 'multilateralism', 'South–South co-operation' and 'North–South co-operation'.

Seeking a Multilateral Approach to Global Governance

In the past few years, China has moved to what some scholars like Chen Zhimin call the 'reform from outside' strategy (Chen 2016, pp. 780–781). Beijing has sought to influence global governance rules by forming 'plurilateralist parallel orders' (Hooijmaaijers 2019, p. 34) supported by new institutions like the New Development

Bank established by the BRICS countries. In the words of Javier Solana (2015, p. 3), the idea behind such moves is the veiled threat that 'if new powers are not given access to existing global governance structures, they will create structures of their own'. For instance, one of NDB's goals is to move away from the conditionalities imposed by the Bretton Woods Institutions (henceforth BWIs). China was piqued when the US Congress did ratify the verbal promises made by the Obama administration for a larger role in the BWIs. To address its concerns, China sought to adopt a two-pronged approach to one of its core concerns regarding existing global governance mechanisms – reforming the global financial system. On the one hand, it sought to establish its own international financial institutions like the BRI and the AIIB. Simultaneously, China has partnered with the BRICS countries to share concerns of underrepresentation in global economic and financial governance. It is very pertinent to note that, since 2015, China has gradually sought to combine its two-pronged strategy. For instance, China has sought to combine the BRICS and BRI initiatives.

One of China's defining features in the first decade of the twenty-first century was deploying the 'harmonious world' concept. The idea of a 'harmonious world' comprises four principles of global governance reform, namely, a) democratisation of international relations, b) justice and common prosperity, c) diversity and tolerance, and d) peaceful resolution of international conflicts (Wang and Rosenau 2009). Given the enormity of the task involved in realising such a lofty goal on its own, China has been very keen to build a platform like BRICS. The BRICS mechanism was perceived as a potent tool to strengthen multilateral co-operation with emerging powers and as an enabler in building new coalitions to form co-ordinated North-South dialogue positions (Cui 2013). In short, active participation in the BRICS mechanism is part of China's new concrete diplomatic practice in the twenty-first century. It results from its 'international responsibility consciousness' and a reflection of the reality of China's economic strength (Cui 2013, p. 57).

The BRICS as a political project keeps China interested in the immense possibilities it has to explore various ways in which non-traditional security threats like poverty, environment, climate change, and anti-terrorism can be tackled. For instance, China has portrayed its Xinjiang problem as one that stems from poverty. Beijing has sought to justify its BRI plans in the western regions of China and Central Asia as a serious attempt to alleviate poverty and the problem of terrorism stemming from it (Cheng 2015, p. 366). Chinese officials believe that international governance needs to effectively contend with poverty issues and to address the glaring inadequacies of existing institutions in overcoming human development issues. China seeks to form coalitions to tackle such problems and possibly exert some pressure on other BRICS member states facing similar developmental problems. Such alliances in the appropriate platforms in various international bodies will help China form pressure groups to negotiate outcomes favourable to it. Moreover, this will help China deal with specific criticisms on human rights by projecting these as developmental concerns rather than human rights issues as the Western world had projected them.

Finally, the development of the BRICS mechanism comprises an essential ingredient of China's development strategy and, therefore, is intricately linked to China's national interests. To cite an example, the Chinese leadership has undertaken a major diplomatic offensive to champion the Belt and Road Initiative benefits. It also played a very pro-active role in setting up the new development bank (NDB/BRICS bank) and the various platforms that BRICS has provided. Further, a quick look at China's trade and economic engagement with the external world reveals that the interdependence between the Chinese and global economies has increased manifold, especially in the last decade. It is also evident that trade and commerce and other forms of economic engagement have become more diversified. All this necessitates that China deals with developing countries more consistently and keeps in mind their unique sensitivities. Many of these countries have an abundance of raw materials and are lucrative markets that China finds difficult to resist. More importantly, engagement with these countries is an indispensable part of China's economic growth and development strategy. Therefore, to maintain stable and sustainable growth, China needs to find new and more substantial economic partners. BRICS countries, as representatives of emerging markets, fulfil this diplomatic goal.

Conclusion: Making Sense of 'China's Approach to BRICS

Chinese leadership and diplomacy have always projected BRICS as one that has been promoting democracy in international relations. BRICS countries, China contends, stand for global equity and justice. Further, Beijing argues that the BRICS grouping has always aspired to emerge as the voice of emerging markets and developing countries on various international and regional issues. Delivering his keynote speech at the seventh BRICS Summit in Ufa, Russia, President Xi Jinping expressed confidence in the BRICS co-operation mechanism's future. He stated, 'the more difficulties we face, the more confidence we must have'.[9] In his address, Xi called on BRICS countries to build a four-pronged partnership – '*safeguarding world peace, boosting common development, promoting diversified civilisation and strengthening global economic governance*'[10] and should forge a *community of shared interests* and build a closer economic partnership.

On strengthening global economic governance, Xi urged the BRICS countries to push for IMF reforms by expanding its representative character and raising the voices of emerging market economies and developing countries. BRICS countries should work together to elevate their position and role in the global governance system and push the international economic order to conform to the historical trend of the rising influence of emerging economies and developing countries. Further, BRICS countries have worked to boost world economic growth and improve global economic governance. It sought to enhance the representation and voice of emerging markets and developing countries in international economic and financial affairs. It instilled new momentum in the World Bank, the International Monetary Fund, and other international financial institutions. From time to time, these statements have shown that China, in partnership with other BRICS countries, is keen to negotiate and bargain with the established institutional mechanisms of global governance in the international system.

In recent times, China's foreign policy strategy has been based on the realisation that they are advocated and implemented in collaboration with others (Heilman, Rudolf, Huotari, and Buckow 2014). For instance, in the financial and monetary policy domain, in partnership with BRICS countries, China has not hesitated to play a critical role in launching multiple initiatives with the BRICS countries. China's enthusiastic participation after its initial reluctance to India's proposal to set up the New Development Bank is a pointer in this regard. Apart from the active support for the New Development Bank, China played a crucial role in setting up the BRICS Contingency Reserve Arrangement (CRA), which provided a reserve pool of USD100 billion for dealing with any situation caused by a liquidity crisis (Heilman, Rudolf, Huotari, and Buckow 2014, p. 4). China contributed 41% of the financial capital required to set up the CRA.

Interestingly, China has also invested in Chiang Mai Initiative Multilateralisation (CMIM) in the financial policy domain, providing a reserve pool of USD240 billion to tide over the liquidity crisis in the ASEAN region. The inspiration to establish these new institutions came from China's keenness to move beyond the era of WB's and IMF's pre-eminence in the international financial architecture. This desire is commensurate with its growing economic prowess. China has adopted a similar policy with some of the other alliances to establish parallel structures in essential policy domains. For instance, in the security domain, it has played a critical role in advancing its interests by showing a substantial interest in the Conference on Interaction and Confidence Building Measures in Asia (CICA), a security forum first initiated by Kazakhstan.

In a similar vein, China also perceives the immense potential of BRICS to collaborate and collectively voice grievances against the post-second world war US-led Western order. It seeks to capitalise on the collective voice of the BRICS to set new agendas and bring incremental changes in current global governance structures and espouse the need for new institutions reflecting the BRICS countries' values.

China observers are divided over the magnitude of power that a country like China commands in the international system. However, there is unanimity among all of them that China has come a long way from being a country used to abide by Deng Xiaoping's sagely advice that China should not assume the mantle of leadership too soon (*bu dang you*). In the wake of the 2008 crisis, the US-led West credentials have suffered a moral blow. The expansion of G8 to G20 and China's simultaneous rise and its growing assertiveness is a reality that one cannot wish away. It has always been a critic of Western values, especially those manifested in the US-led international order. China firmly believes that today, it is militarily strong enough to raise its voice to achieve and effect significant changes in tune with its foreign policy ambitions. In recent times, especially since Xi Jinping's elevation as the President of China, it has become more vociferous in its pronouncements on reshaping institutional mechanisms of global governance. These pronouncements reflect today's international politics and the values that are not necessarily an offshoot of the liberal order. In the case of China, these values can be traced to Confucianism and Daoism. As exemplified by the Presidential addresses in the BRICS Summits and its diplomats in various other international fora, the diplomatic language is replete with 'justice', 'equality', and 'mutual trust'. However, the most formidable challenge for Chinese diplomacy is to overcome the suspicions of the rest of the world, which is unsure of dealing with China. Unless Chinese diplomacy invests in addressing concerns emanating from these suspicions and bridges the apparent gulf between what it says and what it does, it will be increasingly difficult for China to realise its ambitions of reshaping the rules of global governance.

Notes

1 The details of this idea were contained a report to the ASEAN Regional Forum (ARF) Inter-sessional Support Group on Confidence-building Measures in Tokyo in January 1996.
2 The Washington consensus refers to policy prescriptions for developing countries by the Bretton Woods Institutions, namely, the IMF and the World Bank. These prescriptions are arrived at in consultation with the US Government's Department of treasury
3 South Africa joined the BRICS group in December 2010.
4 People's Daily is the largest newspaper group in China. It provides a very credible source of information on various developments including policy matters and viewpoints within the Chinese Communist Party
5 Ministry of External Affairs, Press Release, https://mea.gov.in/press-releases.htm?dtl/33197/12th+BRICS+Summit
6 Xinhua, November 18, 2020
7 *Xinhuanet*, 29 November 2012
8 Radebe, H. (2012). Brics a force for world peace, says China. *Business Day BDlive*, *8*.
9 BBC Monitoring Asia Pacific – Political, July 10, 2015, China president voices confidence in BRICS future
10 'Chinese President Xi Jinping Attends 5th BRICS Summit in Durban and Delivers an Important Speech', 2013. www.fmprc.gov.cn/mfa_eng/topics_665678/xjpcf1_665694/t1026742.shtml

References

Abdenur, A. E. (2014). China and the BRICS development bank: Legitimacy and multilateralism in south – south cooperation. *IDS Bulletin*, *45*(4), 85–101.

Acharya, A. (2016). The future of global governance: Fragmentation may be inevitable and creative. *Global Governance*, *22*(4), 453–460.

Beeson, M., and Li, F. (2016). China's place in regional and global governance: A new world comes into view. *Global Policy*, 7(4), 491–499.

Bergsten, C. F., Freeman, C., Lardy, N. R., and Mitchell, D. J. (2008). *China's rise: Challenges and opportunities*. Peterson Institute for International Economics. Center for Strategic and International.

Bremmer, I. (2010). Article commentary: The end of the free market: who wins the war between states and corporations? *European View*, *9*(2), 249–252.

Brütsch, C., and Papa, M. (2013). Deconstructing the BRICS: Bargaining coalition, imagined community, or geopolitical fad? *Chinese Journal of International Politics*, *6*(3), 299–327.

Chan, L. H., Lee, P. K., and Chan, G. (2008). Rethinking global governance: A China model in the making? *Contemporary Politics*, *14*(1), 3–19.
Chen, Z. (2016). China, the European Union and the fragile world order. *JCMS: Journal of Common Market Studies*, *54*(4), 775–792.
Cheng, J. Y. (2015). China's Approach to BRICS. *Journal of Contemporary China*, *24*(92), 357–375.
Cui, Y. (2013). Why the BRICS? A Chinese view. *Culture Mandala*, *10*(1), 5905.
Deng, Y. (2014). China: The post-responsible power. *The Washington Quarterly*, *37*(4), 117–132.
Flockhart, T. (2016). The coming multi-order world. *Contemporary Security Policy*, *37*(1), 3–30.
Glosny, M. A. (2010). China and the BRICs: A real (but limited) partnership in a unipolar world. *Polity*, *42*(1), 100–129.
Goldstein, A. (2008). Power transition, institutions, and China's Rise in East Asia. *The United States and Northeast Asia: Debates, Issues, and New Order*, 39–78.
Gu, J., Humphrey, J., and Messner, D. (2008). Global governance and developing countries: The implications of the rise of China. *World development*, *36*(2), 274–292.
Guo, Y. (2004). *Cultural nationalism in contemporary China*. Routledge.
Hachigian, N., and Peng, Y. (2010). The US – China expectations gap: An exchange. *Survival*, *52*(4), 67–86.
Haynes, K. (2017). Diversionary conflict: Demonizing enemies or demonstrating competence? *Conflict Management and Peace Science*, *34*(4), 337–358.
Heilmann, S., Rudolf, M., Huotari, M., and Buckow, J. (2014). China's shadow foreign policy: parallel structures challenge the established international order. *China Monitor*, *18*(10), 1–9.
Hooijmaaijers, B. (2019). China, the BRICS, and the limitations of reshaping global economic governance. *The Pacific Review*, *34*(1), 29–55.
Hughes, C. R. (2005). Nationalism and multilateralism in Chinese foreign policy: Implications for Southeast Asia. *The Pacific Review*, *18*(1), 119–135.
Jacobson, H. K., and Oksenberg, M. (1990). *China's participation in the IMF, the World Bank, and GATT: Toward a global economic order*. University of Michigan Press.
Jacques, M. (2009). *When China rules the world: The end of the western world and the birth of a new global order*. Penguin.
Jintao, H. (2007). Hold High the Great Banner of Socialism with Chinese Characteristics and Strive for New Victories in Building a Moderately Prosperous Society in All Respects. In *Report to the seventeenth national congress of the communist party of China* (Vol. 15). Beijing Review.
Johnston, A. I. (2013). How new and assertive is China's new assertiveness? *International Security*, *37*(4), 7–48.
Lardy, N. R. (1994). *China in the world economy*. Peterson Institute Press: All Books.
Levy, J. S. (1989). The diversionary theory of war: A critique. *Handbook of War Studies*, *1*, 259–288.
Liao, N. C. C. (2018). Domestic politics and China's assertive foreign policy: Why China's rise may not be peaceful. In *Decoding the rise of China* (pp. 85–106). Palgrave Macmillan.
Li, M. (2009). China's participation in Asian multilateralism: pragmatism prevails. *Rising China: Power and Reassurance*, 147.
McNally, C. A. (2012). Sino-capitalism: China's reemergence and the international political economy. *World Politics*, *64*(4), 741–776.
Mitter, R. (2003). *An uneasy engagement: Chinese ideas of global order and justice in historical perspective*. Oxford University Press.

Nathan, A. J., and Zhang, B. (2021). 'A shared future for mankind': Rhetoric and reality in Chinese foreign policy under Xi Jinping. *Journal of Contemporary China*, 1–15.

Öniş, Z., and Kutlay, M. (2020). The new age of hybridity and clash of norms: China, BRICS, and challenges of global governance in a postliberal international order. *Alternatives*, *45*(3), 123–142.

Richards, D., Morgan, T. C., Wilson, R. K., Schwebach, V. L., and Young, G. D. (1993). Good times, bad times, and the diversionary use of force: A tale of some not-so-free agents. *Journal of Conflict Resolution*, *37*(3), 504–535.

Solana, J. (2015). China and global governance. *The Project Syndicate*, *30*.

Theiler, T. (2018). The microfoundations of diversionary conflict. *Security Studies*, *27*(2), 318–343.

Wang, H., and Rosenau, J. N. (2009). China and global governance. *Asian Perspective*, 5–39.

Whiting, A. S. (1983). Assertive nationalism in Chinese foreign policy. *Asian Survey*, *23*(8), 913–933.

Zemin, J. (2002). Build a well-off society in an all-round way and create a new situation in building socialism with Chinese characteristics. Report at 16th National Congress of the Communist Party of China (CPC), November 8.

Zhao, S. (2005). China's pragmatic nationalism: is it manageable? *The Washington Quarterly*, *29*(1), 131–144.

15
SOUTH AFRICA AND BRICS

Subodh N. Malakar and Khush-Hal S. Lagdhyan

South Africa's entry into BRICS raised a number of questions about its role in the formation of the transcontinental grouping, BRICS. The British economist, Jim'O Neil, who coined the term BRIC in 2001, doubted the relevance of the collective grouping of five emerging economies – Brazil, Russia, India, China and South Africa. In his opinion, South Africa did not fit into the league of emerging economies, and therefore, the inclusion of South Africa was incongruous and would only weaken the 'club'. In his words, South Africa's presence in the powerful grouping is a 'drag on the dynamics of the BRICS grouping' (O'Neil in Naidoo, 2012). Nigeria has been favoured by many including Jim O'Neil as a country that fit the role of the leading country in Africa better.

However, there were many reasons why South Africa was preferred over other candidates. Its economy and a long history of struggle against colonialism were the prime reasons for the inclusion of South Africa. But its inclusion has not been without controversy and many sceptics from Africa as well as outside raised doubts about its inclusion in BRICS. From the perspective of South Africa, its inclusion put a final stamp on its capability as a leading regional player. It came to be identified in a league that was viewed as the drivers of growth in the twenty-first century.

Global Context and Emergence of BRICS

Post-colonial nations remained sceptical of market economies in the beginning. Their economies were mostly closed due to their stress on sovereignty and a quest for self-reliance. They faced tremendous hardship as newly independent states. Their economies were in a shambles and societies were divided. In South Africa, racism continued in various forms even after independence. But with liberation came the realisation of the extent of damage that colonial governance had inflicted. The rebuilding of the nation was an uphill task for the leaders of South Africa.

DOI: 10.4324/9781003148074-17

Emphatic initiatives of self-reliance were undertaken initially but with the unleashing of the forces of globalisation, the economies started to open up under domestic and external pressures. For a long period, however, the process of opening up their economies was extremely slow, and the market economy did not take root. Crony capitalism developed in several states. Gradually, these societies embraced capitalism and a market economy. The West attempted to formalise intervention through the International Monetary Fund (IMF), the World Bank (WB) and the World Trade Organization (WTO).

Most developing nations adopted the Structural Adjustment Program and liberalisation, privatisation and globalisation under pressure from the IMF. The resistance from developing nations was largely absent and the only challenging force was the Soviet Union. The collapse of the Socialist Bloc in 1990 resulted in the USA emerging as the leader of a unipolar world. This unipolarity was transitory to be challenged soon by the European Union and China. Many regional organisations in Asia, Latin America and Africa contributed to the diffusion of power.

The international economic order did not really serve the interests of developing countries, which continued to languish with crushing underdevelopment. It is not surprising, therefore, that in the first decade of the twenty-first century, several intercontinental organisations such as the IBSA and BRICS began to emerge. Whether such forums managed to address the issues of emerging states is can be disputed. However, they did generate hopes for challenging unipolarity.

The emergence of BRICS can be explained in multiple ways. Patrick Bond and Ana Garcia (2016) doubt the rationale of BRICS and have dubbed it as subimperial (Bond and Garcia, 2016: 6–7). Those who view the emergence of BRICS as a favourable development hold that BRICS is an outcome of the same globalisation process. The structure of international economy has changed fundamentally in the last three decades. The economic influence of developing states has grown significantly. They became the engines of growth of the world economy after the financial crisis of 2008 (Griffith Jones, 2014: 1).

Goldman Sachs' report (2003) projected that BRICS states would catch up with the Western economy and become the pivot of new demand-led growth in less than four decades (Wilson and Purushothaman, 2003: 2). In this report, BRIC was conceptualised as a group of countries with somewhat identical economic profile and global standing. Later, South Africa was given membership and BRICS came to represent all the regions of the world.

The Rationale behind South Africa's Inclusion

As mentioned earlier, the inclusion of South Africa in 2010 had raised a lot of eyebrows. Its case as a suitable match for inclusion was questioned. Many of the objections had valid grounds on the surface. Jim O'Neil's argument for the inclusion of Nigeria in the grouping had merit in it. Nigeria's economic performance was better than South Africa's on some variables and it had the characteristics to be considered a leading African nation. However, its overdependence on oil makes its economy weak and vulnerable. Nigeria is the seventh largest exporter of crude oil and the 10th largest holder gas reserves in the world. But paradoxically, the average per capita income and its ranks in the Human Development Index remain very low. The amount of per capita debt is also very high. About 70% of its 180 million population, according to the National Population Commission (2017), live in poverty. Nigeria ranks high in Corruption Perception Index reports (Dele, 2017: 2–3). These indicators stand against its ambition to emerge as a regional leader in Africa. South Africa

South Africa fares better in terms of diversification and being technologically advanced. According to World Bank figures for 2020, Nigeria's GNI per capita was US$2000 as opposed to US$5,410 of South Africa; 68.2% of South African population uses the internet as opposed to 33.6 of Nigeria; life expectancy is 64 in South Africa and 55 in Nigeria and the mortality rate under five is 35 in South Africa and 117 in Nigeria (Worldbank, 2021). It can be inferred, therefore, that on many of the parameters, South Africa fared much better. However, economic considerations may not have been the only ones when it came to the inclusion of South Africa as a full-fledged member of BRICS. Although there is a lot of truth in the argument of the incongruence of South Africa vis-à-vis other members in terms of its size and economy, it competes rather well on some other counts.

It is apparent from Table 15.1 that South Africa's parameters are comparable with other BRICS countries. For example, 68.2% of its people use the internet as compared to 41% in India, its mortality rate under-5 is 35, just a little above India's 34, and life expectancy at birth is 64 as against 70 in India, the next higher figure among the BRICS countries. South Africa, therefore, does possess the wherewithal to compete in relative terms with other members. However, it would be limiting to say that its inclusion only rested on its promising profile. There are several factors, including geopolitical ones, that ultimately tilted the scale in favour of South Africa. As Philip Harrison points out,

> the idea of BRIC(S) has evolved beyond the analytical construct developed by O'Neill and his Goldman Sachs' colleagues into a political construct with the pragmatic purpose of developing a geopolitical note of influence as an alternative to the historically dominant alliance of North America and Western Europe. In terms of this understanding, there is a credible, even compelling rationale for South Africa's membership of BRICS.
>
> *(Harrison, 2014: 68)*

The rationale for its membership, therefore, cannot be understood in economic terms only as BRICS has already carved for itself a geopolitical construct as an alternative to the current international order. South Africa brings a lot to the table as a 'gateway to Africa' (Kahn, 2011), bringing enormous possibilities for BRICS' engagement in Africa, and making it look more representative of the world. Along with this, the legacy of the South African struggle against apartheid, which continued into the 1990s, grants it a global stature. The legacy of the iconic figure of

TABLE 15.1 Comparative Indicators of BRICS States

S. No	*Variable*	*South Africa*	*Brazil*	*India*	*China*	*Russia*
1	Population, Total(millions)	59.31	212.56	1,380.00	1,402.11	144.10
2	GNI per capita, Atlas method (current US$)	5,410	7,850	1,900	10,610	10,690
3	Income shared by lowest 20%	2.5 (in 2010)	3.1	8.1 (in 2010)	5.1 (in 2010)	7.1
4	Mortality rate under-5 (per 1000live births)	35	14	34	8	6
5	Life expectancy at birth, total (years)	64	76	70	77	73
6	Individuals using the internet (% of population)	68.2	73.9	41.0	70.6	85.0
7	External debt stocks, total (DOD, current US$) (millions)	170,767	549,234	564,179	2,349,389	475,518

Source: Based on 2020 data from the World Bank (2021). Some figures, according to the site, have been extrapolated from earlier ones due to non-availability of 2020 figures.

Nelson Mandela and his acceptance as a global hero added ideological strength to BRICS. It would be disingenuous if one does not count South Africa as a model of democracy for other states in Africa, despite all its flaws and infirmities. The presence of South Africa added the much-needed African dimension and made BRICS a formidable international grouping. Following summits in Yekaterinburg in 2009 and Brasilia in 2010, the Sanya summit on 14 April 2011 included South Africa as a member, adding a new dimension to South–South co-operation. In the following pages, the factors underlying South Africa's significance are enumerated briefly.

South Africa's Geo-Strategic Importance

As one of the biggest economies in the continent, South Africa was symbolically, economically and strategically the most important contender in the continent (Gumede, 2014). This served to facilitate its entry into BRICS. Its political leadership, especially under President Jacob Zuma, pursued the case of its entry into the elite club. South Africa's 'soft power' allows it to become the voice of the continent, and its economic stability provides credence to its ambition to represent the region (Harrison, 2014: 67). The idea of South Africa as the undisputed leader of the continent has always been problematic and has been contested fiercely by other powerful countries such as Nigeria, Egypt, Angola and Mozambique along with others of the PALOP (African countries with Portuguese as official language), which include Cape Verde, Guinea-Bissau, Sao Tome and Principe.

South Africa has a unique place because of its geostrategic location. It has historically been extremely important as it contains the southernmost tip of the African continent, Cape Agulhas, which is the dividing point of the Atlantic and the Indian Ocean. Together with another great cape, the Cape of Good Hope, on the South Atlantic side, they were two important points on early eastbound sailing routes. South Africa is also a part of the ZOPACAS (South Atlantic Peace and Co-operation Zone), an initiative spearheaded by Brazil under the aegis of the UN to bring together a host of countries from Africa and South America to de-nuclearise the South Atlantic and foster peace. Although there are some places in the region like the Falkland Islands that are not signatories to the ZOPACAS, the formation itself, much like BRICS, is symbolic of the Global South.

South Africa has the most powerful economy in Sub-Saharan Africa. Its relatively stable economy, its population of nearly 50 million and the presence of big companies make it a powerful player in the region. Its economy contributes nearly one-third of Africa's economy, and 17 of the top 20 companies in the continent are based in South Africa (Carmody, 2013: 49). It must, however, be acknowledged that in recent years, the status of being the largest economy has been also claimed by Nigeria. Its influence over the region is through trade, investment, aid and tourism. Like other BRICS states, it has also invested in the agricultural sector, especially in Tanzania and Zambia.

Table 15.2 demonstrates interactions between South Africa and Sub-Saharan Africa (Carmody, 2013: 52).

TABLE 15.2 South Africa's regional engagement

Types of Impact	*Trade*	*Outward foreign direct investment*	*Foreign portfolio investment*	*Labour and private capital flow*	*Government regimes and ideas*
Capital extractive (results in net flow of capital to SA or overseas)	Consumptive (e.g. cars from SA) and competitive (e.g. textiles from SA).	Market serving (e.g. retail bank and cell phone investment from SA).	Capital flows into SA stock market and banks.	The regional brain drain of skilled workers and professional and economic/trade tourism to SA.	EU-SA free trade agreement (SA as regional entrepot for EU goods)
Resource extractive (flow of resources to SA for further processing).	Extractive (e.g. copper to SA).	Export Platform (e.g. minerals to SA).	Global FPI transformed in SA to outward FDI, often in the resource sector.	Associated migration of South African 'expats' and local resentment.	Private sector driven idea of South African-centred regional economy
Developmental (contributing to economic growth and poverty reduction).	Complementary (e.g. mining equipment from SA)	Various	Capital flows from SA into regional stock markets and banks	Return migration to country of origin and remittances	NEPAD (infrastructural and educational development. Africa as a region of 'good governance')

In the Southern African Development Community (SADC), comprising of 13 states, the contribution of South Africa is more than 75%. South Africa invested almost a billion dollars per year between 1994 and 2004, and it was the third largest in terms of foreign direct investment in these countries.

South Africa has expanded its influence beyond Sub-Saharan Africa (SSA). It is one of the most influential actors in the African Union. Nkosazana Dlamini-Zuma, a South African woman, headed that institution from 2012 to 2017. South Africa has also mediated in conflicts in the African continent.

After its inclusion in BRICS, South Africa's role expanded in Africa due to bilateral trade and developmental projects. All members of BRICS have interests in the African market (Ouma, 2015). The role of China in exploiting the African market has been extremely conspicuous. The expansionism of China in Africa, though under the framework of respecting sovereignties, has been seen as problematic by some. Historically, Brazil and India too have considerable presence in Africa and the formation of BRICS will extend their influence further. As Padraig Carmody says, 'The projection and penetration of Chinese and South African state/capital interests into South Africa represents a form of geo-governance, where power is projected across borders'. China operates through existing African agencies and formal and informal power networks (Carmody and Kragelund, 2016; Carmody, 2019). China's influence has grown significantly in the last few years.

South Africa's Strengths: Is It Punching Above Its Weight?

As mentioned earlier, when the term BRIC was coined by Jim O'Neill, South Africa did not figure in it. He was most astonished when South Africa was included. South Africa was considered a 'minnow' given its size of economy and population (Harrison, 2014: 6). This, however, may not be entirely true as South Africa fares well with other BRICS members across several variables.

As is evident from Table 15.3, South Africa was not a 'minnow' and it ranks high on several indicators. For instance, the population below the poverty line is lower than in India.

Notwithstanding these indicators of the past and the vast possibilities of trade and commerce that exist for South Africa, the truth is that it has not performed so well economically in the recent past. The problem of rampant corruption at the highest levels has impeded overall development. Further, the already fragile economy was faced with the pandemic and subsequent lockdown. The Covid-19 crisis wreaked havoc on the economy of South Africa, as has been the case with most countries (Roy Choudhary, 2020). The handling of the ongoing crisis left much to be desired and South Africa looked vulnerable without any visible, robust vaccine plan or strategy (van der Heever et al., 2021).

South Africa, as we know, was globally known for its liberation struggle against apartheid and had received a lot of support globally. After South Africa's transition to a democratic regime, a new perspective was brought to bear on the country's foreign policy. It initiated the integration of its economy with the global economy

TABLE 15.3 Comparative social indicators across BRICS countries (figures for 2012 unless otherwise indicated)

Indicator	*Brazil*	*Russia*	*India*	*China*	*South Africa*
GDP Per Capita (USD), 2013, IMF	12221	17884	4077	9844	11259
GDP Per Capita IMF Global Rankings, 2013	79th	58th	133rd	93rd	84th
Gini Coefficient	54.7	40.1	33.4	42.5	63.1
% of population with income below PPP US$1.25 day	6.1	0.0	32.7	13.1	13.8
Infant mortality (per 1000 live births)	20.3	8.7	47.0	12.1	37.9
Life expectancy at birth (years)	73.8	69.8	69.1	73.7	53.4
Fertility rate per woman	1.6	1.6	2.5	-	2.4
Natural increase of population (per 1000)	7.9	0.02	14.9	5.0	9.3
Urbanisation level (percentage)	84.6	73.8	31.3	53.7	62.0

Source: BRICS Joint Statistical Publication, 2013, Human Development Report 2013.

in the 1990s. The country managed to attract a large number of nations and was on the road to becoming a player in the global arena. In 2003, South Africa joined the India, Brazil, and South Africa (IBSA) forum. Thabo Mbeki was a staunch supporter of a trilateral forum. Christ Landsberg points out that 'IBSA is widely recognized even by India and Brazil as the brainchild and strategic idea of South Africa' (Harrison, 2014: 70).

A dilemma erupted when BRIC emerged as a new forum. BRIC was bound to receive greater notice than IBSA, and experts felt that IBSA may lose its sheen and even become irrelevant (Bhatia, The Hindu, 30 April, 2011). China and Russia in BRICS comprise the heavyweights, and its influence was global. It also helped China, which was searching for a platform to counter IBSA.

South Africa's Interests in BRICS

South Africa considers BRICS advantageous for the following reasons: first, it will lead to enhanced mutual trade and investment; second, it will put a stamp on South Africa as an undisputed regional leader; and finally, it can play an active role in global governance by joining the club of leading powers in the world. Thus, BRICS has commercial as well as status-centric benefits for South Africa. BRICS, on the other hand, views South Africa as a gateway for Africa and expects it to perform an integrative function in the continent.

Pretoria's perspective on BRICS can be gauged from the 'BRICS Strategy' adopted by its Cabinet in 2012: strengthen economic and political co-operation, pursue a pan-African agenda and promote sustainable development, and push for global governance reforms and, intra-BRICS co-operation (Harvard International Review, August 2019). South Africa is the only member from Africa in the G20 and the Group of 5. South Africa is seen as representing the voice of Africa in several multilateral forums.

Africa, consisting of 54 countries, opens an enormous opportunity for BRICS. The fifth and tenth BRICS Summits were held in South Africa in 2013 and 2018 respectively. The eThekwini Declaration of the fifth Summit stressed the significance of emerging markets in Africa in following words, 'We are open to increasing our engagement and co-operation with non-BRICS countries, in particular, the Emerging Market and Developing Countries (EMDC's), and relevant international and regional organisations, as envisioned in the Sanya Declaration'. They decided to hold a meet with other African leaders after this Summit (Harrison, 2014: 69). As is evident from this declaration, South Africa is clearly seen as a facilitator of connecting BRICS with other countries in the continent.

The Durban summit held in 2013 stressed Africa's regional integration for sustainable growth, poverty eradication, and development (eThekwini Declaration, 2013). It decided to support the industrialisation process in Africa through FDI, capacity-building, diversification of export, sharing of knowledge and aid to poorer countries. The leaders reiterated that infrastructure development was key to unlock the potential of African states. They recognised the role of the African Union in developmental projects especially through Programme for Infrastructure Development in Africa (PIDA), the AU NEPAD Africa Action Plan (2010–2015), the NEPAD Presidential Intrastate Championing Initiative (PICI) and the Regional Infrastructure Development Master Plans (Landerberg, 2006: 4–7).

The 10th BRICS Summit at Johannesburg in 2018 was an important event for South Africa. It reiterated the vision of earlier summits for infrastructural development, industrialisation, digital connectivity and integration of Africa. In the words of Stuenkel, it provided a 'massive status boost on the international stage'. South African leaders view BRICS as a bridge to connect with other emerging states of the South, and as a necessary forum to raise its voice on the global stage (Stuenkel, 2015).

How Do Other Member States View South Africa?

All the states of BRICS have historical, commercial and political ties with South Africa. Since BRICS is largely seen as an organisation of the global south, South Africa brings an immense political legitimacy to this organisation. South Africa is known for its political struggle against colonialism, its vibrant economic growth after independence, and a strong cultural legacy. And therefore, no organisation of the global south can ignore this country. All the countries view South Africa as a gateway to the resource rich continent of Africa. Its relative political stability and economic growth are the key reasons why BRICS prefers this country over others in Africa. Every member of this organisation also carries its own interests in Africa.

Brazil has a long history of relationship with Africa. It dates back to the slave trade started by Europeans in the age of mercantilism and imperialism. More than 50% of its population is of African descent. It ranks second after Nigeria in terms of people of African origin, and therefore, Brazilian civilisation is intrinsically linked with that of Africa (The BRICS Report, 2012: 39). There are several Brazilian companies with investments in Africa. Brazilian firms which invested in Africa include Andrade Gutierrez, a big multinational company involved in infrastructure, services and telecom. Camargo Correa is another firm to have invested heavily in infrastructure, real estate, cement production and shipbuilding. It invested US$8 billion in Africa. Another company called Odebrecht has invested in construction, water management, waste treatment, energy production and transport. Petrobras, Queiroz Galvao and Vale are other corporations engaged in infrastructure, hydrocarbon, and public services.

Russia has had a long history of association with Africa dating back to Soviet years. But following the collapse of the USSR, it could not retain its erstwhile influence and its influence has diminished drastically in the last three decades. However, it is trying to re-establish its relations in Africa. President Putin visited a number of countries in Africa and has committed investment in building infrastructure there. Russian companies operate in almost all the countries of Africa. Russia's experience in the production of oil and gas can be helpful for hydro-carbon rich states of Africa. Russia also supplies arms and weapons to many countries in Africa.

India has cordial relations with African states. India supported the African liberation movement and is viewed favourably in most of the states. It has a strong diasporic presence there. There are nearly 2.5 million people of Indian origin in Africa. A civilisational link exists between India and Africa. India's foreign policy had been consistent until 1990, but it changed considerably afterwards. It began to emphasise on the Indian Ocean Rim with members of East Africa. In its Africa Focus policy, the focus was on East African states. Given its high oil requirements, India is keen to explore the hydro-carbon resources in West Africa. It became part of the TEAM 9 (also called Techno-economic Approach for Africa-India Movement), which included eight countries of West Africa. Further, taking a cue from the Chinese engagement in Africa, New Delhi went for a big plan and created the India Africa forum. It is actively engaged in hydrocarbon sector, agriculture, telecom, services, real estate, construction and other retail sectors.

New Delhi views South Africa as a gateway to African continent. It has a long history of commercial and political interaction with the continent. It has a strong diasporic presence in Africa with nearly 80,000 people categorised as Persons of Indian Origin. The India-Africa Forum Summit started in 2008, and it met again in 2011 and 2015. In the last two decades, it has extended a concessional credit of nearly US$11 billion to various countries. In just one decade, Indian-African trade shot up from USD51.7 billion in 2010–2011 to USD 66.7 billion in 2019–2020. India is the eight largest investor in Africa. India continued to supply medicines and vaccines to Africa during the pandemic. India worked closely with South Africa and demanded a patent waiver for vaccines at the World Trade Organization, which the US agreed but the European Union rejected. In contrast with China's massive economic investments, India focuses on capacity-building, digital technology, education and health care (Pant and Mishra, 2021).

China, as mentioned earlier, has emerged as one of the biggest investors in Africa. It has entered almost all African countries. It has invested heavily in infrastructure, oil and gas, construction and service sectors. The Chinese diaspora in Africa is the primary source of infrastructural activities in Africa. Some scholars argue that the long-term goal of China is to displace the US as the leading player in Africa (Blumenthal, 2021). The biggest investment in Africa was still from the US, amounting to US$78 billion, followed by the UK with US$65 billion, and then France with US$53 billion. Chinese investments have increased rapidly in the last few years. China's foreign direct investment (FDI) to Africa amounted to US$44 billion in 2019 (Stein and Uddhammar, 2021). China exported products worth US$113 billion in 2019, while its imports amounted to US$78 billion (ibid.). In terms of total trade, China has emerged as Africa's biggest trade partner. China's export to South Africa amounted to US$16.6 billion in 2019, which was roughly 14.6% of its export to Africa. Other exporting destinations are Nigeria, Egypt, Kenya and Ghana. Chinese investment amounted to US$6.1 billion in 2019 (ibid).

As discussed earlier, all BRICS are engaged in Africa. Their presence varies depending on their capacity to invest and ability to mobilise the African elite. As a continent endowed with rich resources, it offers huge opportunities for the investors and entrepreneurs. But these resources are still unutilised. Therefore, two most immediate requirements are infrastructure development and capacity-building. The financial institutions of BRICS are providing assistance to several infrastructural projects in Africa. They claim to provide alternative sources of funding without the conditionalities associated with loans from the IMF and the World Bank.

The nature of BRICS funding, however, has also come under serious scrutiny by scholars from Africa. They argue that the NDB does not yet appear as an alternative to the Washington-centric development finance that is rife with problems. The NDB funding may in fact amplify uneven development by financing some of South Africa's notoriously corrupt institutions (Bond, 2021). There are several general problems associated with the NDB: its oversight of corruption, lack of a strong regulatory mechanism, neoliberal orientation, lending amount and mechanisms, and failure to engage communities (Bond, 2021).

Further, South Africa witnessed political violence and ethnic tussles in 2021. In a recent development, Jacob Zuma, the former president of South Africa, was sent to prison in July 2021 for refusing to appear before a court probing allegation of corruption during his nine-year tenure. This led to massive violence in different parts of the country, killing more than 200 persons, the worst since the end of apartheid regime in 1994. Cyril Ramaphosa, who leads a moderate faction of the ruling African National Congress party, became the president (The Guardian, September 5, 2021). These developments have adversely affected South Africa's positioning as a leading regional power. BRICS is concerned about political instability and ethnic violence in South Africa. It does not intervene in domestic matters, but South Africa's stability is a concern common to all BRICS states.

Conclusion

To sum up, the entry of South Africa was crucial for BRICS to claim to be symbolically representative of the global south. South Africa cannot be compared to other countries of this grouping as there is a huge asymmetry in terms of population, the size of economy and military capacity. But the inclusion of South Africa cannot be dismissed as mere symbolic. All the countries of BRICS view it as gateway to the continent of Africa. Its economic and other human-index indicators are far better than other countries in the continent. Moreover, a long history of political struggle against colonialism rendered it a natural candidate for an organisation of the global south.

Each of the BRICS countries in Africa seeks to maintain cordial ties to ensure access to resources and markets. We can argue, therefore, that the entry of South Africa in BRICS was an outcome of recognition of mutual interests. South Africa views BRICS as a crucial instrument to enhance its influence at the continental and the global level. BRICS trade and investments have grown significantly in the last few years in the whole of Africa. The growing interdependence, however, has raised concerns that Africa may become the new 'periphery' supplying raw materials to the emerging 'core' states of Asia and Latin America. The exploitation of natural resources by BRICS states has raised the fear of neo-colonialism. Such fears, however, are baseless. BRICS has diverse interests and is too heterogenous to pursue a common exploitative agenda. On the contrary, it can provide huge opportunities for trade, investment and infrastructural developments in the region. African states will have a new option in the form of BRICS, and their dependence on the West is likely to diminish in the coming years.

References

Bhatia, Rajiv. 2011. 'BRICS set to outshine IBSA', *The Hindu*. 30 April 2011. https://www.thehindu.com/opinion/lead/BRICS-set-to-outshine-IBSA/article13874888.ece

Blumenthal, Dan. 2021. 'Beijing's Grand Strategy', *National Review*, 15 July.

Bond, P. 2021. 'BRICS New Development Bank Corruption in South Africa', *CADTM*, 5 September. www.cadtm.org/BRICS-New-Development-Bank-Corruption-in-South-Africa (Accessed on 20 November 2021).

Bond. P. and Ana Garcia. 2016. *BRICS – An Anti-Capitalist Critique*. Delhi: Aakar Books.

The BRICS Report. 2012. *A Study of Brazil, Russian, China, India and South Africa with Special Focus on Synergies and Complementarities*. London: Oxford University Press.

Carmody, P. 2013. *The Rise of BRICS in Africa: The Geopolitics of South-South Relation*. New York: Zed Books.

Carmody, Padraig. 2019. 'Global Political Economy: The BRICS Connection: Contemporary Challenges and New Directions', *The Geography of South Africa*, pp. 223–227, DOI: 10.1007/978-3-319-94974-1-29 (Accessed on 29 November 2021).

Carmody, Padraig and Peter Kragelund. 2016. 'Who is in Charge? State Power and Agency in Sino African Relations, *Cornell International Law Journal*, 49: 1–23. https://ww3.lawschool.cornell.edu/research/ILJ/upload/Carmody-Kraglund-final.pdf

Dele, Ishaka. 2017. 'Over- Dependence on Oil and Its Implication for Development in Nigeria', *HUMASS*, 1(2): 25–33 (Accessed on 29 November 2021).

eThekwini Declaration. 2013. 'Fifth BRICS Summit (Durban: 27 March 2013)', *BRICS and Africa: Partnership for Development, Integration and Industrialization*, 2–9.

Goldman Sachs report. 2003. https://www.goldmansachs.com/our_firm/investor_relations/financial_reports/annual_reports/2003/

Griffith-Jones. S. 2014. *A BRICS Development Bank: A Dream Coming True?* Unctad/OSG. The United Nations. https://unctad.org/system/files/official-document/osgdp20141_en.pdf

Gumede, William. 2014. 'South African and the BRICS Alliance', *Transnational Institute*, 4 September. www.tni.org/es/node/1624 (Accessed on 12 October 2021).

Harrison, Philip. 2014. 'South Africa in the BRICS', *OASIS*, 19: 67–84.

Harvard International Review. August 2019. https://hir.harvard.edu/tag/winter-2019/

Kahn, Michael. 2011. 'The BRICs and South Africa as the Gateway to Africa', *South African Institute of Mining and Metallurgy*, 111(7): 493–496.

Landerberg, C. 2006. 'IBSA's Political Origins, Significance and Challenges', *Policy Studies Bulletin of CPS*, 8(2): 4–7.

Naidoo, Sharda, 2012. 'South Africa's Presence Drags BRICs Down', *Mail and Guardian*, 23 March 2012. Mg.co.za/article/2012–03–23-sa-presence-drags-down-brics/ (Accessed on 29 November 2021).

Ouma, Stefan. 2015. Review of *The Rise of BRICS in Africa by Padraig Carmody: London: Zed Books, 2013*', *Economic Geography,* 91(2), DOI: 10,1111/ecge.12085 (Accessed on 29 November 2021).

Pant, Harsh and Asbhishek Mishra. 2021. 'Is India the New China in Africa?' *Foreign Policy*, 17 June. https://foreignpolicy.com/2021/06/17/india-china-africa-development-aid-investment/ (Accessed on 13 December 2021).

Roy Choudhary, Dipanjan. 2020. 'South Africa's Active Role in BRICS: Key to Boosting African Economy', *The Economic Times,* 5 December. (Accessed 22 October 2021).

Stein, Peter and Emil Uddhammar. 2021. 'China in Africa: The Role of Trade, Investments, and Loans amidst Shifting Geopolitical Ambitions', 25 August. www.orfonline.org/research/china-in-africa/ (Accessed 12 December 2021).

Stuenkel, O. 2015. *India-Brazil-South Africa Dialogue Forum (IBSA): The Rise of the Global South?* London and New York: Routledge.

Stuenkel, Oliver. 2018. 'The 10th BRICS Summit in Johannesburg: An Analysis', 29 July. www.oliverstuenkel.com/2018/07/29/johannesburg-declaration-analysis/ (Accessed on 12 October 2021).

The Guardian. 5 September 2021. https://www.theguardian.com/world/cyril-ramaphosa

Van der Heever, Alex et al. 2021. 'How Series of Missteps Led to South Africa's Covid 19 Vaccine Crisis and What Can be Done Now', *scroll.in,* 6 July. (Accessed 22 October 2021).

Wilson, D. and R. Purushothaman. 2003. 'Dreaming with BRICS: The Path to 2050', *Global Economics Chapter No. 99*, Goldman Sachs. p. 2.

World Bank. 2021. 'Country Profile'. www.data.worldbank.org (Accessed on 29 November 2021).

PART III

New Vistas of Cooperation within BRICS

Lacunae and Possibilities

16

THE COVID-19 PANDEMIC AND THE BRICS RESPONSE

Cooperation, Constraints, and Geopolitics

Ashok Sharma

COVID-19, a disease caused by a novel coronavirus, has proven to be the most destructive catastrophe since World War II, wreaking havoc on human lives and economy. As of 4 January 2021, COVID-19 has infected more than 85,083,468 people and killed 1,842,455 people globally. The highest fatality has been in the United States, followed by Brazil, India, Mexico, Italy, the United Kingdom, France, Russia, Iran, Spain, Colombia, Argentina, Peru, Germany and South Africa, surpassing the reported deaths of 4,784 people in China where the disease originated (JHU Coronavirus Resource Centre, 2021). Governments across the world imposed a state of emergency, lockdowns, and social distancing, took other non-pharmaceutical measures to stop the spread of the outbreak, and announced economic stimulus packages to help people in hardship and protect their economies.

So far, COVID-19 data indicate that some countries have done well, and some, despite having advanced health care capability, have failed to contain the spread of the outbreak resulting in an unexpectedly high number of confirmed coronavirus cases and deaths. Countries such as New Zealand, Vietnam, Thailand, South Korea and Australia have been able to contain the outbreak reasonably well. However, countries such as the United States and West European developed countries with highly advanced health care systems have failed to contain the pandemic. The successful containment of the pandemic has been mainly due to a combination of factors: executive competency of the governments reflected in timely action on pandemic containment measures, proper co-ordination between various agencies and levels of government, appropriate use of their health care resources and capability, and implementation of containment measures at the national level.

However, the pandemic is a global crisis and its transnational character requires international co-operation as well. The World Health Organization (WHO), a formally organised institution, has failed in its responsibility to tackle this unprecedented humanitarian crisis. In these circumstances, multinational organisations and regional

DOI: 10.4324/9781003148074-19

and economic groupings of nations such as the European Union (EU) and BRICS – a grouping of Brazil, Russia, India, China and South Africa – could have played an important role in assisting nations and strengthening the spirit of co-operation and internationalism to mitigate the challenges of the pandemic. The EU failed miserably and has seen the worst fatality rates. BRICS too could have leveraged the opportunity created by the outbreak. Instead, BRICS has failed to play any meaningful role and has been the worst affected and weakened by the COVID-19 outbreak.

An assessment of BRICS' handling of COVID-19 raises questions on its ability to play a significant role in the global crisis. Despite a promising beginning amidst the outbreak, BRICS has failed to co-ordinate at the bloc level, although there was some bilateral co-operation among BRICS nations to contain the disease. Struggling economies and society further devastated by the COVID-19 pandemic, existing internal differences, political values, varying health care capability and resources, and strategic rivalry among the member countries hampered BRICS' ability to play a meaningful role in containing COVID-19. Despite being a grouping of nations with a considerable share in the global economy and population, BRICS could not leverage the opportunity created in the wake of COVID-19 and failed to show its efficacy as an influential bloc in global governance.

The chapter elaborates the observations in four sections. The first section provides an overview of the BRICS nations' COVID-19 containment strategy. The second section critically examines the effectiveness of the containment measures. The third section deals with co-operation among BRICS nations on the issue of COVID-19 containment. The following section deals with the strategic rivalry between India and China and the complex geopolitics that hampered BRICS' capability as a bloc to co-ordinate during COVID-19. The conclusion sums up BRICS' performance during COVID-19 and the way forward.

BRICS COVID-19 Containment Strategy

Brazil

Brazil is among the top three countries hit the worst by COVID-19 in the world. The first confirmed coronavirus case in Brazil was reported on 25 February 2020 and the virus spread to every state in Brazil by 21 March 2020. On 19 June 2020, Brazil reported its one-millionth case with about 49,000 reported deaths (Charner, 2020). On 17 July 2020, Brazil reached 2 million cases, and, on 8 August 2020, the country reached its three millionth case, with deaths exceeding 100,000. Brazil occupied the second spot in terms of people infected with the novel coronavirus for a long time only to be overtaken by India on 5 September 2020. As of 4 January 2021, Brazil, with 7,733,746 people infected and 196,018 deaths, had the third highest number of confirmed COVID-19 cases and the second highest number of COVID-19 deaths in the world (JHU Coronavirus Resource Centre, 2021).

The virus prompted federal, state, and local governments to take various containment measures, affecting politics, education, the environment, and the economy.

To combat the spread of the virus, Brazil placed temporary restrictions on foreign flights on 27 March 2021, and most state governors announced lockdowns and quarantines. Despite having a reasonably good health care system and infrastructure, the country became one of the worst hit by the pandemic. Brazil's handling of COVID-19, unlike other BRICS nations, resembles that of the US.

Brazil, a large middle-income country with deep social and economic inequality and uneven infrastructure development, has a modern and well- structured universal health-care system and infrastructure. The Brazilian health care system is credited with having have brought relief to millions of its poor (Jurberg, 2018). Despite the availability of a good health care system, Brazil failed in containing the disease. Executive incompetence, reflected in untimely action and a non-serious approach towards the pandemic by the federal government, complicated further by the lack of co-ordination between the federal and state governments, were the main reasons for Brazil's failure to contain the disease. Besides, the federal government prioritised the economy over health. Brazilian President Jair Bolsonaro opposed the COVID-19-related lockdowns. President Bolsonaro and the economy minister justified the opposition to strict lockdowns by arguing that Brazil's economy was on the verge of collapse, and the fallout from social distancing measures could be worse than the novel coronavirus disease itself (ABC News, 8 May 2020). This was in May 2020, when projections indicated that worse was to come. During this time, countries such as India, China and Russia had imposed complete lockdowns with far less cases than Brazil. Brazil's case was that of a non-serious approach to the pandemic in a country that had better resources to deal with the virus.

The lack of co-ordination between the federal government and state governments was reflected in a tussle between the federal, state and local governments on the issue of imposing lockdowns. While the federal government opposed the lockdowns, some state and municipal governments went for full lockdowns. This resulted in a tussle between the judicial and executive branch as Brazil's Federal Supreme Court consistently upheld the state governments' physical distancing policies that President Bolsonaro was against, and barred the federal government from adopting measures against social distancing taken by states (Human Rights Watch, 2020). The state governments took more appropriate and proactive actions to contain the disease by increasing intensive care units in the public health system and emergency field hospitals, moving COVID-19 patients from highly affected areas to areas where demand for health services was lower, and by rapidly increasing the emergency bed capacity in intensive care units (Barberia and Gómez, 2020).

Russia

Unlike Brazil, which showed laxity in taking appropriate action to contain the spread of the virus, Russia took a serious approach from the beginning. When Russia had confirmed cases in the single digits and no evidence of community spread, the Putin Government began to enforce tough COVID-19 containment related measures.

Russia shares a 4,300-km land border with China and, at the beginning of March itself, 16 of its neighbouring countries had confirmed cases of COVID-19. The COVID-19 virus was confirmed to have reached to Russia on 31 January 2020, when two Chinese citizens tested positive though both cases were contained. The virus spread throughout Russia around mid-April 2020. Russia imposed a lockdown on the vast majority of its federal subjects including in the capital city of Moscow by the end of March 2020. Russia took an early decision to restrict borders with China, and ban air travel to stop the spread of the virus. Extensive testing, cancellation of activities, closure of schools, theatres, and museums, closing the border, and proclaiming a non-working time were all used to limit the epidemic, which lasted until May 11, 2020, after two extensions.

Some of the harsh and comprehensive containment strategies taken were as follows. Non-Russian citizens travelling from pandemic affected nations were banned from entering Russia; air and land travel routes and cities along the Chinese border were closed; large-scale public events were cancelled; Russian citizens and foreign nationals entering from abroad were put under voluntary quarantine, and random temperature checks were conducted on Moscow metro passengers (Twigg, 2020).

Russia's aggressive containment strategy could be seen from two perspectives. The main concern was that the spike in cases could have overburdened Russian infrastructure and capacity for mitigation. This would have resulted in a heavy death toll due to the pandemic. Furthermore, the Russian worry was to protect its already hard-hit economy. Russia's tough containment measures from the beginning were to prevent a worsening of the economic consequences for Russia because of declining oil prices, the depreciation of the rouble, the fall in the main RTS stock index, the downgraded OECD forecast for the Russian economy, and the declaration of *force majeure* on natural gas import contracts by PetroChina (OECD, 2020).

According to figures from the national coronavirus crisis centre, as of 14 September 2020, Russia has 1,068,320 confirmed cases, 878,770 recoveries, 18,635 deaths, and over 40.9 million tests performed (Russia Business Today, 2020). According to mortality data published by the Federal State Statistics Service, 37,490 people with COVID-19 died from April to July 2020, with the virus determined or assumed to have been the main cause of death for 22,063 of them (The Moscow Times, 2020). Despite strict virus containment measures, as of 4 January 2021, Russia, with 3,203,743 confirmed cases and 57, 803 deaths, has the world's fourth highest number of confirmed COVID-19 cases and stands eighth in the number of COVID-19 deaths. Russia tops Europe with the highest number of confirmed cases, and ranks the fourth highest affect country in the world after the United States, India, and Brazil (JHU Coronavirus Resource Centre, 2021).

India

India imposed the world's largest lockdown on its 1.3 billion people on March 24, 2020, for 21 days as a preventive measure to contain the spread of the disease. When India imposed the lockdown, the confirmed positive cases of coronavirus in India was 500. Nevertheless, India had to extend the lockdown further from 14 April until 3 May 2020 with conditional easing of the lockdown after 20 April 2020 for those states where the disease was under control. However, the lockdown was again extended until 17 May and then until 31 May 2020. India's districts were divided into three zones based on the spread of the virus – green, red, and orange – and the restrictions were eased according to the number of COVID-19 cases in particular districts. The classification was based on the incidence of cases, doubling rate, the extent of testing, and surveillance feedback (The Indian Express, 2020).

From 1 June 2020, India began to relax restrictions and states were to decide on further lockdowns depending on the status of coronavirus cases in their states. The relaxation was partly because of the recognition of the growing difficulties and stress that people were facing and the need for resumption of economic activities. India initiated a phase wise easing of restrictions with the first relaxations in the lockdown beginning from 1 June to 30 June 2020, then from 1 July to 30 July 2020, the third from 1 August to 31 August, and fourth from 1 September. India coherently followed the COVID-19 containment policy.

The lockdown helped India slow down infections at the initial stage. By 6 April 2020, the rate of doubling was every six days – falling to 1.55 on 11 April from 1.83 on 6 April. By 18 April 2020, the rate of doubling climbed to every eight days (Ramesh and Basu, 2020; Gupta, 2020). The lockdown brought most economic activities to a halt. According to estimates, if India had not imposed strict lockdowns initially, the situation would have been worse. India would have reached 820,000 coronavirus infected cases by mid-April. By September, perhaps India would have crossed all countries in both the number of cases and fatality rates (Jha, 2020).

However, after keeping the number of cases low for almost two months since the lockdown was imposed, India's COVID-19 cases started to rise in the last week of May with 165,386 confirmed cases, and 4,711 COVID-19 deaths by 29 May 2020 (JHU Coronavirus Resource Centre, 2021). On the same day that the WHO declared COVID-19 a public health emergency, India reported its first case of the virus. Before that, India began screening international passengers from China and Hong Kong at its three major airports in Delhi, Mumbai, and Kolkata as early as 18 January 2020, and the testing was quickly extended to include other nations and all airports. On 25 March, India enacted a nationwide lockdown, except for vital services, after the WHO declared COVID-19 a pandemic on 11 March (Jha, 2020).

One of the main aspects of the Indian government's pandemic containment strategy was that state governments were allowed to both impose and lift lockdown restrictions. This move was mainly because state governments would have a better understanding of local conditions than the union government. This decision was also in line with the constitutional rights of state governments within India's federal structure.

Besides, unlike other BRICS nations, India had a unique challenge to tackle. The 40 million migrant workers in different parts of the country faced hardship because of the lockdown. Migrant workers lost their jobs and became desperate to go to their hometowns and villages. India's social security system is negligible and the government could not give much needed economic help. Arrangements were made to help them return to their homes from the big cities. Despite precautions taken, the virus too travelled from big cities to small towns and villages across India. This became the cause for the subsequent spike in COVID-19 cases in India.

The spread of the virus in India in the beginning has also been attributed to the Tablighi Jamaat. The gathering of nearly 2,500 Muslim delegates, some from Malaysia, Sri Lanka and Kyrgyzstan, became the reason for the sudden increase in COVID-19 cases. They infected Indian attendees and spread the disease across the country. At one point, the delegates and those infected by them accounted for a third of the total COVID-19 cases in India (Haq, 2020). Apparently Tablighi Jamaat's action was seen as an act of act revenge against the Indian government's decision to revoke Article 370, which stripped Kashmir of its special status and the Citizenship Amendment Act. It has also been reported that the Islamic State appealed to its adherents in India and the world to spread the virus to every corner of the country (Williams, 2020).

Although India has the second-highest confirmed COVID-19 cases, its case-fatality rate is reasonably low when compared with the EU, the US, and other BRICS nations. From the beginning, India's challenge was to adopt a containment strategy that could protect both human lives and the economy. India's virus containment strategy has been much better than that of countries (including the US, the UK, Italy, France, and Germany) with far more advanced health systems. The data released in June 2020, when India announced its first phase of easing restriction, indicated that India's recovery rate was steadily rising and the death rate steadily falling. Seventy per cent of India's COVID-19 cases were in 13 clusters, with the city of Mumbai accounting for 25 per cent of all COVID-19 cases (The Economic Times, 2020).

India, with its patchy health system and densely populated cities, was projected to be the COVID-19 hotspot from the beginning. After defying this projection for a long time, India faced an economic crisis and could not continue the lockdown. On 10 September 2020, India surpassed Brazil to the second spot in the number of infected cases. India reported a record daily high of 97,570 cases on September 11 and on 15 September 2020, India recorded the highest number of positive cases in the world as the Health Ministry reported 90,123 new cases in the previous 24 hours, raising the confirmed total to more than 5 million, about 0.35 per cent of India's nearly 1.4 billion population, and the total number of deaths to 82,066. The fatality rate among Indian coronavirus patients continues to be low at 1.6 per cent in comparison to 3 per cent in Brazil and the US. However, India, which was expected to surpass the United States in terms of COVID-19 cases, has been able to slow down the spread of the virus. As of 4 January 2021, India, with 10,323,965 confirmed COVID-19 cases and 149,435 deaths, has the second highest number of cases and third highest number of COVID-19 deaths in the world (ABC News, 16 September 2020). Apart from the easing of restrictions, India's under-resourced, patchy, and inadequate healthcare system in tens of thousands of impoverished towns and villages is the main reason for India's failure to contain the surge in COVID cases and deaths.

China

China's COVID-19 containment response has been in phases. In its first phase of containment measures, China's focus was first to stop the disease spreading from Hubei province to the rest of the mainland. China took stern measures, imposing an extreme lockdown in mid-January 2020. China's virus containment measures, which included the stopping of movement in and out of Wuhan, the centre of the epidemic, and 15 other cities in Hubei province, were unprecedented. Overall, China went for strict lockdown and other measures such as the closure of schools, universities, transport, and workplace shutdowns to contain the virus. In addition, trains and flights were suspended, and transportation through roads were blocked. People were asked to stay at home across China and movement was allowed only for essentials food and medical needs. Almost half the population of China were confined to their homes (Zhong and Mozur, 2020). The highlight of the lockdown was that Hubei province was under strict lockdown, and no transport or airways were allowed to operate from Hubei to the rest of China.

After containing the disease reasonably well, China began to lift these strict lockdowns and work on its next phase of public health response to mitigate the risk of COVID-19 across the general population in the long run. The strategy was physical distancing, good hygiene practices, restricted gatherings, and testing and contact tracing and isolation. This became the daily routine, which China strictly followed.

Among the BRICS nations, China emerged as an outlier from being the epicentre of the COVID-19 pandemic to almost having contained the disease. China as the biggest manufacturer of PPE was able to use them to contain the disease at home first. In addition, the Chinese authoritarian system allowed it to impose the lockdowns strictly.

China also got the support of the WHO, which has been at the forefront of China's COVID-19 containment strategy and efforts. The WHO Country Office in China, supported by the Regional Office for the Western Pacific and global headquarters, gave all kinds of support from technical advice on detection, testing, isolation, and quarantine measures to the Chinese government for quick action to stop the spread of COVID-19 (World Health Organization, 2020). By the time the virus was declared a pandemic, the WHO's resources and capacity became inadequate to assist other nations with China receiving the maximum attention. Both China and WHO have been accused of hiding the truth about the severity of the outbreak, which did not allow other countries to prepare well (BBC News, 8 July 2020).

The number of reported cases and deaths released by the Chinese authorities in the case of Wuhan Province has been questioned. China has a history of hiding casualties, be it in the 1962 Sino-India War, the deaths because of the famine in 1959–61, or COVID-19 casualties (Sharma, 2 July 2020).

China's containment measures have been criticised as, after the detection of the virus in Wuhan, China stopped incoming flights to China but continued outward flights from China to spread the disease to the world. China's actions were delayed and, initially, the country tried to hide the information regarding the disease to save its image. According to epidemiologists, China's unprecedented authoritarian lockdown measures were too late. When the outbreak was first reported in December and January, the authorities in Wuhan were first slow to report the mysterious cases, and then delayed the measures taken to contain the disease. This untimely action is responsible for its becoming a pandemic. A model simulation by Lai Shengjie and Andrew Tatem at the University of Southampton, UK, demonstrates that if China had implemented its control measures a week earlier, it could have prevented 67% of all cases there. Implementing the measures three weeks earlier, from the beginning of January, would have cut the number of infections to 5% of the total (Lai *et al., 2020*). China's COVID-19 containment measures, though harsh, doubtful, and criticised heavily, have been able to contain the virus at home.

South Africa

As of 4 January 2021, South Africa, ranked 17th in the world in terms of the number of cases (1,100,748 confirmed COVID-19 cases) and 13th in terms of the number of deaths (15,499 deaths). South Africa has the highest number of COVID-19 cases in Africa with a relatively low fatality rate (Johns Hopkins University Coronavirus Resource Centre, https://coronavirus.jhu.edu/, Accessed on 4 January 2021). On 5 March 2020, the first confirmed case of the virus was reported in South Africa, and the first two deaths to have occurred from the disease were reported on 27 March 2020. On 15 March 2020, President Cyril Ramaphosa declared a national state of disaster, and imposed measures such as immediate travel restrictions and closure of schools from 18 March 2020. On 17 March 2020, the *National Coronavirus Command Council* was established to guide South Africa's strategy to contain the spread and mitigate the negative impact of the coronavirus (Hunter, 2020). On 23 March 2020, the South African government announced a national lockdown starting on 26 March 2020. On 21 April 2020, the government announced a ZAR500-billion stimulus package to tackle the economic hardship. From 1 May 2020, the government adopted a gradual easing of the lockdown restrictions strategy. As a result, the national alert was lowered to level 4, from 1 June 2020, to level 3 and then to level 2 on 17 August 2020 (Businesstech, 2020).

South Africa could have been in a better position as far as the number of cases and COVID-19 deaths are concerned for the following reasons. After an initial slow start, COVID-19 infections cases began to rise rapidly in South Africa. South Africa's case resembled Brazil more than it did countries in its home continent. COVID-19 exposed the healthcare infrastructure system and its uneven distribution and access. The country's authorities always believed that a pandemic would occur and that it would be difficult to contain. Other countries' epidemiologists were working with their governments to find ways to curb the epidemic, but South African medical scientists, almost unanimously, believed that fighting a pandemic would be difficult. Experts attribute this to the fact that South Africans compared themselves to the countries of West Europe and the United States instead of comparing themselves with the countries in Asia and Africa where the pandemic was reasonably well controlled in comparison to the global North (Friedman, 2020).

South Africa boasted of a high testing rate but failed in contact tracing and quarantining positive cases. Inadequate facilities and lack of technical expertise further complicated the problem.

Despite appearing to have given up before the fight began, South Africa could have contained COVID-19 had it done what its government said it would: create an effective testing and tracing programme that would identify people with the virus, trace their contacts and isolate them if they were infected (Friedman, 2020). In June and July 2020, when South Africa was ranked fourth in the number of people infected and 17th in terms of the infection rate among 215 countries battling the pandemic, Health Minister Zwelli Mkhize said, 'A hard lockdown will always remain a possibility, it may become necessary. When that situation comes, we'll talk about it'. South Africa could not see the seriousness of the disease (Medical Brief, 2020). The problem also got complicated because of delayed testing reports. All these highlighted the medical capacity problem in South Africa and the stark reality of inequalities where one-third of its people's standard of life resembles that of the First World while two-thirds of the population lived in third world conditions. Still, it could not emulate its poor neighbouring countries such as Senegal where COVID-19 cases were almost contained and was far better managed.

Assessing the Impact of COVID-19 Lockdowns in BRICS

Lockdowns are time-tested strategies for containing pandemics. Although COVID-19 lockdowns have saved lives, the actual impact of lockdowns is still being debated. It is not yet known how much voluntary social isolation helped reduce the number of cases. Questions are being raised on the lockdowns as they were imposed without verifiable data, leading to great stress among people, higher unemployment and an increase in the incidence of poverty. Evidence suggests that the state's 'command and control' was successful in containing the virus in countries as diverse as Vietnam, South Korea, New Zealand and the Indian southern state of Kerala in the beginning. This also increased the importance of state control in delivering basics during the crisis (Pegram, 2020). State response to the pandemic has resulted in an unprecedented expansion of state powers, and countries such as China and Russia, known for their authoritarianism, are expected to see an increase in government power. However, South Africa, India, and Brazil have also been criticised for some of the harshest measures to contain the disease. Those who profess limited government control worry that the lockdowns may have increased the tendency of governments to be more authoritarian and that they will not give up that power after the crisis is over. Due to the perceived severity of such measures and the increase in government power, there has been much controversy surrounding lockdowns with some favouring and some opposing the lockdowns (Sault, 2020).

Although countries have struggled to formulate a strategy to both counter the disease spread and handle its economic fallout, well-accepted countermeasures to tackle the outbreak have proved hard to find. This became obvious even in the case of countries with the most advanced health systems, which failed to contain the outbreak. Most countries were not in a position to ascertain what strategy would work. Sweden's chief medical scientist criticised the government for too many deaths and attributed it to not imposing a strict lockdown (Lindeberg, 2020). After witnessing having the highest number of fatalities in Europe, the UK imposed a strict lockdown. The US approach was inconsistent and lacked proper co-ordination between the federal and state governments on the issue of strict lockdowns, leaving the country with the highest number of COVID-19 cases and deaths.

BRICS nations also struggled to follow a consistent strategy. There was no similarity in their approach. China, India, and Russia went for strict lockdowns, Brazil adopted a more casual approach, and South Africa had a pessimistic view about the measures to contain the virus from the beginning.

South Africa's early lockdown allowed the government to prepare the health care system, and ensure widespread testing and other necessary virus containment measures. However, the South African virus containment measures have been questioned because of uncertainties around the length and intensity and the way lockdowns were imposed and implemented. Concerns have been raised about the threat to the South African Constitution as a result of the erosion of civil liberties and lockdowns. The use of the military to enforce night curfews, ban on e-commerce, restricted exercise hours, and the lack of parliamentary oversight in the National Disaster Management Act and its constitutional validity was challenged in the courts (Khumalo, 2020).

In the case of India, though the right step, the sudden nationwide lockdown imposed by the Indian government was criticised because it did not give people enough time to prepare themselves for the lockdown. The worst affected were people trapped in cities away from their homes, especially 40 million migrant workers across India who were trapped without adequate shelter and food arrangements. The Indian government justified its actions on the ground that India was among the most vulnerable to the pandemic and that it needed to be prepared to tackle an increase in COVID-19 cases (The Economic Times, 2020). India's lockdown has been accepted by most as the right decision (Hindustan Times 2020) as it allowed the country with a patchy health system to build its capacity, make temporary hospitals, manufacture ventilators and PPE kits at home, and increase the production of generic medicines such HCQ for domestic and international supply.

While Brazil was criticised for not imposing a lockdown, Russia was criticised for imposing harsh restrictions even when there were not many cases and then rushing out of the lockdown when the number of cases was mounting (The Guardian, 2020). China's lockdown has been under the scanner. China has been always on the radar for its blatant misuse of state power and human rights violations. Lawrence O. Gostin, director of the WHO Collaborating Center on National and Global Health Law at Georgetown University, points to 'major human rights' concerns with the lockdown techniques pioneered in China and now – to a different degree – adopted in many countries (Feldwisch-Drentrup, 2020). Several reports suggest that China used draconian measures to contain the virus and law-enforcing agencies treated the people inhumanely. China's COVID-19 containment strategy also came under the scanner for using its influence and hobnobbing with the World Health Organisation (WHO), and for severely mismanaging and covering up the spread of coronavirus (Gebrekidan *et al.*, 2021). In the beginning, China tried to cover up and deny the severity of the outbreak. While China successfully contained the COVID-19 outbreak, it was too late and coronavirus spread to many parts of the world. China's hiding of the severity of the virus and untimely action delayed much needed global response. Besides, China used medical aid diplomacy for its geopolitical goals. China used the WHO for hiding the severity of the outbreak (Gilsinan, 2020). WHO experts were not allowed to enter China until Director-General Tedros Adhanom visited President Xi Jinping at the end of January. Until then, the WHO was uncritically repeating information from Chinese government sources, ignoring warnings from Taiwanese doctors, and did not declare the virus outbreak a 'public health emergency of international concern'. After the meeting, the WHO declared the virus outbreak a public health emergency of international concern on 30 January 2020 and declared it a pandemic on 1 March 2020, even though the virus was exported to the world more than a month earlier (Feldwisch-Drentrup, 2020).

The correct number of Chinese fatalities will probably never be known. On China's success, the WHO reported, 'The community has largely accepted the prevention and control measures and is fully participating in the management of self-isolation and enhancement of public compliance'. The WHO also left many questions open about how exactly public engagement was managed in its report. The report says that the Chinese people accepted and adhered to the starkest of containment measures. This may have applied for many, but many would have followed the decree of the Supreme People's Court that states, 'People carrying the virus who don't follow quarantine restrictions face jail terms ranging from three to 10 years if the consequence is not serious. Otherwise, they could face a life sentence or death' (The Supreme People's Court of the People's Republic of China, 2020). In fact, it was China's strict enforcement of COVID-19 containment measures that prevented the spread of the disease.

One positive trend visible in BRICS nations is that the observed case-fatality rate is quite low when compared with the EU member nations and in the Americas. On 1 June 2020, the global case-fatality rate was 6.19%. It was the highest in France at 19.35%, followed by Belgium at 16.25%, Italy at 14.33% and the UK at 14.07%. The recovery rate was high in India among the BRICS nations. For example, according to the Health Ministry, the fatality rate or the percentage of deaths was registered at 2.83% on 1 June 2020, 3.15% on May 18, 3.25% on May 3, and 3.3% on April 15. Similarly, the recovery rate form the coronavirus infected people in India increased gradually and attained 48.19% amongst COVID-19 patients on 1 June 2020 as compared to 38.29% on May 18, 26.59% on May 3, and 11.42% on 15 April 2020 (The Economic Times, 2020). Overall, the case-fatality rate has been lower in the BRICS bloc as compared to other blocs such as the EU. China has fewer cases than other BRICS nations, but its case-fatality rate is 5.2 % (JHU, Coronavirus Resource Center, 22 September 2020). A combination of containment measures such as timely lockdown, detection and treatment, case identification and clinical management of the coronavirus cases are cited as reasons for the comparatively low case-fatality rate in the BRICS nations.

BRICS Co-operation on COVID-19: Constraints and Geopolitics

In the beginning, co-ordination in fighting COVID-19 among the BRICS countries looked promising. On 28 April 2020, the Indian External Affairs Minister S. Jaishankar, Chinese Foreign Minister Wang Yi, Brazilian Foreign Minister Ernesto Araujo, and South Africa's Minister of International Relations and Co-operation Naledi Pandor attended the BRICS Foreign Ministers' Extraordinary Conference on COVID-19 via video link, organised and chaired by the Russian Foreign Minister Sergei Lavrov. In the meeting, the BRICS members reached a consensus on enhancing collaboration to combat COVID-19, and the attendees shared their views on safeguarding multilateralism, combating COVID-19, and enhancing co-operation among BRICS countries. The meeting emphasised the need to intensify information and experience sharing, work towards collaboration in research on drugs and vaccines, contribute to global public health security, and mitigate the effects of COVID-19 (Xinhuanet, 2020). Speaking at the conference, the Chinese representative said that BRICS should come together in the spirit of partnership to combat COVID-19 and acknowledged the moral and verbal support by the BRICS nations to China (Yi, 2020). The foreign ministers' meeting was followed by a meeting of senior health officials of BRICS members to draw up an action plan to fight the pandemic.

Before the BRICS Foreign Ministers' Extraordinary Conference on COVID-19, Indian Foreign Minister S. Jaishankar discussed with his Russian and Brazilian counterpart strategies to fight the pandemic (Outlook, 2020). In April ahead of the BRICS foreign ministers' meeting, a Russian think tank Valdai Club released a report, 'BRICS and the Rivalry Pandemic', that emphasised the importance of BRICS amidst the global health crisis caused by the pandemic. Pavel Knyazev, Deputy Director, Department of Foreign Policy Planning of the Russian Ministry of Foreign Affairs, emphasised the need to pay more attention to speed up implementation of the projects and decisions that were agreed on and to accelerate the work to establish the BRICS Centre for Research and Development for vaccines. They also exchanged their views on the application of digital technologies to contain the pandemic.

During these virtual meetings on COVID-19, BRICS demonstrated remarkable solidarity, compassion, and co-operation among the member states (Kondratieva, 2020). Unlike the US, India did not blame China or called it the China Virus; it kept its strategy confined to containment at the domestic level and to co-operation at the international level. India's export of generic medicine and China's export of PPE and medicines demonstrated the significance of the BRICS during the pandemic. The BRICS nations' only goal seemed to be to help each other contain the pandemic.

However, political differences soon cropped up with self-interest taking centre stage. While there was bilateral co-operation among the BRICS countries, the co-operation at the BRICS bloc level was missing. Then Indian and Chinese defence ministers attended Russia's commemoration of 75 years of victory in World War II, and again in August 2020, the defence ministers of the two countries visited Russia. The Russia-China-India format dialogue was against the backdrop of the violent India-China border clash and strategic issues became the primary focus. The tense situation at the India-China border, China's complex strategic relations with other BRICS nations, and the tense strategic rivalry between the US and China further pushed COVID-19 backstage (Sharma, 2019; Ridel, 2015; Sharma, 1 April 2020).

China's flaunting of its global influence to pursue its geopolitical agenda and the geopolitical complexities surrounding China's assertiveness hampered an excellent opportunity for collaboration among the BRICS countries to display their strength. COVID-19 intensified the geopolitics, and the debilitating impact on social, economic, and political aspects triggered a spillover effect on the complex geopolitics in which China's military aggression became the main issue. COVID-19 ignited the US-China strategic rivalry, and the violent India-China standoff further hampered any meaningful collaboration among BRICS nations on COVID-19. Political differences and strategic rivalry watered down the opportunity that could have been the foundation stone for future cohesiveness and co-ordination for BRICS to contribute to handling the COVID crisis at the global level.

The Way Ahead for BRICS

The BRICS nations followed the standard COVID-19 containment measures. Nevertheless, they differed in their approach and implementation. This was due to the different political set-ups, healthcare-related capability, and the conditions within their boundaries. Those with stricter controls were able to contain the disease better. The difference in the political system affected the extent of control exercised over people to follow virus containment measures.

Despite being criticised for its ineffectiveness and doubt over its survivability, the BRICS grouping has not only survived but also been institutionalised with the setting up of the BRICS New Development Bank in 2015 (Kondratieva, 2020). However, the pace of progress has not been as desired. BRICS, a conglomeration of rising powers and emerging economies with almost 40 per cent of the world population, has the potential to play a pivotal role in global governance and crisis management in flattening the world order in the post-COVID-19 world. COVID-19 provided BRICS the opportunity to bring narrow down differences among the members and exert an influence in the shaping the post-COVID-19 world order and governance.

However, the economic downturn, social, health, and mental and other problems at home arising because of the disastrous effects of COVID-19 will hamper the capacity of the BRICS bloc to play a meaningful role on the world stage. The unemployment rate has gone up in Russia up to 30%. South Africa registered 30% unemployment in the first quarter of 2020, and Brazil reported a staggering number of about 1.2 million people becoming jobless in the first half of 2020 (Pham, 2020). India too has faced a similar contraction in its economy and the unemployment rate has gone up. China, although in a better position in comparison to its fellow BRICS nations, will be constrained by falling demand for its products and the growing concern regarding the over-reliance of global supply chains on China – both factors that are likely to make the outlook for China dim.

References

'14–29 lakh COVID-19 Cases Averted Due to Lockdown, 37,000–78,000 Lives Saved: Government'. 2020. *The Economic Times*, 22 May, https://economictimes.indiatimes.com/news/politics-and-nation/14-29-lakh-covid-19-cases-averted-due-to-lockdown-37000–78000-lives-saved-government/articleshow/75901257.cms (accessed on 22 May 2020).

Barberia, Lorena G. and Gómez, Eduardo J. 2020. 'Political and Institutional Perils of Brazil's COVID-19 Crisis'. *The Lancet*, 396(10248), 8 August 2020.

Businesstech. 2020.'South Africa Moves to Level 2 Lockdown on Monday – Here Are the New Rules', 15 August. https://businesstech.co.za/news/government/425708/south-africa-moves-to-level-2-lockdown-on-monday-here-are-the-new-rules/ (accessed on 22 October 2020).

Charner, Flora. 2020. 'Brazil tops 1 million Covid-19 Cases. It May Pass the US Next, Becoming the Worst-Hit Country on the Planet'. *CNN*, 19 June, https://edition.cnn.com/2020/06/19/americas/brazil-one-million-coronavirus-jair-bolsonaro-cases-intl/index.html (accessed on 26 September 2020).

'Coronavirus Has Brazil on Verge of Economic Collapse and Food Shortages, Leaders Warn'. 2020. *ABC News*, 8 May, www.abc.net.au/news/2020-05-08/coronavirus-warnings-brazil-economy-on-verge-of-collapse/12227298 (accessed on 26 September 2020).

Coronavirus: What are President Trump's Charges Against the WHO? 2020. *BBC News*, 8 July, www.bbc.com/news/world-us-canada-52294623 (accessed on 16 October 2020).

'Covid-19 Lockdown: Centre Identifies Red, Orange, Green Zones for Week after May 3'. 2020. *The Indian Express*, 2 May https://indianexpress.com/article/india/covid-19-lockdown-centre-identifies-red-green-orange-zones-for-week-after-may-3-check-full-list-here-6388654/ (accessed on 7 August 2020).

Feldwisch-Drentrup, Hinnerk. 2020. 'How WHO Became China's Coronavirus Accomplice'. *Foreign Policy*, 2 April. https://foreignpolicy.com/2020/04/02/china-coronavirus-who-health-soft-power/ (accessed on 26 October 2020).

Friedman, Steven. 2020. 'South Africa is Failing on COVID-19 Because its Leaders Want to Emulate the First World'. *The Conversation*, 17 July, https://theconversation.com/south-africa-is-failing-on-covid-19-because-its-leaders-want-to-emulate-the-first-world-142732 (accessed on 29July 2020).

Gebrekidan, Selam, Apuzzo, Matt, Qin, Amy and Hernández, Javier C. 2021. 'In Hunt for Virus Source, W.H.O. let China Take Charge'. *New York Times*, 9 February. www.nytimes.com/2020/11/02/world/who-china-coronavirus.html (accessed on 7 November 2021).

Gilsinan, Kathy. 2020. 'How China Deceived the WHO'. *The Atlantic*, 12 April, www.theatlantic.com/politics/archive/2020/04/world-health-organization-blame-pandemic-coronavirus/609820/ (accessed on 7 November 2021).

Gupta, Shekhar. 2020. 'Covid Hasn't Gone Viral in India Yet, But Some in the World & At Home Can't Accept the Truth'. *The Print*, 18 April, https://theprint.in/national-interest/covid-hasnt-gone-viral-in-india-yet-but-some-in-the-world-at-home-cant-accept-the-truth/404178/ (accessed on 14 July 2020).

Haq, Jia. 2020. 'Jamaat Brought Collective shame and Islamophobia, Muslims Say'. *Hindustan Times*, 13 April, www.hindustantimes.com/india-news/jamaat-brought-collective-shame-and-islamophobia-muslims-say/story-ermZoPYGGZ8HBMNeErSnvM.html (accessed on 14 October 2020).

Human Rights Watch. 2020. 'Brazil: Bolsonaro Sabotages Anti-Covid-19 Efforts', 10 April, www.hrw.org/news/2020/04/10/brazil-bolsonaro-sabotages-anti-covid-19-efforts (accessed on 27 September 2020).

Hunter, Qaanitah. 2020. 'EXPLAINER | What Exactly is the National Coronavirus Command Council?' *News 24*, 13 May. www.news24.com/news24/southafrica/news/explainer-what-exactly-is-the-national-coronavirus-command-council-20200513 (accessed on 20 October 2020).

'India's Coronavirus Cases Pass 5 million as Hospitals Scramble for Oxygen'. *ABC News*, 16 September, www.abc.net.au/news/2020-09-16/india-coronavirus-case – pass-5-million/12670756 (accessed on 16 October 2020).

'India's COVID-19 Recovery Rate Improving, Fatality Rate Declining: Health Ministry'. 2020. *The Economic Times*, 2 June. https://economictimes.indiatimes.com/news/politics-and-nation/indias-covid-19-recovery-rate-improving-fatality-rate-declining-health-ministry/articleshow/76140228.cms (accessed on 14 October 2020).

'Jaishankar Speaks to His Counterparts from US, Russia, Brazil, Saudi Arabia'. 2020. *Outlook*, 23 April. www.outlookindia.com/newsscroll/jaishankar-speaks-to-his-counterparts-from-us-russia-brazil-saudi-arabia/1812628 (accessed on 22 June 2020).

'Jamaat Tablighi Event Caused Coronavirus to Spread to "Many Persons": MHA'. 2020. *Indian Express*, 21 September. https://indianexpress.com/article/india/tablighi-jamaat-coronavirus-spread-centre-rajya-sabha-6604521/ (accessed on 14 October 2020).

Jha, Raghbendra. 2020. 'India's Response to the Coronavirus Crisis'. *Australian Outlook*, 11 June. www.internationalaffairs.org.au/australianoutlook/indias-response-to-the-coronavirus-crisis/ (accessed on 14 July 2020).

Johns Hopkins University Coronavirus Resource Centre. 2021. https://coronavirus.jhu.edu/ (accessed on 4 January 2021).

Johns Hopkins University of Medicine, Coronavirus Resource Center. 2020. 22 September. https://coronavirus.jhu.edu/data/mortality (accessed on 22 September 2020).

Jurberg, Claudia. 2018. 'Flawed but Fair: Brazil's Health System Reaches Out to the Poor'. *World Health Organization*, 86: 4. www.who.int/bulletin/volumes/86/4/08-030408/en/ (accessed on 26 September 2020).

Khumalo, Junior. 2020. 'Avalanche of Cases Against State on Covid-19'. *News24*, 24 May. www.news24.com/citypress/news/avalanche-of-cases-against-state-on-covid-19-20200524 (accessed on 25 October 2020).

Kondratieva, Ksenia. 2020. 'For BRICS, Challenges and Opportunities'. *The Hindu*, 4 May. www.thehindu.com/news/international/for-brics-challenges-and-opportunities/article31433942.ece (accessed on 1 June 2020).

Lai, Shengjie, Ruktanonchai, Nick W., Zhou, Liangcai, Prosper, Olivia, Luo, Wei, Floyd, Jessica R., Wesolowski, Amy, Santillana, Mauricio, Zhang, Chi, Du, Xiangjun, Yu, Hongjie and Tatem, Andrew J. 2020. 'Effects of Non-Pharmaceutical Interventions for Containing the COVID-19 Outbreak'. *Nature*, 4 May. www.worldpop.org/events/COVID_NPI (accessed on 20 October 2020).

Lindeberg, Rafaela. 2020. 'Man Behind Sweden's Controversial Coronavirus Strategy Admits Mistakes'. *Sydney Morning Herald*, 3 June. www.smh.com.au/world/europe/man-behind-sweden-s-controversial-coronavirus-strategy-admits-mistakes-20200603-p54z99.html (accessed on 25 October 2020).

Medical Brief. 2020. 'Mkhize warns of "Exponential Rise" of COVID-19 Infections'. 1 July, www.medicalbrief.co.za/archives/mkhize-warns-of-exponential-rise-of-covid-19-infections/ (accessed on 29 July 2020).

OECD Interim Economic Assessment. 2020. 'Coronavirus: The World Economy at Risk', 2 March. www.oecd.org/berlin/publikationen/Interim-Economic-Assessment-2-March-2020.pdf (accessed on 5 October 2020).

Pegram, Tom. 2020. 'Coronavirus is a failure of global governance – now the world needs a radical transformation'. *The Conversation*, 5 May. https://theconversation.com/coronavirus-is-a-failure-of-global-governance-now-the-world-needs-a-radical-transformation-136535 (accessed on 29 July 2020).

Pham, Phuong. 2020. 'How the COVID-19 Pandemic Undermines the Role of BRICS'. *Geopolitics Monitor*, 24 August. www.geopoliticalmonitor.com/how-the-covid-19-pandemic-undermines-the-role-of-brics/ (accessed on 28 October 2020).

'Putin to ease Russia Lockdown Despite Record Number of New Infections – as it Happened'. 2020. *The Guardian*, 12 May. www.theguardian.com/world/live/2020/may/11/coronavirus-live-news-white-house-task-force-hit-by-infection-us-usa-vp-mike-pence-donald-trump-boris-johnsons-uk-lockdown-plans-criticised (accessed on 25 October 2020).

Ramesh, Sandhya and Basu, Mohana. 2020. 'R0 Data Shows India's Coronavirus Infection Rate Has Slowed, Gives Lockdown a Thumbs Up'. *The Print*, 14 April. https://theprint.in/science/r0-data-shows-indias-coronavirus-infection-rate-has-slowed-gives-lockdown-a-thumbs-up/399734/ (accessed on 7 August 2020).

Ridel, Bruce. 2015. *JFK's Forgotten Crisis: Tibet, the CIA, and the Sino-Indian War*. Washington, DC: Brookings Institution Press.

Russia Business Today. 2020. 'Over 5,500 New Coronavirus Cases Recorded in Russia in Past Day'. 14 September. https://russiabusinesstoday.com/health/over-5500-new-coronavirus-cases-recorded-in-russia-in-past-day/(accessed on 5 October 2020).

Sault, Samantha. 2020. 'Why Lockdowns Can Halt the Spread of COVID-19'. *World Economic Forum*, 21 March. www.weforum.org/agenda/2020/03/why-lockdowns-work-epidemics-coronavirus-covid19/ (accessed on 25 October 2020).

Sharma, Ashok. 2019. *India's Pursuit of Energy Security: Domestic Measures, Foreign Policy and Geopolitics*. New Delhi. Sage Publications

Sharma, Ashok. 2020. 'India-China Standoff Ends India's Hopes for Asian Unity'. *Australian Outlook*, 2 July. www.internationalaffairs.org.au/australianoutlook/india-china-standoff-ends-indias-hopes-for-asian-unity/ (accessed on 2 July 2020).

Sharma, Ashok. 2020. 'Great Power Politics in the Post-COVID-19 World'. *Australian Outlook*, 1 April. www.internationalaffairs.org.au/australianoutlook/great-power-politics-in-the-post-covid-19-world/ (accessed on 1 April 2020).

The Moscow Times. 2020. 'New Figures Suggest Russia's Coronavirus Death Toll Underreported', 10 July. www.themoscowtimes.com/2020/07/10/new-figures-suggest-russias-coronavirus-death-toll-underreported-a70848 (accessed on 5 October 2020).

The Supreme People's Court of the People's Republic of China. 2020. 'Guideline Aims at Deliberate Novel Coronavirus Spreaders'. 13 February. http://english.court.gov.cn/2020-02/13/content_37533573.htm (accessed on 26 October 2020).

Twigg, Judy. 2020. 'Russia's Not Ready for Coronavirus'. *Think Global Health*, 6 March. www.thinkglobalhealth.org/article/russias-not-ready-coronavirus (accessed on 5 October 2020).
'Unlock 1.0: Coronavirus Lockdowns Saved Many Lives and Easing Them is Risky. Here's How'. 2020. *Hindustan Times*, 9 June. www.hindustantimes.com/more-lifestyle/unlock-1-0-coronavirus-lockdowns-saved-many-lives-and-easing-them-is-risky-here-s-how/story-LJqbnMeJkCZADE2BdQYtMP.html (accessed on 12 June 2020).
Williams, Brian Glyn. 2020. 'Islamic State Calls for Followers to Spread Coronavirus, Exploit Pandemic and Protests'. *The Conversation*, 25 June. https://theconversation.com/islamic-state-calls-for-followers-to-spread-coronavirus-exploit-pandemic-and-protests-136224 (accessed on 12 November 2020).
World Health Organization. 2020. 'China shows COVID-19 Responses Must Be Tailored to the Local Context'. *Regional Office of Europe*, 3 April. www.euro.who.int/en/health-topics/health-emergencies/coronavirus-covid-19/news/news/2020/4/china-shows-covid-19-responses-must-be-tailored-to-the-local-context (accessed on 16 October 2020).
Xinhuanet. 2020, 'BRICS Countries Agree to Boost Cooperation on COVID-19 Fight', 29 April www.xinhuanet.com/english/2020-04/29/c_139016152.htm (accessed on 26 October 2020).
Yi, Wang. 2020. 'Deepening BRICS Cooperation to Combat COVID-19'. Statement by H.E. Wang Yi, State Councillor and Minister of Foreign Affairs of The People's Republic of China. Ministry of Foreign Affairs of People's Republic of China, 28 April, www.fmprc.gov.cn/mfa_eng/wjdt_665385/zyjh_665391/t1774323.shtml (accessed on 26 October 2020).
Zhong, Raymond and Mozur, Paul. 2020. 'To Tame Coronavirus, Mao-Style Social Control Blankets China'. *New York Times*, 15 February. www.nytimes.com/2020/02/15/business/china-coronavirus-lockdown.html (accessed on 16 October 2020).

17

BRICS AND THE COVID PANDEMIC

Challenges and Opportunities

Shradha

Introduction

The Covid pandemic, which has affected 215 countries, is perhaps among the worst global crises to hit the world since the Second World War. It has wreaked immense economic damage globally as governments tried to contain the spread of the pandemic through the imposition of strict lockdowns in several countries that have resulted in the winding down of economies and hit international trade severely. Despite the patent need for concerted and co-ordinated action by countries to both control the pandemic and mitigate its disastrous economic efforts, global institutions like the World Health Organization (WHO) have been struggling to ensure co-operation and co-ordination among nations. The WHO's seeming inability to play an effective role in combating the pandemic has arisen primarily because of a tussle between the United States and China on the origin of the virus and the United States' dissatisfaction with both the WHO's handling of the crisis and its alleged collusion with China to hide the extent of the crisis (Associated Press, July 2, 2020). The US administration's decision to withdraw its funding of the WHO and its threat to withdraw membership (the decisions were reversed after President Joe Biden took over as the president of the United States) have also weakened the WHO's capacity to deal with the pandemic. The US administration's withdrawal from its international obligations to participate in efforts to mitigate a global crisis of such magnitude has provided BRICS an opportunity to take the lead in the fight against the pandemic (Kumar and De Conti, 2020).

The following discussion is a broad overview of the impact of Covid on BRICS nations, the challenges they face, and their response to the threats posed by the pandemic.

DOI: 10.4324/9781003148074-20

Coronavirus and Its Impact on BRICS Nations

Covid is caused by the Severe Acute Respiratory Syndrome Coronavirus 2 (SARS-CoV-2). It is a type of virus that may have mild symptoms of common cold initially but may aggravate to severe conditions like pneumonia, MERS, and SARS. The virus is reported to have originated from a seafood market in China's Wuhan city. The WHO declared it a pandemic in late January 2020. In their initial response, the governments of the affected nations responded through strict containment measures like border sealing, flight ban, lockdown, and closure of all non-essential services. Preventive measures like social distancing, use of facemasks, and sanitisation have become the new normal across the world.

Brazil

The impact of Covid on Brazil has been severe as the pandemic claimed over 550,000 lives (the second-highest death toll worldwide) (IMF, 2021). The country recorded its first case of Covid infection on 26 February 2020 and its first confirmed death from the virus on 17 March 2020. There was a sharp rise in confirmed corona cases in Brazil from early May 2020, with its first peak in August 2020 and a steady fall from November 2020 to a new peak in April 2021 with the second wave (IMF, 2021). In the second wave, the situation worsened due to the detection of a highly transmissible variant of the virus – P1 – in early 2021, leading to a virtual collapse of its health system. Reports indicated a serious shortage of oxygen supplies, ICU beds and equipment in April and May. Experts believe the mortality average from the pandemic has been over four times higher in Brazil in comparison to other countries of the world. Brazil's Jair Bolsonaro government was under the scanner for its alleged mishandling of the pandemic. The government has also been criticised for the delayed start of its vaccination programme interrupted due to supply shortages (The Guardian, 2020a). Brazil also suspended the contract for the purchase of 20 million doses of vaccine worth $325 million from the Indian company Bharat Biotech following graft allegations in its purchase. The deal is being probed by its Senate panel (The Times of India, 2021). However, as the vaccination programme progressed, it has resulted in a gradual decline in the Covid death rate.

Brazil responded to the pandemic by imposing travel ban, border sealing, and closure of schools and businesses. The adverse impact of Covid on Brazil's economy became visible as early as April 2020 when growth forecasts indicated an economic slowdown. Its economy shrank as gross domestic product (GDP) growth rate dipped by 4.1 per cent in 2020 (the last worst dip was 4.35 per cent of GDP in 1990) (McGeever, 2021). The healthcare sector was badly affected by the pandemic as the Latin American country was already struggling to combat tropical diseases like Dengue, Zika, and Chikungunya. In order to bail out its economy from the impact of the pandemic, Brazil's Congress declared a state of 'public calamity' and drew up a separate emergency budget with financial measures to support vulnerable sections of the population. The country injected upto 12 per cent of the GDP into its economy, including cash transfers, advance payments for unorganised sector, low-income workers, and employment support by expanding the Bolsa Familia programme (partial compensation and tax breaks to workers suspended or facing pay cuts). Emergency grants were sanctioned for workers and mothers supporting the family. A digital platform was created to facilitate smooth connectivity between health professionals and support systems such as hospitals, clinics, and laboratories in their fight against Covid (IMF, 2020).

Brazil's central bank undertook a host of steps to infuse liquidity into the financial system, such as the provision of loans to financial institutions. Public banks lowered policy rates by expanding credit lines for businesses and households, adding up to 4.5 per cent of the GDP, to support working capital. An amount worth 1 per cent of GDP was used to initiate special support schemes to extend credit lines to small and medium enterprises (SMEs) and small businesses to cover salaries, working capital, and investment. In order to stabilise the exchange rate, the central bank pumped a huge amount of money (US$41 billion) into the foreign exchange market in several attempts starting from mid-February 2020. It also infused US$9 billion into the money market until September 2020 (IMF, 2020). Most measures expired in 2020 end, except a few like emergency aid, employment, and credit support were renewed in mid-2021 (IMF, 2021)

Russia

Russia's confirmation of its first Covid case came on 31 January 2020, after two Chinese nationals who had returned from China tested positive. To check the spread of Covid, Russia sealed its borders, which helped delay the further spread of the pandemic until March 2020. However, once Russian tourists headed home from Italy and other destinations, the virus started spreading among the wider population. Russia's delay in initiating the lockdown until March end led to the sudden rise in Covid cases. The number of confirmed corona cases in Russia increased steeply from mid-April 2020, with a total of 76, 661 deaths as on 7 February 2020. Moscow was the worst-affected metropolis. However, a number of preventive measures such as social distancing and closure of non-essential services undertaken since March 2020 did pay dividends in checking the spread of the virus (Statista Research Department, 2020). A three-stage reopening had been planned, allowing outdoor exercise, small business, and services to reopen first, followed by schools and large shops in the second stage, and the rest in the third stage, depending on the infection rate in the region. The economy had almost fully reopened; however, in June 2021, Russia was again hit by a steep surge in Covid cases due to the highly infectious Delta variant. Mass vaccination had started in January 2021, but only 12 per cent of the population had been vaccinated by the end of June 2021 (IMF, 2021).

Russia suffered a huge economic downturn as the impact of the pandemic was aggravated by a steep fall in oil prices and its repercussions on financial markets. In the second quarter of 2020, the adverse impact of lockdown and restrictions on the economy was visible as its economy shrank by 9.6 per cent (Ostroukh, 2021). The government came up with an action plan to provide support to households and businesses. They identified the worst-hit sectors such as transport, aviation, entertainment, and tourism. However, there was a spurt in demand in certain sectors such as Fast Moving Consumer Goods, personalised gym equipment, electronics, and pharmacy. Containment restrictions resulted in increased consumption of TV, surge in food delivery, as well as internet traffic (Melkadze, 2021).

Russian authorities undertook a series of fiscal measures to arrest the downward slide of the Russian economy. It formulated a National Economic Recovery Plan worth 5 trillion roubles to bring the economy back on a steady growth path. Its fiscal package, which amounted to 3.4 per cent of the GDP, included a host of welfare measures, such as the provision of sick leave pay equivalent to the minimum wage for those under quarantine and the provision of unemployment benefit equivalent to five months minimum wages for job losers post March 1, 2020. A tax holiday was also announced on all taxes (excluding value-added taxes), and the registered self-employed were granted full tax refund for 2019 and partial for 2020. Rent payment for all levels of government functionaries was deferred until 2020 end. Retail trade has recovered fast to pre-corona levels, but large malls are still struggling for survival (KPMG Russia, 2020).

On 24 July 2020, the Central Bank of Russia (CBR) introduced regulatory relief measures for credit institutions to incentivise loan restructuring. It also introduced temporary long-term refinancing instruments as well as a measure to protect retail borrowers. As a relief measure, citizens and SMEs could defer loan repayments for up to six months. It also introduced a subsidised loan facility for SMEs and affected industries. A fresh 500 billion roubles facility for SME lending and an additional 50 billion roubles for non-SME borrowers were introduced. Besides, import duties for sectors like pharmaceuticals and medical supplies were reduced to zero, and a subsidy for the sectors such as airlines and automobiles was introduced at the end of July 2020 (IMF, 2020).

India

India experienced exponential growth in the number of pandemic cases from May to October 2020 during the first wave and again a sharp rise in cases during the second wave, at its peak from April to July 2021. Initially, coronavirus cases appeared in India as a result of foreign contact. The first three confirmed cases of infection in India were reported between 30 January 2020 and 07 February 2020 in Kerala. The infected persons had returned from China's Wuhan Province. However, within a month, a number of corona cases were reported among the people who had returned from Italy, Dubai, and other places (worldometers.info India, 2020). Reports indicate that the imposition of a lockdown arrested the rise in Covid cases until May 2020, but once India reopened, it registered a steep rise in Covid cases as well as Covid deaths from June to October 2020. In order to combat the pandemic, the Indian government issued travel advisories and imposed restrictions and a four-phased lockdown starting from 24 March to 31 May 2020. Reopening began in a phased manner from 20 April 2020, with large-scale migration of stranded people, graded relaxations in economic activities in designated areas, and commencement of domestic air travel on 25 May 2020. Restrictions on metro rail were removed in August end, followed by gradual removal of other restrictions (IMF, 2020).

The proverbial Indian resilience was once again on display. The people and the government quickly got their act together. India's medical infrastructure was geared up to meet emerging requirements, laboratory testing facility for Covid increased from one per day in January 2020 to roughly 15,000 per day by December 2020. Quarantine facilities were created in colleges, hotels, and railway coaches, while stadiums were converted into isolation wards to manage Covid cases. The *Arogya Setu* mobile app was launched to track the movement of Covid-infected people. In January 2021, India had geared up to eradicate corona from the country as it kicked of the world's biggest vaccination drive on 16 January 2021. Initially, the government had permitted two vaccines – Covishield, developed by UK-based company AstraZeneca, and Covaxin, developed by Indian firm Bharat Biotech (Al Jazeera.com, 2021). Later, it also allowed Russia's Sputnik V vaccine. The vaccination programme has been undertaken in three phases – the first began on 16 January 2021 for healthcare and frontline workers, and the second from 1 March 2021 in two parts, for those above 60 years of age and another for those above 45 years. From 1 May 2021, the third phase for those above 18 years began (Joseph, 2021).

The Covid pandemic hit the Indian economy hard. The April–June quarter of financial year 2020–2021 registered a negative growth of 23.9 per cent. However, there was an improvement in the second quarter with the growth rate at (−)7.5 per cent. International rating agencies such as Moody's Investors Service have projected India's GDP growth rate for 2020–2021 at a negative 10.6 per cent (The Hindu, 2021). The sudden enforcement of a lockdown on 24 March 2020 to check the spread of the pandemic had a severe adverse impact on people's income and employment. The unorganised sector consisting of wage labourers, migrant workers, and so on were the worst hit. The adverse impact of Covid was most visible in sectors like aviation, tourism, hospitality, real estate, poultry, entertainment, exports, and shipping. Virtually no sector of the Indian economy escaped the impact of Covid. Even the agricultural sector, which registered a positive growth rate 3.2 per cent for the first two quarters, was badly hit due to the breakdown of the supply chain of agricultural commodities. India also witnessed the second-largest reverse mass migration in its history since partition in 1947. Over 50 million migrant labourers residing in Maharashtra and Delhi were forced to head home to Assam, Bihar, Uttar Pradesh, and so on without any public transport facility. The education system in rural areas was disrupted due to Covid because of both lack of access to the Internet and non-availability of digital devices. However, educational institutions in urban areas shifted to the online mode, resulting in high demand for Wi-Fi connectivity, which served to boost the telecom sector. There was also a reduction in pollution levels as a few power plants were closed down due to low demand. Closure of non-essential services meant lesser vehicles on road, which led to an improvement in the air quality index in various cities. The impact was also visible among birds and wildlife, as South Asian River Ganges dolphins (a critically endangered species) were spotted back in the river after a gap of 30 years. Similarly, thousands of flamingos were spotted in Navi Mumbai (Khan, 2020).

The government undertook a host of measures to ward off the adverse impact of the pandemic on India's economy. These include tax relief – for example, the government extended the last date for filing the returns from 31 March 2020 to 30 June 2020 – employment, social security, liquidity, relief for micro, small, and medium enterprises (MSMEs), non-banking financial companies (NBFCs), power utilities, and so on (Ministry of Finance, 2020). Income tax concessions were granted in the case of Covid treatment. In May 2020, the Indian prime minister announced a relief package of around 10 per cent of the GDP, including monetary and fiscal measures, and launched the 'Atmnirbhar Bharat Abhiyan Yojana' (to create a self-reliant India) targeting farmers, migrant workers, cottage industries, middle class, and others. An additional INR150 billion (about 0.1 per cent of GDP) was allocated for health infrastructure.

In early March 2020, India's central bank announced a number of measures to infuse liquidity in the economy. It directed banks to provide concessional credit to farmers as well as street vendors and ordered a resolution plan for loans stressed due to Covid. This was followed by a business support package for MSMEs and NBFCs in August 2020.

As India was still struggling to tide over the adverse consequences of the first wave of the Covid pandemic, it was badly hit by a second wave around the end of March (2021). The second wave, which saw an exponential rise in Covid cases, had devastating consequences. The country reported a record of 414,188 cases in 24 hours on 7 May 2021 (Firstpost, 2021). As the infection spread at a very fast pace in every age group, India's health infrastructure nearly collapsed. Several states were affected badly, with reports of an acute shortage of oxygen, medicines, and hospital beds, with people desperate to seek help on social media platforms. Disturbing reports of people dying unattended for want of timely treatment poured in from across the country during the month of April and May 2021. Crematoriums in many districts were reported to be running day and night during the two months. To add to the woes, a large number of those who had contracted Covid were also found to be infected by a rare fungal disease called mucormycosis, or 'black fungus', which affected the brain, eyes, and nose in most patients and reportedly had a 50 per cent casualty rate. Many Indian states even declared 'black fungus' an epidemic (Sen, 2021). Large religious gatherings, reopening of most public places, and crowded election rallies have been blamed for the sudden sharp rise in Covid cases (Al Jazeera, 2021). The government's handling of the two waves has been different. The second wave was primarily handled in a localised manner, driven by the state government. However, the centre was forced to intervene and announced a lockdown on 19 April 2021. The situation was finally brought under control by June 2021. Taking a cue from the second wave, several state governments have been creating new facilities to cope with an expected third wave (Sheriff M, 2021).

China

There are contradicting reports about the pandemic's origin date in China. The *South China Morning Post* traces the first case in China to 17 November 2019, while Chinese state media traces it to the end of December 2019. International media has widely criticised China over its attempt to cover up Covid outbreak in its initial weeks, including the crackdown on doctors who warned of the emergence of the virus in a seafood market at Wuhan city in Hubei Province. On 8 January 2020, a new coronavirus was identified as the cause of the pandemic, but it was only on 21 January 2020 that authorities conceded that there was a human-to-human transmission of the virus. By January end, Covid had spread to all provinces of mainland China (The Guardian, 2020b). Reports indicate a steep rise in Covid cases from January to March 2020. However, subsequently, China has seen only a marginal rise in confirmed cases, suggesting it has been able to restrict the rise in Covid cases since it lifted its lockdown in April 2020.

Stringent restrictions were in place in the early months of 2020; non-registered persons were denied access to residential flats and restaurants were closed. Large-scale temperature checks across the country were carried out, with Commands for Epidemic Control formed across different regions (Xinhua, 2021). A quarantine period of 14-day upon arrival at destination was imposed on domestic and international travel. Amidst all this, media outlets reported concerns of the Chinese government's deliberate under-reporting of the extent of infections and deaths (Kevin, 2020). By mid-February 2020, the government started to ease out mobility and activity restrictions and prioritised certain sectors, industries, regions, and population groups based on risk assessments. Most businesses and schools across China reopened with Covid protocols in place, and foreign entry remains restricted. Restrictions were re-imposed in new hotspots.

China's GDP suffered a 6.8 per cent decline during the first quarter of 2020 as certain sectors such as food and beverages and travel and tourism were worst hit and their employees laid off. SMEs have suffered the most as they are not financed by mainstream banks but through shadow banking system, out of the purview of central government bailouts. Migrant workers, particularly in the construction sector, were among the worst hit. However, reports suggest that nine months after the pandemic outbreak, China seems to have brought the situation largely under its control (Livermore, 2020). It has undertaken a host of measures to put the economy back on track. It allocated around RMB4.6 trillion amounting to 4.5 per cent of the GDP to fight the pandemic. It also introduced a smartphone-based app indicating the risk level faced in public places, as well as research based on mathematical models for contact tracing and identifying virus transmission. A new focus was on developing new diagnostics and methods with the support of artificial intelligence in the health sector (Hira and Pathreya, 2020).

The People's Bank of China undertook several measures to provide monetary policy support such as liquidity infusion into the banking system; re-lending and re-discounting facilities worth RMB1.8 trillion to support manufacturers of medical supplies and daily necessities, MSMEs, firms, and the agricultural sector; and credit line to private firms and MSMEs (RMB350 billion). Further measures include those to encourage lending to SMEs, postponement of loan payments, and tolerance for higher non-performing loans (IMF, 2020). China has been forced to restructure the debt obligations of other countries (it has given loans), mainly those arising from the $1trillion One Belt and One Road initiative (Campbell, 2020).

South Africa

The Covid pandemic grew rapidly in South Africa after its first confirmed case was reported on 5 March 2020. The government responded promptly, and the country was able to slow down the transmission rate by declaring a state of disaster, border closure, and enforcing lockdown on 27 March 2020. On 17 March 2020, the National Coronavirus Command Council was formed to check the spread of the disease and mitigate its negative impact. This was followed by a curfew and a ban on alcohol. The country was reopened on 1 May 2020 in a gradual and phased manner, and by 21 September 2020, almost all restrictions were removed with the pandemic brought under control.

There was a net capital outflow (bonds and equities) from South Africa amounting to 3.6 per cent of the GDP (since the beginning of the pandemic), while the Rand depreciated by about 15 per cent vis-à-vis the US dollar. On 27 July 2020, the International Monetary Fund (IMF) approved emergency assistance equivalent to US$4.3 billion. The South African government initiated a phase-wise response to revive its economy. In mid-March, it initiated several measures such as tax relief, disaster relief funds, and special programmes from the Industrial Development Corporation. A temporarily raised social grant amount was released to the most vulnerable families for a period of six months. Measures were introduced to ease liquidity, reduce policy rates, and facilitate banks to provide debt relief to borrowers. In April 2020, the South African president also announced a socio-economic support package of ZAR500 billion (almost 10 per cent of its GDP) to assist health support measures. Financial assistance and tax holidays were provided to the affected SMEs in sectors like tourism, hospitality, and livestock. The Africa Medical Supplies Portal was launched in June 2020 to enable all African countries to access critical medical supplies from across the globe at competitive prices (Tralac, 2020).

BRICS Co-operation in the Fight Against Covid

Amidst rising corona cases across the globe, the road ahead for BRICS nations as well as the organisation seems to be an uphill task. However, the pandemic has opened up new opportunities as well. The extent to which BRICS as a platform is able to collectively deliver in these testing times matters to all its five members. All five nations face similar issues and developmental challenges, and therefore, they have reliable allies in BRICS in a crisis situation. The platform can also serve as a valuable resource in terms of access to medicines, equipment, personnel, technology, and research. Equally important is the co-ordination among BRICS nations to present the group as a collective front to have an impact at the international level during any discussion or negotiation. BRICS needs to use this adversity as an opportunity to establish its credentials as a leader. However, rebellion within the group may lead to look out for new allies and coalition partners for outsiders.

Ever since Covid emerged, BRICS member states have expressed support for each other and stood in solidarity. However, the co-operation has been marred to some extent by the India–China stalemate following clashes between their troops in Galwan Valley in May 2020. BRICS nations have undertaken various co-ordination and co-operation efforts in their fight against Covid. BRICS nations have held various online conferences/meetings hosted by current chair Russia, a sign of their commitment to collective action and cooperation. Russia hosted the 12th BRICS Summit on 17 November 2020, primarily to step-up efforts for anti-pandemic co-operation. Moreover, BRICS nations have also made a direct contribution to the G20 comprehensive package aimed at countering the negative consequences of the pandemic (Huaxia, 2020). South Africa highlighted the trade disruptions and supply chain challenges and called for a 'New Global Deal' for reforms to address such issues. India stressed the need to promote digital health care and traditional medicines among BRICS nations (MEA, 2021).

Their co-operation and unity of purpose are clear from a statement issued at a meeting of BRICS Sherpas/Sous-Sherpas on 11 February 2020 chaired by Russia, where they stressed on avoiding discrimination, stigma, and overreaction in BRICS nations' response to the pandemic outbreak. At the outbreak of Covid in China, Russia supported China and provided humanitarian supplies, medicine, test kits, medical specialists, and so on to fight the pandemic. Similarly, India delivered emergency medical supplies to Wuhan through its military aircraft. On 7 May 2020, a virtual meeting of BRICS nations was organised by Russia's Health Ministry where they pledged to adopt collaborative steps to eradicate the pandemic (Kester, 2020). Sports Ministers of BRICS nations also held a virtual meeting on 25 August 2020 to assess the impact of the pandemic on sports and ways to revive it (ANI, 2020). Similarly, the National Security Advisors of BRICS nations met on 17 September 2020 via video link and discussed a wide range of issues, including bio-safety, anti-terrorism, and cyber security.

Leaders of intellectual property offices in BRICS nations held a conference on 26 August 2020 to discuss measures taken to mitigate the impact of the pandemic and the progress in granting patents to drugs meant to treat coronavirus. Similarly, a virtual meeting of the sixth BRICS communications ministers was held on 17 September 2020 to share technology initiatives at the governmental level to check the pandemic (Press Trust of India, 2020). On 24 August 2020, BRICS industry ministers held a video conference to boost co-operation in various areas, including 5G, artificial intelligence, digital economy, digital transformation of enterprises, and innovation capabilities during the Covid pandemic (The Economic Times, 2020).

As far as financial assistance during Covid is concerned, on 19 March 2020, BRICS' New Development Bank granted an emergency loan of RMB 7 billion mainly to assist China's worst-affected provinces of Hubei, Guangdong, and Henan in their fight against Covid. Subsequently, the NDB also disbursed US$1 billion emergency loans to India, South Africa, and Brazil to fight Covid. BRICS foreign ministers held a virtual meeting on 28 April 2020 and agreed to create a US$15 billion loan instrument to meet emergency expenses incurred in responding to the pandemic. Intra-bloc trade, which is also an important sign of co-operation and co-ordination among the member states, has shown positive signs despite the pandemic. Russian Foreign Minister Sergei Lavrov at an online ministerial-level meeting of BRICS said that trade among BRICS nations has risen by 45 per cent as compared to 2015 levels (Chakraborty, 2021). In another sign of BRICS collaboration, India has received 3 million doses of Sputnik V vaccine from Russia in June 2021 (Press Trust of India, 2021).

Disagreements and Disputes Within the BRICS

Alongside efforts to co-operate and collaborate on combating the pandemic, there have been signs of dissension as well as polarisation within the multilateral group. China has been blamed for secrecy and cover-up of the Covid, which finally led to its global spread. To make things worse, it has also been accused of manufacturing the virus as a biological weapon for economic and political gains. China has also allegedly tried to benefit from the pandemic by supplying substandard medicines and testing kits to several countries. Such allegations were circulated widely on informal social and vernacular media and had led to even BRICS members echoing the same sentiment or reacting to it. Brazil's minister of foreign affairs had warned that the virus was China's strategy to spread communism across the globe. Even the Indian Council of Medical Research was reported to have rejected imported Rapid Test Kits from China for being faulty. Thus, there was rising resentment against China, not a very good sign for BRICS as a multilateral group, coming to the fore (Kumar and De Conti, 2020).

The Indo-China stalemate has been another factor that has hindered intra-bloc co-operation. Tension between the two member states cropped up as a result of a deadly border skirmish in eastern Ladakh's Galwan Valley (June 2020) taking ties between the two neighbours to their lowest ebb. It has also fuelled anti-Chinese sentiment in India and resulted in actions such as a ban on all Chinese apps like TikTok, WeChat, and Helo. Calls for boycott of Chinese products could be heard from various quarters in India (The Indian Express, 2020). However, another BRICS member, Russia, has been successful to some extent in defusing tension between the two sides. Russia had facilitated a Sino-India meeting on the sidelines of the SCO meet in Moscow in early September 2020, which resulted in a five-point roadmap for de-escalation of tension along the Line of Actual Control (Hindustan Times, 2020).

These are positive moves, but insufficient to fight a global pandemic. China and India are the two largest economies in the multilateral grouping. Deteriorating ties between the two could significantly undermine the group's coherence and sway. Given that three other countries are also plagued by the pandemic, it is even more difficult for the BRICS to co-ordinate with each other to fight against the crisis.

BRICS must realise that the battle against Covid is likely to be long and protracted and the road to recovery quite challenging and arduous. Its members need to sort out their differences and restore trust, which seems to be lacking at the moment. They must also guard against any kind of Sinophobia and verify facts before resorting to any move that would leave the bloc in disarray. Its members need to refrain from resorting to restrictive trade practices to ensure fast revival of their economies. The New Development Bank and its contingency arrangements may be significant in bailing out economies in crisis, if utilised adequately. Nonetheless, it is also important for China to be considerate and avoid aggressive designs in its economic and security pursuits in order to restore confidence among other member states. This is important if BRICS wants to resolve issues within the group and emerge as a powerful grouping in the international arena (Rajan and De Conti, 2020).

Conclusion

The Covid pandemic has raised questions over the ability of nation states to fight emergencies like the corona pandemic. Be it superpowers like the United States or Britain, a substantial part of the globe is struggling to fight the pandemic's horrendous consequences. It is in this backdrop that the role of BRICS is significant as it comprises the world's two most-populated countries, with one being the source of origin of the lethal virus. On the positive side, BRICS seems to have taken the pandemic as a challenge and has been playing a significant role in handling the global crisis.

Once the corona crisis began in European countries like Italy, Russia was quick in flying medical supplies to Italy. It also dispatched a Russian aircraft, *Antonov-124*, full of medical supplies comprising PPE kits, masks, ventilators, and so on to New York on the request of the US president. Meanwhile, South Africa, the (then) chair of the African Union, was engaged in coordinating a pan-African response to Covid. India is already providing pharma assistance to over 150 countries, including many countries in Africa, to counter the pandemic. Even China under its Health Silk Road diplomacy has provided PPEs and test kits to hotspots across the world. Even though international institutions have been criticised for failing to adequately respond to the Covid pandemic, BRICS nations have been proactive in reaching out to hotspots across the globe and supporting them. Moreover, both India and South Africa backed by 62 other nations are trying to seek waiver on patent protections for Covid vaccines at the WTO. The nations also stressed on the transfer of technology and expansion of vaccine production capacity to fight the pandemic (Laskar, 2021).

The pandemic has also highlighted that member states need to expedite the implementation of the projects and decisions agreed upon. Apart from this, BRICS countries at its 13th summit in New Delhi pledged support to establish an early warning mechanism to detect the outbreak of infectious diseases. The member states have also agreed to work towards enhanced diagnostic and preventive techniques as well as conduct joint epidemiological exercises. BRICS' New Development Bank would provide the required financial support to its members in the fight against the pandemic (Kondratieva, 2020). Moreover, BRICS also needs to enhance its public health governance, make it a priority on the international agenda, and work together to build a community of health for all (Nilsen and Holdt, 2020).

References

AlJazeera. (2021). Rallies, religious gatherings aggravate India's worst COVID surge. www.aljazeera.com/news/2021/4/9/rallies-religious-gatherings-aggravate-indias-worst-covid-surge (last accessed October 20, 2021).

ANI. (2020). Impact of Covid-19 on sports discussed during meeting between BRICS sports ministers. Available at www.aninews.in/news/sports/others/impact-of-covid-19-on-sports-discussed-during-meeting-between-brics-sports-ministers20200825201611/ (last accessed November 15, 2020).

Breuninger, Kevin. (2020). China hid extent of coronavirus outbreak; US intelligence reportedly says. Available at www.cnbc.com/2020/04/01/coronavirus-china-gid-extent-of-outbreak-us-intelligence-reportedly-says.html (last accessed November 10, 2021).

California News Times. (2021). India sees record 4.14 lakh COVID-19 cases in 24 Hrs; Karnataka, Goa, Telangana Impose Fresh Curbs. Available at https://californianewstimes.com/india-sees-record-4-14-lakh-covid-19-cases-in-24-hrs-karnataka-goa-telangana-impose-fresh-curbs-india-news-firstpost/322661/ (last accessed October 10, 2021).

Campbell, Charlie. (2020). How can I get through this?' The impact of coronavirus on China's economy is only just beginning. Available at https://time.com/5824599/china-coronavirus-covid19-economy/ (last accessed September 10, 2021).

Chakraborty, Subhayan. (2021). Government focuses on ramping up trade with BRICS nations, barring China. Available at www.msn.com/en-in/money/topstories/exclusive-government-focuses-on-ramping-up-trade-with-brics-nations-barring-china/ar-AANxrYn (last accessed September 10, 2020).

The Economic Times (2020). China plans to Establish BRICS innovation base: Minister. Available at https://economictimes.indiatimes.com/news/international/world-news/china-plans-to-establish-brics-innovation-base-minister/articleshow/77743119.cms (last accessed December 10, 2020).

Hindustan Times. (2020). Virtual BRICS summit on Nov 17; PM Modi, Xi set for a face-off. Available at www.hindustantimes.com/india-news/brics-summit-to-be-held-virtually-on-nov-17-cooperation-strengthening-global-stability-on-genda/storyIo-02j2Xpb81KAx03C13O1M.html (last accessed December 10, 2021).

Hindustan Times. (2021). Serum Institute to begin Sputnik V vaccine production in September. Available at www.hindustantimes.com/india-news/serum-institute-to-begin-sputnik-v-vaccine-production-in-september-101626167092874.html (last accessed September 10, 2021).

Hira, Pathreya. (2020). Covid-19 learnings from China on reopening of the economy. Available at www.bloombergquint.com/coronavirus-outbreak/covid-19-learnings-from-china-on-reopening-the-economy (last accessed October 10, 2020).

Huaxia. (2020). Putin advocates more BRICS cooperation to fight pandemic. www.xinhuanet.com/english/2020-11/17/c_139523096.htm (last accessed on 10 November 2021).

IMF Country Focus Brazil. (2021). Sustaining a strong recovery. Available at www.imf.org/en/News/Articles/2021/09/22/na092221-brazil-sustaining-a-strong-recovery (last accessed October 10, 2021).

IMF. (2020). Policy response to Covid-19. Available at www.imf.org/en/Topics/imf-and-covid19/Policy-Responses-to-COVID-19#B (last accessed September 02, 2020).

India TV. (2021). Consignment of 3 million Doses of Sputnik V Vaccine from Russia Land in Hyderabad 2021. Available at www.indiatvnews.com/news/india/sputnik-v-vaccine-3-million-doses-consignment-land-in-hyderabad-from-russia-708459 (last accessed November 10, 2021).

Joseph, K. Arun. (2021). What is the State of India's vaccination program as of May 2021?' Available at https://carnegieindia.org/2021/05/19/what-is-happening-to-india-s-covid-19-vaccine-program-pub-84570 (last accessed September 15, 2021).

Khan, I. Mohd. (2020). COVID-19 lockdown a blessing for the Endangered Gangetic Dolphin in Bihar: Experts. Available at www.downtoearth.org.in/news/wildlife-biodiversity/covid-19-lockdown-a-blessing-for-the-endangered-gangetic-dolphin-in-bihar-experts-70470 (last accessed October 10, 2021).

Klomegah, K. Kester. (2020). Covid -19 hits hard, but challenges BRICS. *Modern Diplomacy*. Available at https://moderndiplomacy.eu/2020/05/23/covid-19-hits-hard-but-challenges-brics/ (last accessed August 10, 2021).

Kondratieva, Ksenia. (2020). For BRICS, challenges and opportunities. *The Hindu*. Available at www.thehindu.com/news/international/for-brics-challenges-and-opportunities/article (last accessed November 10, 2020).

KPMG, Russia. (2020). Government and institution measures in response to COVID-19. Available at https://home.kpmg/xx/en/home/insights/2020/04/russia-government-and-institution-measures-in-response-to-covid.html (last accessed August 05, 2021).

Kumar and De Conti. (2020). Combating the coronavirus pandemic: The BRICS must step in and lead from the front. *Financial Express*. Available at www.financialexpress.com/defence/combating-the-coronavirus-pandemic-the-brics-must-step-in-and-lead-from-the-front/1944584/ (last accessed on September 10, 2020).

Laskar, H. Rezaul. (2021). At BRICS foreign ministers meet, focus on Covid-19 pandemic, access to vaccines. *Hindustan Times*. Available at www.hindustantimes.com/india-news/at-brics-foreign-ministers-meet-focus-on-covid-19-pandemic-access-to-vaccines-101622554080380.html (last accessed November 10, 2021).

Livermore, Adam. (2020). The social and economic impact of COVID-19 on China and its recovery potential. Available at www.china-briefing.com/news/social-economic-impact-covid-19-china-recovery-potential/ (last accessed November 10, 2020).

McGeever, Jamie. (2021). Brazil GDP drops 4.1% in 2020, COVID-19 surge erodes rebound. Available at www.reuters.com/article/us-brazil-economy-gdp-idUSKBN2AV1FZ (last accessed April 15, 2021).

Melkadze, A. (2021). FMCG sales growth in Russia 2019–2020, by sales channel. Available at www.statista.com/statistics/1207385/fmcg-sales-growth-in-russia-by-sales-channel/ (last accessed September 10, 2021).

Ministry of External Affairs, Government of India. (2021). 12th BRICS summit calls for global stability and shared security. 2020. Available at https://indbiz.gov.in/12th-brics-summit-calls-for-global-stability-and-shared-security/ (last accessed September 15, 2021).

Ministry of Finance. (2020). Finance Minister announces several relief measures relating to Statutory and Regulatory compliance matters across sectors in view of COVID-19 outbreak. Available at https://pib.gov.in/PressReleaseIframePage.aspx?PRID=1607942 (last accessed October 10, 2020).

Nilsen A. G. and Holdt K. V. (2020). BRICS and COVID: Rising powers in a time of pandemic. Available at https://thewire.in/world/brics-and-covid-rising-powers-in-a-time-of-pandemic (last accessed November 10, 2020).

Ostroukh, Andrey. (2021). Russia's economic recovery faces COVID-19, inflation. Available at www.reuters.com/article/us-russia-economy-outlook-idUSKCN2EB0W7 (last accessed November 10, 2020).

Press Trust of India. (2020). BRICS Communications Ministers' meet: Dhotre shares India's. Available at http://timesofindia.indiatimes.com/articleshow/78174269.cms?utm_source= m_ contentofinterest&utmedium=text&utm_campaign=cppst (last accessed December 2021).

Press Trust of India. (2021). RBI announces liquidity measures for sectors hit hard by COVID-19. *Financial Express*. Available at https://www.financialexpress.com/industry/rbi-announces-liquidity-measures-for-sectors-hit-hard-by-covid-19/2265212/ (last accessed December 2021).

Rajan & De Conti. (2020). Combating the coronavirus pandemic: The BRICS must step in and lead from the front. *Financial Express*. Available at www.financialexpress.com/ defence/combating-the-coronavirus-pandemic-the-brics-must-step-in-and-lead-from-the-front/1944584/ (last accessed on September 10, 2020).

Sen, Meghna. (2021). Black Fungus: These 5 states account for over 65% of India's 11,717 mucormycosis cases. Available at www.livemint.com/news/india/black-fungus-these-5-states-account-for-60-of-india-s-11–700-mucormycosis-cases-11622018575067.html (last accessed October 14, 2021).

Sheriff, M. Kaunain. (2021). Readying for third wave, govt plans most pediatric O2 Beds in 6 States. Available at https://indianexpress.com/article/india/readying-for-third-wave-govt-plans-most-paediatric-o2-beds-in-6-states-7452913/ (last accessed November 10, 2021).

Statista Research Department. (2020). Coronavirus in Russia statistics & facts. Available at www.statista.com/topics/6205/coronavirus-covid-19-in-russia/ (last accessed November 20, 2021).

The Associated Press. (2020). AP report raises concerns about China and WHO; China denies. Available at pnews.com/article/understanding-the-outbreak-united-nations-public-health-health-virus-outbreak-3937a18aa4f0ccbe69b82907640c792f (last accessed December 2020).

The Guardian. (2020a). 'We're being left behind': anger and confusion in Brazil as vaccine program lags. Available at https://www.theguardian.com/world/2020/dec/31/brazil-coronavirus-vaccine-jair-bolsonaro (last accessed September 2021)

The Guardian. (2020b). First Covid-19 case happened in November; China government records show – Report. Available at www.theguardian.com/world/2020/mar/13/first-covid-19-case-happened-in-november-china-government-records-show-report (last accessed June 15, 2021).

The Hindu. (2021). Moody's revises India's 2020-21 GDP contraction to 10.6%. Available at https://www.thehindu.com/business/Economy/moodys-revises-indias-2020-21-gdp-contraction-to-106/article33131396.ece (last accessed February 2022).

The Indian Express. (2020). PUBG Mobile, 117 Chinese apps banned in India. Available at https://indianexpress.com/article/technology/tech-news-technology/india-bans-pubg-mobile-116-chinese-apps-full-list-6580365/ (last accessed November 10, 2020).

The Times of India. (2021). Centre announces tax concessions on money received for covid treatment. Available at http://timesofindia.indiatimes.com/articleshow/83842271. cms?utm_source=contentofinterest&utm_medium=text&utm_campaign=cppst (last accessed October 15, 2021).

Tralac. (2020). South Africa's policy response to the COVID-19 pandemic. Available at www.tralac.org/news/article/14617-south-africa-s-policy-response-to-the-covid-19-pandemic.html (last accessed August 10, 2021).

Worldometer. (2020). Coronavirus. Available at www.worldometers.info/coronavirus/ country/india/, (last accessed September 15, 2020).

Xinhua. (2021). Fighting Covid-19 China in action. Available at www.xinhuanet.com/ english/202006/07/c _139120424.htm (last accessed September 15, 2021).

18

BRICS

A Study of Its Cooperation and Challenges

Aparaajita Pandey and Huma Siddiqui

BRICS is a novel and unique grouping of diverse nations. It is not a regional grouping like the EU or the ASEAN. Nor is it a commodity-based club like the OPEC, or a security-centric formation such as NATO. What brings together its members is the joint strategic will of BRICS countries to reshape the world order and engage with others in their quest for inclusive growth and sustainable solutions.

The Origin

BRICS is clearly distinct from other international entities. Generally, such organisations are born out of a need for greater political stability, economic progress, collective security, trade and/or administrative and governmental interactions. However, unlike these conventional forms of international groupings, generally tinkered and cobbled through diplomacy, the idea of BRICS germinated in 2001 in the chambers of the Goldman Sachs' chief economist Jim O' Neill. O'Neill coined the term BRIC, since he was inspired by the idea that Brazil, Russia, India, and China genuinely had great economic potential and that their growth trajectories were so strong that they would eventually outdo economies that have traditionally held the top positions in the world. Although the RIC or the Russia-India-China group already existed as a precedent to nation states coming together with an agenda to reshape the world order among other things, BRICS still is an organisation of its own kind and a key role in its formation was played by the prophesied trajectory of the economic growth of the member countries. However, many still doubted the future and the relevance of the organisation. It is imperative to keep in mind that from the very beginning this idea, of BRICS was not believed to be an organisation of much consequence. It was a group of countries whose economies were supposedly on an upward surge. Thus, these could serve as great markets for investors.

DOI: 10.4324/9781003148074-21

Brazil, Russia, India, and China were just countries that were capriciously congregated together in the files of an economic brief. These were predicted to achieve growth rates that were robust enough to ensure that they surpassed the six of the largest economies of the West by the year 2041. The predictions were later twice revised to reach that goal – first to 2039 and then to an even earlier date; that of 2032. To predict growth for decades on the basis of present economic trends and believing that the trends and their direction would remain unchanged and unhindered is unheard of and would not be considered sound evaluation by any parameters of conventional research.

It is also important to note that since Jim O' Neill was an economist, he did not concern himself with the political dimensions of BRICS. Nor was he burdened by the necessity of giving BRICS organisational value for ease of evaluation by political scientists. The shift that global politics and economics was experiencing during the first decade of the twenty-first century could be attributed to the long-term ramifications of the transformation first from a bipolar to a unipolar world, and later to the rise of alternatives to unipolarity. The shift in the global order in the repercussion of the decline of the erstwhile Soviet Union led to conditions for economic growth for countries that had until then been burdened by the global operating systems dictated by the terms of the Cold War. The beginning of the decade of the 1990s gave most of the world an opportunity to emerge out of the shadows of the two global superpowers and build themselves to become contributing members to global supply chains (Newman 2020).

The term BRICS was scoffed at by most in the beginning. Charles Dumas, a London based economist had opined that the term carried no real significance and was at best a marketing gimmick. He saw it as being hyped for profit. According to others equally or more cynical of the concept of BRICS, the term was a profit-driven campaign for one of the largest firms in the world. But Jim O'Neill stated that the concept of BRICS was not just an economic projection but a reflection of his faith that the conventional economic frameworks of the world that were driven by and vested in the proverbial West or the global North were beginning to shift to other poles around the planet that had emerged and grown since the advent of globalisation.

Open economies and a renewed or general acceptance of capitalistic or neo-liberal policies started proving to be extremely beneficial to those with an inherent economic advantage. These included developed economies and large multinational corporations. At the same time, it also allowed other nations to rebuild or build their economic prowess. They moved to either develop manufacturing capabilities, or a service sector, or provide cheap labour in the open market. Besides these, many countries also took to serving as both markets and a raw material base for bigger economies. By no means does this indicate any economic benevolence and/or egalitarianism as a result of the process of globalisation. However, the process did play a role in the rise of alternatives to conventional Western economies. The Russia, India, China grouping or RIC was one such formation before the BRICS. Both organisations are akin to each other in the context of their functions and ambitions. RIC, however, is a regionally coherent organisation. Although BRICS emerged later, it does share some of its core philosophy with the RIC. They are both organisations that have an agenda and the potential to counterbalance the Western alliance. The countries involved in RIC and BRICS command huge chunks of the global economy as well as population (Kapoor 2020).

BRICS, however, is more than a strategic organisation. It was built in the backdrop of the 9/11 attacks. It got a further push with the global financial crisis that hit the world in 2008. Both events were not only of global significance but also emblematic of a need for change. The West has always dictated the global order, which is still largely tilted towards it. However, a need was felt in the 2000s for an alternative to the traditional global order. BRICS, formerly BRIC, was seen as the manifestation of the need for a new order. Brazil, Russia, India, China and South Africa are the five leading emerging powers that are spread over the continents of Asia, Africa and Latin America. These countries are consistently and incrementally rewriting the rules of global engagement and savouring their collective economic and diplomatic heft to recast the international landscape.

What started as a new pole of opportunity for global investors looking to plough their money in emerging markets has now morphed into a formidable multilateral grouping marked by a striking convergence of interests on a range of global issues. This meant that the BRICS nations were not intrinsically captives of the constraints of geography. Nor did the member countries need similarity in their political frameworks, or multilateral or, in some cases, bilateral co-operation (Dresen 2011). Its emblematic of colossal shift of power from the north to the south and from the west to the east.

A group that had the bare minimum in common and was conceived of in an investor's brief rather than out of any significant political movement or economic consensus has surprisingly withstood the test of time so far. Its survival and growth signify the fact that diverse countries can come together and find paths towards collective functioning despite their traditional disputes.

The Evolution

Although the term BRIC was coined in 2001, it took a few years before the term picked up currency. The term first took off in academic circles and universities. As these started offering electives on BRIC, and investment forums devised portfolios for the BRIC grouping, the associated countries began to perceive it as a tangible opportunity to co-operate and gain collective bargaining power in a world unfairly tilted towards the West (Purshottam 2018).

In the year 2008, the world was hit by the Lehman Brothers crisis in the US banking. Soon it overtook and rocked most open economies the world over. Yet countries like India, China, and most Latin American nations showed surprising economic resilience in the face of the crash. It crippled not just the American economy but also the economies and the banking sector through most of Western Europe. On the margins of the G8 meeting in 2008, the leaders of China, India, and Russia met each other. Hu Jintao, Manmohan Singh, and Medvedev, who then headed their respective countries, met in St. Petersburg as the city hosted the G8 summit.

The following year the first summit of BRIC leaders took place in the Russian city of Yekaterinburg. The summit included the original four nations and their leaders – Hu Jintao, Dmitry Medvedev, Lula Ignacio de Silva, and Dr Manmohan Singh. The countries and their leaders recognised that the formation of a forum like BRIC could turn out to be a great opportunity not just in the economic context but also as an opportunity for South–South co-operation.

In 2010, a meeting of the foreign ministers of the original four participating nations took place and it was unanimously decided that an invitation to South Africa must be sent. By the 2011 summit, BRIC had transformed to BRICS with South Africa becoming an integral part of the group. It is important to note that Brazil, India, and South Africa were already part of another trilateral forum called IBSA. Like BRICS, the acronym is derived from the names of its member nations (Dresen 2011).

The term BRICS came to denote not only the names of its member nations as was originally intended but also of emerging markets around the world. Its transcontinental character liberates it from the proverbial 'tyranny of geography', a phrase that is becoming less and less significant with each minute, courtesy the advent of newer and more advanced technology to facilitate real-time communication.

However, its lack of clarity regarding a common thread other than the newfound status of its member countries as emerging markets continues to be an unwavering trend. There are certainly more differences than commonalities between these nations with regard to their polity and economy. The member states have also never tried to hide these differences. China and Russia are the two members of the group that enjoy the status of permanent members of the Security Council. Their status as a member of the P-5 in the council definitively gives both a qualitatively larger role in global governance than Brazil, India, and South Africa.

The differences do not end here as China and Russia, right from the time of Hu Jintao and Dimitri Medvedev to Xi Jinping and Vladimir Putin, represent authoritarian structures of power. Against this, Brazil, India, and South Africa have been democracies for long. Although one could argue about the changes that democracy in Brazil and India has of late been undergoing, they are democracies nonetheless (Kapoor 2020).

An evaluation of the Joint Communiques issued at the BRICS Summits highlights the fact that the main idea behind BRICS was to underline and draw the world's attention to emerging markets with huge potential. This made these countries ideal destinations for investment. BRICS also began to focus its attention on initiating discourse and discussion towards the need for greater egalitarianism in global governance. It was an ambition quite clearly recognisable from the discourse around BRICS. This hung on the premise that the multilateral forum for emerging markets deserved to have a greater voice in global governance. The Joint Statement issued at the BRIC summit in 2009 amid the aftershocks of the 2008 economic crisis revolved around the primacy of a co-ordinated financial policy. As per the statement, the economic crisis of 2008 was an event that had an impact on economies around the world and its adverse repercussions were not isolated; therefore, a need was felt to collectively combat the crisis. Such emphasis on collective action was not only symptomatic of a thought process that believed in composite response but also of a new worldview that saw all players as being equally important and welcome at the high table (Li Li 2019).

The communiques also reiterated the need to create an environment that facilitated 'greater voice and representation', especially from countries identified as emerging economies. These included not only the BRICS nations but also several mentioned in the N-11[1] grouping. BRICS also emphasised the need for greater transparency in global governance including in the process of selecting the leadership of world forums.

The statements often targeted the leadership traditions of the World Bank and the IMF. Usually, the President of the World Bank tends to be of American origin and the Managing Director of the International Monetary Fund (IMF) happens to be European. It has been noticed since the very beginning of these institutions that their voting and quota shares are tilted towards the Western economies. This anomaly was also pointed out in the communiques. In essence, these statements became a means of highlighting the glaring tendency of world systems to favour Western economies.

Yet there is an obvious and undeniable difference in the status and role of China and Russia vis-à-vis India, Brazil, and South Africa. This is more so when it comes to global governance. This difference, as mentioned earlier, is due to the permanent status of China and Russia in the Security Council. In 2011, the Joint Statement mentioned China and Russia's reiteration of the importance they attached to the status of Brazil, India, and South Africa in the broader arena of international affairs. The two powers acknowledged the aspirations of the three BRICS partner nations to play a greater role in the United Nations. Although such an endorsement had its significance, the rhetoric did not translate into action at the United Nations. This was so courtesy both China and Russia (Stuenkel 2014).

The dragging of feet by Russia and China at the UN did not go unnoticed. Yet it could not hamper the growth of BRICS as a bloc. It has also been emphasised by BRICS that their collective strength in world politics and economics remains unmatched. Thus, these countries tried to summon greater strength and a higher degree of legitimacy via BRICS on the world stage. The 2012 BRICS Summit was held in New Delhi and the joint statement of the year went on to highlight the fact that approximately forty-three per cent of the world's population resided in the BRICS nations. It was not just a mere statement of fact but a bid to gain greater legitimacy and representation at the global level than has traditionally been the case.

BRICS, since its commencement, has gradually but consistently extended its diplomatic engagements. It initiated with the annual meeting of heads of states and finance ministers. Since the focus behind its beginning was economic in nature, greater co-ordination and co-operation among the economies was an organic development. However, the augmentation of BRICS' diplomatic activities now comprises not only co-ordinated policy positions but also larger people-to-people contact and dialogue. This is notwithstanding the fact that the issues under discussion and the discourse in general are cautiously fashioned so to circumvent any possible conflict (Cheng et al. 2007).

The annual summit diplomacy that was limited to conformist track one dialogue has now been expanded to include specialists from various fields. It is not unusual to find the governors of central banks, national security advisors, ministers of science and technology, those from the agriculture ministry, disaster response authorities, environment ministers, health ministers, labour ministers, and heads of think tanks, members of parliaments, prominent industrialists, and members of chambers of commerce taking part in BRICS Summits. This culture of inclusivity is not just a measured expansion of ties but also an acknowledgement of the fact that there is greater cohesions between BRICS nations than was formerly thought. It also reiterates the belief of the nations that common solutions and co-ordinated public policy would produce better outcomes for those involved in the decision-making process.

As BRICS was making headway in becoming the voice of those who often went unheard on the world's stage, it also provided the world an alternative to the conventional global political economy. The BRICS New Development Bank (NDB) was established in 2014 in Fortaleza, Brazil. The bank was introduced and established along with a Contingent Reserve Arrangement. This institution came to life once it became clear that the proposed reforms in IMF and the World Bank were a distant dream. The NDB was not just supposed to be an economic oasis for the members of BRICS but also a beacon of change and a shift from dependence on the IMF and World Bank for economic assistance (Stuenkel 2014).

The NDB is operational, with the five member countries contributing equally to the initial subscribed capital of US $ 50 billion. This equality in the initial share also gave each of the countries an equal voice in the bank. This is so despite the size of their economies being vastly different. Along with the NDB, a Contingent Reserve Arrangement worth USD100 billion was also established in 2014. The Contingent Reserve Arrangement, as the name suggests, is meant to provide immediate assistance in times of a liquidity crisis. Past experiences of member countries indebted to the IMF made the need for an alternative to the IMF. Brazil famously witnessed and, to an, experienced Latin America's 'lost decade' of the 1980s. Much of this unfortunate part of the world was made to sacrifice its sovereign pride and economic growth at the altar of strict austerity measures imposed by the IMF (Singh 2013).

The NDB and, more importantly, the Contingency Reserve Agreement do not just focus on being alternatives to the IMF and the World Bank. The two also function in a manner that facilitates economic growth without giving rise to domestic political challenges. There have often been comparisons between the NDB and China-led Asian Infrastructure Investment Bank (AIIB). As compared to the NDB, the AIIB was considered more durable. The exponential growth of the Chinese economy and the amplification of its position and influence in global politics was perhaps the reason for such a perception. The comparison between the NBD and the AIIB is perhaps not fair though it may look unavoidable. While the NBD was born out of the BRICS agenda to provide a substitute for the IMF and the World Bank and to offset traditional economic patterns, the AIIB is part of the greater Chinese strategy not just challenging the existing global economic order but also of expanding its geopolitical influence.

In the recent past, the BRICS has attained a clear strategic hue. The five countries have come to hold joint positions on global issues of importance like the nuclear issue in Iran, the continuing humanitarian crisis in Syria and the turmoil in Mali and West Africa. The annual conclave of national security advisers of BRICS countries has turned into a veritable forum for evolving common positions on numerous kinds of security threats that confront different parts of the world. The broad areas, narrowed down for BRICS co-operation, are counter-terrorism, maritime security and cyber security (Chand 2010).

Besides the economic and geopolitical issues faced by BRICS nations, it has evolved a mechanism of interactions that cover as many as 20 areas that relate, directly or indirectly, to the lives of over three billion people living in the member countries. Now BRICS countries co-operate in areas like education, health, disaster management, urbanisation, and science and technology, besides having partnerships in research and innovation. Experts from the BRICS countries, besides their ministers and officials dealing in myriad areas, regularly meet for meaningful interactions to exchange ideas and weigh fresh initiatives (ibid).

Although BRICS has been quite cohesive, it would be fallacious to assume that there are no disputes between the member nations. The BRICS members for long have been thought to be incongruent. China's economy is much larger than that of other members; it has been assessed that the Chinese economy is approximately thirty-nine times the size of the South African economy. The Russian and Chinese status as permanent members of the UN Security Council gives them a greater share in decision making and global governance. At the same time, their lack of initiative and support on the question of reforming in the council in the context of increasing its membership has on no occasion been condoned by the other member countries.

Besides this, there are other problems between the member countries. The border dispute between India and China as well as the Sino-Indian dynamics regarding Pakistan are a constant bone of contention between the two neighbouring countries. Yet the two have found a way to circumnavigate their differences with regards to BRICS and carry the association under it so far.

Challenges of BRICS

Berating BRICS as a decrepit forum that is irrelevant and redundant has become an annual ritual for economists and journalists alike. Predictions of its demise and suggestions for its disintegration are usually served with the BRICS Summit and 2020 was no different. Sadanand Dhume (2020) of the Wall Street Journal was quick to point out the 'the five- member club makes less sense than ever' and recommended that 'instead of building up BRICS, India should help dismantle it'.

Such comments are neither new nor particularly scathing. In 2011, or a decade or so ago, it was Philip Stevens of the Financial Times, who had announced that it was 'time to bid farewell to BRICS'. Those who do not perceive BRICS as unnecessary tend to focus on the geopolitical and economic realities of the nations and often point to the inevitable demise of the association. However, BRICS has shown great strength and tenacity and even growth in the face of opposition. The growth is not just in spreading the agenda of an alternative to traditional global politico-economic institutions but also expanding its diplomatic agenda as well as establishing NDB.

While these are not insignificant, an unforeseen consequence of the perseverance of BRICS has been the reaction of far-right and conservative governments to it as well as a perceptible change not only in their rhetoric but also in their attitude towards BRICS. Stuenkel (2020) discusses the transformation in the response of the Brazilian premier towards BRICS. Fuchs once called Jair Bolsonaro, the admittedly far- right Brazilian President, the proverbial bull in a China shop in the context of BRICS (2019). Bolsonaro, who has vehemently opposed multilateral engagements, soon reformed not only his rhetoric but also his policy and supported the group's commitment to continuous institutionalisation.

Moreover, it can be argued that differences between the BRICS nations are at times disproportionately played up. This conveniently overlooks the factors that unite them, their status as emerging economies, their perseverance in ensuring the growth of BRICS and the fact that three out of five countries want reform in the United Nations Security Council, and all five of them explicitly advocate it.

Bolsonaro also highlights the fact that EU, NATO and/or the G7 are not questioned despite disagreements between their member states. The existence of disagreements does not necessarily end in the dismantling of a group. The BRICS countries have shown tremendous economic growth; even though their growth rates have differed, their economic growth is undeniable. BRICS could also play a role in stabilising bilateral ties. It is reflected in Bolsonaro giving up his anti-China rhetoric and the adoption of a more pragmatic approach during the eleventh BRICS Summit that was held in 2019 in Brazil. The grouping has also brought India and China to the table despite the escalation of tensions at their borders.

BRICS also provides the member nations with legitimacy not only on the world stage but also in domestic politics. The diplomatic victories that BRICS provides along with global recognition become great campaign material and are often used by leaders during their election campaigns. Hosting the BRICS Summit in 2019 was a pivotal moment for the Bolsonaro administration. The Russian online BRICS Summit a year later amidst the restrictions of the pandemic followed a similar pattern of glorification of the regime's capabilities.

Conclusion

It is important to recognise that while BRICS seems like a grouping that could dissipate at any moment, it has exhibited tremendous resilience since 2008. The forum is not just significant to its members as a framework for South–South co-operation and an economic security network but is also an alternative to most traditional options of political and economic associations. It indicates the rise of a multipolar world that is prepared to challenge conventions. It is emblematic of a global system that might eventually be more egalitarian in nature. BRICS is essential for the perpetuation of an alternative narrative to the existence of multiple global systems.

Notes

1 The N 11 members were Bangladesh, Egypt, Indonesia, Iran, Mexico, Nigeria, Pakistan, the Philippines, Turkey, South Korea, and Vietnam.

References

Cheng, H., Gutierrez, M., Mahajan, A., Shachmurove, Y. and Shahrokhi, M. 2007. A Future Global Economy to be Built by BRICs. *Global Finance Journal*, Vol. 18(2):143–156.

Dhume, S. 2020. Sadanand Dhume – News, Articles, Biography, Photos – WSJ.Com. *WSJ*. <www.wsj.com/news/author/sadanand-dhume> [Accessed 14 December 2020].

Dresen, Joseph. 2011. BRICS: Shaping the New Global Architecture. *Wilson Center*. <www.wilsoncenter.org/publication/brics-shaping-the-new-global-architecture>, [Accessed on 03 March 2021].

Kapoor, N. 2020. Russia's BRICS Chairmanship: The 2020 Summit and Challenges Ahead | *ORF*. <www.orfonline.org/expert-speak/russia-brics-chairmanship-2020-summit-challenges-ahead/> [Accessed 14 December 2020].

Li Li. 2019. BRICS: A Limited Role in Transforming the World. *Strategic Analysis,* Vol. 43(6):499–508. DOI: 10.1080/09700161.2019.1677017.

Newman, Catherine. Jim O' Neill Created BRICS: What does he Think Two Decades On? 18 November 2020, CGTN. Available at: <https://newseu.cgtn.com/news/2020-11-18/Jim-O-Neill-created-the-term-BRICS-What-does-he-think-two-decades-on–VuS1f56FcQ/index.html#:~:text=CGTN%20Europe%20spoke%20to%20Jim,2010%2C%20to%20include%20South%20Africa.> [Accessed on 16 February 2021].

Purshottam, Uma. 2018. Why RIC is as Important to India as JAI and BRICS, ORF. [online] *ORF*. <www.orfonline.org/expert-speak/why-ric-is-as-important-to-india-as-jai-and-brics-46213/> [Accessed 21 February 2021].

Singh, S. 2013. Future of Golden BRICS. *Strategic Analysis*, Vol. 37(4):393–397.

Stuenkel, O. 2014. Emerging Powers and Status: The Case of the First BRICs Summit. *Asian Perspective*, Vol. 38(1):89–109.

Stuenkel, O. 2020. Why The BRICS Grouping is Here to Stay. [online] *Thediplomat.com*. <https://thediplomat.com/2020/11/why-the-brics-grouping-is-here-to-stay/> [Accessed 14 December 2020].

19

BRICS, DEVELOPMENT-AID AND DISASTER-AID MANAGEMENT

A Framework for Cooperation in Disaster Management

Himanshu Shekhar Mishra

Introduction

The worst public health disaster in the world since the Spanish Flu pandemic of 1918–1919, the COVID-19 pandemic has exposed the fault lines in the existing public health management systems worldwide. It has brought to fore the inherent structural weaknesses in the public health management strategy of the most developed countries in the world, as it has caused maximum damage to life and economy in nations with the most advanced healthcare infrastructure like the United States, the United Kingdom and Italy. In fact, the spread of the coronavirus pandemic from Wuhan, China, to almost every part of the world has also raised fundamental questions about the efficacy of existing global health surveillance mechanisms for monitoring the spread of epidemic-prone infectious diseases beyond national boundaries. This has made it imperative for the global community to put in place a new institutional disaster management framework to combat such a pandemic in future. This is especially significant for BRICS since all the five member countries – India, Brazil, Russia, South Africa and China – have figured among the worst COVID-19 affected countries in the world at different stages/waves of the deadly pandemic.

The World Health Organization data show the number of COVID-19 infected people within BRICS member countries had crossed a staggering figure of 14.2 million by the second week of October 2020, confirming their high degree of vulnerability to the pandemic, with India accounting for around half of the total number of cases within BRICS (1). To combat such a public health disaster incident in future, BRICS urgently needs to collectively formulate a cooperative disaster management framework to initiate institutional measures within BRICS member countries to strengthen their collective ability to combat this challenge. In fact, the BRICS member states have shown a very high level of vulnerability to

DOI: 10.4324/9781003148074-22

many types of disasters in recent decades, apart from the COVID-19 pandemic. It is significant to note that BRICS member states have reported a gradual increase in the number of climate-related disasters within BRICS member states, which is increasingly threatening both human life and development processes. A study by the United Nations Office for Disaster Risk Reduction (UNDRR) and the Centre for Research on the Epidemiology of Disasters (CRED) has found that the frequency of disaster events rose in China from 248 in 1996–2005 to 306 in 2006–2015. India too witnessed a sharp rise in the number of incidents of floods from 67 in 1996–2005 to 90 in 2006–2015 (2). China and India figured among the five worst disaster-affected countries in the world in terms of the number of people affected and killed in disasters in 2018. Both the countries suffered from 22 disaster incidents each in 2018 of the total 315 disaster incidents recorded worldwide. India was the worst-affected country in the world with 22 disasters affecting lives of 23.2 million peoples, which accounted for 35% of the total 68-million people affected worldwide (3). The flash floods in Kerala in August 2018 was the largest flood event of the year in the world; it killed 504 people, and two-thirds of the state's population was affected.

These figures consequently translate into egregiously high human cost of disasters. Three of the BRICS member countries – China, India and Russia – figure in the global list of ten worst disaster-affected countries in the world between 1996 and 2015. As per the official estimates, China alone lost 123,937 people, while India lost 97,691 precious lives in disaster incidents in these two decades alone (4). Russia has suffered the most from extreme weather incidents. According to data compiled by CRED and UNDRR, a total of 55,736 Russians died due to a severe spell of heat wave between June and August in 2010. It is widely considered one of the deadliest disasters in the last two decades (5). The World Bank has estimated that weather-related disasters cost the Russian economy anywhere between USD1 billion to USD2 billion every year. Russia is especially vulnerable to the impact of climate change and weather-related disasters in the Far East, Siberia and Southern Russia. Brazil too is struggling to cope with the impact of climate change. The drought in Brazil affected 27 million people and caused losses up to USD5 billion in 2014 alone (6). As per the data analysed by the Global Facility for Disaster Reduction and Recovery, Brazil's average annual losses caused by disasters are estimated at USD3.9 billion with poor being the most vulnerable (7).

In the wake of the rising threat posed by disasters, this chapter highlights the urgent need among the BRICS member states to develop a cooperative disaster management framework and offers a future roadmap for an institutionalised collaborative effort in this regard. BRICS also has the potential to play a significant role in disaster-aid management in high disaster-prone zones of the world. The chapter offers a new perspective on how BRICS can leverage its position in global political arena by weaving a disaster-aid management component in its larger development-aid objectives in the global arena. It also attempts to address the concerns and apprehensions states have with regard to accepting 'foreign aid' during a disaster. It offers an 'autonomy-respecting' development assistance model developed by ASEAN countries. The 'ASEAN Agreement' lays down a mutually agreed framework for member states to provide 'disaster aid' in a disaster-hit zone within the ASEAN region. The chapter studies the broad contours of the 'ASEAN Agreement' to understand how BRICS can develop its own framework to supply disaster-aid while protecting the sovereign rights of the member states.

The basic empirical facts used in this chapter have been drawn from research documents and published reports of UNDRR, CRED, Emergency Events Database (EM-DAT), the Internal Displacement Monitoring Centre (Norwegian Refugee Council) and the World Health Organization (WHO). It also draws important empirical facts from official reports tabled in the Indian Parliament by the Parliamentary Standing Committee on Home Affairs and Water Resources respectively on disasters and post-disaster reconstruction and rehabilitation work in disaster-hit zones. Official documents of the Ministry of Home Affairs and the Ministry of External Affairs, research reports of the re-insurance agency Aon Benfield Analytics and documents accessed from the New Development Bank and ASEAN Secretariat have also been analysed and discussed.

Disaster Aid as a 'Soft Power' Tool

As BRICS takes the next step towards increasing its influence in the global arena, it urgently needs to formulate development-aid strategies which are viable and have the potential to transform the global aid landscape and make them more pluralistic and equitable. BRICS member states should create new structures for utilising development-aid as a 'soft power' tool to transfer their respective experiences in disaster management to the emerging market economies and under-developed countries. BRICS should weave this idea in its larger development-aid strategy, both within BRICS and outside. Major disaster incidents in recent years have exposed the limitations of traditional global institutions of governance in carrying out effective rescue, relief and rehabilitation measures. Significant gaps exist in the response mechanism of global institutions and governance structures to disaster incidents; it makes it incumbent for BRICS to intervene and occupy this space by facilitating financial and material aid in disaster-affected zones, especially for post-disaster reconstruction and rehabilitation work.

In recent years, major disasters on the African continent have caused huge losses to human life and property and also highlighted the inability of African states to launch effective relief and rescue operations. These disasters have also exposed the growing vulnerability and limitations of African states in terms of launching effective rehabilitation and reconstruction measures, especially in the post-disaster phase. The absence of requisite funds has often incapacitated the ability of state agencies to launch efforts to rebuild lives of disaster victims. For instance, Cyclone Idai, the worst tropical cyclone to hit the Southern African region in decades, affected more than 3 million lives and killed nearly 1,300 people in Mozambique, Zimbabwe and Malawi in March this year. It caused damages worth more than USD2.2 billion (8). UN Assistant Secretary General Mohamed Beavogui has highlighted the failure of Mozambique, Malawi and Zimbabwe governments respectively to mobilise required financial, logistical and humanitarian resources to help the disaster-affected populace (9). Referring to the institutional problem Africa as a whole is facing in terms of strengthening the resilience of member states to climate change, Beavogui has argued:

> Africa faces major hurdles, including fiscal constraints and lack of appropriate policy and institutional framework, to prepare for, manage, and respond to disaster risks that are increasing because of climate change. For example, the agriculture system on the continent, mostly rain-fed, is likely to suffer from a reduction in crop yields, which will increase rural-to-urban migration. As a result, more than 85 million people (4 percent of the overall population) are estimated to have to relocate within their own countries by 2050.
>
> *(10)*

Disasters Impede Development

The damages caused by disasters to life and property within BRICS are rising. In September 2014, the devastating floods in India's most sensitive and strategically important border region of Jammu and Kashmir caused extensive damage to agricultural crops and critical infrastructure like power, drinking water supply, communication/telecom services and development projects, leading to losses running into many billions of dollars. The Annual Disaster Statistical Review 2014 estimated that it was the costliest disaster of the year in the world as it caused USD16 billion in economic losses (11). The scale of damages to the local business and state's economy was so extensive that it disrupted the income generation process itself in Jammu and Kashmir. Jammu and Kashmir Finance Minister Haseeb Drabu argued in his Budget Speech in the then Jammu and Kashmir assembly on 22 March 2015:

> The total income of the state has declined by 1.5 per cent in 2014–15 to a little less than 88,000 crore rupees. With this the average per capita of a common man in J&K has declined from 59,279 rupees to 58,888 rupees.
>
> *(12)*

Nearly four years later, the devastating floods in Kerala in August 2018 severely crippled the state's economy and industrial infrastructure, causing economic losses up to 40,000 crore rupees (approximately USD5.7 billion). The scale of the devastation unleashed by the worst floods in this coastal state since 1924 was so high that the government of India allowed companies engaged in relief and rehabilitation work to include their contributions under their mandatory 2% spending on Corporate Social Responsibility (CSR) initiatives as mandated by the Companies Act, 2013. It again highlighted the threat climate-related disasters posed to India's leading urban centres and industrial clusters.

The increase in frequency of disaster incidents has been recorded at a time when investments in critical infrastructure are gradually increasing worldwide. India's nodal disaster management agency, the National Disaster Management Authority (NDMA) has estimated that the global annual investment in transportation, power, water and telecom sectors alone is estimated to reach USD53 trillion, almost 2.5% of the world's GDP. This has made it imperative for disaster-sensitive countries to increase their investments in disaster risk reduction measures (13). This is especially significant for India with 58.6% of its landmass highly prone to earthquakes; 14% of its geographical area highly prone to floods; 5,700 km long coastline prone to cyclones and tsunamis; 68% of its cultivable area vulnerable to drought; and hilly areas highly prone to landslides and avalanches (14). In fact, the Indian economy has suffered from disasters for many decades. A World Bank study found that India had lost about 2% of its GDP between 1991 and 2005 due to disasters (15).

China too has lost trillions of dollars over the decades because of the devastation unleashed by disasters. A study of disasters in China between 1985 and 2014 alone pegged the overall economic loss at USD874.6 billion with floods accounting for more than 70% of the total economic losses (16). Importantly, the United Nations Office for Disaster Risk Reduction (formerly known as 'UNISDR') has estimated that the average annual losses caused by disasters globally is expected to increase from an annual average of USD 260 billion in 2015 to USD 414 billion by 2030. This is bound to further weaken efforts to achieve sustainable development goals (17).The low penetration of insurance culture in high disaster-prone regions of the world has aggravated the threat from disasters. The Willis Re Summary of Natural Cat Events 2016 Report argues:

> The insured loss estimates from major natural catastrophes in 2016 of about USD 39.5 billion are the highest since the annual market losses of USD 60 billion observed in 2012. These losses do not include man-made disasters. . . . The economic losses have been much higher than the insured losses which show low insurance penetration in the selected regions affected by the catastrophes.
>
> *(18)*

Human Displacement and Loss of Livelihood

Beyond the officially recorded damages disasters have caused to human life, property, livelihood opportunities, critical infrastructure and developmental projects, they have also led to a large-scale displacement of hundreds of millions of underprivileged and poor people within the BRICS who have lost livelihood opportunities. According to the Internal Displacement Monitoring Centre's 'Global Report on Internal Displacement (2017)', a total of 7,434,000 people were displaced because of disasters in China, while 2,400,000 disaster-affected people were forced to migrate in India in 2016. As per official figures, most of the displacement in India was associated with floods in the northern state of Bihar, which alone accounted for 1.6 million displacements between mid-July and October. China, in fact, accounts for the highest number of people displaced because of disasters. India ranks third in the global list in 2016 (19). The growing threat posed by disasters is apparent from the fact that they displaced three times more people than conflicts and violence in 2016. The 'Global Report on Internal Displacement 2017' claims:

> There were 24.2 million new displacements by disasters brought on by sudden-onset of natural hazards in 118 countries and territories in 2016. They outnumbered new displacements associated with conflict and violence by more than three to one. In the nine years since 2008, 227.6 million such displacements have been recorded, or an average of 25.3 million per year.
>
> *(20)*

Udaipur Declaration: The First Step

BRICS has taken the first step towards addressing the rising threat of disasters. It has identified disaster management as an important area for mutual cooperation among member states. The Ufa Declaration signed by BRICS nations on 9 July 2015 identified the need to promote cooperation in preventing disasters and developing collective responses to deal with emergency situations. As part of this endeavour, ministers in charge of disaster management met in Udaipur, Rajasthan, on 23 August 2016 and agreed on a new framework of cooperation within BRICS called the 'Udaipur Declaration' (21). They agreed to setup a Joint Task Force for disaster risk management, which would function as an official forum for regular dialogue and facilitate intra-regional cooperation within BRICS on disaster management. According to the 'Udaipur Declaration', the BRICS Ministers agreed to work on enhancing mutual cooperation on the following issues:

> Flood risk management particularly with regard to flood risk assessment, flood forecasting, early warning and emergency response;
>
> Forecasting of extreme weather events – heat and cold waves, episodes of extreme rainfall – particularly in the context of a changing climate;
>
> Collaboration between institutions of respective BRICS countries in the area of flood risk management and extreme weather related events; Lessons learnt for ensuring last mile connectivity/community level action on early warning.
>
> *(22)*

Buffalo City Declaration

Nearly two years later, the BRICS ministers in-charge of disaster management met in Buffalo city in Eastern Cape Province of South Africa in July 2018 and adopted a Buffalo City Declaration. It reaffirmed the commitments made in St. Petersburg Declaration (April 2016) and Udaipur Declaration (August 2016) with regard to enhancing mutual cooperation in monitoring and forecasting emergencies, risk assessment and a framework for mutual assistance in case of emergencies. The Buffalo City Declaration broadened the agenda and scope of cooperation between and among the BRICS member states by calling for a commitment towards a 'risk-informed' development process and sought to align BRICS' priorities with disaster risk reduction targets enshrined in the United Nation's Sendai Framework 2015–30. The Buffalo City Declaration called upon BRICS member states to

> [c]ommit to risk-informed development by reducing existing risks and preventing new risks, through the implementation of integrated and inclusive measures that prevent and reduce hazard exposure and vulnerability to disasters and increase preparedness for response, recovery and reconstruction thereby strengthening resilience . . . (and) contribute to substantially reduce disaster risks and losses in lives, livelihoods and health and in the economic, physical, social, cultural and environmental assets of persons, businesses, communities and countries as echoed in the Sendai Framework for Disaster Risk Reduction: 2015–2030.
>
> *(23)*

The New Development Bank and Development Aid

The broad challenge before BRICS is to effectively implement and operationalise both the objectives and goals enshrined in the Udaipur Declaration and Buffalo City Declaration. The New Development Bank (NDB) setup by BRICS in July 2015 can play a crucial role in this process. The NDB has identified sustainable development, both within BRICS and outside, as its main purpose of operation. Article 1 of the main text of Agreement on NDB categorically states:

> The Bank shall mobilise resources for infrastructure and sustainable development projects in BRICS and other emerging economies and developing countries, complementing the existing efforts of multilateral and regional financial institutions for global growth and development
>
> *(24)*

Significantly, the NDB's Annual Report 2016 lists 'Climate Change' as one of its guiding principle. The Report states:

> The Bank seeks to promote mitigation and adaptation measures to address climate change. NDB aims to build upon existing green economic growth initiatives and provide support for new ones at regional, national and sub-national levels, as well as private sector. The Bank also encourages climate proofing of its infrastructure financing and investments to build resilience to climate change.
>
> *(25)*

This gives the NDB the requisite mandate to supply disaster-aid and launch disaster mitigation projects in disaster-prone regions of the world. The BRICS member states need to facilitate a new institutional framework to help the NDB direct development aid both within BRICS and outside in a structured way. BRICS can play an important role in helping emerging economies and under-developed disaster-prone countries in setting up disaster resilient structures, formulating disaster mitigation strategies and offering development aid, especially for initiating effective post-disaster reconstruction and rehabilitation measures in disaster-affected regions. In this regard, it is imperative for BRICS to integrate a disaster risk management vision within its global development-aid strategy. Mutual development aid committed by BRICS nations could be a crucial factor in facilitating such policy-level integration. During the COVID-19 pandemic, NDB has taken the first policy steps in this direction. The NDB launched a 'Fast Track COVID-19 Emergency Assistance Response Facility' of up to $10 billion to assist the BRICS member countries cope with the unprecedented economic crisis. Under this facility, sovereign loans of RMB7 billion to China (19 March 2020) and $1 billion to India (30 April 2020) were disbursed within a month of approval by the NDB Board (26). Later, South Africa and Brazil were also given USD1 billion each to combat the impact of COVID-19 (27).

BRICS Disaster Response Fund

To achieve the global development-aid objectives of BRICS, member states should consider setting up a BRICS Disaster Response Fund to help launch development aid in disaster-hit zones. BRICS can utilise development-aid funds to help build disaster resilient communities and assist in post-disaster reconstruction and rehabilitation work in disaster-prone countries. The NDB can play an important role in creating and operationalising this Special Fund. It is significant that the NDB has already identified promotion of mitigation and adaptation measures as its guiding principle to address the challenge of climate change. This Special Fund could be utilised to set up new specialised institutions like a BRICS Coordinating Centre for Humanitarian Assistance on disaster management; a BRICS Rapid Response System to fight Disasters; a BRICS Earthquake Information Centre; a BRICS Specialised Meteorological Centre; and a BRICS Disaster Management Centre to strengthen the capacity-building and disaster mitigation-related measures in member states.

A BRICS University Network

BRICS needs to create an institutional academic platform to facilitate exchange of information and new knowledge among engineering and disaster research institutes among BRICS member states. Considering the varied challenges posed by disasters in BRICS, the experience of member states and their institutional response mechanisms needs to be shared among the member states. It would help facilitate the creation of new knowledge and regular exchange of ideas on initiating post-disaster reconstruction and rehabilitation in member states and better utilisation of development aid within BRICS.

A BRICS Foreign Disaster Assistance Programme

BRICS should consider setting up a BRICS Foreign Disaster Assistance (BRICS-FDA) Programme to help streamline its aid priorities with regard to disaster aid management. It can function on the lines of the Office of US Foreign Disaster Assistance, the leading official agency which leads the US government's efforts to launch disaster relief and rescue operations in different parts of the world (28).

The BRICS-FDA Programme can run in active coordination with nodal agencies in BRICS member states dealing with disaster management. Leading disaster management experts from BRICS member states can be assigned the responsibility to prepare a framework to help disaster-affected countries in an institutionalised manner. BRICS can send a team of disaster experts and trained personnel to launch relief and rescue measures in disaster-affected zones in coordination with the local state agencies. BRICS can also help launch programmes specially designed to develop community resilience in disaster-prone zones, offer development aid in initiating disaster risk reduction measures like early warning systems and support economic revival and reconstruction of life and infrastructure in disaster-affected zones.

A BRICS Disaster Management Centre

To sensitise the government and private institutions in BRICS member states, it would be worthwhile to set up a BRICS Disaster Management Centre. It can function as a nodal centre with the responsibility to both facilitate capacity-building and help launch disaster risk reduction initiatives within and outside BRICS. It can also help setup a BRICS Action Plan on Cooperation on Climate Change by creating institutional linkages with leading regional and international organisations. It can also help restructure urban planning processes and building codes and by-laws by weaving a disaster resistance component in them and set up earthquake-resistant infrastructure in both public and private sectors. This is especially significant in the light of rapid urbanisation expected in developing and under-developed countries in the coming decades. As the Cancun Communique categorically states (Section-9):

> Some 60 per cent of the area expected to be urbanised by 2030 remains to be built and trillions of US Dollars are expected to be invested in new infrastructure annually. Meeting the needs of a global population that will reach nine billion by 2050, achieving the SDGs by 2030 and responding to the adverse effects of climate change will require considerable investments in resilient infrastructure, including green infrastructure and housing. While the cost of retrofitting infrastructure and building is often high, making new investment resilient is not and pays off over the long term.
>
> *(29)*

BRICS can orient its development-aid initiatives on making cities resilient in disaster-prone countries. It can work on delineating current and future risk scenarios, enhance the financial capability of local institutions to launch disaster mitigation initiatives, and help restructure and revise urban development policies by incorporating disaster management components. In this context, it would be significant to also focus on the state of governance structures in aid recipient countries, the quality of institutions through which the development-aid funds will be routed to reach the needy populace.

ASEAN Model on Disaster Aid

BRICS needs to formulate development-aid strategies which are effective and address the concerns of recipient countries with regard to their 'autonomy'-related concerns. As BRICS member states deliberate on creating new institutional norms to enhance mutual cooperation in disaster aid management, it would be worthwhile to study the ASEAN experience in this regard. The ASEAN Agreement on Disaster Management and Emergency Response ('The ASEAN Agreement') codifies the roles and responsibilities of member states and also specifies the terms of engagement for cooperation in disaster-related subjects. It lays down a framework for enhancing mutual cooperation between and among the Member States in the wake of the increasing frequency and scale of disasters in the region.

The 'ASEAN Agreement' also puts in place an institutionalised system of cooperation which respects the sovereign rights of the member states in order to avoid any conflict at the time of launching disaster-relief. It clearly states:

> The sovereignty, territorial integrity and national unity of the Parties shall be respected, in accordance with the Charter of the United Nations and the Treaty of Amity and Cooperation in Southeast Asia, in the implementation of this Agreement. In this context, each affected Party shall have the primary responsibility to respond to disasters occurring within its territory and external assistance or offers of assistance shall only be provided upon the request or with the consent of the affected Party.
>
> *(30)*

Importantly, the 'ASEAN Agreement' also lays down the ground rules of cooperation. It categorically specifies that 'The Requesting or Receiving Party shall exercise the overall direction, control, co-ordination and supervision of the assistance within its territory' (31). It is significant to note that the 'ASEAN Agreement' also outlines the steps member states have to undertake to identify, prevent and reduce risks in their respective domain:

> Each Party shall undertake measures to reduce losses from disasters which include:

a) developing and implementing legislative and other regulatory measures;
b) strengthening local and national disaster management capability and coordination;

c) promoting public awareness and education and strengthening community participation;
d) promoting and utilizing indigenous knowledge and practices.

(32)

BRICS: The Road Ahead

The Buffalo City Declaration commits BRICS to significantly contribute to global efforts to reduce disaster risks and losses in lives as per the goals outlined in the Sendai Framework for Disaster Risk Reduction: 2015–2030. The BRICS Foreign Ministers' meeting in Rio de Janeiro on 27 July 2019 reaffirmed the commitment of member states to the 2030 Agenda for Sustainable Development and the implementation of the Paris Agreement (33). In his intervention at an informal meeting of BRICS leaders on the sidelines of the G20 summit, Prime Minister Narendra Modi urged leaders of BRICS to join India's initiative for Coalition for Disaster Resilient Infrastructure to develop resilient infrastructure in the least-developed and developing countries (34).

BRICS urgently needs to evolve a new cooperative strategy to jointly initiate policy measures to effectively deal with the threat posed by climate change and the consequent rise in climate-related disasters which has followed abnormal changes in global weather. A joint study by UNISDR and the Centre for Research on Epidemiology of Disasters of the climate-related disasters has revealed that, 'the number of weather- and climate-related disasters more than doubled over the past forty years, accounting for 6,392 events in the 20-year period 1996–2015, up from 3,017 in 1976–1995' (35). This is expected to seriously threaten sustainable development processes in high disaster-risk zones, especially in the least-developed countries.

In the wake of the COVID-19 pandemic, BRICS member states have decided to intensify cooperation to combat the threat posed by new infectious diseases. They have decided to strengthen cooperation in bio-safety governance and vaccine research and development. Efforts are being expedited to operationalise the proposed BRICS Vaccine Research and Development Centre as per the schedule finalised at the Johannesburg Declaration (2018) (36). To address the challenge posed by COVID-19, the BRICS STI Framework Programme also gave a call for research projects facilitating cooperation among the researchers and institutions within BRICS member countries on the following thematic areas:

> 1. Research and development of new technologies/tools for diagnosing COVID-19.2. Research and development of COVID-19 vaccines and drugs, including repurposing of available drugs. 3. Genomic sequencing of SARS-CoV-2 and studies on the epidemiology and mathematical modelling of the COVID-19 pandemic. 4. AI, ICT and HPC oriented research for COVID-19 drugs design, vaccine development, treatment, clinical trials and public health infrastructures and systems. 5. Epidemiological studies and

clinical trials to evaluate the overlap of SARSCoV-2 and co-morbidities, especially tuberculosis.

(37)

As BRICS member countries struggle to cope with the worst epidemic in the last hundred years, they need to collectively formulate a multi-pronged strategy to combat the threat of disasters and prioritise their development-aid objectives accordingly. BRICS needs to synchronise its development-aid objectives with these larger goals set by the international community. It should formulate sustainable development strategies by weaving in a disaster risk reduction component in its larger developmental agenda. In this era of climate change and increasing threat of disasters, it is important for BRICS to formulate a collective strategy to align its larger development-aid objectives with the challenges posed by disasters.

References

1) World Health Organisation. 'Coronavirus Disease (COVID-19) Dashboard', https://covid19.who.int/ (accessed on 11 October 2020).
2) Centre for Research on the Epidemiology of Disaster (CRED) and UN Office for Disaster Risk Reduction (UNDRR). 2016. 'Poverty & Death: Disaster Mortality, 1996–2015'. (ed.) Robert Glasser and Debarati Guha-Sapir. Brussels: CRED.
3) Centre for Research on the Epidemiology of Disasters (CRED), USAID and US Louvain. 2018. 'Natural Disasters 2018'. p-5, www.cred.be/natural-disasters-2018 (accessed on 19 December, 2021).
4) Centre for Research on the Epidemiology of Disaster (CRED) and UN Office for Disaster Risk Reduction (UNDRR). 2016. 'Poverty & Death: Disaster Mortality, 1996–2015'. (ed.) Robert Glasser and Debarati Guha-Sapir. Brussels: CRED.
5) CRED and UNDRR. 'Human Cost of Disasters, An Overview of the last 20 years: 2000–2019'. 2020. p-15, www.undrr.org/publication/human-cost-disasters-overview-last-20-years-2000-2019 (accessed on 18 December 2021).
6) CRED, Institute of Health and Society (IRSS) and Universite catholique de Louvain. 'Annual Disaster Statistical Review 2016, The Numbers and Trends'. p-48.2016. (ed.) Debarati Guha-Sapir, Philippe Hoyois Pascaline Wallemacq and Regina Below. Brussels: CRED.
7) World Bank. 'Coping with Losses: Options for Disaster Risk Financing in Brazil''. p-8.2014. Washington DC: World Bank.
8) AON. Global Catastrophe Recap: First Half of 2019. July 2019. p-7. http://thoughtleadership.aon.com/Documents/20190723-analytics-if-1h-global-report.pdf (accessed on 17 December 2021).
9) Beavogui, Mohamed. 'Cyclone Idai exposes the gap of disaster risk relief financing in Africa'. Africa in Focus, Brookings. 01 April 2019.
10) Beavogui, Mohamed. 'An African-owned initiative to manage natural disaster and climate risks'. Africa in Focus, Brookings. 14 March 2019.
11) Debarati Guha-Sapir, Philippe Hoyois and Regina Below. 'Annual Disaster Statistical Review 2014, The Numbers and Trends'. Brussels: CRED, 2015, 2.
12) 'Budget Speech 2015–16: Haseeb A Drabu', Government of Jammu & Kashmir, https://jkpdp.org/budget-speech-2015-16/ (accessed on 19 December, 2021).

13) National Disaster Management Authority. International Workshop on Disaster Resilient Infrastructure. 2018. p-1, www.cdri.world/sites/default/files/publication/iwdri2018_summaryReport.pdf (accessed on December 17, 2021).
14) Ministry of Home Affairs, Government of India. 'National Policy on Disaster Management 2009'. p-1. New Delhi: Magnum Custom Publishing.
15) Ministry of Home Affairs (MHA), Government of India. 'Disaster Management in India 2011'. 2011. p-13. New Delhi: MHA.
16) Han, Weixiao, Liang, Chen, Jiang, Baofa, Ma, Wei and Zhang, Ying. 2016. 'Major Natural Disasters in China, 1985–2014: Occurrence and Damages', *International Journal of Environmental Research and Public Health*. 13(11): 1118.
17) United Nations. 'Sendai Framework for Disaster Risk Reduction 2015–30'. 2015. Geneva: UNDRR.
18) Willis Re. 'Willis Re Summary of Natural Cat Events 2016 Report'. 2017. Volume 5, Issue 3, p-1.
19) Internal Displacement Monitoring Centre, Norwegian Refugee Council. 'Global Report on Internal Displacement'. 2017. p-3.
20) Internal Displacement Monitoring Centre. 'Global Report on Internal Displacement'. 2017, http://internal-displacement.org/global-report/grid2017/pdfs/2017-GRID-part-1.pdf (accessed on 19 December 2021).
21) Press Information Bureau. 'BRICS Disaster Risk Reduction meet adopts Udaipur Declaration'. 23 August 2016, http://pib.nic.in/newsite/PrintRelease.aspx?relid=149135 (accessed on 19 December 2021).
22) Press Information Bureau. 'Second Meeting of BRICS Ministers for Disaster Management to be held in Udaipur, Rajasthan on August 22–23, 2016', http://pib.nic.in/newsite/PrintRelease.aspx?relid=148977 (accessed on 19 December 2021).
23) Department of Cooperative Governance and Traditional Affairs, Government of South Africa. 'Buffalo City Declaration 2018'. 2018, www.cogta.gov.za/index.php/2018/07/01/brics-in-africa-collaboration-for-inclusive-growth-and-shared-prosperity-in-the-4th-industrial-revolution/ (accessed on 19 December 2021).
24) New Development Bank. 'Agreement on the New Development Bank – Fortaleza, July 15'. 2017, www.ndb.int/wp-content/themes/ndb/pdf/Agreement-on-the-New-Development-Bank.pdf (accessed on 18 December 2021).
25) New Development Bank. 'Towards a Greener Tomorrow, Annual Report 2016'. 2017, www.ndb.int/wp-content/uploads/2017/10/NBD-ANNUAL-REPORT-SINGLE.pdf (accessed on 19 December 2021).
26) New Development Bank. 'New Development Bank Policy on Fast-track Emergency Response to COVID-19'. 10 June 2020, www.ndb.int/wp-content/uploads/2020/07/Policy-on-Fast-track-Emergency-Response-to-COVID-19.pdf (accessed on 18 December 2021).
27) New Development Bank. 'COVID-19 Emergency Program'. 19 June 2020, www.ndb.int/covid-19-emergency-program-sa/ and www.ndb.int/emergency-assistance-program-in-combating-covid-19-brazil/ (accessed on 19 December 2021).
28) USAID. 'Office of US Foreign Disaster Assistance'. 2017, www.usaid.gov/who-we-are/organization/bureaus/bureau-democracy-conflict-and-humanitarian-assistance/office-us (accessed on 17 December 2021).
29) UNDRR Global Platform for Disaster Risk Reduction. 'The Cancun High-Level Communiqué – 24 May 2017'. 2017. p-3.
30) ASEAN. 'ASEAN Agreement on Disaster Management and Emergency Response, Article 3, 6', http://agreement.asean.org/media/download/20140119170000.pdf (accessed on 19 December 2021).

31) Ibid.
32) ASEAN. 'ASEAN Agreement on Disaster Management and Emergency Response, Article 3, 9', http://agreement.asean.org/media/download/20140119170000.pdf (accessed on 19 December 2021).
33) Ministry of External Affairs, Government of India. 'Press Statement at Meeting of the BRICS Ministers of Foreign Affairs/International Relations'. 27 July 2019.
34) Ministry of External Affairs, Government of India. 'Translation of Prime Minister's intervention at the BRICS Leaders Informal Meeting on the margins of G20 Summit'. 28 June 2019.
35) Centre for Research on the Epidemiology of Disaster (CRED) and UN Office for Disaster Risk Reduction (UNDRR). 2016. 'Poverty & Death: Disaster Mortality, 1996–2015'. p-5. (ed.) Robert Glasser and Debarati Guha-Sapir. Brussels: CRED.
36) Ministry of External Affairs, Government of India. 'Media statement – Meeting of the BRICS Ministers of Foreign Affairs/International Relations'. 04 September 2020.
37) BRICS STI Framework Program-Joint Call Secretariat. 17 June 2020, http://brics-sti.org/files/BRICS_STI_Framework_Programme_Call_2020.pdf (accessed on 19 December 2021).

20

CONCLUSION: BUILDING ALTERITY[1] AND INCLUSION

BRICS' Journey thus Far

Meeta Keswani Mehra and Meenakshi Sundriyal

The incongruence among the BRICS member states has been a point of reference for many critics of the BRICS idea and its significance beyond a talking shop. While it is true that each of the BRICS members is significantly different from each other in terms of their economies, foreign policy thrusts and domestic political environments, these differences could be also seen as its strength, as a coming together of international players with a vision that is more inclusive and that better represents the diverse cultural value systems of the world. Most of them have the shared experience of being at the receiving end of colonisation of some form or another. Most of them suffer from challenges of socio-economic inequalities and can share and learn from each other's efforts to overcome inequalities. That BRICS has so far managed to evolve institutions that are non-hierarchical in nature adds to the appeal of BRICS' vision as something to be offered to the world community as a possible future pathway, especially in view of the signs of duress that the prevailing world order is showing in the face of the United States' recent retreat from Afghanistan. The retreat has left a trail of disruption in its wake in Afghanistan and thrown the entire region into a state of uncertainty. The Afghanistan events place a great responsibility and at the same time offer an opportunity to BRICS, some of whom share their boundary and neighbourhood with Afghanistan, to take appropriate measures to ensure peace and stability in the region.

Despite continued scepticism about the role and relevance of BRICS in the evolving global order, and persistent bilateral demands and conflicts, the emerging economies of Brazil, Russia, India, China and South Africa have continued to hold their own, unilaterally and as a group. BRICS nations have been striving to enhance co-operation on matters of mutual interest, while continuing to balance these against their own national interests and foreign policy objectives (Kapoor, 2020). Setting aside differing economic performances, changing political regimes, the impact of the Covid-19 pandemic, the complex India-China dynamics, India's

DOI: 10.4324/9781003148074-23

and Brazil's poising act with the United States and the rising Russia–China association, the fact that BRICS has been able to assiduously work out a consensus on an expanded agenda for the group implies that it continues to matter.

The key takeaways from the different chapters of the book emanate precisely out of the potential of BRICS members to work along the lines of this broadly defined agenda, within the realms of their individual national pursuits, and to co-operate in specific domains pertaining to evolving non-partisan institutions and governance mechanisms, improved economic growth and development, enhanced commodity trade and capital flows, recognition of maritime co-operation, concerns of the political economy of growth processes, response to the Covid-19 pandemic and natural disasters, and intersecting cultural paradigms. It is these themes along which the role and relevance of BRICS need to be located in the changing world order.

We have seen in the chapters on the evolution of BRICS that the idea of creating an alternate space had been felt for long in global governance where countries' concerns, which were often short-changed by the current international order, could be aired and addressed in a constructive manner. It was expressed in the form of the RIC and the IBSA. Although it has never been the BRICS agenda to actually leave the Bretton Woods Institutions, it has been vocal about the urgent need to substantially reform these. The eventual formation of BRICS institutions like the NBA and the CRA points to the joint desire of the BRICS nations to assert themselves and be in a better bargaining position. The liberal international order has not been very clear or shown to be truthful on the principle of sovereignty or its violation in specific cases where it has been carried out. This sharply contrasts with the BRICS' vision, which upholds sovereignty.

In spite of the challenges posed by the disproportionality among its members, the BRICS continues to be more or less guided by its desire for a better say in the global arena. Despite the different nature of their political systems with democratic structures in India, Brazil and South Africa and more authoritarian systems in Russia and China, the BRICS institutions have managed to steadily work out egalitarian systems and are desirous of working towards strengthening them further. BRICS has exhibited far greater resilience than was originally believed to be the case.

The various BRICS nations have their own specific interests and expectations of BRICS. Despite the many predictions of its collapse, especially with the political shifts witnessed in Brazil and India, the BRICS countries have so far not shown any inclination to abandon ship. The member countries look at BRICS as a potential furtherer of their self-interests in a fast-changing world political environment in which multipolarity seems to be a better way forward. Among the BRICS countries, Russia and China share common features of strong political authority and assertiveness in the international arena with Russia being a strong military power and China a strong economic power. India, Brazil and South Africa is another cohort made up of democracies looking for partnerships to defend their strategic and economic interests.

India has historically associated itself with the non-aligned movement as an alternate vision during the Cold War period. Its interest in BRICS has to be seen in the light of its foreign policy, which mostly has been remarkably uniform over the years. India has followed a policy of risk aversion and non-alignment, which could be termed a straddle policy to better protect its interests. It maintains its neutrality and so far has been able to execute the balancing act between building close ties with the US and maintaining historically friendly ties with Russia. But it has not been able to resolve its conflict with China on the border issue, which makes it not just a bilateral conflict but also puts into jeopardy the viability of BRICS each time it is played out in real time. Notably, however, both China and India have been brought to the table, often with friendly interventions from Russia. Despite this relationship with China, India sees potential in BRICS as an agent of reforms in global governance as well as for its own interest in being relevant as an important player in the South Asian region, especially vis-à-vis Pakistan. It has successfully been able to push the agenda of counterterrorism in BRICS' official discourse.

Brazil was a vociferous protagonist of the BRICS grouping under the regimes of Lula and Dilma Rouseff. It was supported by the general upward trend of economic growth and poverty eradication measures, which brought about substantial changes in the lives of the poor in this vast Latin American country. However, drastic political changes were rung in by Temer after Rouseff was overthrown. With the arrival of Bolsonaro, the regime took a definitive right turn, and he gave explicitly pro-US statements and set out an agenda to overturn everything that Lula and Rouseff had envisaged. All this made scholars of BRICS extremely sceptical of the future of BRICS. However, it was soon observed that even Bolsonaro reformed himself in terms of BRICS, and Brazil participated in BRICS as before, although not with the same vision as that of Lula or Rouseff.

Russia, though economically not one of the strongest, brings to BRICS the Eurasian dimension and assertive power play. It has time and again asserted that BRICS is very important for it. After its definitive fallout with the liberal order, Russia has to look at other alliances like the CSTO and BRICS to not only buffer itself but also posture as an assertive player in international politics. It nurtures a nostalgic consciousness of having been a great power and works towards being as near to that as possible in the present scenario. In the Russian discourse, BRICS is often featured in terms of 'civilisational values', which is something much broader than is represented by the concept of the Global South. It asserts that the BRICS countries represent the distinct historical-cultural perspectives of diverse lands that have thus far not found prominence, and, hence, there should be efforts to harmoniously synergise these value systems for peaceful co-existence (Concept of the Foreign Policy of the Russian Federation, 2013). The US-led current international order has kept the countries that assert sovereignty on the margins even as they participate in their neo-liberal system by opening up their economies and executing reforms. Russia has opined that the US-led multipolar system is detrimental to global security. The concept of multipolarity or polycentricism, therefore, lies at the core of Russian foreign policy. But it clearly positions itself as distinct from Western multilateralism or multipolarity, which often works on the principle of great power exceptionalism. It is within this framework that Russia's interest in the BRICS can be understood.

In the period after the 2008 financial crisis, China emerged as a major player in the globalised world. It had earlier successfully dodged the intentions of the US-led system to integrate its domestic policy by default with liberalism by making it participate in the Liberal International Order (LIO). China learnt instead to balance its ideological core and a strong sense of state authority with preserving its self-interests by participating in the US-led world order and globalised economy. This enabled it to reap benefits while preserving its ideological core, eventually emerging as one of the major global economic powers, much to the chagrin of the West. This recent avatar of China that has been in the making for many years has allowed it to exercise its say in global governance. Its interest in BRICS is based on a well-thought out mix of ideological rigidity and flexible pragmatism. On the one hand, China brings its economic might to the BRICS table and, in that sense, is a major mover in the establishment of BRICS financial institutions, which fosters greater co-operation among BRICS nations. On the other, it faces trust issues within BRICS as it is perceived to be less open about its conduct. It has long-standing border issues with India, which have periodically led to conflicts, often violent ones, as we saw in May 2020. The resolution of this conflict could lead to a greater possibility of BRICS acting in a cohesive manner in order to further impact global governance.

South Africa has the distinction of being a later inclusion in the BRICS grouping. It was not included in the original mention of emerging economies by Jim O'Neil. However, its inclusion in 2010 made the grouping more representative of the world as it now could count as an access point to the African continent. South Africa is one of the leading economies of Africa and had, since its inclusion, opened up several fora for BRICS nations to interact and engage with the other African countries. Although, as compared to other BRICS countries, it comes across as the odd one, being much smaller, it adds to the BRICS vision of inclusivity and equity. It also counts with the legacy of a strong anti-apartheid movement led by Nelson Mandela, which further connects with the southernity paradigm of BRICS. And although it is small, it compares well on several counts of social indicators when compared with other BRICS countries. Conversely, South Africa views its inclusion as the only African country in BRICS as something that greatly enhances its role within Africa and projects it well into the world.

In terms of economic performance, BRICS as a group has been emerging along the pathway envisioned for it (O'Neill, 2021). According to IMF projections, BRICS nations could contribute close to 50% of world GDP by 2030 in comparison with the current 22% or so. They are economically influential in several dimensions. China boasts of the world's largest industrial and manufacturing capacity and is an important R&D hub. India has taken big strides in science and technology, especially information and communication technology and services, as well as its pharmaceutical industry. Brazil and South Africa are significantly endowed with mineral, water, and other natural and ecological resources, while Russia has emerged as one of the largest energy (oil and natural gas) suppliers to the rest of the world.

Demographic trends are also favourable for the realisation of the economic prospects of BRICS. Brazil, India and South Africa currently have significant populations below the working age of 0–14 years that could potentially join the workforce by 2030–2040, implying that the dominating position of BRICS in this respect is likely to be sustained over the next two to three decades. Utilising its human capital potential lies at the core of a robust recovery for BRICS in the post-Covid-19 era.

As shown in one of the chapters, the intra-BRICS commodity trade patterns also hold significant promise. In the case of specific commodity groups, indicators such as Revealed Comparative Advantage (RCA) and Trade Intensity Index (TII) point to a high comparative advantage and trade intensity within the BRICS countries. These trends are likely to deepen further in case the group endeavours to become a more cohesive global entity and chooses to lower trade barriers to strengthen trade ties. The import gravity analysis corroborates this viewpoint. It is seen that, even though the distance between countries affects imports negatively, gross fixed capital formation in the partner countries works towards boosting exports towards the BRICS nations. Furthermore, commodity import inflows of the individual BRICS countries are affected negatively by their tariffs, implying that lowering of trade barriers could lead to substantial gains from trade. It is also promising to find that the formation of the BRICS group and freedom of trade have had positive effects on commodity imports.

The impressive performance of BRICS in attracting direct investment has been a key driving factor for its economic growth and the internationalisation of financial flows, technology and resources. In fact, FDI inflows have been steady for most BRICS countries in spite of the Covid-19 pandemic. BRICS countries are emerging economies endowed with rich stocks of natural resources and low-cost labour. These also provide large markets for absorbing the sale of goods and services. These features of BRICS provide a fillip for FDI inflows. Given their importance, FDI inflows into BRICS require closer scrutiny in terms of their key drivers; these have been studied in greater detail in another chapter of the book. A closer analysis indicates that there has been a significant increase in investment inflows into the BRICS economies, especially when compared with the OECD countries. Specifically, factors such as market size, economic stability, interest rates, and availability of natural resources and labour have been the most important determinants of FDI inflows into BRICS. Thus, both market-seeking and labour- and natural resource-seeking behaviour of FDI is found to exist, which can help boost economic growth in the post-Covid recovery period.

As for maritime interactions, despite the BRICS linkages transcending the trans-oceanic zone originating in Russia and reaching up to South America, linked through the Indian Ocean, their full potential remains to be achieved. It is being increasingly brought to the fore that overcoming the challenges posed by political economy and the promise of opportunities from BRICS' emerging maritime interactions could well allow it to occupy a more distinctive position in the context of the new global realities.

In the face of the Covid-19 pandemic and climate-induced and other natural disasters, a realisation has dawned that the ill effects of globalisation and transnational spill overs cannot be simply addressed by the conventional multilateral institutions alone. In fact, a lot can be accomplished through the expression of certitude and co-operation among groupings such as the BRICS (Chaturvedi and Saha, 2021). Accordingly, the governments of BRICS nations have responded to the pandemic, both individually and collectively. Country governments have relied on a range of fiscal and monetary policy measures as well as new programmes and schemes to mitigate the adverse welfare effects on their citizens. BRICS has also sought co-operation for freer trade and more integrated supply networks, public health, provisioning of humanitarian and medical supplies, artificial intelligence and digitisation along with financial assistance in terms of loans from the New Development Bank. The existing standoff between India and China and growing polarisation among the countries may have slowed their progress; efforts have been made to overcome disagreements and work co-operatively to expedite the implementation of planned projects. In fact, BRICS envisages working on an early warning mechanism for the outbreak of viral diseases, development of diagnostic and preventive measures for such diseases, as well as joint epidemiological R&D with financial support from the New Development Bank. Similar co-operative responses are also envisaged to tackle climate and other nature-induced disasters within and outside BRICS. Going forward, these include the need for building institutions, such as a Disaster Response Fund and a Disaster Management Centre. The need to rope in the BRICS Network universities for knowledge sharing and strategic management of these concerns is also being discussed. In spite of the fact that the strategic rivalry between India-China and problematic geopolitics may have hampered BRICS' efforts to co-ordinate action to cope with Covid-19, transfrontier environmental issues and disaster management, yet common and differentiated responses to these problems have been sought time and again, and BRICS has continued to survive and evolve institutionally.

The BRICS idea intersects with culture in a variety of ways. It could be seen as what it brings to the ideational horizon of perceiving IR. It could also be understood as what kind of cultural praxis pervades the area that comes under the BRICS countries. In each of these perspectives, the key takeaway is the creation of an alternate space informed by a value system, which is more egalitarian than the present one. The vision of southernity founded in the postcolonial/decolonial discourse of most of the BRICS countries adds ideational value to the BRICS idea even as each of these countries struggles with wide disparities among its citizens.

The BRICS's inception and journey so far can be called moderately successful. The idea of gathering a rather incongruent group of countries representing almost half the world from major continents is indeed novel and has raised hopes as well as apprehensions in a fiercely competitive global environ. As a platform guided by ideals of mutual co-operation in all fields based on egalitarian values, it has not only survived but also met with some success at institution-building. It also offers immense scope for economic and social co-operation. On an ideological level, it provides a vision of southernity and a more inclusive world order.

Note

1 Broadly, the conceptualisation of an alternative in opposition to the dominant/prevailing one.

References

Chaturvedi, Sachin and Saha, Sabyasachi (2021). The BRICS way to multilateralism amid crisis. In *"The Future of BRICS". BRICS India 2021*. Observer Research Foundation and Research and Information System for Developing Countries.

Foreign Policy Concept of the Russian Federation (2013). www.mid.ru/en/foreign_policy/official_documents/-/asset_publisher/CptICkB6BZ29/content/id/122186. Accessed on 5 October 2021.

Kapoor, Nivedita (2020). BRICS and its future: The challenges of multilateralism. *Raisina Debates*, May 13, 2020. www.orfonline.org/expert-speak/brics-future-challenges-multilateralism-66053/. Accessed on 27 September 2021.

O'Neill, Jim (2021). Is the emerging world still emerging? Two decades on, the BRICs promise lingers. *International Monetary Fund: Finance and Development*. Summer 2021. www.imf.org/external/pubs/ft/fandd/2021/06/jim-oneill-revisits-brics-emerging-markets.htm. Accessed on 20 September 2021.

INDEX